MW01620406

ArtScroll® Series

Rabbi Nosson Scherman / Rabbi Gedaliah Zlotowitz

General Editors

Rabbi Meir Zlotowitz ז״ל, *Founder*

MILTON OSTREICHER EDITION

FOREVER

Published by

ARTSCROLL®
Mesorah Publications, ltd

Infusing the essence of Rabbi Shlomo Freifeld into the next generation

TALMID

THE CHINUCH LEGACY OF RABBI CHANINA HERZBERG

RABBI YITZCHOK HERZBERG

FOREWORD BY YISROEL BESSER

FIRST EDITION
First Impression ... January 2023
Second Impression ... February 2023

Published and Distributed by
MESORAH PUBLICATIONS, LTD.
313 Regina Avenue / Rahway, N.J. 07065

Distributed in Europe by
LEHMANNS
Unit E, Viking Business Park
Rolling Mill Road
Jarrow, Tyne & Wear NE32 3DP
England

Distributed in Australia & New Zealand by
GOLDS WORLD OF JUDAICA
3-13 William Street
Balaclava, Melbourne 3183
Victoria Australia

Distributed in Israel by
SIFRIATI / A. GITLER — BOOKS
POB 2351
Bnei Brak 51122

Distributed in South Africa by
KOLLEL BOOKSHOP
Northfield Centre, 17 Northfield Avenue
Glenhazel 2192, Johannesburg, South Africa

ARTSCROLL® SERIES
FOREVER A TALMID

ITEM CODE: FORTH
ISBN 10: 1-4226-3283-0
ISBN 13: 978-1-4226-3283-3

Typography by CompuScribe at ArtScroll Studios, Ltd.
Printed in PRC

This book is dedicated in memory of

Milton Ostreicher ז״ל

מנחם אברהם בן משה בנימין ז״ל

נפ׳ כ״ז שבט תשפ״א

My father and "Mr. O." were cut from the same cloth. They were both scrupulously honest, had an incredible work ethic, and were loved by all those who knew them. Mr. O., as he was fondly called, was someone we all knew as a close friend and confidant of Abba *z"l.*

It was only natural that when I set out to make a *parnassah,* Mr. O. was the first call that my father made for me. He became a cherished mentor from whom I learned many lessons — namely, how to treat your employees, that if you are not five minutes early then you are late, and most importantly, how to make a *kiddush Hashem* in the workplace.

My father always stressed the importance of showing *hakaras hatov.* This dedication allows me, in a small way, to express how much Mr. O. meant to me and to the entire Herzberg family. I feel that it is most fitting that a book perpetuating the legacy of our father will be closely linked with Mr. Milton Ostreicher.

Yudi and Chumi Herzberg

In memory of

Rabbi Chanina Herzberg ז״ל

The ultimate *mechanech* and friend

Mark and Barbara Silber

Alex, David, Jonathan

and families

We are among thousands of families
who owe heartfelt *hakaras hatov* to

Rabbi Chanina Herzberg ז״ל.

His brilliance in *chinuch*, both of boys and girls, young and old, was remarkable. His wise guidance has left an impression that will endure for generations. We valued his friendship and cherish his memory. May his legacy serve as an inspiration for his many *talmidim* and his wonderful family.

יהי זכרו ברוך

The Golombeck and Kleiner families

RABBI NAFTALI JAEGER
ROSH HAYESHIVA

בס"ד ג' טבת תשפ"ג מכתב ברכה

הנה אצל יבלחט"א ידידנו הדגול נכבד הגה"ר חנינא הערצבערג זצ"ל ראינו קיום הפסוק "וכ"מ דבאו"ר ופרנ"י וכ"מ שהם טובים לך שהן ימי התלהבות ימי נעורך כן יהיו ימי זקנותך שהם דומים צדיקים ומתמוטטים על היינו דכל ימיו היה משפיע כמו שלמד אצל מורו ורבו [מורי חמי] הגה"צ רבי שלמה פריינד זללה"ה המחבר ספר היה אומר הרבה פעמים לתלמידיו [בין הדבר דס' חוט המשולש] אני הייתי תלמיד נאמן לרבי הסטמרי זצ"ל ושאבתי מים עד דלות עד אשר עמדה לי עד כן ראינו אצל רבי חנינא ונמשך עליו מפה דס' ארץ צבי פרנקים דעם הגדמו"ל מוהר"א בחוטר ציון היינו שחתר עצמו לבאר מ"מ היינו שמשפיע תורה לישראל עד - מספר ח"י של רבי חנינא הטעים והתאים עם מורו ורבו כשם והיה תלמיד נאמן דמלא המצוות

תמן בניו אדות והעמידו תלמידים הרבה והיינו לא רק ללמד לתלמידיו אלא גילה להם עמידה שידעו לכוון ולבוא מה רבם היה עושה ונבאמת דסלכה כה ולא אמר דבר שלא שמע מפי רבו מעולם - היינו שלא רק היה דולה ומשקה מתורת רבו אלא היה מוציא היסודות נאמנים שלמד וקיבל ממורו ורבו והשפיע כן על תלמידיו הימרוקים דעשרות שנים דעיבת גלגלת חיים דסאטמאר ממש עד היום.

ועתה יגדה הוא לי שהספר על ח"י של רבי חנינא [שלא יהיה רק סיפורי מעשיות ועובדות אלא ספר נעזר למחנכים ולמחונכים כדי לגדול ולהשפיע] נכתב ע"י בנו חביבו ידיד בן ידיד מצה בן מצה תה מעין ומחוך דחסד עליון היה יצחק נ"י וכבר אותו גברא ואיתמחי קמיה שהיה יודע דלית מדכרינו כמה שנים והיה כותב את הנעלמים דברכות ודברכות ובן כשמד הרבה שנים דמתיבתא רבנו חיים ברלין - כולל גוראריה נגד את שיעורי המעמרים של מרן ראש הישיבה הגאון רבי אהרן שכטר שליט"א הקב"ה ימלאנו וישלח לו רפואה שלמה וגם לרבות הלכות שיש לאמו של המחבר אשת חבר כחבר תחי' שתמ"ד היתה עזר ואחיסמך לעבודת הקדושה של בעלה. מנשים באהל תבורך

ואין לי אלא לברך בכבת הדיוט אידידי הנ"ל יזכה וכל משפחת הערצבערג ששפר צה יהיה נחת כוח לנשמתו הזכה ויהיה תועלת לרבים. ומילתא בפומיה דמו"ג זללה"ה דברי התניא סוף דבלא דמוהר"ן לשון צרכים. מנהג נבגו מצי יליכה מדהירן שמי שמא ולפי שלשון מוהר"ן כי לנרך נכאה לי שכך פירושו של רבו מוהר"ן כלומר אלא רבו שלזה נעשה מוהר"ן ומילא מוהר"ן מוסר על תלמיד ושמם בעצמו סימן מוהר"ן מוסר מוהר"ן על הסימן שהסימן הוא מוהר"ן ובה"ר ונוגה לו כמשעט ועי"ל ימיד בספר זה נלמד איך רק מוציא רצון שהתלמיד עצמו יקרין אוכיר הכותב מותם לכבוד המחבר הדגול ולכל המשפחה

נפתלי הלוי יעגר

שאר ישוב
SH'OR YOSHUV
INSTITUTE

ONE CEDARLAWN AVENUE • LAWRENCE, NY 11559 • (516) 239-9002 • FAX: (516) 239-9003

Table of Contents

Introduction

THE MOMENT IS ETCHED IN MY MEMORY FOREVER.

My father *zt"l* had recently been diagnosed with a dreaded illness, and I was visiting him in his home. He sat in his big, brown leather armchair deep in thought, as I sat next to him quietly, waiting for him to open the conversation. After a few moments of silence, he had a request. "Yitzy, can you please pass me the phone? I need to make an important phone call to Rav Aaron Schechter (rosh yeshiva of Mesivta Yeshiva Rabbi Chaim Berlin). I must give him my name and ask him to daven for me."

I dialed the number. My father anxiously waited for R' Aaron to pick up the phone, which he did. Before voicing his request, my father clearly identified himself. "It's Chanina Herzberg, and I was a *talmid* of Rav Shlomo Freifeld *zt"l* (rosh yeshiva of Yeshiva Sh'or Yoshuv)..."

R' Aaron stopped my father before he could continue and forcefully shouted so loudly I could hear him through the phone, "No! You ARE a *talmid l'olam va'ed*! You are FOREVER A TALMID!"

I looked at my father, and my father looked at me, and he broke down in tears, tears that spoke volumes.

Tears of comfort.

Tears that emanated from the very essence of his being.

Tears that defined his 69 years of accomplishment in this world.

It was at that moment that I realized that anything my father — with the constant support of my mother, *she'tichyeh*, and, of course, with the help of Hashem — merited to accomplish in life came to fruition only because he had a rebbi: R' Shlomo Freifeld *zt"l*. R' Shlomo formed him, made him. And as my father was *mevatel* every fiber of his being to him, as he was *forever a talmid*, my father became his.

In a certain sense, what R' Shlomo accomplished with adults, my father accomplished with children. His life's mission was to infuse R' Shlomo's essence into the next generation, inspiring, elevating, and transforming the lives of his family, thousands of *talmidim, mispallelim,* and scores of people with whom he came in contact throughout his life.

Just as my father was *forever a talmid* of R' Shlomo Freifeld, so are each one of the thousands of people he had the *zechus* to mold *forever a talmid* of R' Chanina Herzberg.

Anyone acquainted with my father knows he was a private person, entirely focused on his mission of being *mechanech Yiddishe kinder,* without becoming lost in the "glitz and glamor," even as he became well-respected and well-known throughout the *chinuch* world. Although an excellent speaker who was frequently asked to speak at public events, he rarely accepted, instead focusing all his *kochos* on his *tafkid* as menahel, rav, and family man.

Therefore, we — my mother, my siblings, and myself — approached this project with trepidation. We all agreed that our father would not be happy with a biography written about him. However, we also agreed that now that he is no longer with us and can no longer, as a *mechanech,* continue his calling of infusing the essence of R' Shlomo into the next generation, he would agree that his teachings, his path, should live on through the written word.

This book serves as my father's *chinuch* legacy. As such, it is not a typical biography. It is the story of Charlie, a young boy from East New York, a boy born into an American Jewish family of the 1940's, who became R' Chanina, a Jew whose very essence proclaimed, "I am an *eved Hashem.*" A Jew who impacted thousands of Yidden over the course of his life. A Jew who became a legendary *mechanech,* elevating children and positioning them forward on their life's path.

True, our father's story is an extraordinary one, glimpses of which are found within this book, but that's not the point. Rather, the purpose of this book is to serve as a practical "*chinuch* handbook," expressed through countless stories about our father. A handbook from which parents, *mechanchim, mechanchos,* as well as anyone seeking a full picture of R' Shlomo Freifeld's *chinuch* approach, can glean and apply to their lives.

And hopefully, as you read this book, digesting it slowly and internalizing the message in its lessons, you will, in some way, become *forever a talmid.*

ACKNOWLEDGMENTS

IT IS IMPOSSIBLE TO PROPERLY EXPRESS *SHEVACH V'HODA'AH* TO the *Ribbono shel Olam* for the tremendous amount of *siyata d'Shmaya* He granted me in producing this book. "*Hodu la'Shem ki tov ki l'olam chasdo* — Give thanks to Hashem for He is good; His kindness endures forever" (*Tehillim* 136:1).

During the *shivah* for my father, numerous stories we'd never heard began pouring in. My family and I listened in awe, realizing his incredible impact. Following the *shivah,* I shared some of these stories with Rav Hillel David, *shlita,* who had known my father. After hearing the stories, he encouraged me to write each of them down to ensure they are not forgotten. The stories kept coming, and after a couple of years of writing and categorizing them, we — my siblings, my mother, and I — realized that here was a treasure trove of practical *chinuch* insight, as well as a tangible link to the essence of Rav Shlomo Freifeld *zt"l* and his teachings.

At that point, we discussed the idea of writing a book, and my family asked me to take on this project. I approached my rebbi, Rav Shlomo Halioua, *shlita,* rosh yeshiva of Mesivta Yeshiva Rabbi Chaim Berlin, and he encouraged me to undertake it — and the work on this book began.

Now that the project is coming to its conclusion, I would like to take the opportunity to express my gratitude to all those who have helped bring me to this point.

My father ingrained in me the importance of having a rebbi. I was *zocheh* to spend my formative years as a *bachur* in Yeshiva Sh'or Yoshuv, where my rebbi, the rosh yeshiva, **Rav Naftali Jaeger,** *shlita,* was and is a shining example of *ameilus baTorah,* and the fulfilling life that comes along with it. It means so much to my whole family that his letter graces this book. When I entered Mesivta Yeshiva Rabbi Chaim Berlin as a kollel *yungerman,* I was *zocheh* to acquire my rebbeim, and those rebbeim — the rosh yeshiva, **Rav Aaron Schechter,** *shlita,* and the rosh yeshiva, **Rav Shlomo Halioua,** *shlita* — have always been there to provide guidance, inspiration, and strength in every aspect of my life.

R' Avrohom Fruchthandler's excitement about this book early in the process helped give me strength to carry it through, and his invaluable insights truly enhanced the manuscript.

R' Yisroel Besser's words of encouragement throughout this project were instrumental in bringing it to fruition. Through his work on the book about R' Shlomo Freifeld, *Reb Shlomo* (Judaica Press), R' Yisroel got to know my father well, and I am honored that he wrote the foreword to this book.

R' Benjie Brecher, one of my father's closest friends, has done so much to perpetuate the legacy of R' Freifeld, especially through the biography, *Reb Shlomo.* Thank you for the consistent encouragement and for allowing me to use some important information contained in the *Reb Shlomo* book, which added so much to the final product.

My father and **Rav Mordechai Kamenetzky,** *shlita,* dean/rosh yeshiva of Yeshiva Toras Chaim Bais Binyamin at South Shore, enjoyed a very close relationship. R' Mordechai, with the help of his son R' Shmuel, director of advancement at Yeshiva Toras Chaim, made himself available throughout this process, clarifying important information, providing many pictures, and sharing articles and letters, all of which added immensely to this volume.

I cannot thank my close friend **R' Dovid Hertzberg** enough for his continued friendship, guidance, and listening ear.

I've come to learn that finding the right editor is difficult. *Baruch Hashem,* **Mrs. Tova Salb** was willing to take on this project. In truth, she was not only an editor, but an adviser, as well. She taught me the ins and outs of structuring a book and pulling it all together. There are no words to express my appreciation for going above and beyond in ensuring that this book came out the way it did.

Both the **Silber families** and **Golombeck families** enjoyed a close bond with my father. How appropriate that both families agreed to sponsor this book. I am truly appreciative of their generosity.

R' Raziel Stone's notes of R' Shlomo Freifeld's weekly Shabbos *derashos* added so much to this book. Thank you!

Thanks to **Gi Orman** of **Big Productions** for giving me access to hours of interviews from the many close *talmidim* and friends of my father, originally filmed for Yeshiva Toras Chaim's dinner honoring my father's legacy.

Thank you to **Hamodia** for allowing me to glean from the research of **R' Binyamin Zev Karman** for an article about R' Yitzchok Schmidman. Thank you to **Mishpacha Magazine** for use of the information contained in an article about R' Shlomo Freifeld by **R' Yisroel Besser.** Thank you to the **Jewish Heritage Society of the Five Towns** for the historical background of Yeshiva Toras Chaim, both of East New York and South Shore.

Thank you to all those who came forward to share personal memories and stories, and to all those who wrote articles and letters following my father's *petirah.*

After becoming acquainted with the inner workings of **ArtScroll,** I was able to see how **R' Gedaliah Zlotowitz** leads with dignity, dedication, and a pleasant demeanor. Thank you for your words of encouragement and for believing in this project.

R' Nosson Scherman, the "pen" behind the ArtScroll product, continues to enrich every project put forth by ArtScroll.

R' Sheah Brander's attention to detail and keen insights ensured that the final product is truly worthy of the ArtScroll stamp. As a beloved *mechutan* of my father, his involvement in this project was especially meaningful.

R' Avrohom Biderman's wise advice and counsel are always on target and always valued.

Mrs. Judi Dick augmented this volume with her spot-on edits and astute observations. Her vote of confidence and appreciation for this project kept me going, even when the work seemed interminable.

R' Yitzchok Hisiger's excitement, energy, and *chizuk* injected me with renewed *kochos* when the task appeared overwhelming.

R' Eli Kroen's talent and quest for perfection always come through. This cover, which encapsulates the essence of both my father and R' Shlomo Freifeld, provided a challenge, which R' Eli met with his usual professionalism.

Mrs. Estie Dicker paginated the book and inserted edits and numerous photographs, all with efficiency and skill.

Chanie Ziegler's work on the photographs is very much appreciated.

Mrs. Mindy Stern proofread the book from cover to cover, with precision and proficiency.

Mrs. Esther Feierstein made many important suggestions.

To **Mommy:** You stood behind Abba in everything he did with incredible *mesiras nefesh*. This book, in a certain sense, is really a tribute to you. May you continue to lead the *mishpachah* with strength and vigor, together with your husband, **Rav Tzvi Flaum,** in good health.

To **Bubby Sarah,** who is an inspiration to the entire family. May you see continued *nachas* from your children, grandchildren, great-grandchildren, and great-great-grandchildren, for many years.

To my in-laws, **R' Yitzchok** and **Miriam Skolnik:** May you be blessed with continued good health and much *nachas*. Your constant availability, support, and advice are of inestimable value.

To my **Aunt Sharon:** I cannot adequately describe what you mean to the entire Herzberg family. As my father's only sibling, we turn to you for your wisdom, your logic, and your humor. May you and Uncle Harris see much *nachas* from your family, along with the entire *mishpachah.*

Baruch Hashem, our parents raised my siblings and me as a very close and tight-knit family. We laugh together, we cry together, we grow together; we call each other frequently for advice. As close as we were at the time of our father's *petirah,* through this project we became even closer. All of you and your spouses added so much to the final product.

To **Moshe:** Thank you for your sage advice throughout this journey, and for always being the voice of reason when making the difficult decision of what to include and what to leave out.

To **Mendy:** Through this project, I got a closeup view of the important work you do at ArtScroll on a daily basis. You are akin to the conductor of a magnificent symphony, pulling it all together with poise, grace, and calm. Your know-how and experience in taking a book from beginning to end cannot be overstated. It was only through your constant guidance that this book came to fruition.

To **Eli:** As you are also *zocheh* to spend your time being *mechanech Yiddishe kinder,* the two of us have spent countless hours discussing the many *chinuch* conversations each of us had with Abba, especially regarding his general *chinuch* approach and the *mesorah* transmitted to him by his rebbi. Your initial writings, sent out to hundreds in the few months following Abba's passing, entitled "Chinuch Daily," were invaluable to this project. Particularly helpful was the fact that you spent over seventeen years working side-by-side with Abba, and therefore had the unusual "in the trenches experience," which helped convey Abba's *chinuch* legacy.

To **Brochie:** Your knack of cutting through all the nonsense in deciding if and how something should be conveyed was much appreciated.

To **Rivky:** Your levelheadedness and on-point edits contributed so much to the final product.

To **Yudi:** You were the apple of Abba's eye, and you have done so much to perpetuate his legacy. You undertook the task of raising funds and purchasing a house in your growing Monsey neighborhood of Pomona East, to become Khal Zichron Chanina Getzel, named for Abba. Yudi, it was your financial backing that allowed this book to happen, and we are all forever grateful. Abba would be proud that you took upon yourself to dedicate this book to his *yedid*, R' Milton Ostreicher *z"l*, as *hakaras hatov* for getting you started in the workforce.

To my brother-in-law, **Aharon Kaplan:** Your trademark humor and wit provided a breath of fresh air, all the while keeping us focused on the goal.

To my brother-in-law, **Shua Nachman:** For months, we could not think of an appropriate title for the book. It was you who came up with the magnificent title, *Forever a Talmid*. For that, and everything else, we are all thankful.

To my sisters-in-law, **Sara, Yocheved, Sara,** and **Chumi:** Thank you for your input and insight throughout this project.

To **my children,** who sacrificed so much of the time that should have been spent with me so that this book about "Zeidy Rockaway" could come to fruition. Mommy and I are so proud of each and every one of you. May you continue to be a source of *Yiddishe nachas* to Mommy and me.

To my wife, **Rivki:** Suffice it to say that none of this would have been possible without you, and whatever I write is not enough. Thank you for everything.

May this book find its place in the minds and hearts of Klal Yisrael, and become a valuable resource to parents, *mechanchim, mechanchos,* and anyone looking to grow in their service of the *Ribbono shel Olam*.

And, of course, through this book, may the essence of R' Shlomo Freifeld come alive and call out to each and every one of us to grow, expand our dimensions, and become "big Jews."

Yitzchok Herzberg
ח׳ טבת תשפ״ג
יארצייט של אבי מורי הרב חנינא געציל בן ר׳ משה זצ״ל

Note to reader:

After much deliberation, it was decided to write this book in third person.

In addition, in many stories, names (and details) were changed to protect privacy, as indicated by an asterisk.

PHOTO CREDITS

AE Gedolim Photos
Ari Hirsch/ Jewish Vues
Benjie Brecher
Dovid Bashevkin
Herzberg family
Ira Thomas Creations
Jewish Heritage Society of the Five Towns
Menachem Butler
Naftoli Goldgrab Photography
Orthodox Jewish Archive of Agudath Israel of America
Avrohom Monczyk
Mordechai Schiller
Shaul Kessler
Telushkin family
Tsemach Glenn
Yeshiva Darchei Torah
Yeshiva Rabbi Chaim Berlin
Yeshiva Sh'or Yoshuv
Yeshiva Toras Chaim

Foreword

By Yisroel Besser

THE GIFTED MUSICIAN STANDS ON THE STAGE OF THE GREAT HALL and plays to an enchanted audience.

Take that same musician out of the concert hall, without the soaring ceilings and impeccable acoustics, and the sound will become thinner, more distant.

Now, take away his instrument, and the music is diminished yet further.

However, if that musician, displaced from his usual venue, deprived of his usual instrument, can still enthrall the people with his song, it is testimony to both the beauty of the music and the talent of the one who plays it.

Slabodka was a song, an approach developed by the greatest virtuoso of his time, its strains of the majesty of man imbedded on the souls of dynamic, brilliant young men.

They were enraptured by the song of the Alter of Slabodka, committed to teaching it to others.

A generation later, Rav Yitzchak Hutner — one of several Slabodka *talmidim* who filled similar roles — stood alone in a field. Gone was Slabodka and the Olam HaYeshivos that had spawned it. How does one transmit glory when there is only numbness and shock, mourning all that has been lost?

But he found a way, somehow recreating the Alter's song in America, investing young men who had never seen Kovno or Warsaw or Bialystok with the reverence and appreciation for the beauty Torah has to offer.

But then, for some people, the music began to be drowned out by sounds of the street, America playing a song of its own, its noise raucous, deafening, and devoid of substance.

Could the song continue?

Rav Hutner had a *talmid*, Rav Shlomo Freifeld, and he played the song of Slabodka not just in the *beis medrash*, but in the noisy streets of New York, its melody pulling not just the close ones closer, but even those who appeared distant.

The original instrument was long gone, the concert hall of old in ruins, but the *niggun* played on.

But what about the children? Could someone take sophisticated harmonies and convey them to those who barely knew how to sing?

These children had not come to America, but had been born into its excess and superficiality: there were those who thought they were not suited to this sort of learning, and others who did not notice them at all.

And then came Reb Chanina. He knew the song, because he had learned it from the best, and he knew that the children were not just capable, but eager.

This book is the story of that song, and the one who believed not just in its power, but also in the greatness of the audience.

Eventually, they all caught on: see them as great, and they will be great. See them as capable, and they will be capable. See them as thirsty, and they will thirst.

He was among the first though, and so many others were sustained on the *shvil Chanina bni*, the *chinuch* path he forged.

I discovered the world of Rav Shlomo Freifeld in 2005 and during those first few months, I would often stop and marvel at what I was seeing. This Yid, with his vision, his *chiyus*, and his pure Yiddishe instinct, had created a kehillah of old, a family, really, of *talmidim* connected to the Rebbi.

And just as in a family, different children had different roles, so too in that *chaburah*.

Interviewing people for the book on the Rebbi, I spoke with many different *talmidim*, but somehow, I kept making my way back to Reb Chanina.

Not just for his stories, but because he "got it." I was hearing so many other stories — some made sense, some seemed implausible, and others were great, but did not belong in a book. He understood all of this, able to guide me with the easy coolness of someone who has no agenda, who takes up no space in the stories of others, blessed with the *mechanech's* eye for which stories would have impact.

Driving in the Catskills on a summer day after a particularly weighty interview, I felt like I needed Reb Chanina to help me process it, and I drove to his home in Woodridge.

As I sat there, someone else came to visit, having just arrived from the city. Reb Chanina asked him which route he had taken, since the weekend traffic was especially heavy.

The visitor smiled, and said some combination of Van Wyck to the Hutch to the Deegan or whatever it was — I wasn't really paying attention to the how. As he spoke, Reb Chanina's eyes opened wide and he said, "No way, that's brilliant, tell me again."

The visitor's stance got a bit straighter, his voice a bit more confident as he retraced his route and Reb Chanina stood up. He reached out and gave the other man a "high five," the echo of that perfect slap ringing in the house, and commented admiringly one more time on the *chiddush*, the ideal route to beat traffic.

I looked on and knew I was seeing a story about the Rebbi, Reb Shlomo, and that the conversation I had just seen had nothing to do with congestion and the Van Wyck.

Reb Shlomo would say that there is a mandate to emulate the Creator, to reflect His conduct. *Mah Hu rachum*, just as He is compassionate, so too must you be compassionate.

In davening each morning, Reb Shlomo said, we proclaim that Hashem gives life to every living being: *Ve'atah mechayeh es kulam.*

"If Hashem gives life, then 'emulating His ways' means that we too should try to give life to every person we meet," said the Rebbi.

"You *chapped* to get off at that exit, you're a genius," said the *talmid*.

Ve'atah mechayeh es kulam.

That was what the Rebbi did, and Reb Chanina, his *talmid*, found myriad ways each day to do the same, having learned from the master.

No wonder the pain and heartbreak when Reb Chanina slipped away was so profound... so many people had relied on him to give them life.

Maybe this book will remind them of who they are. Maybe this book will remind us. And perhaps, if we are *zocheh*, this book will teach us how to carry around that sort of *chiyus*, that special combination of wise eyesight and a good heart, so that we too can bring life to others.

Just as Reb Chanina did. May we be *zocheh* to make others feel, as he made us feel.

Yisroel Besser
Chanukah 5783

Chapter 1

The Seed Is Planted: Early Influences

R' Yitzchak Schmidman

SUMMER, 1955 (5715). 6-YEAR-OLD CHARLIE HERZBERG COULDN'T WAIT. In just a few weeks, he would be joining the "big boys" in the local public school. Charlie's parents were like many of the observant Jews in America at that time who valued Yiddishkeit; they understood the importance of a yeshiva education. However, they could not afford the yeshiva tuition and felt uncomfortable sending their son without payment. In their way of thinking, they had no other option but to send him to public school.

Not everyone agreed with their decision. And one such person was about to voice his disagreement.

It was the week before the school year began. In the Herzberg apartment on Blake Avenue in East New York, Charlie and his parents were at home when there was an unexpected knock at the door. Mrs. Herzberg opened it

Chanina Herzberg as a young child with his sister Sharon

Yeshiva Toras Chaim of East New York

and was taken aback to see none other than R' Yitzchak Schmidman, menahel of Yeshiva Toras Chaim of East New York, standing at the door.

"What brings the rav to our apartment?" she asked deferentially.

With tears in his eyes, R' Schmidman responded in a pleading tone,

R' Yitzchak Schmidman with Yeshiva Toras Chaim staff in the early 1930's; R' Schmidman is seated in the center.

"Mrs. Herzberg, *tein li hanefesh*, give me your child (based on *Bereishis* 14:21). Please, send Charlie to yeshiva!"

"But R' Schmidman, we can't afford the tuition," Mrs. Herzberg answered regretfully.

R' Schmidman was accustomed to this response, and he had his own rejoinder ready. "Don't worry about the tuition. For Charlie, we have a special rate of one dollar a month. I expect to see him in yeshiva on the first day of school."

Although he had stated his wish, R' Schmidman knew his clientele. The morning of the first day of school, Mrs. Herzberg once again heard a knock on the door. When she opened it, again she could not believe her eyes. It was none other than R' Schmidman back for another visit, despite his packed agenda that morning.

R' Schmidman explained the reason behind the morning visit. "Charlie needs to go to yeshiva. But when I left your apartment last week, I sensed

Chanina's first-grade class in Yeshiva Toras Chaim of East New York, with their rebbi, R' Mechel Scholar (left) R' Yitzchak Schmidman (back right)

some hesitation on your part. Therefore, I decided not to take any chances and I came myself to pick him up and bring him to yeshiva." With that, he took Charlie's hand, and hand in hand they walked to yeshiva. With this began Charlie's lifetime of yeshiva education.

Yes, Charlie's life — and the life of his entire family, his future generations, and his *talmidim* — was changed forever. R' Schmidman had planted a seed right where it belonged, in the fertile environment of a yeshiva.

Yiddishkeit in the East New York neighborhood of the late 1940's was a struggle. In the aftermath of the war years, the world in general was in turmoil, and the future of world Jewry in particular was at stake. On one hand, Jews wished to preserve the Yiddishkeit of their parents, many of whom had been born in the *shtetlach* of Europe. On the other hand, they were overwhelmed by the vast ocean of American culture, which presented opportunities that had never been available in Europe. Unfortunately, many parents could not keep their children's Yiddishkeit afloat, and future generations drowned in the tumult of the times.

It was in this environment that Chanina Getzel Herzberg was born to Moish and Florence Herzberg on April 20th, 1949 (*Acharon shel Pesach*, 5709). His mother gave him the English name Charles Gilbert, because from the time of his birth, she foresaw her son taking advantage of the opportunities America had to offer; her dream was for him to become a doctor. "The name Charles Gilbert Herzberg, MD, will look impressive on the nameplate outside his office," she would say. In fact, the blurb near his picture in his Mesivta Yeshiva Rabbi Chaim Berlin yearbook informs its readers that Chanina wanted to become a dentist. When Chanina was engaged, his *kallah,* Naomi,

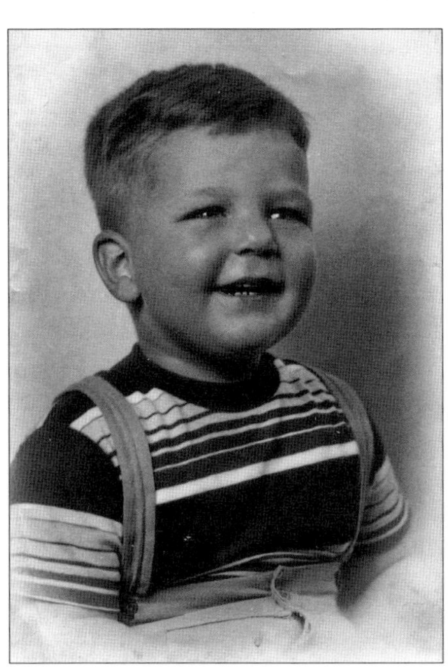

Chanina as a little boy

CHARLES HERZBERG
Rabbinical Academy, Yeshiva University
dentist
•
G. O. alternate
"A man in earnest finds means, and if he cannot find, creates them"—Channing

Yearbook picture and write-up stating Chanina's ambition to become a dentist

browsed through the yearbook and asked, "What is this all about?" To which he replied, "I wrote it to make my mother happy."

Little did Chanina's mother realize. He was indeed destined to be a doctor, just a different type of doctor — a doctor of the soul.

As Charlie grew up, many people helped shape whom he would eventually become. However, R' Yitzchak Schmidman was the one to plant the seed that would eventually blossom into R' Chanina Herzberg, a *mechanech* par excellence.

R' Schmidman was born in 1898 (5658), in Pahost (Pogust), Belarus. An accomplished *talmid chacham,* he learned under the Alter of Novardok, R' Yosef Yoizel Horowitz, in Yeshivas Novardok, and in several other leading yeshivos. At one point, R' Schmidman was sent by Yeshivas Mir in Poland to fundraise in the United States. One of the board members of Yeshiva Toras Chaim of East New York was present at a speech he gave and was captivated by his fervor and spirit. The board member persuaded R' Schmidman to remain in America, for that was where he was needed. He was given the position of menahel of the yeshiva.

R' Schmidman possessed a fiery enthusiasm for spreading Torah. He would walk the streets of East New York and Brownsville, trekking from house to house. "*Tein li hanefesh,* give me your children," he would call out to the Yidden, pleading with them to send their children to yeshivos.

He would quote the *pasuk* (*Yirmiyahu* 2:2), which speaks of Hashem's interminable love for His nation, and His gratitude for their devotion. "*Lechteich acharai ba'midbar b'eretz lo zeruah* — how you followed Me into the Wilderness, into an unsown land." R' Schmidman stated that America was not only a *midbar,* a wilderness, but also an *"eretz* ***'lo'*** *zeruah,"* a land where the word "no" was planted, where an attitude of negativity and pessimism regarding a Jewish future had already set in. He saw it as his mission to combat that "no," to demonstrate that it is feasible to nurture frum Yidden, even upon American soil.

Thousands of children passed through the doors of Yeshiva Toras Chaim at 631 Belmont Avenue, where they received an authentic Jewish education. It made no difference who you were, where you came from, or how much tuition you could pay. Every child was accepted by R' Schmidman with open arms and an open heart.

Though there were approximately 100,000 Jews living in East New York at the time, most Jewish children attended public school. On Rosh Hashanah and Yom Kippur, when the shuls filled with the local Jewish children, the public schools reported 10,000 absences. Yet, even in its heyday, Yeshiva Toras Chaim in East New York had a maximum enrollment of 600 children.

Many of the future leaders of American Jewry attended Yeshiva Toras Chaim, where their lives were shaped by R' Schmidman. Among them were R' Dovid Feinstein, rosh yeshiva of Mesivtha Tifereth Jerusalem; R' Shlomo Freifeld, rosh yeshiva of Yeshiva Sh'or Yoshuv; R' Yaakov Perlow, the Novominsker Rebbe; and R' Aaron Schechter, rosh yeshiva of Mesivta Yeshiva Rabbi Chaim Berlin.

Moetzes Gedolei HaTorah meeting with R' Aaron Schechter, R' Dovid Feinstein, and R' Yaakov Perlow, all of whom attended Yeshiva Toras Chaim, sitting side-by-side (on left side; second, third, and fourth from the left respectively)

Years later, when the Novominsker Rebbe visited Yeshiva Toras Chaim in Hewlett, he looked at the students and said with a smile, "You are *talmidim* of Yeshiva Toras Chaim, and I am a *talmid* of Yeshiva Toras Chaim," imbuing the *talmidim* with feelings of *chashivus* and pride. R' Aaron Schechter once told a *talmid*, "If not for R' Schmidman, who knows where I would be today!"

It was R' Schmidman's cry of *"Tein li hanefesh*!" that left a major imprint on Chanina's life, as well, and he never forgot it. Over 50 years after Charlie joined Yeshiva Toras Chaim, R' Chanina was on the phone with his son Eli who worked in Camp Dora Golding. Eli inquired about a camper whose last name was Schmidman: Was this boy related to R' Yitzchak Schmidman? When R' Chanina was told that the camper was the great-grandson of R' Schmidman, tears formed in his eyes. In a voice choked with emotion, he asked Eli to go over and thank the boy. "His great-grandfather saw to it that I attended yeshiva in East New York. Without him, I would have gone to public school." Echoing the words of R' Aaron Schechter and most likely many others, he avowed, "Who knows what would have become of me if that had happened!"

Far From a Star

YOUNG CHARLIE WAS NOT BORN INTO GREATNESS. HE WAS A REGULAR American boy. His family spent their summers in a bungalow on 85th Street in the Rockaways, and they would frequently go to the beach. Charlie loved sports, played baseball regularly, and was the star linebacker on his football team.

Playing baseball

A childhood friend shared how Charlie was a great third baseman, but more importantly, he was the kindest person on the team. "He never said a bad word about anyone, and no one ever said a bad word about him."

He may have been very kind and a star ballplayer, but he was far from a star student. When it came to the classroom, Charlie just could not get it right. The phone calls from his rebbeim and teachers were almost a nightly occurrence. "Mrs. Herzberg, Charlie needs to work on his classroom behavior," or "Mrs. Herzberg, Charlie failed his test again."

Years later, when R' Chanina served as menahel of Yeshiva Toras Chaim, a couple approached him at a parent-teacher conference with a concern regarding their son, a very challenging student.

"I was a challenging student, as well," R' Chanina admitted with a smile. "When my mother would speak to my rebbeim at parent-teacher conferences, they would tell her, 'Mrs. Herzberg, there's one in every family. It's fine, he'll turn out okay.'

"Don't worry," R' Chanina now assured the boy's parents, "look at me. I think I turned out all right. Your son will, too."

One year, Charlie's rebbi set up the rows in the classroom according to achievement. *Shurah aleph,* row one, was for the top boys; *shurah beis,* the second row, for the next level; and so on. Charlie's seat was in *shurah hei*, the fifth and last row, for obvious reasons. Many years later, he met that rebbi and introduced himself as Herzberg.

"Herzberg from *shurah hei*?" the rebbi inquired.

"Yes."

"Tell me," the rebbi wanted to know, "what do you do today?"

"You won't believe it, but I'm the menahel of Yeshiva Toras Chaim," R' Chanina informed him.

The rebbi nearly fainted on the spot.

But through it all, R' Schmidman never gave up hope on his precious *talmid*.

R' Shlomo Pfeiffer — s'gan menahel of Yeshiva Ketana of Long Island, who previously served on the staff of Yeshiva Toras Chaim — stated that R' Chanina never sought to give the *talmidim* of Yeshiva Toras Chaim the impression that he was a perfect child growing up. To the contrary, he made a point of telling them that he was far from perfect — but he worked on himself and grew. And he never gave up hope on his precious *talmidim* either.

Davey,* an eighth-grader who attended public school, moved with his family to the Five Towns of Long Island. Soon after the move, he came to Yeshiva Toras Chaim for an interview. Davey was extremely apprehensive, wondering how he could possibly make the difficult transition from public school to yeshiva. When he sat down across from R' Chanina, taking in his impressive stature and all, he was nonplussed by the menahel's opening question.

"Davey, do you think I'm successful?"

"Yeah," Davey responded hesitantly, not sure where this was going. "You're a rebbi, you're a menahel."

"Would you believe me if I told you I probably have ADD?" the menahel asked him.

After letting that revelation sink in, R' Chanina continued gently, "Look what I was able to do even though it was hard for me!"

Hearing this, Davey's face lit up with a huge smile. R' Chanina's words gave him such hope and *chizuk*. R' Chanina didn't yet know the extent of what Davey had been through; he merely sensed it and said exactly what Davey needed to hear.

When R' Chanina was *niftar*, Davey came home with tears in his eyes. "Mommy, I'm so sad that R' Herzberg passed away. Do you remember how he made me feel comfortable and gave me hope at my interview?"

The Will to Learn

WHEN CHARLIE WAS IN EIGHTH GRADE, IT WAS TIME TO MAKE THE critical decision regarding which high school to attend. Attending a mainstream yeshiva was not a given. He was not a good student and was not into his learning. Little wonder he had his eyes set on the high school with the best basketball team.

"But then R' Schmidman came to the rescue again and dragged me to meet R' Yitzchak Hutner, rosh yeshiva of Mesivta Yeshiva Rabbi Chaim Berlin," R' Chanina would say as he shared the story. "One day, R' Schmidman walked up to me and said, 'Today we're going to meet R' Hutner. I hope you'll be accepted to his yeshiva.'

"However, I did not do too well," R' Chanina admitted to his listeners as he recounted the story.

But R' Hutner could see beyond the surface. When the disastrous *farher* finally wound down, he had one final question for Charlie.

R' Yitzchak Hutner, rosh yeshiva, Mesivta Yeshiva Rabbi Chaim Berlin

"Do you want to learn?"

"Yes!" Charlie replied.

R' Hutner extended his hand to Charlie and told him, "Chanina, I want you in my yeshiva."

Charlie smiled. "Then I want to come."

"Well then, you're in!" R' Hutner smiled back.

Reflecting on that critical moment in his life, R' Chanina would later stress the power of words. "It was an extremely difficult decision for my parents and for me. I was unsure if I wanted to go to Yeshiva Rabbi Chaim Berlin or not. But those few words, 'I want you in my yeshiva,' changed everything!

"R' Hutner believed in me; he believed that I could do it. *And so I started believing in myself.*" At that moment, Chanina became one of the many *talmidim* who were positively impacted by R' Hutner, a rebbi who believed in the potential of every *talmid.*

As a menahel, R' Chanina would repeat R' Hutner's words, "Do you want to learn?" to help his *talmidim* understand that the desire to learn is the key to success. Those words of R' Hutner helped shape R' Chanina's approach in giving all types of boys the opportunity to attend Yeshiva Toras Chaim. If the boy wanted to learn and the environment of the yeshiva was the best place for him to grow, then Yeshiva Toras Chaim was the right place for him.

With a *talmid* at a Yeshiva Toras Chaim graduation

Furthermore, he used this story as a lesson for eighth-grade boys as they contemplated which high school to attend. "Remember," he would assert, "this decision is a major decision; it could be life-altering. Be careful which high school you choose to attend!"

Enduring Lessons

THROUGH HIS OWN EXPERIENCE WITH R' SCHMIDMAN, R' CHANINA learned that if a person feels a true *achrayus* toward every Yid in Klal Yisrael, and he has the strength and courage to carry through on his mission, he can affect people's lives in unfathomable ways.

A mother of a child in a local yeshiva, Mrs. Friedman,* was insulted by how a rebbi treated her son. Terribly upset, she overreacted, not only by taking her son out of yeshiva, but also taking her daughter out of Bais Yaakov, placing them both in public school. A short time later, she called her friend Mrs. Goldbaum* and asked, "How terrible is it if my daughter attends a Halloween party?"

Mrs. Goldbaum was so shaken by the question that she started calling local rabbanim, asking them to convince Mrs. Friedman to reenroll her children in yeshiva. They tried, but to no avail. Someone told her, "Call R' Chanina Herzberg. He knows the family, and he'll know what to do."

As soon as he received the call, R' Chanina immediately responded, "I'll take care of it."

That Friday afternoon, there was a knock on the Friedman family's door. There stood R' Chanina, with a fresh, hot potato kugel in his hands. After being welcomed into the house, he announced, "I'm not leaving this house until you tell me that you are sending your children back to yeshiva. I'll stay here the entire Shabbos if I have to!"

Mrs. Friedman was so impressed by the strength and courage behind his words that she decided then and there to reinstate her children in Jewish schools.

Chanina at his bar mitzvah

Another boy, Baruch,* was having a hard time. Due to his academic and behavioral issues, no mesivta wanted him. Distraught, his father approached R' Chanina and sadly informed him, "I've been told there is nothing to be done for my son."

R' Chanina banged on the table and declared, "This is a *Yiddishe neshamah*! What do you mean, there is nothing to do?!"

He promptly called the menahel of a mesivta that he thought would be a good fit. In no uncertain terms, R' Chanina let the menahel know, "I'm not hanging up the phone until you agree to accept Baruch into your yeshiva."

At his bar mitzvah with his parents and sister Sharon

The menahel relented and called Baruch's father. "R' Herzberg just called me and 'beat me up,'" he disclosed. "Your son is now welcome to come to our yeshiva."

There is another aspect to this *achrayus,* also gleaned by R' Chanina from R' Schmidman. On the Shabbos morning of Charlie's bar mitzvah, he was surprised that R' Schmidman, who lived two miles from the shul, had come to wish him and his parents mazel tov. Remembering how important this made him feel, R' Chanina later found the strength, as a seventh-grade rebbi and then as a menahel, to attend the bar mitzvahs of his own *talmidim.* He would go to every bar mitzvah, at times walking several miles in the rain, snow, or heat. Only when it was physically impossible to go did he stay home.

R' Schmidman implanted in Charlie a true love and appreciation for Eretz Yisrael and for every Yisrael. When Charlie was in fifth grade, R' Schmidman was the Navi teacher for his class. On the first day, he walked into the classroom, the students opened their *sefarim* to the very first *pasuk* of *Yeshayahu,* and R' Schmidman began to chant, in the tune reserved for *Eichah* on Tishah B'Av, "*Chazon Yeshayahu ben Amotz asher chazah al Yehudah vi'rushalayim...* — The vision of Yeshayahu the son of Amotz, which he saw concerning Yehudah and Yerushalayim..."

That's when R' Schmidman veered from the expected script, as tears immediately began to stream down his face. He was so choked with emotion that it took him 10 minutes to read the entire *pasuk.* R' Chanina later said that he always visualized this image of R' Schmidman during the Three Weeks, in which we mourn the destruction of the *Beis HaMikdash.* Already in fifth grade, Charlie saw a living example of what it means to truly mourn the *Churban.* To R' Chanina, the *Churban* was real, the loss of the *Shechinah* a horrific tragedy. The longing for the rebuilding of the *Beis HaMikdash* was genuine as well, not mere lip service.

R' Chanina at the Kosel

R' Schmidman taught another vital lesson that day. "We all know that the *Beis HaMikdash* was destroyed because of *sinas chinam,* unwarranted hatred. How can we rectify that?" Taking a piece of chalk, he wrote two words on the blackboard: *"ahavas chinam,"* unconditional love.

After he wept, R' Schmidman demonstrated the unconditional love he felt for every Yid. "Do you know how many children are on the street, not keeping Shabbos?"

R' Schmidman didn't merely preach love of Eretz Yisrael or love of other Jews; he taught both in a living, vibrant fashion.

As a product of some of Europe's leading yeshivos, R' Schmidman related stories of European *gedolim,* with the hope of connecting young American boys to the greatness of prewar Europe. For example, when Charlie was in eighth grade, R' Schmidman spoke to his class about the importance of controlling one's anger. To drive the point home, he told the boys a story about R' Yosef Yoizel Horowitz, the Alter of Novardok. Whenever the Alter felt the need to rebuke a student for an inappropriate act, he would first ask someone to bring him a special coat from his office; he called it "the coat of anger." Only after donning the coat would the Alter begin to reprove the student.

When asked about this seemingly odd behavior, the Alter explained, "We must deliver rebuke when we are calm, not when we are angry. It takes a few minutes for someone to bring me my coat and for me to put it on. That gives me time enough to calm down and put myself in the correct frame of mind so I can properly deliver the reproof."

After hearing this story from his menahel, Charlie asked in disbelief, "Rebbi, do you really believe this story is true?"

R' Schmidman countered, "I know for a fact it's true, because I was a *talmid* in Novardok, and I'm the one who brought the Alter his coat!"

R' Chanina kept this lesson with him throughout his life. Dr. Eli Shapiro, Ed. D, LCSW, who worked in Yeshiva Toras Chaim as a social worker for several years, noted, "When R' Chanina had to raise his voice at a student, it was an exterior action. There wasn't any emotional negativity. He was doing what he had to do because that's what the student needed."

As a *bachur* in mesivta, Chanina had the opportunity to connect with R' Hutner, as well. Chanina was one of the few *bachurim* who had a car, affording him the opportunity to occasionally chauffeur R' Hutner from place to place. It was during these rides that R' Hutner would talk to R' Chanina about *hashkafas hachaim*, sharing many stories of *gedolim*, further implanting in him a desire for *gadlus*.

R' Yitzchak Schmidman planted the seed, which he continued to water and care for, soon passing it to the able hands of R' Yitzchak Hutner. In time, it began to sprout, ready to be nurtured further until it flourished and blossomed and was ready to scatter its own seeds.

R' Nissen Telushkin

FROM THE TIME CHARLIE WAS YOUNG, VARIOUS INDIVIDUALS INFLUenced him, each one watering and nurturing the seed a bit more. In East New York and neighboring Brownsville, there were many noted rabbanim. One of the most prominent was R' Nissen Telushkin, a *gadol baTorah*. Born in 1881 (5641) in the city of Bobruisk, Belarus, R' Nissen learned in Karson and Slutzk, where his rebbeim included R' Isser Zalman Meltzer, R' Yaakov Dovid Wilovsky (the Ridvaz), and R' Baruch Ber Leibowitz. R' Telushkin received *semichah* from R' Shmuel Moshe Shapiro of Bobruisk and R' Shmaryahu Noach Schneerson.

After serving as rav in the towns of Bobruisk, Dukar, and Pechovitz, R' Telushkin immigrated to New York in 1924 (5684) and became the rav of Bnai Yitzchak Nusach Ari on Georgia Avenue in East New York. He also served as editor of *HaMesilah,* the Torah journal published under the auspices of the Vaad HaRabbanim of New York. R' Telushkin dedicated much of his time toward improving the *mikvaos* in New York, and wrote a two-volume work on the topic, *Taharas Mayim.*

R' Nissen Telushkin

R' Telushkin was Chanina's grandparents' rav. When his grandmother, Mrs. Bertha Laxer, had a *shailah* for the rav, she frequently sent Charlie with the question, and he slowly established a relationship with the rav and learned many lessons from him and from his approach.

R' Chanina's grandparents, Max and Bertha Laxer

One Erev Pesach, Mrs. Laxer sent Charlie to R' Telushkin with an "important" question. She had forgotten to purchase cinnamon and wanted to know if she was permitted to make *charoses* without it. R' Telushkin pulled a large volume of *Shulchan Aruch* from his bookshelf and spent several minutes studying it.

Finally, he closed it and instructed Charlie, "Tell your grandmother that this year she may make the *charoses* without cinnamon. However, next year she must be careful to purchase kosher-for-Pesach cinnamon immediately after Purim." The rav then went into a side room and emerged with a bottle of wine. "Give this to your grandmother and tell her the rav wishes her a *gut Yom Tov.*"

Obviously, the question is not discussed in the *Shulchan Aruch,* nor did it require any research on the rav's part. However, by giving Charlie the impression that he took his question seriously, R' Telushkin was ensuring that Charlie would not be embarrassed to seek guidance on future occasions. Many years later, R' Chanina still reminisced about the story and the imprint it left.

On another occasion, his grandmother had a question regarding glassware she was *kashering* for Pesach. According to halachah, the process involves soaking the glasses for three days in water, and changing the water every 24 hours. During the course of the three-day period, his grandmother couldn't remember if she had changed the water in the last 24 hours, so she sent Charlie to find out how to proceed. "Your grandmother is a *yerei Shamayim,*" R' Telushkin responded. "I know her and there's no way she forgot to change the water."

When Charlie was in eighth grade, Yeshiva Toras Chaim held a fundraiser before Pesach, where they sold wine and for a fee delivered it to families in the neighborhood. R' Chanina later said in a *shiur,* "I was very good at making these deliveries, since half the time I wasn't in class anyway. And I knew how to work it out that I would be the one to deliver the wine to R' Telushkin." That year, when he came to R' Telushkin's apartment, Charlie learned an important lesson.

R' Telushkin could have thanked Charlie for the delivery and sent him on his way. Instead, he invited him into his apartment, sat him down, gave him a candy and a drink. When recalling this incident, R' Chanina explained that there are many ways to do a mitzvah. From R' Telushkin, he learned to do it all the way, in the best way possible.

R' Telushkin also taught Charlie what it means to be a true *talmid chacham,* a rav, and a man with an *achrayus* for the *tzibbur*. To Charlie, R' Telushkin was the picture of perfection, both in *chochmah* and in character. R' Chanina shared with his *talmidim* how R' Telushkin would march down the street on Shabbos to try to convince the Jewish storekeepers to close their businesses, which, unfortunately were open on Shabbos. "As R' Chanina spoke about it, you felt you were part of it," R' Shlomo Pfeiffer recalled.

Interestingly, many years earlier, R' Telushkin had also been the rav of R' Shlomo Freifeld, rosh yeshiva of Yeshiva Sh'or Yoshuv and R' Chanina's rebbi. R' Shlomo credited R' Telushkin with ingraining within him the desire to become a *talmid chacham*. "When I was 5 years old," R' Shlomo reminisced, "I was exposed to true Torah aristocracy. The way my rav walked, the way he talked, the way he ate... all made me realize that there is nothing quite as noble as being a *talmid chacham*."

Years later, R' Shlomo was very sick and seriously in need of major surgery. Aware of R' Chanina's connection to R' Telushkin, R' Freifeld called in R' Chanina and asked him to daven at R' Telushkin's *kever* that the operation should go well.

Matzeivah of R' Nissen Telushkin

R' Yaakov Yosef Greenberg

WHEN CHANINA WAS A TEENAGER, THE HERZBERG FAMILY MOVED from East New York to Canarsie. They joined Congregation Beth Tikvah and forged a close relationship with R' Yaakov Yosef (Jacob J.) Greenberg, the rabbi of the shul. A kind and compassionate rav, R' Greenberg believed all Jews could grow in Yiddishkeit, if dealt with in a loving and practical manner.

R' Greenberg came to Canarsie in 1963 (5723), when it was a Jewish wilderness. In the beginning, he could barely gather a *minyan*. But in time, the shul grew and boasted an active membership of several hundred people.

R' Greenberg was much more than the rabbi. He *leined*. He blew shofar. Sometimes, he was the *mohel*. He mopped the floor. No task was too big or too small.

With his erudition, engaging personality, and marvelous sense of humor, he was able to be *mekarev* many people. His congregation grew in Yiddishkeit, each one according to his own level. Tens of congregants became *shomer Shabbos* and sent their children to yeshivos; some of those children pursued roles in *chinuch,* in the rabbinate, and as lay leaders.

R' Yaakov Yosef and Rebbetzin Malka Greenberg not only tended to their flock, but they also became their congregants' family. What the rav did for the men, the rebbetzin did for the women. She gave *shiurim* and was *mekarev* many women. Their home was open to all, at all hours of the day and night; there was no need to call in advance — or even knock on the door.

The Herzberg family also benefited from R' and Rebbetzin Greenberg's caring and love. In time, R' Greenberg became a mentor to Chanina, enabling the seed that had been planted to flourish even more. Especially precious to Chanina was the time before the start of Shabbos. R' Greenberg would come early to shul to learn on Friday afternoons, and Chanina would join him for part of the time. That was when they had their weekly talks about life, yeshiva, and basically whatever was on Chanina's mind.

Many years later, when R' Chanina opened his own shul, Beis Medrash Ohr Shlomo in Far Rockaway, he took a page from R' Greenberg's book. Every week, one hour before Shabbos, he could be

At R' Chanina and Naomi Herzberg's *chasunah*
(l-r): R' Elchanan Yochanan Spiegel (Mrs. Naomi Herzberg's grandfather), R' Chanina, R' Shlomo Freifeld, R' Yaakov Yosef Greenberg

found in the shul with an open *sefer.* As people came in, he would talk to them about the week that had just passed, as well as life in general, providing much-needed *chizuk* and guidance to his *mispallelim.*

Chanina was growing in his *avodas Hashem.* At one point, he and his friend, Avraham Monczyk, went to the rabbi with an idea. They wanted to start an early "yeshiva *minyan*" within the shul. R' Greenberg encouraged them, and Chanina served not only as the *baal korei,* but very often as the *baal tefillah.*

As a seventh-grade rebbi in Yeshiva Toras Chaim, Eli Herzberg, R' Chanina's son, had the honor of having the menahel, his father, visit his class and converse with his *talmidim,* frequently playing a special game. Boys would open a Chumash to any spot, begin reading the first few words, and R' Chanina would complete the *pasuk* from memory. It seemed like he knew the entire Chumash by heart. When Eli asked his father how he had mastered the whole Chumash, R' Chanina attributed much of it to his days in Canarsie when he *leined* every Shabbos.

As Chanina continued to grow, he maintained contact with R' Greenberg, who was always proud of Chanina's success.

Chapter 2

The Seed Blossoms: R' Shlomo Freifeld

FOR MANY YEARS, R' YUSSIE LIEBER SERVED AS A REBBI IN AN AFTERnoon Hebrew school primarily for children from secular homes. He once brought his students to meet R' Shlomo Freifeld, rosh yeshiva of Yeshiva Sh'or Yoshuv. They stood around the table — cautious, uneasy, uncertain — as he began to speak.

A Slow Evolution

"What's your name?" he asked one child.

"Howie," replied the boy.

"No, not Howie. I want your Jewish name," prodded R' Shlomo, ever so gently.

"Oh, it's Chaim."

R' Shlomo beamed at him. "Do you realize what a potent name you have? Life... sparks of life, of perpetual movement and growth..."

Then R' Shlomo continued, revealing to David and Ilana, to Erez and Hadassah, the splendor of their names. Once he had generated a current powerful enough to arouse dormant sparks in these

R' Shlomo Freifeld, R' Chanina's rebbi

neshamos, he smiled broadly. "At my *bris milah*, my father named me Shlomo, yet my mother still preferred to call me Seymour. Do not let the hat and beard fool you. I was Seymour, not Shlomo."

R' Shlomo Freifeld as *mashgiach* in the mesivta of Yeshiva Rabbi Chaim Berlin

R' Shlomo paused, letting the idea sink in. "Life is an evolution, not a revolution. We have to work to tap into the unlimited potential of our names, but it's a mission that's within our reach. Today, I am Shlomo."[1]

After his own momentous encounter with R' Shlomo Freifeld, Charlie began to realize the potential that lay within, and slowly Charlie became Chanina and all that the name represented. And his own evolution began.

But first, the auspicious encounter.

Initially, Chanina's mesivta days were not that different from his days in elementary school, and he frequently found himself roaming the hallways. One day in tenth grade, R' Shlomo, who at that time served as mashgiach in Yeshiva Rabbi Chaim Berlin, found Chanina hanging out in the hallway during class.

"Why are you in the hallway?" he questioned him.

"The rebbi sent me out because I wasn't learning and I was fooling around," Chanina confessed.

"Let's go for a walk," R' Shlomo suggested. They started walking and R' Shlomo asked him, "Are you *matzliach*?"

"Not really."

"Would you like to have *hatzlachah* in your learning?" R' Shlomo probed.

"I think I would," Chanina acknowledged, "but I just don't know how."

"I'll tell you what, we're going to learn Mishnayos every day for five minutes," R' Shlomo decided. "You'll come to the *beis midrash* and we'll sit together and learn."

1. Based on *Mishpacha*: "Wings With Which to Fly," 12 Tishrei, 5767, R' Yisroel Besser.

R' Shlomo Freifeld learning with *talmidim*,
(l-r): Aharon Horowitz, Chanina Herzberg, Binyomin Monczyk

They continued walking and R' Shlomo invited Chanina to join him for a coffee and Danish at the local coffee shop.

R' Chanina would reminisce about that meeting. "R' Shlomo knew what I needed. Instead of reprimanding me, he offered to learn with me and took me for a coffee and a Danish. He won me over with that coffee and Danish!"

R' Chanina had acquired his rebbi for life.

In the meantime, for a few minutes each day, R' Shlomo learned Mishnayos with Chanina, teaching him just a few lines, but insisting on total comprehension. He had him review and review and review, enabling Chanina to experience his first taste of success.

Slowly, success bred success. Through those mini-learning sessions of Mishnayos and numerous hours of discussions, R' Shlomo unlocked the treasure chest within Chanina. As Chanina finally learned how to learn, he started to grow, developing a desire to become a *talmid chacham*, to expand his dimensions and become a "big Jew."

R' Avraham Kleinkaufman, his eleventh grade rebbi, recalled that Chanina was one of those *bachurim* who were motivated and fully involved in the *sugya*. A classmate from those years remembers that already back in mesivta, Chanina aspired to accomplish great things, to make a difference.

At the Mesivta Yeshiva Rabbi Chaim Berlin breakfast
(l-r): R' Yisroel Meir Lasker (executive director of MYRCB), R' Simcha Lefkowitz
(rav of Congregation Anshei Chesed in Hewlett, New York), R' Chanina

Indeed, after connecting with R' Shlomo, everything changed. R' Shlomo took a special liking to Chanina and as their relationship developed, Chanina blossomed. He continued to flourish in his learning, his *avodas Hashem,* and in the *chinuch* realm. Years later, in Sivan 5760, R' Chanina was honored at a breakfast that Mesivta Yeshiva Rabbi Chaim Berlin held in the Five Towns. There he was presented with a plaque:

> "Presented in recognition and esteem *l'yedideinu hanechbad,* Harav Chanina Herzberg, *shlita,* a renowned *mechanech* by the grace of Hashem, whose ways in his *avodas hakodesh* add honor, praise, and glory to our yeshiva. May Hashem reward his deeds, and may his reward be complete from the *Ribbono shel Olam.*"

Chanina wasn't the only *bachur* to grow close to R' Shlomo Freifeld. Any *bachur* who had behavioral issues, or who, for whatever reason, could not function in the conventional classroom setting, would become one of R' Shlomo's "boys," part of the ever-increasing group of *bachurim* who surrounded him.

R' Hutner was pleased with what his *talmid* was accomplishing, at

R' Shlomo Freifeld (r), with his rebbi, R' Yitzchak Hutner (c)

the role he was beginning to fill in the lives of these *bachurim*. When R' Hutner decided to move Mesivta Yeshiva Rabbi Chaim Berlin from Far Rockaway back to Brooklyn, the time was ripe for a new yeshiva in Far Rockaway.

With R' Hutner's blessing, R' Shlomo established Yeshiva Sh'or Yoshuv.

Chanina was part of the first group of *talmidim*. As he once stated in an interview, "We all needed to be in yeshiva; otherwise, we could be drafted into the army, for the Vietnam War." Practical considerations

R' Yitzchak Hutner visiting Yeshiva Sh'or Yoshuv (l-r): R' Shlomo Freifeld, Heshy Markovits, Shaya Novak, R' Yitzchak Hutner, Benjie Brecher

R' Shlomo Freifeld flanked by his *talmidim* at Moshe Herzberg's bar mitzvah (l-r): Sitting: H. Markovits, R. Cohen, R' Shlomo Freifeld, D. Perlman, R' N. Jaeger, R' Y. Kurland. Standing: R' S. Brazil, R' Z. Zelman, R' A. Halpern, S.Z Gutfreund, Moshe Herzberg, Mendy Herzberg, R' D. Sitnick, Y. Goldfeder, M. Kay, R' Chanina Herzberg

aside, Chanina continued to flourish under R' Shlomo's warmth, encouragement, and belief in him.

In those early days of Sh'or Yoshuv, Chanina and his friends gained so much from their rebbi. R' Chanina later recalled, "We saw him in a different way than later *talmidim*. He learned with us, he grew with us. We were all very close. We went on trips to *gedolim* together, we spoke a lot about life, our aspirations in life..."

R' Shlomo would bring his *talmidim* to visit R' Hutner on Succos. As they drove from Far Rockaway to Brooklyn, R' Shlomo would spend the time speaking with the *talmidim*. However, as they drove across the Marine Parkway Bridge, which connects the Rockaways to Brooklyn, his whole demeanor would change. His entire being began to feel the awe and reverence of his rebbi. This seriousness and *pachad* for a rebbi remained with R' Shlomo throughout the visit in the succah, providing an invaluable lesson for his *talmidim*.

R' Chanina continued, "R' Shlomo brought us back to places like Ger and Slabodka. We saw the Chazon Ish, R' Dessler, and older European *gedolim* as if they were right in front of us. The Alter of Slabodka came to life before our eyes. ...When R' Shlomo told us something, we listened, and more importantly, we responded to him, because he helped us have our first real taste of success in Torah learning."

R' Avrohom Moshe Spiegel being presented with a plaque at an Agudah dinner, in appreciation for his assistance in founding Agudath Israel of Long Island (l-r): R' Moshe Feinstein, Mr. Abe Septimus, Mr. Yisrael Katz, R' Avrohom Moshe Spiegel, R' Moshe Sherer presenting the award

When R' Shlomo made the decision to remain in Far Rockaway and open his own yeshiva, he needed a place where the *bachurim* could learn. He approached *baalei batim* of Agudath Israel of Long Island (located in Far Rockaway) and asked if they could host his yeshiva until he secured his own building. Some of the *baalei batim* hesitated; they weren't sure if the old house in which their shul was located could withstand such heavy-duty use. But R' Avrohom Moshe Spiegel, one of the founders of the Agudah, disagreed. Though very ill at the time, he stated his opinion unequivocally, "If a yeshiva wants to open in the community and use our building, we can't say no." The *baalei batim* listened and Yeshiva Sh'or Yoshuv was established.

A short while later, as R' Avrohom Moshe Spiegel lay in bed fighting for his life, R' Shlomo showed his *hakaras hatov* by visiting with the *bachurim* and singing for him. When R' Avrohom Moshe was *niftar* in 1968 (5728), the *levayah* passed by the Agudah, the shul he helped found. R' Shlomo instructed the *bachurim* of Yeshiva Sh'or Yoshuv to escort the *meis*, again to demonstrate gratitude to the man who helped the yeshiva get started.

On R' Avrohom Moshe's first *yahrtzeit,* his daughter Naomi sent a letter to R' Shlomo in which she wrote that since her father had helped the yeshiva, she was sending a donation in his memory. Enclosed was $10, which she had earned by babysitting.

Chanina Herzberg and Naomi Spiegel at their *l'chaim*

Less than a year later, Chanina came to R' Shlomo to discuss a *shidduch* with Naomi Spiegel. Upon hearing the name, R' Shlomo's face became wreathed in smiles. "Go for it. She's a great girl and it's a great *shidduch*. I may not know her, but I know what she does." R' Shlomo then opened his desk drawer and removed the letter Naomi had written him. He had been so impressed by the special deed of a young girl that he had saved the letter.

And so, in November of 1969 (5730), at the age of 20, Chanina Herzberg became engaged to Naomi, the daughter of R' Avrohom Moshe and Sarah Spiegel. R' Avrohom Moshe was a grandson of R' Naftali Aryeh Spiegel, the first Ostrov-Kalushiner Rebbe, and a descendant of R' Yaakov Yitzchak Horowitz, the Chozeh of Lublin. From the time he was young, R' Avrohom Moshe was involved in Agudath Israel of America, in the leadership of Camp Agudah, as well as in other activities alongside R' Mike Tress and R' Moshe Sherer. Mrs. Sarah Spiegel was the granddaughter of R' Yehuda Leib Seltzer, secretary of the Agudath Harabbanim, who was instrumental in securing a visa for R' Moshe

R' Avrohom Moshe and Sarah Spiegel

(l-r): R' Yehuda Leib Seltzer, R' Yisroel Rosenberg, R' Moshe Feinstein, R' Litwak

Feinstein to emigrate to America. R' Avrohom Moshe and Sarah Spiegel raised five children, of whom Naomi is the third.

With Chanina engaged, Mrs. Florence Herzberg was concerned how her son would support his family while learning in kollel. She approached R' Shlomo to discuss the issue.

"Don't worry," R' Shlomo assured her, "he's destined for something special."

Prophetic words.

The wedding was scheduled for September 20th, 1970 (19 Elul, 5730), at the Monsey Park Hotel, with R' Shlomo slated as the *mesader kiddushin*. The preparations were well underway when tragedy struck.

The day was August 18th (16 Av). Planning to buy a tuxedo for the big day, Chanina's father, Moish Herzberg, headed to the Beau Brummel men's clothing store in Forest Hills, Queens, which was owned by his brother-in-law, Sol Laxer. While shopping, Moish suffered a massive heart attack and, tragically, was *niftar* at the age of 56, slightly more than one month before his son's wedding.

Less than three weeks later, on September 6th (5 Elul), R' and Rebbetzin Hutner, along with their son-in-law and daughter, R'

Yonasan and Rebbetzin Bruriah David, were on board TWA Flight 741 from Israel to America, when terrorists hijacked the plane and forced it to fly to Jordan. R' Hutner was not released until close to Rosh Hashanah, with several other hostages freed a few days later. At Chanina and Naomi's *chasunah*, R' Shlomo was focused on the welfare of his rebbi and the other captives; before the *chuppah*, he made a request of the *chassan*. *"Hut dehr rosh yeshiva in zinnen* — Please have the rosh yeshiva (R' Hutner) in mind in your *tefillos*." Yet with it all, R' Shlomo overcame his emotions and pushed himself to be *mesame'ach* his cherished *talmid*.

R' Shlomo walking R' Chanina to the *badeken*

R' Chanina and Naomi at their wedding

R' Shlomo dancing with *talmidim* at R' Chanina's wedding

Following the *chasunah,* R' Chanina joined the Sh'or Yoshuv kollel. Despite his and Naomi's lofty aspirations, life wasn't easy for the young couple. They had no outside financial support; Naomi's mother, Mrs. Sarah Spiegel, and Chanina's mother, Mrs. Florence Herzberg, were both *almanos.*

With remarkable *mesiras nefesh,* Naomi held three jobs so her husband could sit and learn. She taught in a local Talmud Torah, gave art classes, and worked in Stefan's Florist Shop, all while attending college for interior design.

R' Chanina and Naomi Herzberg with their growing family

In time, R' Chanina would leave kollel, become a rebbi, and eventually a menahel. But as the family grew, the yoke of support became increasingly heavy and burdensome. At one point, though R' Chanina entertained the possibility of leaving *chinuch,* Naomi held strong, to the acclaim of her husband's rebbi, R' Shlomo Freifeld.

At a Shabbos morning Kiddush during the week of *Parashas Vayechi,* 5746, R' Freifeld shared his pride with the *kehillah* of Sh'or Yoshuv. "I had so much *nachas* this week. A woman comes to see me…about her husband who is a big *marbitz Torah.* When he first started out, she held several jobs in order to support him, to help him get there. Now he wants to go into business, because he sees how others are making money while he barely has enough *parnassah* to support his family.

"She says to me with a fire in her eyes, 'I don't think it's fair. I helped him get to where he is, and now he wants to leave what he's doing because of the money?! I will take three jobs again. . . I don't want him to leave!' This woman has a *chiyus* about her, a *bren.* She wants to live and grow. I could see from the way she spoke that nothing is going to stop her."

That "big *marbitz Torah*" was R' Chanina, and that woman "with a fire in her eyes," with a "*chiyus*" and a "*bren,*" was Naomi.

This is the full story: When R' Chanina was an established and successful menahel, a wealthy businessman took note of him. Impressed with R' Chanina's leadership skills, the magnate offered him a lucrative job in the business world, a position that would allow him to support his family comfortably. That night, R' Chanina came home and mentioned the proposition to his wife, as he pondered the idea. Seeing that her husband was actually giving the proposal some thought, Naomi called R' Shlomo and arranged a meeting to discuss the matter, to make sure nothing would come of the business offer. R' Shlomo was so taken by her fervor that he mentioned it at the Kiddush that week.

With all the great influences in R' Chanina's life, it was his *eishes chayil* who enabled him to stay the course.

Unconventional Journey Into Chinuch

R' SHLOMO FREIFELD SENT SOME OF HIS TALMIDIM TO TEACH IN THE local afternoon Hebrew schools (Talmud Torahs). It was there that R' Chanina received his first experience in chinuch. In 1971 (5731), he taught first and second grade in the Young Israel of Wavecrest Hebrew School, and from 1972 (5732) to 1974 (5734), he taught grades one through four in the Briarwood Jewish Center Hebrew School in Jamaica, Queens. Even though he taught only part-time, he was quickly recognized as an outstanding rebbi, eventually promoted to assistant principal at Briarwood in 1974 (5734), a position he held until 1976 (5736).

R' Chanina enjoying a light moment with a *talmid* at Briarwood Jewish Center Hebrew School

R' Chanina did not make his way into full-time *chinuch* through conventional channels. He didn't write a resume; he didn't even apply for the job. He was happily learning in the kollel of Yeshiva Sh'or Yoshuv when he received a call from a friend of his parents, R' Yitzchak Brody.

"R' Chanina, as you know, I'm a rebbi in Yeshiva Tiferes Moshe in Queens. Unfortunately, one of our rebbeim just suffered a heart attack. As the father of a large family, the rebbi can't forgo his salary, but the yeshiva can't afford to pay another rebbi's salary. I'm calling to ask you a favor. Please come to the yeshiva without pay and fill in for the rebbi for the second half of the year. We need you."

R' Chanina asked his rebbi, R' Shlomo, what to do. "Rebbi, I feel like my *tafkid* now is to sit and learn in kollel."

"R' Chanina," his rebbi answered with conviction, "right now, it's more important for you to do this *chesed* for the rebbi — and make sure he has money to support his *mishpachah* — than to learn in kollel."

"But Rebbi," R' Chanina wasn't finished yet, "I have a problem. If I'm working for free and also not receiving my kollel check — since I will not be learning here — how will I support my own family?"

R' Shlomo never ran out of ideas. "R' Chanina, you are now officially the first executive director of Yeshiva Sh'or Yoshuv." He proceeded to remove a coat rack from a small closet, replacing it with a small desk and chair. "Every day after you finish teaching, come back here to learn a little bit and I will give you some paperwork to do for the yeshiva. Your salary will be $100 a week."

Thus, while still in his 20's, with the charge of his rebbi, R' Chanina Herzberg began his first full-time "job" in *chinuch*. The *talmidim* instantly fell in love with their rebbi, and the following year, the yeshiva offered him a permanent full-time position teaching a small group of seventh-grade *talmidim* who needed a special rebbi to motivate them to excel in their learning.

R' Yitzchak Brody, to whom R' Chanina felt deep *hakaras hatov*

R' Chanina went back to his rebbi to share his hesitation. "Rebbi, at this point, I really want to return to kollel and continue learning full-time."

"R' Chanina," his rebbi maintained, "it's more important for you to teach children."

Here, too, R' Chanina quickly became known as a stellar rebbi, forging deep connections with *talmidim* and parents alike.

After a short time, he was offered the position of s'gan menahel.

For the rest of his life, R' Chanina had deep *hakaras hatov* to R' Brody for giving him his start in *chinuch.* Furthermore, R' Chanina felt that much of the *siyata d'Shmaya* he merited in his *chinuch* career was due to the *chesed* of filling in for a rebbi without pay.

Full Circle

YESHIVA TORAS CHAIM HAD BEEN ESTABLISHED IN 1927 (5687) IN EAST New York. R' Binyamin Kamenetzky was originally a first-grade rebbi there, beginning in the 1940's. In 1956 (5716), he left to start his own yeshiva, Yeshiva of South Shore, on Long Island.

Several years later, Yeshiva of South Shore desperately needed its own building, but R' Binyamin was having difficulty raising the necessary funds. Though the yeshiva had already purchased land, there were cost overruns, leaving little money after paying the mortgage and leading to many stoppages in construction.

At the same time, R' Schmidman, R' Binyamin's former employer from Yeshiva Toras Chaim of East New York, was dealing with his own issues in regard to his yeshiva. The East New York frum community was fading into oblivion, its shuls vandalized by hoodlums. Ultimately, R' Schmidman decided to sell the East New York building and use a portion of the proceeds to help his former employee build his much-needed building.

In 1963 (5723), the Yeshiva of South Shore merged with Yeshiva Toras Chaim, and the building that began as Yeshiva of South Shore was

R' Yitzchak Schmidman (right) and R' Binyamin Kamenetzky (left) dancing in celebration of the completion of the new building of the newly merged Yeshiva Toras Chaim of South Shore

completed as Yeshiva Toras Chaim of South Shore. The two yeshivos were aligned in *hashkafah,* as well. Anyone who wanted to learn Torah was accepted, whether or not they could afford to pay tuition.

R' Binyamin Kamenetzky and R' Chanina in the early years

At long last, the yeshiva moved into its new campus in Hewlett, Long Island. While R' Binyamin served as rosh yeshiva, R' Schmidman addressed the students at special events and gave *farhers*.

In 2003 (5763), over a decade before his *petirah* in 2017/ 5777, R' Binyamin transmitted the yeshiva's leadership to his son, R' Mordechai Kamenetzky, who was appointed dean/ rosh yeshiva of Yeshiva Toras Chaim of South Shore.

In 1980 (5740), R′ Binyamin sought a menahel, someone who could take the yeshiva to the next level and increase enrollment. R′ Binyamin asked R′ Shlomo Freifeld to suggest a candidate for the position. He recommended R′ Chanina, and he was hired.

At a *melaveh malkah* marking the installation of R′ Chanina as menahel of Yeshiva Toras Chaim of South Shore, R′ Yitzchak Schmidman addressed the assembly and shared the story of how he convinced R′ Chanina's parents to send young Charlie to Yeshiva Toras Chaim, expressing particular *nachas* that R′ Chanina was now menahel of the very yeshiva that had transformed his life.

The seed had blossomed into a full orchard.

Chapter 3

CONTINUING THE MESORAH: REBBI/TALMID

Being Mevatel Oneself

MANY YEARS EARLIER, WHEN R' CHANINA WAS STILL A BUDDING *mechanech,* R' Shlomo Freifeld asked him to attend the Torah Umesorah convention with two other *mechanchim.* He wanted them to raise awareness on behalf of a group of out-of-town girls, who seemed to be destined to enroll in a non-Jewish school because there was no Bais Yaakov high school in their city. R' Chanina took his charge seriously, buttonholing anyone who would listen to his plea, pouring out his heart and his tears as he apprised the attendees of the dire situation. His rebbi had sent him on a mission, and he fulfilled it *b'lev va'nefesh.*

If R' Shlomo instructed R' Chanina to do something, he followed through without hesitation.

R' Chanina recounted what R' Shlomo said in a *hesped* for his rebbi, R' Hutner. R' Shlomo discussed the concept found in Chazal of *rabbo muvhak,* one's primary teacher. This is the teacher from whom one receives and acquires the majority of his *chochmah,* the most significant roots of knowledge, the decisive knowledge that shapes one's life. The Tosafos Yom Tov (*Bava Metzia* 2:11) points out that the word מובהק derives from the root בהק, which refers to something that has a pronounced shine. A *rebbi muvhak* is the rebbi who brings out the student's innate talents and makes him shine. He is the rebbi who unlocks the storehouse, the treasures that lie dormant in the student.

This is a rare concept of teaching.

This is what R' Hutner did for R' Freifeld, and what R' Freifeld did for R' Chanina.

The Midrash in *Parashas Pinchas* (*Bamidbar Rabbah,* 21:14) enlightens us as to why Yehoshua was chosen as the leader of Klal Yisrael after Moshe was *niftar.* Because he served Moshe devotedly and accorded him much honor. He always arrived early and remained late in the *beis midrash.* Additionally, he assisted Moshe, arranging the benches and spreading out the mats in the *beis midrash.* Specifically because he served Moshe with all his strength — and he was totally *mevatel* (nullifying, negating) himself before his rebbi — he merited serving all of Klal Yisrael as their leader.

R' Chanina lamented, "So many people live their lives without a rebbi. They think that if they daven in a shul that has a rav, that means they have a rav. Or if they learn in a yeshiva and a rebbi is teaching them Torah, that means they have a rebbi. People don't realize that in order to have a rebbi, you must work on it. You have to connect yourself to your rebbi with every fiber of your being, until you find yourself asking him how you should think and what you should do in various situations. If you follow these steps, you will become the person you are capable of becoming."

R' Aaron Schechter once commented, "*Shimush talmidei chachamim* requires *yegiah.*" Serving Torah scholars takes effort. R' Chanina invested that *yegiah,* that effort, and he reaped the benefits — because R' Shlomo made R' Chanina who he was. R' Shlomo believed in him, nurturing him every step of the way, bringing out his unique potential, his unique shine.

Quite often, after he finished teaching, R' Chanina drove to R' Shlomo's house, where they would discuss different topics — ranging from the *kehillah* of Sh'or Yoshuv to *chinuch* to current events, and a broad range of other subjects — for close to 45 minutes. Nothing was out of bounds. This took place for many years. It was during these discussions that R' Chanina gleaned many important *yesodos hachaim,* and R' Shlomo transmitted to R' Chanina his *mesorah* of *chinuch habanim.* These meetings were instrumental in fashioning R' Chanina into another link in the *mesorah,* which initiated with the Alter of Slabodka, R' Nosson Tzvi Finkel, continued to R' Hutner, on to R' Shlomo, and now R' Chanina.

R' Shlomo was R' Chanina's *rebbi muvhak,* and R' Chanina was totally

R' Chanina and R' Jaeger dancing together at Eli Herzberg's *chasunah*

mevatel himself to him. At R' Chanina's *levayah*, R' Naftali Jaeger, rosh yeshiva of Yeshiva Sh'or Yoshuv and son-in-law of R' Shlomo, stated that R' Chanina was a *talmid muvhak* of R' Shlomo.

R' Chanina, by example, ingrained in his children and his *talmidim* the importance of having a rebbi, while frequently reiterating, "When you're totally *mevatel* yourself to your rebbi, you expand your dimensions, you become big, you become larger than yourself, you accomplish things you would never have been able to accomplish. If more people had a rebbi to talk to, there would be fewer *shalom bayis* issues and fewer problems raising children."

R' Shlomo pointed out another vital aspect of the rebbi-*talmid* relationship. R' Yehudah HaNasi often engaged in discussions with Antoninus, the Roman emperor. When describing one of these conversations, R' Yehudah HaNasi stated (*Sanhedrin* 91b), "This thing Antoninus taught me." Rashi explains, "From his words I learned." Rashi's explanation seems superfluous. If R' Yehudah didn't learn from Antoninus's words, what *did* he learn from?

Rashi is coming to contrast this teaching of Antoninus to a teaching that comes from one's rebbi. When a *talmid* learns Torah from his rebbi, the *talmid* learns from the person, from his entirety, from his whole being — for the rebbi's very essence is transmitted to the *talmid*. However, when R' Yehudah HaNasi learned from Antoninus, he learned only from his words, and nothing else. Rashi is limiting what exactly was transmitted from one to the other.

When teaching R' Chanina, R' Shlomo gave over his essence.

In turn, R' Chanina gave over his essence to his own *talmidim*.

A Deep-Rooted Connection

IN THE FALL OF 1990 (5751), ONLY WEEKS AFTER R' SHLOMO'S *PETIRAH,* R' Chanina and his wife were honored with the *kesser shem tov* award at Yeshiva Sh'or Yoshuv's annual dinner. R' Shlomo had been the one to designate R' Chanina and his wife as recipients of the award, and he himself chose an antique *sefer* from his library to be gifted to R' Chanina at the dinner. The award was presented by R' Avraham Halpern, R' Freifeld's son-in-law. After discussing how the students of Yeshiva Sh'or Yoshuv, the walls of the yeshiva, the neighborhood surrounding Sh'or Yoshuv, and even the streets of the Five Towns still felt the *roshem,* the impression, made by R' Shlomo Freifeld, R' Avraham moved on to praise the guest of honor, R' Chanina.

"One of the students upon whom the rosh yeshiva has made a great

The Herzberg family in the early 1990's

R' Chanina with R' Shlomo Freifeld in Yeshiva Sh'or Yoshuv at his son Yudi's bris; R' Eliyahu Rominek is speaking

impact is R' Chanina Herzberg. R' Chanina attached himself to his rebbi from the very beginnings of the yeshiva; he took his rebbi's teachings very seriously. And with the encouragement of his rebbi, he decided that he would like to teach others, with the same *mesiras nefesh* and devotion that he saw in his rosh yeshiva. And after years of teaching, he became the principal of Yeshiva Toras Chaim of South Shore.

R' Chanina presenting a talmid with his first siddur

"As the menahel, R' Chanina continues in his rebbi's ways by providing a preferred *chinuch* to each and every one of the students, as he toils to find a way of reaching the hearts of his *talmidim*. Until his rebbi's very last days, R' Chanina would speak to the rosh yeshiva to find new ideas, new methods, to ensure the success of Yeshiva Toras Chaim."

Whether he was dispensing *chinuch* advice or *hashkafas hachaim* in general, R' Chanina's opinion came across with strength, clarity, and conviction — because what he said wasn't his own opinion; it was what he was *mekabel* from his rebbi, and thus emerged fully from the realm of *mesorah.* On occasion, he would say to others, "I hear what you're saying, but to tell you the truth, your opinion on this matter is insignificant to me. I have a *mesorah* from my rebbi, so I know how to deal with such a situation."

R' Chanina would relay a *vort* from the Belzer Rebbe on the *pesukim* of the second paragraph of *Krias Shema.* The command to teach Torah to our children, *"V'limadtem osam es bneichem,"* is placed between the mitzvos of *tefillin* and *mezuzah* (*Devarim* 11:18-20). Just like *tefillin* or *mezuzos* are *pasul* if the writing of the *parashah* is flawed by even the tiniest bit, so, too, our children's *chinuch* can be *pasul,* invalidated, if we veer from the *mesorah* even one iota.

During R' Shlomo's final illness, when his condition worsened and he knew his end was near, he called in R' Chanina and notified him, "I've arranged three people to advise or assist you, if you need advice or help in any area, after I'm gone. I've spoken to all three of them about you and explained who you are and what you're all about. They are R' Aaron Schechter, R' Amos Bunim, and R' Avrohom Fruchthandler."

R' Aaron Schechter, rosh yeshiva of Mesivta Yeshiva Rabbi Chaim

R' Chanina in conversation with R' Aaron Schechter

R' Chanina dancing with R' Amos Bunim

Berlin, was a *yedid nefesh* of R' Shlomo from his youth; the two of them learned under R' Yitzchak Hutner and became his *talmidim muvhakim*. R' Chanina consulted with R' Aaron frequently, appreciating his clarity and *pikchus*. Eventually, R' Chanina sent some of his own sons to learn in Yeshiva Rabbi Chaim Berlin under R' Aaron, so that they, too, could grow close to R' Aaron and become influenced from such an *adam gadol*.

R' Amos Bunim, noted *askan*, was close to R' Chanina's wife's family. Mrs. Naomi (Spiegel) Herzberg lost her father as a young girl, and therefore appreciated the special connection the family maintained with R' Amos, his wife, and his entire family. R' Amos also davened in Yeshiva Sh'or Yoshuv in the early years, further cementing the bond. Those who had the opportunity to experience a Rosh Hashanah davening in Yeshiva Sh'or Yoshuv when R' Amos davened there will never forget his piercing cries during Yamim Noraim davening. Often after davening, R' Chanina would take the opportunity to tell his children how special R' Amos was. "Do you know how much *yiras Shamayim* lives in his cries?"

R' Avrohom Fruchthandler, president of Mesivta Yeshiva Rabbi Chaim Berlin, well-known *askan,* and close *talmid* of R' Hutner, maintained a strong connection with R' Shlomo. After R' Shlomo's *petirah*, R' Chanina developed a rapport with R' Avrohom, conferring with him on a variety of topics, whether pertaining to his personal life or to the klal. R' Avrohom and R' Chanina felt a special kinship.

R' Chanina would highlight what it means to be a rebbi and to have a rebbi. "The relationship is so much more than having someone to talk to when you have a problem, or having someone to hear a *shiur* from. It's a deep-rooted connection, like the bond of father to son. And just as a father will do everything and anything to ensure his son is taken care of even after he passes on, so does a rebbi."

R' Chanina in conversation with R' Avrohom Fruchthandler

R' Chanina upheld the importance of following a rebbi, even when his child's rebbi's opinion was not in sync with his own. One of R' Chanina's children had a major decision to make, a decision that would affect R' Chanina greatly. R' Chanina felt one way, but the child's rebbi, a prominent rosh yeshiva, felt another way.

R' Chanina encouraged his child to follow his rebbi's advice.

The next morning, R' Chanina asked a colleague at Yeshiva Toras Chaim, a rebbi to whom he felt close, to come to his office. The colleague could see that his good friend, R' Chanina, was very disappointed and emotional. He explained his feelings. "I personally felt he should have done differently, but I don't question his decision one bit. He needs to do what his rebbi tells him to do."

When R' Chanina was diagnosed with a dreaded illness, he called R' Aaron Schechter to ask him to daven for him. R' Chanina wanted to make sure the rosh yeshiva knew who his caller was, so he identified himself. "It's Chanina Herzberg, and I was a *talmid* of R' Shlomo Freifeld." R' Schechter stopped him and shouted forcefully, "No! You ARE a *talmid l'olam va'ed*!" Hearing the rosh yeshiva say that he was forever a *talmid*, R' Chanina broke down in tears, as he derived remarkable *chizuk* from that statement.

In *Parashas Bamidbar,* the Torah states (3:1), *"V'eileh toldos Aharon u'Moshe* — These are the children of Aharon and Moshe." If the Torah lists only the children of Aharon in the subsequent *pesukim*, why does it say that these are the sons of Moshe as well? Rashi explains that Aharon's sons are referred to as the sons of Moshe because he was the one who taught them Torah. From here we learn that anyone who teaches his friend's son Torah is considered as if he fathered him.

A student is like a son. And just as a biological son is a son forever, so is a spiritual son a son forever. As R' Hutner once discussed in a *maamar* he gave at Yeshiva Sh'or Yoshuv, "A yeshiva is a place of the infusion of life. It is a place that forges a lifetime relationship between rebbi and *talmid* as a father to son."

At an eighth-grade graduation of Yeshiva Toras Chaim, R' Chanina spoke directly to the *talmidim*. "Chazal tell us that one of the greatest tragedies in the Torah took place when the Jews left Har Sinai, because of how they did so. If you look in the Torah (*Bamidbar* 10:32-36), you see that when Bnei Yisrael were told to leave, they took the *Aron* and followed the *Anan*. Where is the tragedy? '*She'saru me'acharei Hashem... k'tinok hayotzei mi'beis hasefer she'bore'ach lo v'holeich lo.*' They turned from Hashem like a child runs from yeshiva (*Shabbos* 116b; see Tosafos). Though this was the place where they received their *chiyus*, their life-giving sustenance, they did not look back.

"You must go forward," R' Chanina exhorted the graduates, "but don't forget to look back. The yeshiva gave you life, not just an education, but life! Go forward and become the future leaders of Klal Yisrael, but always look back with a sense of pride, accomplishment, and appreciation for what Yeshiva Toras Chaim — your connection to Har Sinai — did for you!"

With only two weeks left to the school year, a boy in Yeshiva Toras Chaim was acting out of line. When his rebbi reprimanded him, the boy shot back, "You're not my rebbi anymore anyway!"

The rebbi brought the boy to R' Chanina, who asked the *talmid,* "How much longer will your rebbi be your rebbi?"

"Only two more weeks!"

R' Chanina paused, then banged on his desk and looked into the *talmid*'s eyes before teaching him an enduring lesson.

"Your rebbi is your rebbi for the rest of your life!"

Living With R' Shlomo

AT THE *BRIS* OF R' CHANINA'S SON YITZCHOK, R' SHLOMO EXTOLLED the praises of his dear *talmid,* whom he described as a hard worker. With all his talents and capabilities, R' Shlomo maintained, R' Chanina could have pursued many opportunities in his life. Instead, he decided, *I want to devote my life to solve the problems that face Jewry; I want to devote my life to harbatzas Torah.* R' Shlomo stressed, "Not only is R' Chanina a *marbitz Torah,* but also a *lomeid Torah,* with toil and sincerity." While praising R' Chanina, R' Shlomo also complimented his wife, Naomi, on her ideals, her willingness to help, and her creativity and talent, which she used to create magnificent centerpieces for Yeshiva Sh'or Yoshuv's annual dinners. Throughout his speech, R' Shlomo's bond with his *talmid* and his family was most evident.

R' Shlomo's respect for his *talmid* was also apparent from the fact that he entrusted R' Chanina with the important role of preparing *chassanim* for married life.

At the *bris* of Yitzchok Herzberg (l-r): R' Chanina, R' Shlomo Freifeld, R' Binyamin Kamenetzky

The *beis midrash* in the Sh'or Yoshuv bungalow colony;
R' Chanina is sitting in the back row under the fan.

Even after R' Shlomo left this world, the bond remained strong. In a *hesped* for R' Chanina, his son Yitzchok shared the words of R' Chaim Vital on this subject. A rebbi who learns with his *talmid* places his *ruach* into his *talmid*, and that *ruach* stays with the *talmid* for eternity — and will never be separated. Indeed, the *ruach* of R' Shlomo was alive in R' Chanina, and lives on in his family.

R' Zev Davidowitz, menahel of the Mechina (middle school) of Yeshiva Toras Chaim, stated, "R' Herzberg lived with his rebbi in real time. When he would reminisce about his rebbi, it wasn't just reminiscing in past tense. It was a *mehalech hachaim.*"

During the summers that R' Chanina and his family spent in the Sh'or Yoshuv bungalow colony, he would occasionally speak to the *bachurim* during *shalosh seudos.* One of those *bachurim,* who was learning in Sh'or Yoshuv at the time, later related that after hearing R' Chanina speak, he and his friends agreed that R' Chanina was similar to his rebbi. They realized and understood the special connection. As R' Shaya Novak, president of Ohr Shlomo and close *yedid* of R' Chanina, reflected, "R' Chanina developed a speaking style similar to that of his rebbi."

The *talmidim* of Yeshiva Toras Chaim felt this way, too, as did the administrators. Any *talmid* who learned in Yeshiva Toras Chaim heard many stories about R' Shlomo. In addition, R' Mordechai Kamenetzky, rosh yeshiva of Toras Chaim, noted that there was hardly a serious conversation with R' Chanina in which he did not "*shtell tzu*" an idea from his rebbi.

The Gemara (*Succah* 28a) teaches that R' Eliezer testified about himself, "I have never said a thing which I did not hear from my rebbi." The commentators ask, how is it possible that in the course of his entire lifetime, R' Eliezer never said anything that he didn't hear from his rebbi? Moreover, *Avos DeRabbi Nassan* (6:3) reveals that R' Eliezer would say things that the world had never heard. Clearly, then, he said things that he had not heard from his rebbi.

R' Chaim Shmulevitz (*Sichos Mussar* 5731:41, *Shaarei Chaim* edition) explains that even when saying new things, R' Eliezer always asked himself, "What would my rebbi say?" And he never said anything his rebbi would not have said.

R' Chanina once informed his children, "I can honestly say that throughout my life, even after my rebbi was *niftar*, I did only what I thought he would do, or what he would tell me to do."

Following R' Chanina's *petirah*, R' Yisroel Besser, the author of *Reb Shlomo*, sent R' Chanina's son Mendy a message. "The *Reb Shlomo* book wouldn't have happened without your father. He made me believe that it was possible — he had R' Shlomo's power and warmth and *seichel* — and explained to me how to express it. It was a pleasure to be around him and soak it in."

When accepting the *kesser shem tov* award at the Sh'or Yoshuv dinner after R' Shlomo's *petirah*, R' Chanina himself expressed it best. At the time, he repeated a *vort* he had once shared with R' Shlomo. Upon hearing it, R' Shlomo had declared, "Chanina, this is a *shtick* Yiddishkeit."

"All of the *avos*," R' Chanina began, "Avraham, Yitzchak, and Yaakov, had dealings with wells. In this week's *parashah*, we learn how Yaakov came to a well, where he met Rochel.

"What are these wells? The *mefarshim* tell us that the wells represent *be'er mayim chaim*, the well of living water, meaning the Torah. The Chiddushei Harim (ad loc.), the first Gerrer Rebbe, comments on the *maaseh* of Yaakov Avinu. When Yaakov Avinu came to Padan Aram, he noticed a huge boulder on the well. However, when Rochel came along with her sheep, he suddenly came up with the strength to push away the rock from on top of the well. The Chiddushei Harim tells us that this was not an impossible feat for Yaakov Avinu. If the well is the well of Torah, the boulder represents all the impediments that prevent us from accomplishing in Torah. And Yaakov managed to push away all the obstacles that stood in the way of his *limud Torah.*

"For 26 years," R' Chanina continued, "we had the *zechus* of having a 'Yaakov,' a person who taught us what it means to push the rock off the well. This is what the rosh yeshiva did. But you can ask the question: What happens after a Yaakov Avinu?

"Once Yaakov Avinu showed the people how to push off the rock, once he forged the path, together, the rest of the shepherds were able to follow his lead and do the same.

"*Baruch Hashem,* for 26 years, I learned under the rebbi, and have been part of the *kehillah* of Sh'or Yoshuv. Now, my rebbetzin and I are *zocheh* that our son Moshe learns in Sh'or Yoshuv, and he comes home with the same warmth and the same desire for learning that I felt under the rosh yeshiva 26 years ago.

"Sh'or Yoshuv lives..."

Many years after his rebbi's *petirah,* R' Chanina was asked, "Are there times in which you wish you could just pick up the phone and speak to your rebbi?"

R' Chanina responded emotionally, "My lot in life is to be a menahel in a yeshiva. *Baruch Hashem,* I am *zocheh* to deal with hundreds of children every day, and many *mishpachos,* as well. *Ba'avonoseinu harabbim,* in today's time it's extremely difficult to navigate.

"But I have a portrait of my rebbi hanging in my office. And I don't think a day goes by in which something comes up and I don't look at that picture and ask myself, 'How would my rebbi have handled this? What would my rebbi have done?' It gives me strength. It gives me courage. It inspires me. I really feel like R' Shlomo is with me every day."

Case in point. R' Chanina had just attended an intense administrative meeting, discussing a serious situation regarding one of the *talmidim* in the yeshiva. The meeting ended without any clarity on the issue, and only R' Chanina and R' Avraham Robinson, R' Chanina's s'gan menahel, remained in R' Chanina's office. R' Chanina looked at the picture of his rebbi hanging on his wall, and then, as if talking to the picture, he asked, "Rebbi, what would you do?" In truth, R' Chanina told his son that he would gaze at the photograph of his rebbi on a daily basis and ask himself, "What would my rebbi do?"

R' Chanina in his office with a *talmid*, with the picture of his rebbi hanging above him

R' Chanina constantly emphasized that the image of a rebbi plays a most important role in a *talmid*'s life. A rebbi in Yeshiva Toras Chaim shared, "I was taking a daily medication that called for a specific number of milligrams every day. One morning, I mistakenly took double the dose, and the side effects hit me while I was teaching. Before I knew it, I had collapsed in front of my class. The boys ran to the nurse, who immediately called Hatzalah. I told everyone I was perfectly okay, and that it was all due to a mistaken dosage. However, protocol required that I be taken to the hospital. As soon as I arrived and the doctor confirmed I was all right, I promptly checked myself out and took a taxi back to yeshiva. On the way, I called R' Herzberg to inform him of my return. He told me to take the rest of the day off, but to please stop by his office before retrieving my car from the yeshiva parking lot.

"I came into R' Herzberg's office and saw my entire class waiting there for me! After the boys welcomed me back, they were dismissed to their next class. I turned to R' Herzberg and asked him, 'Why did you have all the boys here?'

"He replied, 'I didn't want the last image in the minds of the boys to be of you lying on the floor and being taken out on a stretcher. It's not the image *talmidim* should have of their rebbi. They needed to see that you are fine and healthy!'"

This was part of the *mesorah* R' Chanina received from R' Freifeld: The image of a rebbi is of paramount importance, as rebbeim are an integral link in the *mesorah* from Har Sinai.

The picture that a *talmid* retains of his rebbi must be one of aristocracy; a rebbi must stand tall at all times.

The Importance of Having a Rebbi

R' CHANINA, BY EXAMPLE, INCULCATED WITHIN HIS CHILDREN THE importance of having a rebbi. His children knew that Abba didn't make a move without first consulting his rebbi. After his rebbi's *petirah,* his children witnessed how he would constantly ask himself what his rebbi would do in any given situation.

At R' Chanina's *levayah,* the children who spoke all echoed one thought. *The most important thing our father taught us is the importance of having a rebbi.*

It wasn't just about having a rebbi, but also about being willing to accept *mussar* from him. During the *shivah* for R' Chanina, R' Yehuda Kelemer, rav of Young Israel of West Hempstead and R' Chanina's dear friend, shared a *dvar Torah* he had told R' Chanina, which R' Chanina had enjoyed. The Gemara (*Yoma* 37a) states that one who walks on the right of his rebbi is a boor (an uncultivated, uncivilized person).

The Manestricher Rebbe explained: The right side is the side of *kiruv,* as in: "The left hand should always push away, while the right hand draws the person close" (*Sotah* 47a). One who only wants his rebbi to give him compliments, to tell him he's good and wonderful, is, in the

Visiting the *kever* of his rebbi on Har HaZeisim for the first time

words of the Gemara in *Yoma,* an ignoramus, a boor. It takes a wise person to be ready and willing to accept criticism from his rebbi.

Hearing this *vort,* R' Chanina's son told a story about his father. In 1986 (5746), R' Chanina purchased a summer home in Woodridge, New York. That Pesach, the family spent a beautiful Yom Tov there, and R' Chanina decided to spend the Yom Tov of Shavuos upstate, as well, enjoying the refreshing country weather. The preparations were made and the Herzberg family excitedly headed to Woodridge.

Five minutes before Yom Tov, the phone rang. When R' Chanina answered the call, he began to shake. It was his rebbi. "R' Chanina! a Yid in the mountains for Shavuos?!" and he hung up the phone, not even allowing R' Chanina to respond.

R' Chanina told his children what had occurred. "My rebbi is right," he conceded. "I don't know what I was thinking. How could I spend Shavuos away from the yeshiva? I'm lucky to have a rebbi to set me straight."

R' Chanina learned his lesson, as did his children. By that time, R' Chanina had already been out of Yeshiva Sh'or Yoshuv for many years and was already a prominent figure in the community in his own right. Even so, not only did he accept his rebbi's rebuke, he made a point of sharing it with his children — to teach them what it means to be connected to a yeshiva or a shul, and what it means to be totally subservient to your rebbi or rav.

R' Shlomo was *niftar* on Shabbos Chol HaMoed, immediately following the first days of Succos. The Herzberg *mishpachah* was spending the first days in their Woodridge home. Though R' Chanina's son Yitzchok was only 8 at the time, the moment in which his father found out the news about his rebbi's *petirah* will forever be etched in his memory; he still remembers where he and his father were standing at that moment.

R' Chanina was preparing to return home the next day, and Yitzchok was on his way out the door to the succah on the back porch when the call came in. R' Chanina clutched his heart and let out a huge scream, a scream that seemed to shake the house. It was that scream that spoke louder than any words.

At that moment, R' Chanina's children fully understood what R' Shlomo meant to their father, and to the entire *mishpachah.*

In a sense, all the Herzbergs had lost their rebbi.

As menahel, when R' Chanina interviewed a candidate for a position in Yeshiva Toras Chaim, he would ask, "Who is your rebbi?" If the candidate did not have an adequate answer, then even if he had a reputation as an excellent *mechanech,* he wasn't the man for the job. It didn't matter who his rebbi was; he just had to have a rebbi.

R' Chanina firmly believed that if an individual has a rebbi, it says something about his character. "A person who has a rebbi understands what it means to have *hachna'ah* and be a *mekabel,* attributes essential to accepting advice from others." It also meant that he had a sense of *mesorah,* something very important to R' Chanina.

A rebbi in Yeshiva Toras Chaim recalled, "When I interviewed for a position in the yeshiva, R' Herzberg called my rebbeim and asked one question to each: 'Will he be a *mekabel*? Will he accept, hear, and implement what he hears from others?' In R' Herzberg's eyes, being a *mekabel* was integral to being a rebbi."

In a *derashah* on *chinuch,* R' Chanina shared a story involving his friend who was a rebbi, who noticed that one of his students was looking at inappropriate material during class.

"What would you do in such a situation?" R' Chanina asked his audience.

After taking suggestions, ranging from ripping it up to punishing the boy, R' Chanina continued the story. "You know what my friend did? Nothing, at first. He gave the boys a break and went to call his rebbi, R' Shlomo Freifeld, to ask what to do. Now that's a rebbi! He understood that he didn't know how to react and instead of taking the risk of making a mistake, he asked his own rebbi!

"The lesson is simple. Never be ashamed to ask for help in figuring things out."

R' Chanina once received a heart-wrenching letter from a *talmid.* The letter, in which the *talmid* expresses deep regret for not maintaining contact with R' Chanina, demonstrates the importance of having a rebbi and remaining connected to that rebbi throughout one's life, no matter what.

> *R' Herzberg, shlita,*
>
> *I have been beyond negligent in my obligation to give honor to you. I have turned away from my responsibility to give thanks to you. My lack of respect is open for all to see. If it were not for you*

taking me in when you did, who knows what would have been? My connection to Hashem and His Torah is only because of you. My drive for learning and avodas Hashem is only due to you. How much I owe you, yet I have refused to show you my thankfulness and respect. In truth, there is no excuse for what I have done.

Since I knew you would not have approved of certain actions of mine, I decided to cut myself off from you. Cut myself off from the life-giving man, the man who, without him, I would have no life at all. How different things would be if Rebbi had not taken me in when he did. The only one who lost out was I. I was so sure that I was correct in my actions and that you would not understand that I had no choice to act this way. In the end, seven years later, I realize how stupid a choice it was. I was just too afraid to admit that I was wrong, and I did not want to hear that I was at fault for my own conclusions and actions.

So many years without your guidance and advice — this has been a huge mistake. I created a void that could not be filled. So many times I needed you, and so many times I was embarrassed to contact you. With each week that passed, it became more difficult to fill the space that I created. Until I buried my feelings and ignored my true thoughts of calling you. How great a price I paid for this lack of clarity and thought.

How many times I could have used your advice or guidance as a husband or parent. So many times I went against my better judgment and continued to do the stupid thing. How many times you could have helped, and I was too stubborn to pick up the phone. Too haughty and too high on my own high horse to do the right thing. How low I feel now, admitting I was wrong. Is it possible to build a bridge over such a massive span of time and space, in order to attempt to close this gap? I truly hope so.

I truly miss Rebbi with every fiber of my being. I speak of Rebbi as if we are still close. I proudly say the stories about myself and others, as if this is my rebbi. Yet each word I say brings pain, knowing that I have not done even one thing to connect and repair the damage.

A donkey knows its master, a dog knows its owner. Yet I chose to ignore the man who made me a Yid. I chose to ignore the man who taught me the true purpose in this life. I chose to ignore the man who brought me to Hashem. I chose to ignore the man who showed me life. I chose to ignore the man who saved me from tragedy. I chose

BSD

Rabbi Herzberg Shlita,

I have been beyond negligent in my obligation of giving honor to you to say the least. I have turned away from my responsibility to give thanks to you. My lack of respect is open for all to see. If it was not for you taking me in when you did who knows what would have been. My connection to Hashem and His Torah is only because of you. My drive for learning and avodos Hashem is only due to you. How much I owe you how I haverefused to show you my thankfulness and respect. In truh there is no excuse for what I have done.

Since I knew you would not have approved of certain actions that I did seven years ago. I decided to cut myself off from you. Cut myself off form the life giving man. The man who without him my I wuld have no life at all. How different things would be if Rebbe did not take me when he did. The only one that lost was I. I was so sure that I was so correct in my actions and that you would not understand that I had no choice t act this way, In the end seven years later I realize how how stupid a choice it has been I was just to afraid to admit that I was wrong, and did not want to hear that I was at fault for my own conclusions and actions.

So many years without your guidance warmth and advice this has been a huge mistake. I created a void that could not be filled. So many times I needed you and so many times I was to embarrassed to contact you. With each week that passed it became more difficult to fill the space that I created. Until I buried my feelings and ignored my true thoughts of calling you. How great a price I paid for this lack of clarity of thought.

How many times I could have used your advice or guidance as husband or parent. So many times I went against my better judgment and continued to do the stupid thing. How many times you could have helped and I was to stubborn to pick up the phone. To haughty and too high on my own high horse to do the right thing. How low I feel now in admitting I was wrong for what I have done. Is it possible to build a bridge over such a massive span of time and space. In order attempt to close the this gap. I truly hope so. I truly miss Rebbe with every fiber of my being I speak of Rebbe as if we are still close. I say the stories about myself and the others that I know proudly as if this is my Rebbe. Yet each word I would say brought pain knowing that I have not even done one thing to connect and repair the damage.

A donkey knows its masters, a dog knows it's owner and yet I choose to ignore the man who made me a Yid, I chose to ignore the man who taught me the true purpose in this life. I chose to ignore the man who brought me to Hashem, I chose to ignore the man who showed me life. I chose to ignore the man who saved me from tragedy. I chose to ignore my Rebbe who can just as easily be called my Farther. How Ironic since without you I have placed my self in harms way,

Rebbe! Rebbe! Rebbe! I am sorry please forgive me, please if you can find it in your heart to let me come back to you. I would like to call you and hear your voice I would like to call you share good news I would like to call you to share a chidush I would to call you just because I miss you. I need to call you so you can put me in my place when I do wrong. This is truly the biggest loss I have felt in my life. No words can truly be written to describe the foolishness of my actions. I am not sure what has pushed me to write this letter. I am not sure how Rebbe will receive and accept the words this letter, but I know deep down in the depths of my heart the I know the silence has gone to long and this is the right thing to do. Please take me back into your life. Please embrace me again even if I live so far away.

With the Greatest Love and admiration
Always Your Talmid

The heart-wrenching letter written to R' Chanina by a *talmid*

to ignore my rebbi, who can just as easily be my father. How ironic, since without you I have placed myself in harm's way.

Rebbi! Rebbi! Rebbi! I am sorry. Please forgive me. Please, if you can, find it in your heart to let me come back to you. I would like to call you and hear your voice. I would like to call you to share good news. I would like to call you to share a chiddush. I would like to call you just because I miss you. I need to call you so you can put me in my place when I do wrong. This is truly the biggest loss I have felt in my life. No words can be written to truly describe the foolishness of my actions.

I am not sure what has pushed me to write this letter. I am not sure how Rebbi will receive and accept this letter. But I know, deep down in the depths of my heart, that the silence has gone on too long, and this is the right thing to do.

Please take me back into your life. Please embrace me again even if I live so far away...

With the greatest love and admiration,
Always Your Talmid

After reading the letter, R' Chanina cried tears of relief. He was heartened that his *talmid* was mature enough to realize his mistake. The connection was thus reestablished.

In fact, when R' Chanina's son called the *talmid* for permission to include the letter in this book, he immediately granted permission, adding, "You should know that I think about your father several times a day. I ask myself, what would rebbi do in such-and-such a situation? And I know what he would tell me to do. That's how close I feel to my rebbi."

Several months before his own *petirah*, R' Chanina was hospitalized, unsure if he would be able to attend his grandson's bar mitzvah. In case he wouldn't make it to the event, he recorded a message to be played there. At the end of the recording, he conveyed a personal thought, stressing the importance of having a rebbi and the impact a rebbi has on one's life and the life of one's entire family.

"You know, we, the Herzberg family, are determined people. What do I mean that we are determined people? We are determined people because we had a rebbi who instilled in each and every one of us the determination of being an *oveid Hashem*, a servant of Hashem.

"Think about that! Any *hatzlachah* that Mommy and I have had in bringing up our children is because my rebbi instilled in us a certain determination. Any *hatzlachah* that I or any of the children have had in *avodas Hashem* is because my rebbi instilled in us a certain determination.

"We're determined people!

"But we are determined people with a goal in mind. That goal is to be able to make our mark on this world and be able to do *retzon Hashem*."

The night before R' Chanina's youngest child, Yudi, left for Eretz Yisrael to Yeshivas Mir, R' Chanina suddenly began to cry. When Yudi asked his father what was wrong, R' Chanina answered, "Yudi, I'm jealous of you. You're going to Eretz Yisrael to the Mir to find yourself a rebbi. My rebbi was *niftar* almost 20 years ago, and the biggest regret I have in my life is that I didn't go out and find another rebbi to connect to. What am I supposed to do now? I have no one to whom to talk, no one to whom to ask my questions. I'm jealous of some of my friends who, after our rebbi was *niftar*, connected themselves to another rebbi." Of course, R' Chanina had mentors, but he still pined for the rebbi-*talmid* relationship he had enjoyed during R' Shlomo's lifetime.

Yudi listened in awe. Here was his father — 60 years old, a menahel, someone sought after for advice across the gamut, himself a rebbi to many — yet he was broken that he didn't have a rebbi to whom to talk.

That night, the importance of having a rebbi was driven home to Yudi in a most powerful manner.

A Link in the Chain

FOLLOWING R' CHANINA'S *PETIRAH*, R' SHMUEL JUDOWITZ, SEVENTH-grade rebbi at Yeshiva Toras Chaim, wrote, "The first thought that comes to mind when thinking of memories of R' Herzberg is his sense of responsibility in continuing the *mesorah* that he received from his rebbeim, R' Shlomo Freifeld and R' Yitzchak Hutner. This outlook — that he felt that he was a link in the *mesorah* of Torah *chinuch* to the next generation — permeated every action of his as a menahel."

The *mesorah* that the Alter of Slabodka transmitted to R' Hutner.

The *mesorah* that R' Hutner transmitted to R' Shlomo.

The *mesorah* that R' Shlomo transmitted to R' Chanina.

The *mesorah* from which R' Chanina didn't deviate even one iota.

R' Yussie Lieber articulated, "When I visited his class in Yeshiva

Tiferes Moshe, I saw the rebbi's lessons at work in another person other than the rebbi himself."

R' Nosson Tzvi Finkel, the Alter of Slabodka

It came as no surprise during the *shivah* that R' Aryeh Lebowitz — rabbi of Beis HaKnesses of North Woodmere, noted *maggid shiur,* and R' Chanina's *talmid* from Yeshiva Toras Chaim — noted, "The biography of R' Herzberg does not need to be written, since the biography of R' Freifeld has already been written."

R' Lebowitz added, "When I bought the book about R' Shlomo and started reading through it, I felt as if I was reliving my elementary school days. Because everything R' Herzberg did was rooted in R' Shlomo."

The seed of R' Chanina eventually sprouted its own roots and sowed many other plants, yet it always hearkened back toward its origins, from where it stemmed.

Everything R' Chanina did was rooted in his rebbi.

R' Chanina was forever R' Shlomo's *talmid*.

R' Shlomo Freifeld (r) with his rebbi, R' Yitzchak Hutner

R' Chanina Herzberg (l) with his rebbi, R' Shlomo Freifeld

Chapter 4
Spreading the Light: Ohr Shlomo

IN 1998 (5759), R' CHANINA'S MOTHER PASSED AWAY. AS AN *AVEL*, WITH a *chiyuv* to recite *Kaddish* in his mother's memory, R' Chanina was in a quandary. For most of the year, he davened all the weekday *tefillos* in Yeshiva Toras Chaim. However, Motza'ei Shabbos presented a problem. R' Chanina was hesitant about davening in the nearby shuls. He knew that since he was a menahel in the community, the congregants in the shuls would feel obligated to allow him to lead the davening, which made him uncomfortable. "I'm not a member in these shuls, and they shouldn't be giving me precedence to daven for the *amud*, especially over their own members."

A Shul Is Born

As such, R' Chanina decided to start his own *minyan* for Maariv on Motza'ei Shabbos, at 60 minutes after sunset. He invited some neighbors, and they came. As the latest Motza'ei Shabbos Maariv in close proximity, it was convenient in terms of time and location. Thus, even after R' Chanina completed his year of *aveilus*, the *minyan* continued on Motza'ei Shabbos.

R' Chanina's mother had left a small inheritance to her children, and R' Chanina and his wife decided to spend the money on much-needed repairs to their house. Yet as the plans for construction got underway, R' Chanina was struck by a brainstorm. "It will be a *zechus* for my mother if we use a portion of the funds to convert the basement into a *beis midrash*."

A shul was born.

R' Chanina speaking at a shul *melaveh malkah*

With the completion of the renovations in the basement, R' Chanina expanded the *minyan* to include a Friday night and Shabbos Minchah *minyan*, as well. He named the shul Beis Medrash Ohr Shlomo after his rebbi, R' Shlomo Freifeld. His sole intention was to allow others to bask in the *ohr,* the light, of R' Shlomo.

Several years later, in 2004 (5764), R' Chanina opened a Shabbos morning *minyan,* as well. Soon after, Yamim Noraim and Yamim Tovim *minyanim* were added. Though busy as a menahel of a large yeshiva, if people needed *chizuk,* R' Chanina was there to provide it. Not only didn't R' Chanina receive a salary as rav, but he also spent thousands of dollars of his own for the upkeep and basic necessities of the shul.

Through the shul, R' Chanina was able to be *mechanech* his children in working for the *tzibbur.* He appointed his youngest son, Yudi, all of 13 at the time, as *gabbai* of the shul. Yudi looks back at that experience as a key factor in his spiritual growth. His father trusted him, building his confidence and training him to be there for others, not just for the big-ticket items, but also for the small ones. Yudi also learned to take the feelings of everyone into consideration and to look at the broad picture when making decisions. R' Chanina once noted that the entire shul was worthwhile just to give Yudi the opportunity to serve as *gabbai.*

In addition, for that first *Kabbalas Shabbos,* R' Chanina did not seek a seasoned *sheliach tzibbur*. Rather, he asked another one of his sons, who rarely davened for the *amud* and had a slight stutter, to daven for the *amud,* "But I don't know how to lead the davening well," his son, who was 18 at the time, protested.

"Don't worry, you'll be great!" he encouraged him.

Sharing a Blanket

THAT FIRST SHABBOS, *PARASHAS BO,* R' CHANINA SPOKE BEFORE Maariv and shared the goal of the shul, setting the tone with a *vort* he heard from R' Shlomo. At the time of *makkas choshech,* the *pasuk* relates (*Shemos* 10:23), *"Lo ra'u ish es achiv v'lo kamu ish mi'tachtav* — No man could see his brother, nor could anyone rise from his place."

The Chiddushei Harim (*Likkutei Harim,* p. 164) interprets this *pasuk* homiletically. If "no man could see his brother" — when a Yid doesn't feel for another Yid, isn't sympathetic to his plight, doesn't offer him assistance — then, "nor could he rise from his own place" — his own growth will be stunted.

R' Chanina continued with a thought from R' Chaim Shmulevitz (*Sichos Mussar* 5731: 36, *Shaarei Chaim* edition). The Gemara (*Sanhedrin* 20a) teaches that the generation of Rabbi Yehudah bar Ila'i embodied *limud Torah* at its best. What was so striking about that generation? In those days, *"shishah talmidim miskasin b'tallis achas v'oskin baTorah* — six disciples would learn Torah together under a single blanket." According to the basic explanation, the Gemara is praising Rabbi Yehudah's generation, who, despite extreme poverty where six people had to share one blanket, were still devoted to Torah study.

R' Chaim Shmulevitz, however, explains it differently. The only way six people can learn together under one blanket is if every person is looking out for the other, giving a little bit of the blanket to his friend, making sure that all are covered. The true greatness of Rabbi Yehudah bar Ila'i's generation could be found in the way they loved and respected one another, the way they were *b'achdus,* unified as one! These Yidden saw each other's pain and angst and needs. *"Ra'u ish es achiv."*

R' Chanina addressed the *tzibbur.* "This *beis haknesses* is *l'zecher* the *neshamah* of my mother, *Chana Fradel bas Menachem Mendel. B'ezras Hashem,* we will be *matzliach,* for the goal of this *beis midrash* is to come together as *chaverim.* Through this *beis midrash,* may we have the *zechus* of uniting as one, *b'achdus.*"

Along with his wife, R' Chanina cultivated an atmosphere where everyone who came felt welcomed, felt a sense of *chashivus*: R' Chanina

R' Chanina and *mispallelim* at a *simchas beis hasho'eivah* in his succah

with the men, and his wife with the women. An atmosphere in which they all "shared one blanket," where each one really *saw* the other one.

The shul's president, R' Shaya Novak, observed how R' Chanina emulated his rebbi in creating a cohesive *kehillah*. At a *simchas beis hasho'eivah* in the Herzberg succah, R' Chanina spoke to his *mispallelim* and reiterated the importance of togetherness, prefacing his thoughts with a *pasuk* (*Tehillim* 133:1), "*Hinei mah tov u'mah na'im sheves achim gam yachad* — Behold, how good and pleasant is the dwelling of brothers, especially, in unity." R' Chanina exclaimed, "There's a special '*tov*,' a special good, and a special '*n'eemus*,' and a special pleasantness, when it's '*sheves achim gam yachad*,' when we sit together, when we sing together! The *pasuk* is telling us that just being together is a *gurr chashuve zach*. Merely sitting together, crying together, talking together, is in itself a big *zechus*. May we be *zocheh* to always be together."

Dispensing Chizuk and Chiyus

R' CHANINA RELATED TO EACH *MISPALLEL* ON AN INDIVIDUAL BASIS, speaking with them and getting to know their families. As a result, they turned to him for *eitzos* and *hadrachah* regarding life in general, and, of course, *chinuch habanim*. As a young man in Beth Tikvah in Canarsie, Chanina had observed how the rav, R' Yaakov Yosef Greenberg, came to shul early on Friday afternoons to be there for his congregants. Likewise, every week one hour before Shabbos, already bedecked in his

Shabbos attire, R' Chanina went down to the shul, where he sat and learned. As the *mispallelim* entered, he would talk to them about whatever was on their minds, dispensing advice and encouragement as needed.

On the Erev Shabbos of the *shivah* for R' Chanina, his son Yitzchok was preparing for Minchah, when he noticed the silver lead pencil his father had used to write inside his *sefarim*. Knowing that soon the house would be filled with people coming to join the mourners for Minchah, Yitzchok proceeded to put it in a safe place.

A young *bachur* who had been close to R' Chanina noticed and revealed, "That pencil is special to me. I used to get it for your father every Erev Shabbos. I would come to shul early to talk to your father, but first he always asked me to bring him his special pencil. That made *me* feel so special."

Seeing how much the pencil meant to the boy, Yitzchok handed it to him. "My father would want you to have this."

R' Chanina was an expert in benefiting all Yidden, showing them they mattered, and giving them *chiyus*. He frequently cited the *pasuk* (*I Shmuel* 22:2), which describes how Dovid surrounded himself with 400 downtrodden men: "every man in distress, every man with a creditor, and every man embittered of spirit." R' Chanina asserted, "It's easy to take care of important people. Now try caring for those whom nobody cares about!" His whole life was about looking out for the underdogs, for those who are regularly overlooked, serving as their first line of defense.

This, too, was part of the legacy he received from R' Shlomo, which played itself out in his shul. On Simchas Torah, it is customary to grant the honor of *Chassan Torah* to a prominent *talmid chacham*. One year, R' Chanina veered from this practice, instead bestowing the honor upon Mr. Ben Dinkel,* a shul member who had faced many challenges in the past year, particularly in the realm of *parnassah*.

Upon hearing the news, Ben objected. "But R' Herzberg, I don't have any money to pay for the Kiddush that accompanies this special *aliyah*!"

R' Chanina was unfazed. "Don't worry, Ben. Just give whatever you can. I'll take care of the rest." Ben could only contribute five dollars toward the Kiddush. Yet he cherished that moment, as he was elevated to a special status in the eyes of the *mispallelim*.

R' Chanina with his *mispallelim* at *Bircas HaChamah*

Ruvy* grew up in a frum home and attended yeshiva. Unfortunately, as a teenager he strayed from the proper path. One Shabbos, Ruvy, now a young adult, stayed with a friend. Though it had been some time since he had last attended shul, he went with his friend to R' Chanina's shul. However, he didn't bother wearing a yarmulke.

As Ruvy entered the shul during Mussaf, R' Chanina took note of the newcomer and motioned to him to sit next to him at the front of the shul. R' Chanina, who was wearing a hat, removed his yarmulke from under his hat, gave it to Ruvy, and placed his arm around him. R' Chanina remained at Ruvy's side during the Kiddush, as well, making him feel welcome and comfortable. No lengthy conversation, just wise eyes and true love for another Jew.

That was a turning point in Ruvy's return to Torah observance. R' Chanina's warm and selfless act touched his *neshamah,* helping catalyze a complete turnaround. He slowly began to wear a yarmulke more often, always the yarmulke R' Chanina had given him, which he so cherished.

Today, Ruvy is a fully-observant Jew.

To enhance the feeling of *achdus* and provide additional *chizuk,* R' Chanina instituted a weekly Kiddush in shul, where hot kugel, cake, herring, *kichel,* and schnapps were served. He looked at the food as a connector, a means through which the *olam* could first enjoy each other's company and then listen to meaningful *divrei hashkafah.*

All smiles, with a *mispallel* on Purim

Always there to support her husband's undertakings and endeavors, Mrs. Herzberg prepared the Kiddush each week, and did so with *mesiras nefesh.* After ordering the food during the week, she made sure to be home for the deliveries and organized them once they arrived on Friday, and set everything in place on Shabbos morning. Though the *mispallelim* assisted with setting up the tables and chairs after davening and cleaning up afterward, Shabbos was in no way a day off for her.

A *MISPALLEL* AT OHR SHLOMO CONVEYED, "R' CHANINA WAS ABLE TO give over pure Yiddishkeit."

The Weekly Derashos

After R' Chanina's *petirah,* the family received a letter of condolence from a shul family. "When we first moved to Far Rockaway over 15 years ago, we found ourselves at a loss. Our father, the man of the house, found his place, but we, his three daughters, just couldn't find the right shul. Being women meant this wasn't so bad, until the Yamim Noraim rolled around. Someone told us to try out R' Herzberg's shul. 'It's *heimish,*' they said. 'You'll like it.' Indeed, we did. The rabbi spoke with such love and devotion for Klal Yisrael. His short speeches were always about kindness and self-reflection. Somehow, just being around him, you wanted to be better.

"This year, he wasn't able to be in shul all the time, and we felt it. We couldn't see him over the *mechitzah*; he spoke so briefly, and not often.

His absence should not have been so noticeable to three women sitting on the other side, but it was. His presence was palpable, because you knew you were in the presence of greatness."

As rav of Beis Medrash Ohr Shlomo, R' Chanina spoke twice every Shabbos: on Friday night before Maariv, and on Shabbos morning at the weekly Kiddush. His *divrei Torah* were between five and ten minutes, never longer. They contained a question and an answer, with an important takeaway. He could speak about the same theme on a particular *parashah* two or three years in a row, and when people would say, "I heard it last year," R' Chanina would counter, "You remember what I said because you were listening and it spoke to you. If so, it's good to hear it again."

Moreover, he pointed out that if you look through the *sefer Sfas Emes* (one of his favorite *sefarim*), you will see that many times the Sfas Emes, R' Yehudah Aryeh Leib Alter, spoke about the same topic year after year. The Sfas Emes didn't feel he had to speak about a new topic each year. If there was a *limud* in the *parashah* that he felt his Chassidim had to hear, he would talk about it again and again, just to hammer the point home.

After complaining to R' Chanina for relating the same theme in his *derashos* again and again, Dov* went back to him a while later and apologized. One of R' Chanina's main messages was the importance of being friendly and warm to others, to remember to give them *shalom aleichem*. Dov had been having a hard time getting along with an acquaintance. Yet after hearing R' Chanina stress the importance of *ahavas Yisrael,* and hearing the same speech repeatedly, the message began to penetrate and he was able to treat his former nemesis with the love due him and any Jew. As Dov admitted to R' Chanina, the message was drilled into him so many times that it eventually made an impact.

When R' Chanina mentioned a thought from a Rashi on the *parashah,* he had another agenda, too, to teach the importance of learning Chumash with Rashi. As such, he would frequently stress, "There are no great *chochmos* here. It's a *pashute* Rashi!"

Aside from focusing on *ahavas Yisrael* when speaking about the *parashah,* R' Chanina also pinpointed the importance of having a rebbi. And in keeping with the objective of the shul — to spread R' Shlomo's light — R' Chanina generally based his *dvar Torah* on a thought from R' Shlomo.

In the early stages of Ohr Shlomo, several individuals approached R' Chanina with a gripe. "R' Herzberg, we feel like you speak too much about your rebbi." R' Chanina allowed them to vent but didn't respond. Instead, after taking some time to digest the complaint, he voiced his thoughts to his children. "Nobody is going to tell me I can't speak about my rebbi. A person has to do what's right, no matter what." Doing what he knew was right meant spreading his rebbi's Torah.

"Just a Mechanech"

R' CHANINA NEVER LOST HIS HUMILITY, WHETHER HE WAS A REBBI, menahel, or *mara d'asra*. As rav of Beis Medrash Ohr Shlomo, he was in charge of selling the *chametz* on behalf of his *kehillah*. To facilitate this, he joined other *chashuve* rabbanim in the community. One year, the leading rabbi of the group honored R' Chanina with signing the *shtar mechirah*. But R' Chanina refused. "I am just a *mechanech* who happens to be a rav. You're a true rav."

The Herzberg family's *posek* had always been R' Chanina's good friend from his yeshiva days, R' Moshe Dov Stein. R' Chanina repeatedly sang R' Moshe Dov's praises, extolling his vast knowledge and deep understanding of halachah, "Look at R' Moshe Dov," he would mention as he spoke to his children. "He's a great man and he's so normal."

In his capacity as rav, R' Chanina was often asked halachic questions. He would answer the simple questions, but not the complex ones. "I'm not a *posek* and therefore I cannot answer this *shailah*. Go ask R' Stein; he's a real *posek*, and he'll be able to help you." Following R' Moshe Dov's *petirah*, R' Chanina would send his *mispallelim* to R' Tzvi Yaakov Stein, R' Moshe Dov's son. R' Tzvi Yaakov occasionally gave halachah *shiurim* in the shul, as well.

R' Chanina knew how to handle complex situations. One Shabbos, a group of men were talking a little *too* much during davening. An older fellow, who was visiting for Shabbos, started shushing them and telling them off, until heated words were exchanged.

Afterward, the visitor complained to R' Chanina regarding both the talking and the reaction of the talkers to his rebuke. R' Chanina let the man vent, but he didn't agree with his approach, and he told him so. "You shouldn't have gotten involved with them. You don't know them, where they come from and where they are holding, and the trials they may have gone through in their past."

Whereas R' Chanina was all for proper decorum in shul, he rarely administered rebuke in public, and when he did, it was always with a *cheshbon*.

Chapter 5
Making His Mark: R' Herzberg the Menahel

THE DAY AFTER R' CHANINA'S *LEVAYAH*, THE *TALMIDIM* OF YESHIVA Toras Chaim gathered to hear words of *chizuk* and reflect upon their loss. At that gathering, R' Moshe Scharhon, R' Chanina's close *yedid* and a rebbi in Yeshiva Toras Chaim, addressed the boys.

Brick by Brick

R' Binyamin and R' Chanina in later years

"As of yesterday, the ones who built us up are no longer here. All of us here, every one of us, must remember that all we have is because of the hard work of the rosh yeshiva, R' Binyamin Kamenetzky (who had passed away less than two years earlier), and the menahel, R' Chanina Herzberg. R' Binyamin established it and R' Chanina built it up. It's our job to be strong in our learning, strong in our davening, and strong in our *middos*. This is a gigantic yeshiva, a magnificent yeshiva. R' Chanina would have looked at you and he would have had tears in his eyes, looking at such a beautiful yeshiva." This short but poignant speech encapsulated the almost 40 years that R' Chanina was menahel of the yeshiva.

R' Chanina believed that a yeshiva needs to aspire for excellence in every respect: *limudei kodesh, middos tovos,* and *derech eretz,* as well as general studies. And under R' Chanina, Yeshiva Toras Chaim always strove for that standard. Shortly after R' Binyamin hired R' Chanina as menahel, he realized that he had come upon a master *mechanech,* one whom he could entrust with the day-to-day *chinuch* decisions and operations. Which R' Binyamin did, enabling him to focus on the administrative and financial aspects of running the yeshiva. For his part, R' Chanina was forever grateful to R' Binyamin for allowing him to direct all his *kochos* to *chinuch habanim,* not involving him in the school's finances whatsoever.

Under the unusually talented duo, the yeshiva thrived. At the time that R' Binyamin hired R' Chanina as menahel, the yeshiva was small, with one class per grade. In a short time, the yeshiva flourished, growing to 350 *talmidim*. Over the next two decades, it grew to three classes per grade, with a total enrollment of close to 700 *talmidim.*

Yet, as R' Shlomo Freifeld averred at R' Chanina's son's *bris,* in many ways the yeshiva, which he himself attended as a youth, remained the

R' Chanina speaking at a Yeshiva Toras Chaim expansion gathering

The growth of the yeshiva, from one small class in 1981
to three classes per grade in 2003.

same. In R' Shlomo's words, "Yeshiva Toras Chaim is not an ordinary place. It is a yeshiva with a history, a history of pioneering for Torah. And within the tens of years of its functioning from East New York to the Five Towns, I don't think it's lost its velocity, its impact. From its creation, it's always been deeply, deeply concerned with authentic Yiddishkeit."

"HE GAVE THE YESHIVA A HEART," ONE YESHIVA TORAS CHAIM PARENT stated during R' Chanina's *shivah*.

Giving the Yeshiva a Heart

When parents brought their children for an interview with R' Chanina, they were instantly hooked. Many contended that R' Chanina was the reason they chose the yeshiva. Comments such as "R' Herzberg understood my child's *shoresh neshamah*," or "R' Herzberg understood the dynamics of our family," or "R' Herzberg was so warm, welcoming, and non-judgmental," were commonplace.

At R' Chanina's *levayah*, a woman wept with great emotion. A person standing next to her inquired why she was crying uncontrollably, assuming she was a family member or someone very close to the family. "I had a child who graduated from Yeshiva Toras Chaim," she said. "My son was originally in another yeshiva, but then my husband and I divorced, and everything went downhill from there. We both found new spouses, creating a difficult environment for our son, whose learning was affected by the upheaval in his young life. With everything going on, my son needed a fresh start in a new yeshiva. We hoped to register him at Yeshiva Toras Chaim, as we'd heard amazing things about the yeshiva.

"We came for his interview, his father and I, along with our respective spouses. Two couples walked into the office with my son, creating a moment of awkwardness and discomfort for him. With glowing eyes and a big smile, R' Herzberg looked my son in the eye and the first words out of his mouth were, 'Look how lucky you are! You have so many people who love you!'

"With those words, my son knew he was home. My son is now a successful individual, only because of R' Herzberg."

A woman in her mid-30's once said to Eli Herzberg, "I miss your father so much! My family is frum today only because of him!"

She then filled him in. "Although my husband and I were both raised frum, as we grew up each of us struggled with our Yiddishkeit. Several

years ago, we moved to the Five Towns from Eretz Yisrael, and we needed a school for our son. We decided to visit various yeshivos. If we were impressed enough, we'd give yeshiva a shot for our child, and also change our lifestyle. If we weren't happy with what we saw, we were sending him to public school.

"We came to Yeshiva Toras Chaim, to R' Herzberg. In the course of the interview, he offered our 6-year-old son a treat, and asked him kindly, 'Do you know the *berachah* on that candy?' Our son looked at us in confusion; he didn't even know what a *berachah* was! R' Herzberg quickly turned back to my son with a big smile and the warmest look. 'Don't worry, enjoy the candy!' When we saw how your father sized up the situation and reacted with such warmth and sensitivity, we knew right away that this was the yeshiva for us. Because of that choice, over the past several years we've grown step by step, eventually getting back on the right path, and we are once again regular Orthodox Jews! All because of R' Herzberg!"

The acceptance interview wasn't an elaborate one. It wasn't loaded with questions and tests to see where the boy was holding academically. Rather, it was simple and personal.

R' Shlomo had taught R' Chanina that you can't be *mechanech* someone before you understand him as a person; it is not enough to assess only his brainpower. Thus, R' Chanina would talk to the boy on his level. As he connected with the child, R' Chanina would employ his inimitable wisdom until he figured him out to a T, as if he had known him for years.

A mother came with her 5-year-old son for an interview. Halfway through the interview, the child cut off R' Chanina. "Okay, I'm ready to go to Bubby's house now! I want to go!"

Blushing in embarrassment, the mother thought to herself, *That's it. My son is not going to be accepted.*

However, she had underestimated R' Chanina, who responded to the child without hesitation. "You know, you're right. Going to Bubby is much more important than an interview. The interview is over, and you're accepted to the yeshiva."

Interactions like these made people recognize the expert *mechanech* they had in their midst, enabling the yeshiva to flourish.

Toward the end of his life, R' Chanina conveyed his feelings about being menahel of the yeshiva. "Besides my own family, my wonderful family, I get no greater *simchah* than seeing these children as they go from level to level. My rebbi gave me a charge when I was 21 years old. He told me he wants me to go into *chinuch*. He just gave me the feeling and imbued into my being that there is no greater joy, there is no greater job in this world, than to take children and to help mold them into wonderful Jews, into wonderful human beings. I have no greater *simchah* in my life than being here in this yeshiva."

"I have no greater *simchah* in my life than being here in this yeshiva."

As R' Shlomo Freifeld stated at a Shabbos Kiddush (5748) for Mendy Herzberg's bar mitzvah, "Chanina is a Yid whose whole joy comes from being *mechanech Yiddishe kinder*, and his wife is a tremendous force behind him."

R' BINYAMIN KAMENETZKY WAS SELFLESSLY DEDICATED TO HIS ROLE AS rosh yeshiva, as was R' Chanina to his role as menahel, and they made the ideal team. R' Chanina may have been empowered with daily *chinuch* decisions, but he never let that power get to his head, ever aware of his place as menahel, not rosh yeshiva. People marveled at the mutual respect they had for each other. R' Mordechai Kamenetzky, son of R' Binyamin and current dean/ rosh yeshiva of Yeshiva Toras Chaim, beautifully described R' Chanina's unusual relationship with his father, R' Binyamin:

A Unique Relationship

"Throughout his entire career (for lack of a better word), my father was responsible for the yeshiva he founded, Yeshiva Toras Chaim of South Shore. Nevertheless, only a few years after appointing R' Chanina as menahel, he shifted the burden of the day-to-day *chinuch* operations to his discretion. This meant that R' Chanina yielded great power over both the institution and its *talmidim.*

"Still, on countless occasions, R' Chanina would make a difficult decision and then say to my father, 'This is my decision but it's your yeshiva, and I defer to you to have the final say.' This didn't come from fear of jeopardizing his position in the yeshiva; it came from the reverence for authority and *kvod haTorah* with which he'd been inculcated by his rebbi and mentor, the late R' Shlomo Freifeld."

R' Mordechai continued, "I once asked R' Chanina, 'You're a wonderful speaker and terrific *mechanech.* Why don't you go on the lecture circuit?'

"'My rebbi, R' Freifeld, once told me that as long as your father is the head of this institution, I must never position myself in any way that might appear to overshadow him or diminish his position,' he explained. 'He also cautioned me against speaking elsewhere if it'll take time away from my job at the yeshiva.' Indeed, it was rare to see someone who had no aspirations of 'taking over' toil with such devotion. The embodiment of a true *eved ne'eman.*"

R' Binyamin and R' Chanina, presenting a *talmid* with his first siddur

(l to r): R' Binyamin Kamenetzky, R' Shmuel Kamenetsky, R' Chanina, and R' Mordechai Kamenetzky

Furthermore, R' Chanina's children don't remember ever hearing a disapproving word from their father about R' Binyamin, even in instances where there was a difference of opinion. Nor did they ever sense an undercurrent of tension or negativity between R' Chanina and the rosh yeshiva.

His children were not the only ones to take note. One alumnus, Menachem Butler, expressed, "As a student in the yeshiva, I noticed the *kavod* R' Herzberg gave R' Binyamin Kamenetzky and the older rebbeim. He was *mevatel* himself to everyone. It was inspiring." During R' Chanina's *shivah,* one of the rabbanim in the community admired the fact that any time R' Chanina spoke at a *talmid*'s bar mitzvah, he always

R' Binyamin and R' Chanina with students in Yeshiva Toras Chaim

made sure to mention and compliment R' Binyamin. Additionally, although R' Mordechai Kamenetzky was over 10 years younger than R' Chanina, R' Chanina accorded him the same respect and self-effacement he had given his father. For example, while R' Chanina had spoken for years at every bar mitzvah of Toras Chaim *talmidim,* once R' Mordechai became rosh yeshiva, R' Chanina consistently asked him *reshus* before speaking. At one point, R' Mordechai told him there is no need to ask permission. "You speak at the bar mitzvahs as you always did. And as my father always did, I'll speak in the yeshiva when the bar mitzvah boy puts on *tefillin.*" Additionally, R' Chanina would call R' Binyamin, and later R' Mordechai, to give updates on the boys and the classes, to keep each one in the loop.

There was another important aspect to the relationship of R' Binyamin and R' Chanina. Both came from the same strain of *chinuch* ideology, as R' Binyamin's and also R' Chanina's *mesorah* in *chinuch* originated from the Alter of Slabodka: R' Binyamin through his father, R' Yaakov, a *talmid* of Slabodka; and R' Chanina through R' Freifeld and R' Hutner, who was also a Slabodka *talmid.*

The *chinuch* ideology of the Alter of Slabodka was based on the concept of *gadlus ha'adam,* the greatness of man — and every child. And so, from both the rosh yeshiva and the menahel, the yeshiva was saturated with this *chinuch* approach, an approach concentrated on accentuating the positive and building each child to help him realize the greatness that lies within.

Open-Door Policy

BOTH R' BINYAMIN AND R' CHANINA BELIEVED IN AN OPEN-DOOR policy. In this respect, they were both deeply impacted by R' Schmidman: R' Binyamin through his time as a rebbi there, and R' Chanina through his own experience as a child who was "rescued" by R' Schmidman in Yeshiva Toras Chaim.

Following the *petirah* of R' Binyamin, R' Mordechai explained this outlook. "R' Schmidman was an amazing man. He was *moser nefesh* to build *talmidim* in America, and his Yeshiva Toras Chaim in East New York was the sixth *cheder* in America. At one point, he charged a nickel for tuition, and it was he who had an extraordinary impact on my father to offer any child a Torah education, regardless of whether or not he was able to pay tuition. He was not selective and he took in anyone..."

As R' Binyamin's father, R' Yaakov, once told R' Chanina, "A yeshiva is a microcosm of Klal Yisrael." This was an ideal by which R' Binyamin and R' Chanina lived.

Many times, R' Chanina would interview a child who, for whatever reason, was not the type of *talmid* to whom the yeshiva was generally geared. R' Chanina would then turn to Mrs. Elana Fertig, the preschool director. "This is Hashem testing us. Maybe this is our ticket into Gan Eden." He had a very hard time rejecting *talmidim.* And if there was a boy he absolutely couldn't accept into the yeshiva, he helped him find a different place.

L'Sheim Shamayim

ONE FREEZING WINTER MORNING, AT 4:45 A.M., R' CHANINA WAS CONcerned that the boys would arrive in yeshiva and it would be too cold for them to learn. So he went to the yeshiva to turn on the heat. Upon pulling up at Yeshiva Toras Chaim, R' Chanina was shocked to see R' Binyamin's car parked outside the building. He wasn't sure if he should call the police or alert someone. What was R' Binyamin's vehicle doing there at that unearthly hour? R' Chanina tentatively entered the yeshiva building and saw the light on in R' Binyamin's office. He approached the office, where he found R' Binyamin seated at his desk, bundled up in his coat, with a coffee in front of him.

"R' Kamenetzky," he asked, "what are you doing here?"

R' Binyamin flashed R' Chanina his million-dollar smile. Then he explained, "You know, I always lower the heat overnight to save on fuel costs. But it's a freezing day and I was worried that when the boys come in the morning, it will be cold and they won't be able to learn. I came to turn up the heat, so that when they come, it will be warm."

R' Binyamin Kamenetzky, with his "million-dollar smile"

R' Chanina, like R' Binyamin, was focused on spreading warmth and making sure others were comfortable. Both operated for the sake of Heaven.

Perhaps this was the secret of their incredible relationship. All *l'sheim Shamayim,* with no ulterior motives.

All the while helping mold the yeshiva into what it would become.

Chapter 6

Leading the Yeshiva: First One In, Last One Out

IN AN ADDRESS TO MENAHALIM AT A TORAH UMESORAH GATHERING in the 1980's, R' Shlomo proclaimed, "We live in a time in which a menahel has to view himself as a *manhig* in Klal Yisrael."

Follow the Leader

As with everything else in his life, R' Chanina was taught by his rebbi, R' Shlomo, how to be a menahel. After accepting his position as principal in Yeshiva Toras Chaim, he had regular meetings with R' Shlomo on an almost daily basis, in which he dissected his entire day, the challenges and triumphs, and then received training in how a menahel should think, evaluate, and execute what needs to be done.

In short, how to be a leader.

As a leader, the menahel makes sure everything is running properly and smoothly. R' Avraham Fridman, who served as general studies principal of the elementary division of Yeshiva Toras Chaim during R' Chanina's tenure, discussed how a menahel can look at his position: either as the one who can tell people what to do; or as the one with the *achrayus*, who should be doing it all. However, since it's not humanly possible to do everything himself, he has no choice but to ask others for help.

Of course, R' Chanina took the latter view, seeing everything in the school as his personal responsibility. R' Moshe Scharhon stated unequivocally, "He was so willing to do what had to be done, no matter what."

R′ Chanina with R′ Moshe Scharhon and his fifth-grade *talmidim* upon receiving their first Gemara

Mr. Daniel Winkler, principal of general studies of the middle school division of Yeshiva Toras Chaim, conveyed, "R′ Herzberg led by example. He was always the first to enter the building and the last to leave." And he wasn't just the first one there; he was there — before anyone else — with his *tallis* and *tefillin* on. "No matter how hard I tried to get to yeshiva in the morning before him on any given day, he always managed to be there before me," another staff member conceded.

"He came in every single day," added Mr. Winkler, "even when under the weather. He taught us all the true meaning of commitment and work ethic. He cared so much about the boys and wanted to be

Yeshiva Toras Chaim administration (l-r): R′ Avraham Robinson, R′ Chanina, R′ Zev Davidowitz, R′ Avraham Fridman, Mr. Daniel Winkler, Mrs. Elana Fertig

there for them every single day, even toward the end when it became increasingly difficult for him."

Several times, R' Chanina's son Eli drove R' Chanina straight from chemotherapy treatment to yeshiva. He wouldn't have it any other way. He wanted to make sure the boys were having a good day. On top of that, the minute he got into the car, he was already calling his secretary to check in.

To R' Chanina, coming early, not just on time, was vital for a menahel or a rebbi. When R' Zev Davidowitz was hired as menahel of grades six through eight, R' Chanina stressed the importance of coming to school early, before the *talmidim*. He did not perceive this as merely a safety issue, but he also felt that it is crucial that when a *talmid* walks in, he is greeted by a menahel or rebbi.

Congregation Anshei Chesed had its shul in Yeshiva Toras Chaim. In an ad for the Yeshiva Toras Chaim journal, the rav, R' Simcha Lefkowitz, and the board members wrote: "So many of our past and present members were inspired by R' Chanina Herzberg, through his decades-long role as menahel... Many of us on our way back from morning *minyan* at 7:00 a.m. caught a glimpse of him at his desk immersed in learning and the *avodas hakodesh,* which was a hallmark of his legendary commitment..."

R' Chanina at his desk in Yeshiva Toras Chaim

As a seasoned leader, R' Chanina remained cool, calm, and collected under all circumstances. And always with a smile on his face. He understood that he set the tone in the yeshiva and he managed to block out his daily life challenges and focus on the yeshiva. It was clear that here was a man on a mission, and nothing was going to stop him. That tenacity and work ethic rubbed off on those around him, creating an environment where rebbeim, teachers, and staff members were constantly looking to grow and up their game, making the yeshiva into the exceptional institution it is.

He expected that type of leadership from other *hanhalah* members, as well. In an article written for R' Chanina's second *yahrtzeit,* Yeshiva Toras Chaim's preschool director, Mrs. Elana Fertig, shared lessons she and others in authority gleaned from him. These lessons were successfully applied through the COVID-19 shutdown, even when R' Chanina was no longer there to lead them:

While none of us could have imagined what we would deal with on a daily basis in the months of this pandemic, we know there are some specific messages that we learned from R' Herzberg that have helped us battle these waves.

1. Is everyone okay? As we go through the daily routines, we are all constantly checking: Are we okay? Is the staff okay? Are the children okay? Are the parents okay?

While many of these answers are not always yes, we are fully aware of checking in on everybody, and that was a lesson R' Herzberg taught us by example. He checked up on us all the time: seeing that we were okay, asking what we were dealing with, or worrying about and checking up on our own families, too.

2. What should you do when it seems like you just can't make everything better? SMILE!

In the midst of a crisis, when I was worried about a flood from one of the bathrooms, or when the heat broke and the children and *moros* were freezing, while I tried to deal with all the pieces, I obviously looked worried. *Just smile, so everyone will know it's going to be okay,* was a clear message R' Herzberg taught us.

3. Your job at the yeshiva is full-time, 24/7. Even when you might not be here physically, your mind is always caring about the people you take care of.

All of these points were practiced by R' Chanina and passed on to his devoted staff, to be referred to and put into practice when necessary.

R' Dovid Kramer, executive director at Yeshiva Toras Chaim, also merited to observe R' Chanina's leadership from up close. "He had confidence in his staff. He was a *savlan*, with a huge amount of patience. He wore his experience well and had a calming presence."

As well, R' Kramer gleaned so much from witnessing R' Chanina's careful *cheshbonos*. "When a situation came up, he didn't react right away, but he would first think about it. However, if an issue had to be taken care of or warranted a strong reaction, he managed that, too. He thought about every nuance of a conversation before he said it, and whenever he came up with an idea or had to make a decision, he would calculate, *This person will be supportive, this one won't*."

As R' Avrohom Fruchthandler articulated, "R' Chanina thought things through, with hard work and effort, until he reached the *emes*, and his heart and mind were one." This is why others looked to him for guidance.

R' Chanina expended a lot of energy contemplating every detail of each decision and how it would affect everyone involved, whether to make a big deal out of something, or whether to leave it alone. And he knew when to leave things alone. "A menahel has to be a *mevater*," R' Chanina would say. "Not every potential flaw must be addressed at that moment."

And his efforts showed. Before R' Zev Davidowitz undertook his new position as middle school menahel, he visited R' Chanina in his summer home in Woodridge to discuss the coming school year. He later shared one of his first glimpses of R' Chanina's abilities. "He was sitting in the living room in his brown chair, going through the class lists with me. Throughout that meeting, he received over 10 phone calls and each one he navigated with brilliance."

The Core Curriculum

AS A LEADER, R' CHANINA TOOK PRIDE IN DOING WHAT HE FELT WAS right. This was evident in regard to curriculum, where R' Chanina made sure to keep to the cherished *mesorah*, focusing on the core curriculum and ensuring that his rebbeim spent their time teaching the basics of *kriah*, Chumash, Mishnayos, and Gemara, first on an elementary level and then on a deeper one. And, of course, the crucial skills that went along with each *limud*. Although always ready to improve and innovate, R' Chanina would not lose focus by introducing new programs that required the *talmid* to invest significant time on extracurricular subjects and projects. His goal was to incorporate everything — for example, learning about *shemiras halashon* or *yediyos klaliyos* — into the context of the main *limudim.*

R' Mordechai Kamenetzky elaborated, "With regard to the way R' Chanina dealt with the core curriculum, what he got from his own rebbeim was the *ikar*. There are so many new innovations and new ideas, but if they interfered with the Gemara/ Rashi/ Tosafos, and the Chumash/ Rashi, and what he felt the rebbeim were supposed to teach, he had no time for them. Instead, he tried to incorporate the core curriculum concepts into the Gemara, Rashi, and Tosafos. It was a tremendous loyalty to *mesorah*, a tremendous allegiance to how his own rebbeim told him to teach and to learn."

R' Chanina used to share, in the name of R' Mordechai's grandfather, R' Yaakov: "*Ah mohl, vos mihr hut gekent lernen fuhn unzere bubbes, heint darf mehn lernen fuhn Chumash, Rashi, uhn Ramban* — What we were able to learn from our grandmothers years ago must now be learned from Chumash, Rashi, and Ramban." In the olden days, a child could imbibe *hashkafah* and *mesorah* just from observing and listening to his grandmother. As the generations weaken, however, this must be

R' Chanina (right) at a *has'chalas Chumash* event at Yeshiva Toras Chaim

learned in school, from the Torah itself, and from its main commentaries.

R' Mordechai had more to say about R' Chanina's adherence to tradition. "He wasn't into using smartboards. He felt that *talmidim* need to condition themselves to learn from a *sefer,* and smartboards take away from that."

A board member reminisced, "I had the unique privilege of interacting with R' Herzberg on a frequent basis, including many, many discussions about improving the quality of education and upgrading the yeshiva materially and educationally. I may have been one of his most vocal critics, but I was also one of his biggest fans.

"He firmly believed that he must carry on the *mesorah* of his rebbeim, and that there was no need to change anything about the way Torah had been taught in the yeshiva for the last few decades. Times may change, but the Torah and the methodology of teaching Torah remains constant.

"We had many intense discussions, and we often did not agree about how to raise the bar of education. But R' Chanina was very fond of telling me that he appreciated our discussions, because neither of us had personal agendas. We were both passionate about our positions, and although they were not aligned, they were both *l'sheim Shamayim.*"

While R' Chanina was on top of homework and tests, he stated unambiguously, "That isn't what *chinuch* is all about. *Chinuch* is about connecting the children to the *Ribbono shel Olam.*" He kept this goal in mind at all times.

To R' Chanina, there was nothing like sitting and learning from a rebbi. "Routine, routine, routine, that's what the children need." Anything that interrupted the normal routine was frowned upon. It was for this reason that he held as few assemblies as possible, especially first-day assemblies. He maintained: You come into yeshiva, and you learn. Period. He felt that in most cases, the *talmidim* gain more from being in the classroom with their rebbi. To him, assemblies constituted *bitul Torah*, more about PR and the picture than the actual event. That meant no Rosh Chodesh assemblies either. If rabbanim or roshei yeshiva came to visit, they would visit individual classes. Only on special occasions would they speak at an assembly.

The Skverer Rebbe on a visit to Yeshiva Toras Chaim (l-r): Eli Herzberg, Skverer Rebbe, R' Chanina

Whenever there was an assembly, R' Chanina involved himself in the logistics, when and how it would take place. He was careful to think through every detail, ensuring it wouldn't interfere with the *seder hayom*, and that it was short and simple. Each detail was calculated to maximize Torah learning and give the children the best *chinuch* possible.

On May 26, 2013 (17 Sivan, 5773), one-half year after Hurricane Sandy, a *levayah* was held in the White Shul in Far Rockaway for 12 *Sifrei Torah* that were irreparably damaged by the storm. Since a large community gathering was planned, pressure was put on R' Chanina to bring the *talmidim* of Yeshiva Toras Chaim. However, in discussion with R' Mordechai Kamenetzky, R' Chanina opined, "Why should we bring the *talmidim* of the yeshiva? Chazal

R' Chanina speaking at an assembly in honor of R' Yitzchak Scheiner's visit to Yeshiva Toras Chaim; sitting next to R' Scheiner is R' Binyamin Kamenetzky.

(l-r): R' Mordechai Kamenetzky, R' Shmuel Kamenetsky, R' Chanina

instruct us (*Shabbos* 119b), '*Ein mevatlin tinokos shel beis rabban afilu l'vinyan Beis HaMikdash* — We may not interrupt children's learning even in order to build the *Beis HaMikdash*.'"

R' Aaron Schechter explained the reason behind this injunction from Chazal: "*Veil dos is binyan haMikdash. Dorten boint sech di kodesh fuhn Bnei Yisrael* — Because teaching children is considered building a *Mikdash*. There, in a yeshiva, we build the *kodesh* of Bnei Yisrael. Each child is his own edifice of *kedushah*, his own structure, and when we teach him Torah, we are building his *Mikdash*."

R' Chanina and R' Mordechai agreed to ask R' Shmuel Kamenetsky, rosh yeshiva of Talmudical Yeshiva of Philadelphia, for his opinion. R' Shmuel said not to attend, so the yeshiva stayed put and the *talmidim* continued learning according to their regular schedule.

General Studies

AFTER R' CHANINA WAS HIRED AS MENAHEL OF YESHIVA TORAS Chaim, he traveled to Monsey to meet with R' Yaakov Kamenetsky, the father of the rosh yeshiva, R' Binyamin. They discussed various *chinuch* topics, and R' Chanina derived a lot of *chizuk* from the meeting. When R' Chanina was ready to leave, R' Yaakov added one important point. "Make sure you hire the best English teachers. Every part of the day in yeshiva has to follow the same standard of excellence. You never want a *talmid* to think that you, or he, can settle for mediocrity. If you're doing something, you do it all the way. Moreover, if students don't take general studies seriously and waste their time, then the time in which they are not learning constitutes *bitul Torah. Vos mehn lerent darf mehn lernen gut*. Whatever you learn must be learned well."

R' Chanina left with a mandate from one of the *gedolei hador*, a mandate he took seriously. "We need to be great, not just okay. Mediocrity won't fly," R' Chanina would say, reiterating R' Yaakov's words.

To facilitate this, R' Chanina made sure to hire highly competent general studies principals, who also strove for excellence. R' Shmuel Schwebel, former general studies principal at Yeshiva Toras Chaim, recounted two other points that R' Chanina offered in favor of a strong general studies department. "The yeshiva's goal is to produce *talmidim* who will graduate with the tools needed to become whatever they need to become, a kollel *yungerman* or a professional, and striving for excellence affords the *talmidim* that opportunity. In addition, if the general studies program is solid, it makes the *limudei kodesh* program more solid. If the general studies program is a joke, it creates an attitude of *hisrashlus* (negligence, laxity), which extends through the entire day."

To R' Chanina, there was no such thing as a menahel leaving after *limudei kodesh*, not remaining for general studies. He was of the opinion that for a general studies department to maintain proper decorum, the *talmidim* must understand that the comportment expected of them in *limudei kodesh* is expected of them in general studies, as well. When the menahel remains through the afternoon, he is injecting this message into the *talmidim* by his very presence. Though the menahel isn't involved in a detailed way in the running of the general studies department, he is there, overseeing and ensuring that throughout the day, his staff and students are aspiring for the same level of distinction.

R' Chanina used to walk the halls during general studies. From time to time, he'd also visit classes, conveying the importance of general studies and of taking the classes seriously. R' Chanina wasn't just the first to arrive in the yeshiva, he was also the last to leave. Though he gave the general studies principal his space so he could run the department with confidence, there was constant communication. R' Chanina was kept abreast of the happenings during the afternoon, and he was always available for support. "He was a force behind us, and with us," R' Schwebel described. "And yet he wasn't looking to micromanage."

R′ Chanina visiting a class during general studies

Furthermore, the general studies teachers must be not only capable, talented pedagogues, who know how to make the lessons engaging and interesting and how to connect to the students, but also proper role models, befitting the *ruach* of the yeshiva. When it came to hiring teachers, the general studies principals in Yeshiva Toras Chaim were trusted to do the research and take care of the interview process. However, no teacher was hired without R′ Chanina's approval. "He took pride in having a great general studies department," R′ Schwebel shared, "and his eyes would shine when he had great teachers."

One general studies teacher was having trouble controlling his class. Since a Maariv *minyan* took place every evening in that classroom following sessions, R′ Chanina decided to join the *minyan.* However, he came 15 minutes early and sat outside the classroom. The boys saw him sitting outside — and their behavior improved.

R′ Chanina was very proud of the *menschlichkeit* of the *talmidim* at Yeshiva Toras Chaim and the way they treated their general studies teachers, thereby bringing honor to the Name of Hashem.

Mr. Arthur Shield, an English teacher at Yeshiva Toras Chaim, became very close to the *talmidim.* Realizing that he didn't own a pair of *tefillin,* the *talmidim* decided to collect money for *tefillin* for Mr. Shield. They painstakingly raised funds, arranged the purchase with a reputable *sofer,* informed Mr. Shield of their plan, and counted the days until they could present him with the precious gift of *tefillin,* as well as a *tallis* and *tefillin* bag. When the day finally arrived, all the *talmidim* of the upper division

R' Chanina presenting *tallis* and *tefillin* to Mr. Shield

of the yeshiva gathered in the *beis midrash.* R' Mordechai Kamenetzky stood in front of the *beis midrash,* with Mr. Shield next to him sporting a huge grin.

With the *tallis* and *tefillin* in hand, R' Chanina spoke on behalf of the *talmidim.* "Mr. Shield, we know you have been working diligently on the mitzvah of *tallis* and *tefillin.* And you are an inspiration to every one of us here in the yeshiva." Following a round of applause, R' Chanina continued, "The boys here couldn't think of anything more meaningful to express their appreciation than to present you, Avraham Shield, with this *tallis* bag, which contains a *tallis* and a pair of *tefillin.* It is our wish that you wear both in good health, till 120 years!" R' Mordechai then handed the gift to Mr. Shield, to a standing ovation by the packed *beis midrash.*

When the applause died down, Mr. Shield spoke to the students. "For me, coming here every day is not work. I enjoy every single one of you boys, every single one of you! I thank you from the bottom of my heart!"

With overflowing love and emotion, Mr. Shield embraced each of his *talmidim*, followed by dancing with R' Chanina, R' Mordechai, and the *talmidim.*

Another vignette about Mr. Shield and his dear students: When the advertising began for the great MetLife *siyum haShas* of 2012 (5772), R' Mordechai Kamenetzky received a call from his son Zvi, a Yeshiva Toras Chaim alumnus. He asked if Mr. Shield was still teaching in the school.

Mr. Shield embracing a *talmid*

"Of course, he is! He is the best! We would never let him leave," R' Kamenetzky replied.

Zvi asked his father if he could arrange that he receive a ticket together with Mr. Shield to the *siyum.*

"Mr. Shield? *Siyum haShas*? Why?"

Zvi explained, "I was in Mr. Shield's class almost eight years ago. One day, we all packed out of class to go to the *siyum haShas.* On my way out, I saw that he was upset. 'Where is everyone headed?' he asked. When we told him about the large *siyum,* Mr. Shield exclaimed, 'An event where so many Jewish people are gathered and no one invited me? Here is the deal. I will let you leave my class to go to this *siyum* on one condition. Next time you take me.'"

True to their word, R' Kamenetzky and his son Zvi took Mr. Shield and sat with him through the entire *siyum,* explaining every aspect of the powerful event.

To R' Chanina, incidents such as these epitomized the effect of a positive relationship between a general studies teacher and his students.

"Our Rock"

R' CHANINA TREATED HIS STAFF VERY WELL. AFTER ALL, A LEADER IS only as good as the team supporting him, and R' Chanina knew this. He was always there for his team, not only in the practical sense but also in the emotional sense, boosting his rebbeim's confidence. Whenever presented with the opportunity, R' Chanina would build up a rebbi in front of the *talmidim* or parents. "You're so lucky to have such a wonderful rebbi," he'd say to a class, which, of course, gave the rebbi the push to be even better.

Year after year, a certain rebbi was given exceptionally challenging *talmidim.* Whenever he complained to R' Chanina about his class and the difficulties he encountered teaching his students, R' Chanina used the opportunity to give him *chizuk* and encouragement. "*Di greste kronkeit darf di beste doctors* — The worst illness requires the best doctors."

Mrs. Elana Fertig expressed, "He was our rock, the person always checking on us to see how we were doing. If we needed him, he was there. He was constantly calling staff members on the phone and also asking them in person how everything was going.

"In my early years as preschool director at Yeshiva Toras Chaim, R' Herzberg would call me daily. My own mother doesn't call me daily, and at first I didn't understand. Until I learned that R' Herzberg called all his family members every single day.

"Then one day, I noticed that everyone was calling him back. It was then that I realized what he was doing; he was establishing

R' Chanina in discussion with staff members

relationships... He taught us that you have to care about people as people, and then they'll come to you to share things. How can I tell you what's new if you don't know what's old?

"Over time," Mrs. Fertig concluded, "I learned from his example... Keeping lines of communication open builds relationships."

After R' Chanina's *petirah*, the staff members longed for the connection he had created, which was no longer. "If someone is upset at something I did, whom will I tell?" lamented one grieving staff member. "If I did something good, whom will I tell? I miss R' Herzberg."

In the early years: R' Chanina (top left) with rebbeim of Yeshiva Toras Chaim; seated second from the left is R' Binyamin Kamenetzky.

R′ Chanina at a Yeshiva Toras Chaim dinner, arm-in-arm with rebbeim

R′ Chanina encouraged his rebbeim and staff to take good care of themselves, to sleep well and find a healthy way to relax after a long day. "If you've had a stressful day," he'd recommend, "do something before you get home to help you get in a better mood. Buy yourself an iced coffee or Danish."

He also urged them to make good use of their summer break, quoting the aphorism, "What are a teacher's two favorite words? July and August!"

Above all, he told them not to take themselves too seriously!

R′ Chanina was there for his staff in and out of school. A young rebbi in Yeshiva Toras Chaim, who was in need of a ride to school for half a year, relayed, "R′ Herzberg — who would always refer to me as his *yedid* — would go out of his way to pick me up at 7:00 every morning to take me to school. He never made it feel like it was a burden."

A rebbi had a hard time paying his heating bill. The yeshiva gave him a $250 check toward his expenses, and R′ Chanina added a personal check for $100. On a different occasion, R′ Chanina found out that a staff member was in desperate need of funds, and he personally raised thousands of dollars for him. That staff member never discovered the source of the funds. What's more, R′ Chanina personally raised money so his rebbeim could make *simchos* with dignity, simply dubbing the additional funds a bonus.

Mrs. Berman,* the wife of a rebbi in Yeshiva Toras Chaim, took a summer job at a ShopRite in the Catskills. R' Chanina was shopping in that supermarket one summer day and saw Mrs. Berman working the register. It bothered him that one of his rebbeim was so strapped for cash that his wife had to take a job as a cashier, that she had to stand on her feet all day and spend time with the non-Jewish staff members.

On the spot, he took out his phone and called some *baalei batim*, arranging for them to pay Mrs. Berman through the summer. Then he went up to her and said, "Mrs. Berman, go back to the bungalow colony. You are not working here this summer. Take care of your children, relax, and enjoy. Your husband needs you."

Counsel for the Defense

R' CHANINA STOOD BEHIND HIS REBBEIM AND STAFF MEMBERS, AND backed them under almost every circumstance. Just a few weeks into his new position as menahel in Yeshiva Toras Chaim, R' Chanina was faced with his first dilemma. The *baalei batim* wanted to get rid of a certain rebbi; they felt he just couldn't do the job. Of course, R' Chanina discussed the issue with R' Shlomo before making a move, and R' Shlomo advised against letting the rebbi go.

Head held high, R' Chanina told the *baalei batim*, "If the rebbi goes, I go with him."

The rebbi remained, and R' Chanina worked with him, and he soon became a beloved *mechanech.*

A young rebbi, still wet behind the ears, had to discipline a *talmid*. That night, the rebbi received a phone call from the boy's father. After voicing his disapproval at the rebbi's action, the irate father threatened to speak to the board of directors and ensure that the rebbi would lose his job. The next day, after verifying that the father was an active board member and a big supporter of the yeshiva, the rebbi grew apprehensive about his job and his future. Trembling, he approached R' Chanina and repeated the conversation.

R' Chanina looked at him directly and told him bluntly, "There is one person here who decides whether to hire or to fire a rebbi. That person is me! Don't worry. Your job is secure!" The rebbi later revealed that after R' Chanina made it clear that his position was assured, he felt comfortable and stopped worrying that he could be fired at any minute.

R' Chanina in his son Eli's class at Yeshiva Toras Chaim, at the *upsheren* of the son of a Toras Chaim rebbi, R' Binyamin Jacobi (standing)

He also learned not to be so concerned about what the parents thought of him, enabling him to focus on his teaching.

Another time, an excellent rebbi made a mistake and said something to a *talmid* that he shouldn't have. When the boy's parents heard about the comment, they did everything in their power to have the rebbi dismissed. The rebbi walked into R' Chanina's office with a box full of thank you notes from over the years and broke down crying. "I made a mistake; I'm sorry." R' Chanina, feeling his pain, broke down and cried with him — and then saved his job.

R' Daniel Nekritz, mashgiach of Yeshiva Derech Ayson of Far Rockaway, related that his great-grandfather, R' Yosef Yoizel Horowitz, the Alter of Novardok, used to say, "To run a yeshiva, you have to be able to swallow nails." Looking at R' Chanina's children during the *shivah,* R' Nekritz declared, "That was your father."

This, too, was taught to him by his rebbi. A *talmid* in Yeshiva Sh'or Yoshuv was getting married, and his parents very much wanted his rebbeim to walk down the aisle. R' Shlomo was ready to walk down, when he suddenly pulled R' Chanina in to join him. "R' Chanina, it's time for you to learn how to be *sovel bizyonos,* to endure being humiliated."

Though he swallowed his share of nails over the years, R' Chanina never tolerated any insults or signs of disrespect toward his rebbeim or staff members. A young employee grew overwrought, shouting at and berating an elderly employee, Mr. Engel,* who worked in the yeshiva for many years. A witness to the scene, R' Chanina walked right over to the young employee. "Perhaps this is not the best place for you to work.

No one talks to Mr. Engel that way; it's time for you to find a new job."

Mr. Engel tried to intervene. "R' Herzberg, if he talked to *you* that way, you wouldn't be telling him to find a new job!"

"You're right," R' Chanina agreed. "But he wasn't talking to *me*, he was talking to *you*! I won't tolerate such blatant chutzpah from any staff member toward you!"

A rebbi once wronged R' Chanina, leaving him troubled for months. Though he was pressured to ask the rebbi to leave, R' Chanina would not relent. "He is an excellent rebbi. How can I justify asking him to leave? What will be with his *mishpachah*?"

Moreover, R' Chanina made sure that the rebbi never found out what took place behind the scenes, how he had stuck out his neck for him. He felt the knowledge would only hurt the rebbi's confidence and thereby affect his ability to be *mechanech* his *talmidim* properly.

For R' Chanina, it was never about himself. R' Chanina lived his life in others' shoes; he stuck up for the rebbi who fought against him, while defending a teacher who was slighted, constantly thinking outside of himself.

During a Toras Chaim meeting that included a rebbi, a parent, and another *hanhalah* member, the parent grew upset and began to scream and gesticulate at R' Chanina. "What kind of yeshiva do you run? You don't know what you're doing!" Throughout the diatribe, R' Chanina sat quietly, not saying a word, even listening intently. When the parent

R' Chanina dancing with rebbeim and parents at a *has'chalas Chumash* event

was finally finished with R' Chanina, he turned on the other administrator in the room and began to blow off steam.

"Whoa!" interjected R' Chanina. "What are you doing? You think I'm going to allow you to sit here and scream at him like that? It's one thing if you want to attack me, but no one goes after my people!"

R' Avraham Fridman shared another example. "There were times when I was with R' Chanina at board meetings and one of the *baalei batim* would bring up an issue with a rebbi, and it would become a discussion. R' Chanina would respond very strongly, knocking down the complaint. 'Don't say anything bad about one of the rebbeim!' Subsequently, R' Chanina would privately address the issue with the rebbi. He didn't ignore issues; he just didn't want there to be a discussion about them." R' Chanina was clear about the division of labor within the yeshiva. He dealt with *chinuch* while the *baalei batim* dealt with finances.

"One time, I criticized a rebbi in front of the board," a *hanhalah* member revealed. "Following the meeting, R' Chanina called me into his office and gave it to me over the head, warning me to never do that again."

R' Chanina told his son that one of the most important jobs of a menahel is to make sure the rebbeim know he has their back. If this is the case, he explained, "they will be calmer, happier, and more confident. This will filter down to the *talmidim* and parents, and the *chinuch* will be on a totally different level."

Then he clarified. "It doesn't mean that a menahel can't critique a rebbi when needed. In fact, a rebbi should never have to wonder, *What does my menahel think of me?* The rebbeim need to know that if the menahel has something to tell them, he will." If parents called with a valid complaint, R' Chanina would use his wisdom to take care of the issue while still defending the staff member.

Even as R' Chanina treated his rebbeim with utmost respect and looked out for them, he knew when he had to tell it like it is. A staff member at Yeshiva Toras Chaim acted in a manner that was not *l'fi kevodo*. R' Chanina heard about the incident when he was on his way to a *chasunah*, but he didn't wait until the next morning to speak to the rebbi. Right then and there, he made a detour and drove straight to the rebbi's house and told him what needed to be said. The rebbi knew where he stood and what needed improvement, and was able to move on.

R' Chanina developed a rapport with each rebbi, and if he had to administer constructive criticism, he did, but then the next minute the two would be chatting like best friends. The rebbeim understood that he was there to help them be the best they could be, with nothing personal about the criticism.

One rebbi, whose home was a 45-minute drive from Yeshiva Toras Chaim, recalled, "At times, it was inevitable that I would come a few minutes late to school. Any time this happened, I would find R' Herzberg at the door to my class, keeping an eye on them. I would walk in, he would say good morning, and then walk away. He never verbalized that I was late, but his standing there when I arrived was all that was needed."

A boy was sent to R' Chanina for misbehaving in class, and R' Chanina felt that the boy needed to be dealt with firmly, especially for the sake of his rebbi. As he walked with the boy from his office into the hallway outside the boy's classroom, R' Chanina took a look to see if anyone was around. Seeing that the hallway was empty, he raised his voice. "How could you do such a thing? You have a great rebbi; he cares so much about you!"

R' Chanina's son, who happened to be with his father at the time, asked, "Why did you discipline him in the hallway? Why not in your office?"

R' Chanina explained, "This rebbi is having a difficult time with his class and he needs my support. I wanted him to hear me raising my voice at his *talmid,* because I need him to understand that I have his back and I'm there to help him. This will help him gain confidence, enabling him to take control of the class."

A rebbi in Yeshiva Toras Chaim became exasperated with a *talmid* for repeated misbehavior. As he sent the boy out of class, the rebbi stood in the hallway right outside R' Chanina's office and began disciplining the *talmid* vociferously. The rebbi was so agitated that he did not even realize where he was standing and how loudly he was yelling. (At the boy's bar mitzvah, the rebbi asked the boy *mechilah.*)

Hearing the commotion, R' Chanina stepped outside his office and, after the boy walked away, addressed the rebbi in a caring and gentle tone. "Rebbi, you are going to ruin your reputation." The rebbi related that at that moment, he genuinely felt R' Chanina's care and concern for him, how R' Chanina felt the shame the rebbi would experience after

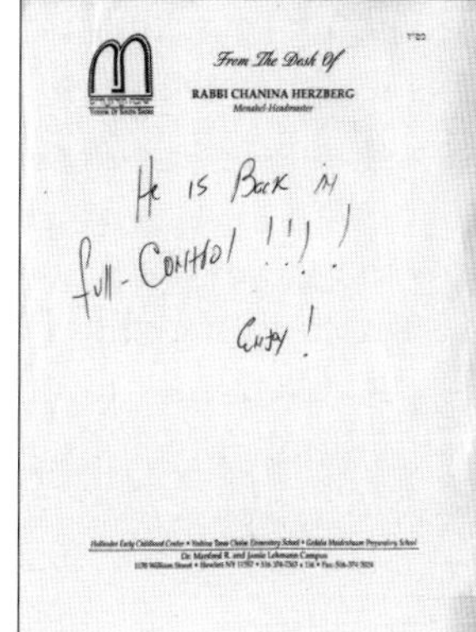

From The Desk Of
RABBI CHANINA HERZBERG
Menahel-Headmaster

He is Back in full-Control !!!! Enjoy!

From The Desk Of
RABBI CHANINA HERZBERG
Menahel-Headmaster

למען לא ניגע לריק

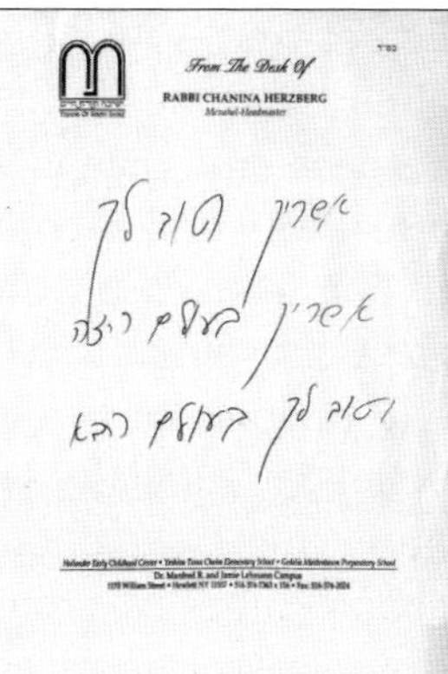

From The Desk Of
RABBI CHANINA HERZBERG
Menahel-Headmaster

אשריך וטוב לך
אשריך בעולם הזה
וטוב לך בעולם הבא

R' Chanina's encouraging notes to rebbeim

losing himself in public. All those sentiments came across loud and clear, proving more effective than any strong words of rebuke. To the rebbi, it was a "wow" moment.

Occasionally, when disobedient children were sent to the principal's office, R' Chanina, sensing that the rebbi could use some *chizuk*, would write him a short note with words of encouragement, depending on the situation. At times, it was the words of *Pirkei Avos* (6:4), "*Ashrecha v'tov lach, ashrecha ba'olam hazeh v'tov lach la'Olam Haba* — You are praiseworthy and all is well with you. You are praiseworthy in this world and all is well with you in the World to Come," with a smiley face accompanying the note. Or the words of *U'Va L'Tzion*, "*L'maan lo niga la'rik* — So that we do not struggle in vain." This was his way of telling a rebbi, *Don't take things too seriously; I'm on it and I have your back.* Other times, he would write, "He is back in full control!!!! Enjoy!"

Be Yourself

JUST AS R' CHANINA WAS PATIENT WITH THE *TALMIDIM,* HE WAS patient with the rebbeim. "He understood that a rebbi is normal and has his challenges," one rebbi stated. "He saw in me many things which I didn't believe I had in myself. And he had a vision and would invest in it."

Yet he was not looking for clones. Rather, R' Chanina cultivated an environment in which individuality was encouraged. R' Mordechai Kamenetzky communicated, "I feel that one of his many attributes was that he let the rebbeim 'do their own thing.' Of course, R' Chanina was on top of the standard curriculum of what each class had to cover that year with innate expectations. But in terms of how to teach, there was no set way. R' Chanina believed that each rebbi has his own unique ability and the way he teaches has to align with his *techunos hanefesh,* because only then is the rebbi truly able to connect with his *talmidim* in a real way and become the best rebbi he could be."

For this reason there were no rules about how long davening in each class should take. Each class's davening session could be different, because each rebbi was different. Additionally, R' Chanina didn't believe in officially observing the rebbi in a class situation. He felt that observing his rebbeim would take a psychological toll, plus create a cookie-cutter environment where rebbeim teach in a way that will make the menahel happy, not based on who they are. In addition, he once told his son, "A menahel should know exactly how the rebbi is doing without having to observe his teaching."

When R' Chanina's son Yitzchok landed his first rebbi position, he called his father to discuss in detail how a classroom should run, expecting clear and effective teaching and discipline methods based on his father's 35 years of experience in *chinuch.*

He was in for a surprise.

"You'll figure it out," his father said. That was the sum total of the *chinuch* advice Yitzchok received from his father.

"It took me six months to figure out what I was doing in the classroom, but at the end of the day, I did figure it out. With those four words, 'You'll figure it out,' my father was teaching me a crucial lesson in being a rebbi. A successful rebbi has to be himself, and he felt that if he gave me advice, knowing how much experience he had as a *mechanech,* I would feel compelled to do what he told me and not be myself. So he felt it better to say nothing."

This sentiment was echoed by R' Avraham Robinson, who received the same guidance when he started out as a rebbi in Yeshiva Toras Chaim: "Figure it out." R' Robinson elucidated, "That was a *chinuch* concept. If you go in with preconceived programs, it's not true *chinuch.* That being said, he was always there for support, and you knew he was there to help if needed."

Before the start of the school year, R' Gedaliah Weiss* attended a workshop on classroom management. Basing his methods on the course, he distanced himself from the *talmidim,* though the discipline in his class was impeccable.

One day, R' Chanina called him aside and asked him, "What are you doing?"

"What do you mean, what am I doing?" R' Gedaliah defended himself. "I'm running my classroom and *baruch Hashem* it's going great."

"I've been watching you through the window," R' Chanina countered, "and I see how you're conducting your classroom. Do me a favor and put the course aside. That's not how you, Gedaliah Weiss, connect and get through to *talmidim*. You have to be yourself."

Following that encounter, R' Gedaliah revealed, everything changed. He started being himself and truly connecting to his *talmidim*. He also began paying close attention to how R' Chanina interacted with *talmidim*. "R' Herzberg was smiley and bubbly, and the *talmidim* flocked to him. He was always running some sort of contest — Mishnayos *b'al peh*, Gemara *b'al peh* — all for a chocolate cookie. This had a big effect on me."

If his staff members planned on attending training courses, R' Chanina cautioned them not to simply take what they were being taught and make that their teaching procedure or discipline methodology. Rather, he advised, "Listen, digest, and then think: *Does that particular approach fit my personality? Is that me?* If you do that, then the course can be beneficial. Otherwise, you may become someone whom you're not, and you won't actualize your true potential in being *mechanech Yiddishe kinder.*"

Though R' Chanina let his rebbeim follow their own path, he insisted on three things. One was being on time for davening. Davening for the older grades started at 7:55 a.m., and R' Chanina preferred when his rebbeim were there by 7:45. "A child shouldn't see a rebbi coming late to davening," he would say. "When a rebbi is on time, it automatically gives the impression that he's in charge, he's running the show."

The second was *shemirah,* watching the children. If something happened, such as a fight or an injury, and the rebbi wasn't there, R' Chanina's first question was, "Where was the rebbi?"

Finally, just as he worked carefully with his team, he wanted his staff members to work together, with each one contributing as a team player.

R' CHANINA WAS SPEAKING TO A NEW REBBI IN THE YESHIVA, GIVING him *chizuk* as he entered the world of *chinuch*. "Don't worry, you're going to make mistakes. I did, and I do. We all do." He smiled as he inserted the wisdom of R' Shlomo. "Every rebbi makes mistakes. However, a great rebbi is one who never makes the same mistake twice."

Making New Mistakes

A rebbi in Yeshiva Toras Chaim traveled down memory lane, as he imparted what took place when he first began teaching seventh grade in Yeshiva Toras Chaim. "The first day was terrifying. I myself wasn't that old, and I was teaching boys who were 12 and 13. The fact that I looked really young wasn't helpful, and my stomach was on a roller coaster ride. I sat in my chair in my classroom and looked at the clock. It wasn't even 7:00 a.m. yet, and I was like a little boy waiting for school to start.

"I walked downstairs and strolled through the hallway. After a few minutes, I realized that the light was on inside R' Herzberg's office. I approached the office and saw the door was wide open. He looked up and motioned me inside. It was my second time in the office, and I remember being scared. I hadn't done anything wrong but being in the menahel's office was never a good thing for me.

"R' Herzberg said, 'You're going to make a mistake today.'

"I froze. What mistake could I be making? I hadn't started teaching yet!

"'A *good* rebbi makes mistakes every day,' he continued. 'A *great* rebbi makes new mistakes every day.' My mind was going a mile a minute.

"R' Herzberg asked pointedly, 'Are you a *good* rebbi or a *great* rebbi?'

"I left his office and walked back upstairs. He was 100 percent correct — I did make a mistake that day. However, after that, I only made new mistakes."

Following R' Chanina's *petirah*, a menahel of a mesivta in the Five Towns communicated, "In the early years that I was menahel, I was very young and inexperienced and, frankly, did not really know what I was doing. During an interview with a Yeshiva Toras Chaim family, I said something that could have been interpreted as a negative comment about Yeshiva Toras Chaim. What did I know? To my surprise, the comment made its way back to R' Herzberg. He called me up and called me out about the comment.

"Still, not wanting me to feel so awful about my mistake, R' Herzberg, who at the time barely knew me, said, 'I hope we work together for many more years. Don't feel so bad about your mistake. A bad principal makes 200 mistakes a day. A good principal makes 200 new mistakes each day.'"

R' CHANINA HAD HIS SHARE OF OPPONENTS AND CHALLENGERS. YET he learned how to pick himself up, dust himself off, and keep going. This, too, served as an example to his staff members.

Getting Right Back Up

When R' Chanina first started as a rebbi in Yeshiva Tiferes Moshe, a boy in his class lost control and began jumping on his desk, until he fell off and broke his arm. That night, R' Chanina received a phone call from the boy's father, who happened to be the president of the school, asking to meet with him the next morning.

Since the accident had taken place on R' Chanina's watch, and to the son of the school's president no less, R' Chanina felt responsible and was sure the president felt the same. Why else would he have set up a

Class picture of R' Chanina and his *talmidim* in Yeshiva Tiferes Moshe

meeting? Certain his job in the school was history, R' Chanina called his uncle who owned a suit store and asked if he could work for him; he had to support his family and it didn't look like his career in *chinuch* had any staying power.

He needn't have worried.

The next day, as R' Chanina sat nervously in front of the president, the president smiled. "Don't worry about it. That's what happens when a boy gets wild, and now he's learned his lesson."

What a relief! R' Chanina saw this as a sign *min haShamayim* that he should remain in *chinuch.*

However, not every influential parent approved of R' Chanina's out-of-the-box, laid-back *chinuch* approach. And though his style made him extremely popular among the students, it made some people nervous. But he stayed true to the *mesorah* of his rebbi, not deviating one bit. And with R' Shlomo's constant encouragement, he forged on.

During his first year or two as menahel of Yeshiva Toras Chaim, R' Chanina was, for the most part, not proactive, at least not overtly. Rather, he sat back and observed while letting the yeshiva run, tackling problems as they cropped up. This was a calculated approach. He wanted to first take stock of how the yeshiva was running and what needed correcting, and only start making changes afterward. He once told a *talmid* starting in a new *menahel* position, "Don't come in like a bull in a china shop. Take it slow; observe, digest, and take the time to think. Then slowly implement changes."

About a year or two into R' Chanina's tenure at Yeshiva Toras Chaim, there were rumblings among parents with clout; they were unsure if R' Chanina was the right person for the job. One influential parent voiced his doubts to a rebbi in Yeshiva Toras Chaim. "Is R' Herzberg doing a satisfactory job leading the school? Because if not, I'll get him out."

The rebbi allayed the parent's misgivings. "R' Herzberg is on top of everything — even though you don't realize it. He has a style all his own. He's very much out to make sure the children are *matzliach* and connect to the *Ribbono shel Olam.* Give it some time and you'll see."

Eventually, this parent became a staunch devotee of R' Chanina.

But he wasn't the only detractor. Early on in his career as menahel, R' Chanina received a letter from a parent attacking him and accusing him of ruining his child. To make matters worse, the letter wasn't even signed. Though R' Chanina strongly suspected a certain parent of

R′ Binyamin and R′ Chanina with *talmidim*;
a sketch of R′ Yaakov can be seen on the wall behind them.

penning the letter, without a signature there was no way for R′ Chanina to defend himself. Perturbed, he went to R′ Yaakov Kamenetsky to discuss the letter and what to do about it. "Rip it up and throw it in the garbage, and never think about it again," R′ Yaakov advised. "An unsigned letter is worthless!"

True, R′ Chanina made it his business to ignore the letter, but he didn't completely forget the incident; he needed to access the experience in order to advise his staff. Over the years, various staff members in the yeshiva received unsigned complaints and asked R′ Chanina how to proceed. He followed in R′ Yaakov's footsteps and said simply, "We are going to do nothing because it's not signed."

On another occasion, a woman shot off a spiteful email, which included her name, to the yeshiva. Another *hanhalah* member wanted to write a strong response. "I know she's going through a hard time at home," R′ Chanina told him. "Just let it be."

A *talmid* of R′ Chanina, who today serves as a menahel of a yeshiva, commented, "The way R′ Chanina dealt with these situations helped frame my mindset. He taught me that dealing with struggles and challenges is a fact of life. As the saying goes, 'Life is not about how many times you fall down. It's about how many times you get back up.' R′ Herzberg taught me to get back up."

R′ Hutner comments (*Igros*, p. 217) on the *pasuk* (*Mishlei* 24:16), "*Sheva yipol tzaddik vakam* — The righteous one may fall seven times, but he will rise." The fools think that this means: Even though a *tzaddik* falls seven times, he will rise. However, the wise know well that the meaning is: Because a *tzaddik* falls seven times, he will rise!

If a disgruntled individual went on a rant and began spreading a false rumor or a complaint about a staff member, R' Chanina would console the individual being maligned. "Don't worry about it. Just be patient. There's a two-week rule. After two weeks, people will stop talking and will pretty much forget about it." And he was right.

Several years following R' Chanina's *petirah, hanhalah* members and rebbeim at Yeshiva Toras Chaim still ask themselves on a regular basis, especially when faced with challenges and tricky situations, "What would R' Herzberg say? What would R' Herzberg do?"

Because R' Chanina Herzberg was the quintessential leader.

Chapter 7
The Adam HaShalem: The Making of a Mensch

R' CHANINA BUILT UP YESHIVA TORAS CHAIM WITH THE FOCUS ON creating a complete person — one who encompasses the three pillars upon which the world stands: Torah, *avodah*, and *gemilus chasadim* (*Pirkei Avos* 1:2) — what is known as a mensch, an *adam hashalem*.

"This Is a Yid!"

A young couple was looking into several yeshivos for their son. When they came to Yeshiva Toras Chaim, they asked R' Chanina a common question. "What is our son going to learn?"

His answer, however, was uncommon. "He'll learn how to be a mensch."

They knew this was the yeshiva for their son.

R' Shlomo Freifeld in the succah

As R' Chanina learned from R' Shlomo Freifeld, being a mensch is the essence of being a Yid. One Succos, R' Shlomo shared with his *talmidim* several stories about R' Yechiel Mordechai Gordon, the rosh yeshiva of Yeshivas Lomza. In the 1930's,

R' Yechiel Mordechai came to America to fundraise for his yeshiva, but when World War II broke out, he was unable to return to Europe, leaving his family behind; unfortunately, his children and other family members were murdered by the Nazis, *yimach shemam*. R' Yechiel Mordechai eventually made his way to Petach Tikvah, where he had years earlier established a branch of Yeshivas Lomza.

In R' Hutner's words, R' Yechiel Mordechai was "a *baki b'Shas mamash,*" a true expert in all of Shas. Yet that was not what R' Shlomo emphasized in the stories he related about R' Yechiel Mordechai. Rather, R' Shlomo wished to teach his *talmidim* about *menschlichkeit* or, in his words, "the dimensions of a *talmid chacham*...and what a Yid has to be." R' Yechiel Mordechai was the perfect paradigm for those teachings, despite the fact that he was steeped in *tzaros*. R' Shlomo instructed his *talmidim* to review these stories, remember them, and then retell them to their children; that is how important they are.

R' Yechiel Mordechai was walking from his house to the yeshiva in Petach Tikvah when, as R' Shlomo expressed it, "you should excuse me, I apologize a thousand times, he saw dog droppings on the sidewalk." R' Yechiel Mordechai reached into his pocket, pulled out a handkerchief, bent down to pick up the filth from the floor, and dropped it into a nearby trash can. Here we had, in R' Shlomo's words, "a Yid, a *baki b'Shas*, a big rosh yeshiva, who embodied the aristocracy of Klal Yisrael," and yet he cared so much about others. He didn't want them to have to step on the filth, so he dealt with it himself. "Can you imagine the prince of Wales, *l'havdil,* doing such a thing?" R' Shlomo asked rhetorically. "This was his sensitivity to *kvod habriyos*."

Another story. Every morning, R' Yechiel Mordechai would stand by a plaque with the name of a certain donor and stare at it. When asked for an explanation, the rosh yeshiva said, "The man whose name is written on this plaque was not a rich man. Yet he loved Torah and he donated a substantial sum to the yeshiva. I never want to forget the *tovah* this Jew did for me, so every day I look at the plaque to remind myself." R' Shlomo concluded this story with, "This is a Yid."

R' Shlomo continued, "I'm not a storyteller, but these stories fall in the category of *shimush talmidei chachamim. 'Gedolah shimushah shel Torah yoser mi'limudah* — One can grow more from serving Torah scholars than from learning Torah from them' (*Berachos* 7b). Do we know what *kvod habriyos* is? We step on people; we step on people as if they're rugs! Do we know what *hakaras hatov* is? We can take and take and take and take and take and take, and then go like this" — here, R' Shlomo put his hand to his mouth with a napkin as if he were wiping his mouth after finishing a meal — "finished, and throw the *baal tovah* away."

R' Yechiel Mordechai Gordon

R' Shlomo then gave some more background before relating one final vignette about R' Yechiel Mordechai. Though most of R' Yechiel Mordechai's children were subsequently slaughtered by the Nazis in Vilna, one son, Shneur, was learning in Eretz Yisrael at the time. In 1938 (5699), he was killed by the Arabs. A *shailah* arose: Would R' Yechiel Mordechai, who had already endured other colossal losses in his life, be able to handle the news that his child had been taken? The *gedolim* of Eretz Yisrael determined that he would not be able to bear it; it was too dangerous to inform him. And since R' Yechiel Mordechai was in America at the time, they assumed he would not find out.

Soon after, an old Yid entered the Lomza Yeshiva office on the Lower East Side of Manhattan to give a donation. Not knowing that the *gedolim* had *paskened* to keep R' Yechiel Mordechai in the dark regarding his son, the man began to console the rosh yeshiva on his loss. Upon hearing the man's soothing words, R' Yechiel Mordechai immediately understood what had happened, yet his face did not betray him; he did not let on that the man had himself just delivered the devastating news. R' Yechiel Mordechai continued speaking to him for 15 minutes, the visitor none the wiser. Only after the man left did R' Yechiel Mordechai fall down in a faint. It had obviously been too much for him to bear.

When he came to, another rav asked R' Yechiel Mordechai, "Why did you spend another 15 minutes speaking to that Yid when it was so difficult for you?"

R' Yechiel Mordechai was incredulous. "I should make a Yid feel that he made such a mistake? Can you imagine the pain that Jew would have felt had he found out that he was the one who told me the bad news?"

"This is another dimension of what a Yid is," R' Shlomo declared, "what a *talmid chacham* is...*Nebach, ba'avonoseinu harabbim,* there aren't too many princes like that walking around today."

R' Chanina constantly echoed the words of his rebbi. "We have to be 'big Jews,' all-encompassing; each of us must be an *adam hashalem*!" In truth, young Charlie Herzberg imbibed the concept of *menschlichkeit* already from the time he was born. The home of Moish and Florence Herzberg preached and practiced *menschlichkeit* from the beginning. Eli, R' Chanina's son, once accompanied his father to the *levayah* of a relative of R' Chanina's father, where one of the speakers said about him, "Moish Herzberg was a mensch." With tears in his eyes, R' Chanina turned to Eli. "You hear that? He called my father a mensch! There's no greater praise!"

R' Chanina liked to retell the story of a Chassidic Rebbe who asked his Chassidim, "What are the three most important words in davening?" One of the Chassidim answered, "*Shema Yisrael Hashem,*" while another suggested, "*Modeh ani lefanecha.*"

The Rebbe smiled and offered his opinion. "I say the three most important words in davening are '*L'olam yehei adam*' (from *Korbanos,* recited before *Pesukei DeZimrah*), which can be translated homiletically: A person should always be a mensch!"

R' Chanina as a *yungerman,* with R' Shlomo Freifeld at a *chasunah*

At an open house in West Hempstead for prospective parents of Yeshiva Toras Chaim, R' Chanina addressed the crowd, taking this one step further. "Let me tell you in one sentence what this yeshiva is all about: '*L'olam yehei adam yerei Shamayim.*' A person must first be an *adam,* a mensch; only then will the *yiras Shamayim* — and everything else — follow. Once a boy is a mensch, then we can educate him!"

R' Chanina once accompanied R' Shlomo to a *chasunah,* entering the hall behind a couple, Reuven* and his wife. After they walked in, R' Shlomo requested of R' Chanina, "I noticed that when our friend Reuven entered the *chasunah* hall, he opened the door and walked in, without holding the door for his wife. He let the door close on her, and she had to open it herself. Please go tell Reuven in my name (*Bereishis* 29:26), '*Lo ye'aseh kein bimkomeinu* — This is not done in our place.'"

Also at a *chasunah*, R' Chanina noticed a young mother struggling with a carriage after the *chuppah* as she tried to bring it down a flight of stairs. R' Chanina ran over and carried it down the stairs for her. No fanfare, no accolades. Just fulfilling the role of a mensch, just like his rebbi adjured.

A Yeshiva Toras Chaim *talmid* recounted, "When I was in eighth grade, a bunch of boys slept over in Far Rockaway for a friend's bar mitzvah. Friday night after the meal, all the boys decided to go over to our English teacher's house to say good Shabbos. When we knocked on the door, she was ecstatic. She invited us in, gave us cookies, and spoke with us for a few minutes.

"Afterward, we all walked over to R' Herzberg's house to say good Shabbos. As R' Herzberg invited us into his house, he realized there were not enough seats at the dining room table for all 15 of us. He asked me to go downstairs to get some chairs from the basement. After giving out the chairs, I sat down near R' Herzberg. He turned to me and asked, 'How's Shabbos going so far?' I said that it was going well, and that we had just come from Mrs. Schwartz's house. He replied, 'Wow, that's so nice of you boys,' and continued to ask me about the visit.

"As I walked out of R' Herzberg's house, my brother and a friend

R' Chanina with *talmidim* in his house

turned to me and asked, 'Do you realize what just happened?' I said no. They explained that the boys who had been sitting there had already told R' Herzberg about the visit to Mrs. Schwartz's house. I would never have known from the way he responded that this was not new information.

"He wanted to lead by example, showing that you don't have to make someone feel uncomfortable even if you know the information already. Let the person tell his story. All the boys were wowed by how R' Herzberg handled the situation."

This is a Yid!

A Fundamental Component

R' SHLOMO ONCE TOLD R' CHANINA ABOUT A SERIOUS *MASMID* WHO used to sit and learn in the *beis midrash* day and night. While learning, he ate sunflower seeds, slowly making a neat pile of the shells on the edge of the table, until the pile was a nice-sized mound. R' Shlomo noticed that after the *bachur* finished learning, he pushed all the shells onto the floor, leaving the mess for the custodian to sweep up as he made his rounds after *seder*.

Appalled, R' Shlomo went to ask R' Hutner, "How is it possible that such a *masmid*, who has so much knowledge of Torah, can behave this way?"

His rebbi replied, "When a person displays such terrible *middos*, it is a sign that he is missing a fundamental component in Torah growth. It's not possible for a true *talmid chacham* to act in such a way!"

R' Shlomo told R' Chanina, "I kept track of this person as the years went by, and unfortunately, he never developed into a true *talmid chacham*. His lack of *tikkun hamiddos* held him back!"

Chazal tell us (*Derech Eretz Zuta* 5:1) that a *talmid chacham* should not eat while standing.

Many years ago, a Kiddush took place in a Far Rockaway shul. A large contingent from Sh'or Yoshuv accompanied R' Freifeld to wish mazel tov to the *baalei simchah*. Unfortunately, the caterer hadn't set enough tables. Taking note of the issue, R' Freifeld asked some of his *talmidim* to bring in a table and chairs. Only then did he make Kiddush and eat something.

R' Chanina told his family that his rebbi never ate while standing, and he himself conformed to this *hanhagah*. He was never seen at a Kiddush or other function eating while standing.

Middos are the basis for everything in life, a point R' Chanina stressed repeatedly. After R' Chanina's *petirah,* his good friend, R' Moshe Scharhon, a long-time rebbi at Yeshiva Toras Chaim, wrote about the loss. "We lost a menahel who would speak to the boys at *minyan* every Friday about the importance of being a mensch. So much so, that at times I would have to remind him that there were other things that had to be mentioned. We lost a menahel who, when I mentioned his name to our mechanic, his response was, 'He was a real mensch.'"

With the importance of *menschlichkeit* in mind, R' Chanina was fond of repeating a *vort* based on *Parashas Chayei Sarah.* When seeking a wife for his son Yitzchak, Avraham gave his trusted servant Eliezer only one directive: not to take a wife from the daughters of Canaan. Notwithstanding Eliezer's trustworthiness, Avraham had him swear that he would abide by this stipulation (*Bereishis* 24:2-4).

Upon reaching his destination, Eliezer davened to Hashem to bring the appropriate girl to him, a girl who was ready and willing to give him a drink and to water his camels, as well (ibid. v. 14). The defining factor was *middos tovos,* and nothing else, not even *yiras Shamayim.* Why?

While answering the question, R' Eliyahu Lopian (*Lev Eliyahu*) teaches us a basic concept in Yiddishkeit. No doubt, the main ingredient for *avodas Hashem* is *yiras Shamayim.* Even so, if a person does not yet possess *yiras Shamayim,* if he has *middos tovos,* he already has the tools, the foundation is already laid, to easily acquire *yiras Shamayim* and to reach lofty *madreigos.* Therefore, Avraham's only command was not to take a wife from the women of Canaan, because they had despicable *middos* and thus nothing would become of them.

This was R' Chanina's refrain. Be a mensch! If you're a mensch, then everything else will come. And if you're not a mensch, then you're like a boat with a hole in it. You can try from today until tomorrow to empty the water from the boat, but the water will keep entering — and the boat will sink!

Mr. Yaacov Lewis, president of Yeshiva Toras Chaim, stated, "The absolutely most important lesson R' Herzberg would impart to every boy, parent, and rebbi was in regard to *middos* and *derech eretz.* He was much less concerned about the number of Rashi's the boys would learn every week. Most important was that the boys would learn *middos, bein adam la'chaveiro,* and *menschlichkeit. Kavod* for the rebbi and respectful play between boys on the playground were of paramount importance in his educational philosophy. He always appreciated a boy who was the epitome of *chesed* and *middos* over a boy with natural genius abilities."

Man Was Not Created for Himself

A FAMILY MEMBER ASKED R' CHANINA HOW HE HAD THE PATIENCE TO talk to so many people over the course of a day. His reply was so genuine, so real. "I can do it because I really care about other people!"

In his introduction to the *sefer Nefesh HaChaim*, R' Yitzchak Volozhin, the son of its author, R' Chaim Volozhin, writes that his father always used to say, "Man was not created for himself (to take care of his own needs), only to benefit others to whatever extent his strength allows." This was a concept R' Chanina absorbed from his rebbi, and in turn demonstrated to others.

Young Shlomo Freifeld and two friends once went on a *bein hazmanim* trip and encountered a sad-looking man staring dejectedly ahead. After Shlomo pointed out the man to his friends, the group approached him and asked the fellow what was wrong, and he shared that he had been employed at a nearby factory for many years — until that morning, when he had unexpectedly been laid off. "I have no skills, no experience in anything else, and nowhere to go." To distract the man from his worries, Shlomo began to tell jokes, and after several minutes, the man was laughing. Shlomo and the others remained with him for a long while, until he felt ready to go home and relay the news to his wife.

Years passed. R' Shlomo opened Yeshiva Sh'or Yoshuv. One day, Chanina was in the office with his rebbi and brought him the mail. He watched as R' Shlomo opened a letter that had originated from a name and address he didn't recognize.

> *Dear R' Freifeld,*
>
> *Many years ago, you gave me the strength to go on when I felt that I couldn't. You saved my life that day. I have been following your career for years and wish you all the best in this new endeavor.*

Enclosed was a check for a significant sum of money. The man continued sending money to the yeshiva every year until he passed away.

Shlomo and his friends, who had never met the man before that day, could easily have said to themselves, "It's not our business." But they didn't. They understood that *chesed* must be done with all Jews, even those with whom one is not acquainted.

After finishing the story, R' Chanina would insert, "You know who the other two friends in the story are? R' Elya Weintraub and R' Aaron Schechter. Let me tell you, it's no coincidence that all three of them became 'big people'!"

R' Shlomo Freifeld (left) and R' Aaron Schechter (right)

R' Chanina made these stories a part of his own life. R' Meir Pam wrote a *sefer, Moreh Tzedek*, in which he compiled many of the speeches and *derashos* of his grandfather, R' Avraham Pam, rosh yeshiva of Yeshiva Torah Vodaath. The *sefer* includes many of R' Pam's talks on *chinuch* topics. R' Chanina loved the *sefer*.

At a certain point, the *sefer* was out of print. R' Chanina's son Yitzchok, looking for a copy, called the author to see if he had any on hand. He introduced himself as Yitzchok Herzberg and R' Meir asked, "Are you related to R' Chanina Herzberg?"

"Yes, how did you know him?"

"I didn't know him," R' Meir explained. "However, when the *sefer* first came out, your father called me and gave me an enormous amount of *chizuk*; he was crying on the phone as he spoke. I received many letters and compliments about the *sefer,* but your father's phone call stood out."

A videographer once came to Yeshiva Toras Chaim to film some footage for the yeshiva's annual dinner. Though he had never met R' Chanina before, they got into a conversation and the man mentioned that he was in the midst of moving to the Five Towns and his wife was looking for a job. R' Chanina took down his information and said he would see what he could do. True to his word, he started making phone calls as soon as he had some free time, eventually finding the man's wife a job.

Likewise, someone informed R' Chanina of a child in another community who didn't have a yeshiva to attend. R' Chanina took it upon himself to call yeshivos in that community, until he managed to find a yeshiva for the boy.

It didn't matter that he didn't know the author of the *sefer,* the videographer's wife, or the boy who didn't have a yeshiva to attend. They were Jews, and that's all that mattered.

One of the non-kosher birds listed in the Torah is the *chassidah,* the stork. Rashi (*Vayikra* 11:19) explains that this bird is called the חסידה because it performs חסידות (kindness) with others of its species, and helps them sustain themselves with food.

Since it is known that a bird's kashrus is connected to its behavior, the Chiddushei Harim (ad loc.) asks: If the *chassidah* does acts of kindness, why is it non-kosher? R' Chanina enjoyed sharing the Chiddushei Harim's answer: Because the *chassidah* performs acts of kindness *only* with her kind. If an animal is not one of her species, she doesn't help it, even with a little bit of food. Therefore, the *chassidah* is non-kosher.

"A Yid must always be on the lookout for ALL Jews!" R' Chanina thundered. "*Chesed* that is performed for an exclusive group is not the way of the Torah!"

R' Chanina was once driving with R' Shlomo in the Catskill Mountains and he ran into a bakery to purchase a coffee for his rebbi, who waited in the car. Upon returning to the car, R' Chanina noticed that his rebbi was perturbed. "Is something bothering Rebbi?" he inquired.

"R' Chanina," R' Shlomo replied, "do you see the pharmacy over there, and the group of Yidden waiting for the bus right near it?"

"Yes, I see them."

R' Shlomo said, "I'm very bothered by the display of inappropriate magazines on the display rack by the front window. As the Yidden wait for the bus, they are directly facing the *yetzer hara*! Please go into the pharmacy and ask the owner to move the magazines to the back of the store."

R' Chanina went inside and asked the owner if he could please remove the magazines, at the request of R' Chanina's rebbi.

The owner responded, "I'm so sorry, but those magazines provide me with a very generous profit. If I move them to the back of the store, people won't see them or buy them. Please tell your rabbi that unfortunately I cannot fulfill his request."

When R' Chanina relayed the storeowner's answer, R' Shlomo took out his checkbook and sent R' Chanina back into the store. "Please ask the owner to accept a check in the amount of the profits he expects to make this summer on the magazines — and to please move them to the rear of the store."

R' Chanina went inside and asked the storeowner to accept the deal. Hearing R' Shlomo's offer, the owner said, "Please go outside and tell the rabbi that if it means so much to him, I will gladly move them to the back. He doesn't need to give me a check!"

R' Chanina later shared his take. "My rebbi was concerned for all of the people waiting for the bus. There were all different types of Jews, and he was worried about all of them!"

Like R' Shlomo, R' Chanina enjoined his children and *talmidim* to think about others: their feelings, their needs, their overall welfare. To that end, he told the story of R' Isser Zalman Meltzer, the noted author of the *sefer Even HaAzel* and rosh yeshiva of Yeshivas Etz Chaim, who was on his way up to his apartment in Yerushalayim. When he reached the top step, he stopped for a moment outside his front door and listened. Suddenly, he turned around and went back down the stairs. About 15 minutes later, he started climbing back up and came back down. Several times he repeated this, wandering outside each time, until finally he returned and entered his home.

His nephew, who had accompanied him, wondered what was going on. "The rosh yeshiva just finished his *shiur* and is tired. Why did you go up and down the stairs and take all those short walks?"

R' Isser Zalman's answer shed light in more ways than one. "When I came to the door of my apartment the first time, I realized the housekeeper was singing to herself. I knew that if I were to go in, she would stop singing, since she knows I am not allowed to hear a woman sing. She is a poor woman who works hard and has very little enjoyment in her life. I felt bad for her and did not want to take away one of her few pleasures, the joy she derives from singing."

R' Isser Zalman Meltzer

"That's a true *gadol*," R' Chanina concluded, "whose first thoughts are for the benefit of the housekeeper. We must learn from this story to always care about others, to think about others, whoever that person may be, including the housekeeper."

R' Yehuda Kelemer once communicated a *vort* to R' Chanina, and R' Chanina derived great pleasure from it because it spoke to him. Moshe Rabbeinu grew up in the palace of Pharaoh, yet went out to the construction sites where his brothers slaved away. The *pasuk* informs us, "*Vayar b'sivlosam* — And he observed their burdens" (*Shemos* 2:11). Rashi explains, "*Nassan einav v'libo liheyos meitzar aleihem* — He focused his eyes and his heart to be distressed over them." R' Chaim Shmulevitz (*Sichos Mussar,* 5732:63, *Shaarei Chaim* edition), R' Kelemer's rebbi, elaborated. Merely feeling with one's heart is not sufficient. Only when one uses his eyes to really see the pain of another can one then feel with his heart. This was how R' Chanina conducted himself.

After R' Chanina's *petirah,* R' Chaim Aryeh Zev Ginzberg, rav of the Chofetz Chaim Torah Center of Cedarhurst/ Woodmere, wrote, "His huge heart and *regesh* for people were inherited from his great rebbi, R' Shlomo Freifeld. He was a large man with a very firm grip. But I have seen him burst into tears at the pain of someone else..."

A number of years ago, R' Chanina was going through his mail on Motza'ei Shabbos when he began to cry. He had come across a letter from a local organization, requesting *tefillos* on behalf of a young woman in the community who was in the throes of an excruciating illness. Whereas R' Chanina, who knew the family, had been aware that the woman was unwell, he had not known to what extent. Now, as he

R' Chanina (right) and R' Ginzberg greeting each other

read about the gravity of the situation, the woman's *tzaar* affected him deeply, moving him to tears.

R' Chanina would put aside his personal pain to focus on the pain of others. In August of 2006 (5766), R' Chanina suffered a massive heart attack, and the family didn't know if he was going to survive. During his stay in St. Francis Hospital, he heard the unfortunate news that his *talmid* from Yeshiva Tiferes Moshe — from over 30 years earlier — had passed away. R' Chanina began to cry uncontrollably. At that moment, he saw nothing of his own pain, weakness, or precarious health, only the *tzaar* that his *talmid*'s family was experiencing.

As R' Yitzchak of Volozhin wrote, "Man was not created for himself (to take care of his own needs), only to benefit others to whatever extent his strength allows."

Acting the Part

A BOY HAD JUST TRANSFERRED TO YESHIVA TORAS CHAIM FOR SIXTH grade. Soon after he arrived in yeshiva, R' Chanina caught him running through the halls. "In this yeshiva," R' Chanina informed him without raising his voice, "we don't run through the halls. We walk like *bnei Torah*."

Thirty-six years later, the *talmid*'s mother told R' Chanina's children, "Your father didn't yell at the boys. His quiet, thought-out reprimand was much more successful."

Another example of how R' Chanina taught *menschlichkeit*, as recalled by another Yeshiva Toras Chaim alumnus: "When I was in seventh grade, our class was invited to a weekend bar mitzvah of a classmate in a hotel. That Friday night when we returned to our rooms, we made a tremendous amount of noise, preventing the other guests from going to sleep. R' Herzberg, who was also there, found out what had happened. Oddly, throughout the rest of the Shabbos, he didn't say a word to us about it.

"That Sunday morning, after davening in yeshiva, R' Herzberg asked the seventh grade to stay in shul while everyone else went to class. 'Boys, your behavior in the hotel on Friday night was inexcusable. That's not the way a *ben Torah* behaves. On account of your actions, many people didn't sleep well that night. Chazal teach us: *Derech eretz kadmah laTorah*; having *derech eretz*, being a mensch, is crucial to becoming a true *ben Torah*. Because of the way you boys behaved Friday night, you don't deserve to learn Torah! I want all of you to stay right here and think about what you did, and about what I just told you!'

"R' Herzberg made us sit in the shul for over a half-hour," the alumnus remembered. "Only then did he allow us to return to class."

That moment lives on in those boys.

When the boys did behave properly, R' Chanina was quick to praise and reward them. R' Noam Singer, a rebbi in Yeshiva Toras Chaim, shared how his class was on the way back from a trip to a 7-11 store when R' Zev Davidowitz called with a message: R' Herzberg wanted to talk to the whole class upon their return to school.

The rebbi and his class went directly to R' Chanina's office, where R' Chanina addressed the boys, "My sister was in the 7-11 when you were there, and she described the exemplary *middos* and behavior of your class. This is what our yeshiva stands for: being a mensch and making a *kiddush Hashem*!"

To top it off, he gave the class a pizza party as a reward. The boys were pleasantly surprised to receive a reward for a trip! Even more important, they realized that being a true *ben Torah* is paramount to all.

R' Shmuel Schwebel gave another example of how R' Chanina taught about *menschlichkeit*. He instituted and took much pride in an organized program designed to encourage *derech eretz* on the school bus. Titled "U'v'lechtecha Ba'derech," the program included points and a reward system. Once, R' Chanina invited the superintendent in charge of busing in the Five Towns to hand out the reward certificates to the *talmidim* with the most points. In addition, with the assistance of R' Moshe Scharhon, R' Chanina created an honor roll for good *middos*, to allow boys who weren't academic stars to shine by being awarded for excellent behavior in the morning and afternoon, as well. The program was given its name, "Bachurei Chemed" (pleasant young men, based on *Yechezkel* 23:6,12, 23), by the rosh yeshiva, R' Binyamin Kamenetzky.

Before 9/11, there was minimal security in the yeshiva building. Since R' Chanina's office was down the hall from the main entrance, visitors entering the building frequently had no clue where to go. R' Chanina was always proud to hear how his students or staff members would stop and ask the visitors if they needed help finding the office or a specific person.

A Yeshiva Toras Chaim parent shared, "Decades ago, when I entered the yeshiva, I didn't know the location of a certain classroom. I asked a student who was passing by where the room was. Instead of pointing me to the room, he stopped in his tracks, walked me to the room, even opening the lunchroom door for me on the way. I knew then what this yeshiva is all about."

R' Chanina with Dovid Bashevkin at Dovid's *hanachas tefillin*

Yeshiva Toras Chaim alumni fondly recall the way R' Chanina trained them to behave at bar mitzvahs. As R' Dovid Bashevkin — noted author and alumnus of Yeshiva Toras Chaim — put it, "To R' Herzberg, the importance of boys behaving at bar mitzvahs wasn't about PR; it was about being a mensch, and bar mitzvahs were the first training ground for what it meant to be a mensch and a *ben Torah* outside the yeshiva."

His *talmidim* were not the only ones who learned about the conduct of a mensch from R' Chanina. Anyone who came into contact with him perceived his *menschlichkeit* and automatically conducted themselves accordingly. After his *petirah,* a friend of his, who had come to Sh'or Yoshuv without any religious background whatsoever, shared, "After R' Freifeld taught me *aleph-beis,* R' Chanina taught me Chumash. He was one of the people who had an everlasting impact on my journey to Torah. I will always remember our friendship of close to 50 years and all that he taught me — especially on being a mensch!"

Showing Your Pearly Whites

SPEAKING ONCE AT A KIDDUSH (*PARASHAS NASSO,* 5749), R' SHLOMO Freifeld communicated, "I was once in Yerushalayim at a *chasunah.* I met R' Aryeh Levin, and he gave me *shalom aleichem.* He did it with such genius, I'm telling you, I felt *epes* an unusual warmth from that *shalom aleichem.*

"The question is: Where did he get this from? And the answer is: *Shalom aleichem* is a *sugya* in the Torah. That's how he knew about it, and that's what put it into his mind to figure out how to do it *b'koach.* After all, giving a proper *shalom aleichem* and making another person feel special is one of the challenges of life."

When Chanina was still a *bachur* in Sh'or Yoshuv, R' Shlomo once walked up to the *bimah* in the middle of first *seder* and gave a *klap,* something extremely unusual. Silence reigned immediately, and in a booming voice, R' Shlomo announced, "I just saw a stranger come

R' Shlomo Freifeld, always with a pleasant smile

into the *beis midrash,* and not one person went over to him to say *shalom aleichem.* If my *talmidim* don't understand the importance of a *shalom aleichem,* then I may as well close the yeshiva!"

In addition, when delineating many of the princely attributes of R' Yechiel Mordechai Gordon in his Succos *shmuess,* R' Shlomo inserted, "R' Yechiel Mordechai Gordon always had a pleasant smile on his face. He greeted every person with a smile. That's also part of *kvod habriyos.*"

Chanina took these messages to heart and then transmitted them further.

R' Chanina would share what Chazal teach (*Kesubos* 111b): "Rabbi Yochanan said: A person who displays the whiteness of his teeth to his friend is better than one who gives him milk to drink, as it says (*Bereishis* 49:12), *'U'leven shinayim mei'chalav* — And white-toothed from milk.' Do not pronounce it לבן שנים (white toothed) but לבון שנים (a whitening of the teeth)." Thus, the *pasuk* should read, "A whitening of the teeth (i.e., sharing a smile) is better than serving a friend milk."

Making others feel welcome with his smile

"You have to show others your pearly whites!" R' Chanina would exclaim. "Like my rebbi used to say, you must greet everybody the way you would want to be greeted. When you say hello to someone and make him feel comfortable, you are showing him that he matters. When you give someone a *shalom aleichem,* you're validating him, you're telling him he's important. A person coming into a strange place has *sfeikos,* doubts, about his *metziyus,* his essence. A *shalom aleichem* says to him, 'You are part of our *tzibbur;* you now have a *metziyus.'* When you give him a *shalom aleichem,* he feels like he's at home. So make him feel welcome. Whether it's with a *l'chaim,* a *shtickel* herring, a good *vort* — say something to him. Let him know that you care, that you are there for him!"

R' Chanina once shared with his son-in-law, Shua Nachman, an important precept in the name of R' Shlomo: As Jews, we do not make a *l'chaim* just because we want to have a drink. Rather, we make a *l'chaim* because at that moment, we can look the other person in the eye and say, "You matter to me," and thereby give him *chiyus.*

He would also quote the famous line from R' Yisrael Salanter, that a person's face has the status of a *reshus harabbim,* a public domain. If one walks around with a sour look on his face, his face is a *bor birshus harabbim,* a pit in a public domain, and he is responsible for any damage caused to someone who falls or hurts himself on account of his "pit."

During R' Chanina's stay in St. Francis Hospital after suffering a heart attack, R' Moshe Shonek, rebbi in Yeshiva Toras Chaim and R' Chanina's close friend, came to visit. As soon as R' Moshe walked into the room, R' Chanina broke down in tears. "This morning, before I went for a big test to see the extent of the damage from the heart attack, I didn't really have time to daven. I put on my *tefillin* for a couple of minutes, and I was thinking: *What zechus do I have? What zechus do I have that I can make it through?"* Emotionally, he continued, "The only *zechus* I could find is that when I meet people, when I give someone a *shalom aleichem,* I have a *koach* to make them feel good, to give them *chizuk.* You hear? That was the only *zechus* I could find!"

Giving *shalom aleichem* to a *talmid*

But it *was* a *zechus,* a very important one. R' Chanina would relay to his *talmidim,* "In Europe there was a yeshiva called Telshe Yeshiva, where the top *bachurim* went to learn. The roshei yeshiva and rebbeim instituted that every morning after davening, the *bachurim* would line up to give a proper good morning to their rebbeim. One young man always took a long time to daven. By the time he removed his *tefillin,* the line of people waiting to say good morning was already very long. He decided that he would forgo the morning greeting to his rebbeim. Instead, he would eat breakfast and be the first one in the *beis midrash,* the first one to start learning.

"After several days, the rebbeim noticed that this boy was consistently absent from the line. The rosh yeshiva called him aside and asked him to explain his absence. The *bachur* proudly replied, 'Rebbi, by doing it this way, I'm getting in more learning!'

"The rosh yeshiva softly responded, 'And saying good morning and *shalom aleichem* isn't Torah?'"

R' Chanina then turned to the group of *bachurim* and concluded, "You need to understand the importance of a *shalom aleichem* or a good morning. Do you know how many people have told me they became *shomrei Torah u'mitzvos* because of a *shalom aleichem*!?" R' Chanina went on to emphasize the importance of giving another *bachur* a friendly good morning or saying a nice word to one's sibling or parent, and doing so with a full heart, doing so with love. "Because those few words can make a big difference!"

Chapter 8
24/7: The Mindset of a Mechanech

AT R' CHANINA'S *LEVAYAH*, HIS SON MENDY CITED THE GEMARA (*BAVA Basra* 8b), which brings a Baraisa quoting the *pasuk* (*Daniel* 12:3): "*U'matzdikei harabbim ka'kochavim l'olam va'ed* — And those who teach righteousness to the multitudes will shine like the stars, forever and ever."

Constantly on His Mind

To whom is this referring? "*Eilu melamdei tinokos* — These are the teachers of young children," the Gemara informs us.

The Gemara asks: Such as whom? Then it gives an example: Rav Shmuel bar Shilas. Rav Shmuel bar Shilas was once standing in a garden. Rav, his rebbi, confronted him, "Did you abandon your *talmidim*?"

Rav Shmuel answered, "I have not been in this beautiful garden for 13 years, and even now, my mind is on my *talmidim*; I am constantly thinking about my students."

"This was our father," concluded Mendy, "never taking his mind off his *talmidim*." Not only were his *talmidim* always on R' Chanina's mind, but he was constantly devising new plans to make each one succeed. He didn't view this as extra credit, but as a part of his job as menahel.

After all, his *talmidim* were his children. On this topic, the Brisker Rav cited the verse, "*V'shinantam l'vanecha* — You shall teach them thoroughly to your children" (*Devarim* 6:7), along with the explanation of the *Sifrei* (*Va'eschanan* 34) that the *pasuk* is not referring to biological children. Rather, *"eilu talmidecha* — these are your students." The Brisker Rav stated that just as a parent is only as happy as his weakest child, so should a rebbi only be as happy as his weakest *talmid*.

Furthermore, just as a parent constantly thinks about his child and how he can bring out the best in him, so R' Chanina thought about his *talmidim* and how he could bring out the best in them. R' Chanina spent his nights worrying about each individual student, losing sleep over the *talmidim* who weren't growing the way they were capable of, tossing and turning while contemplating those in need of extra assistance and extra TLC. His secretary often saw him sitting at his desk just thinking about the *talmidim*.

And he didn't stop until he came up with solutions.

Yehuda,* a middle school student at Yeshiva Toras Chaim, was diagnosed with leukemia and had to undergo chemotherapy. After a round of treatments, he was cleared by the doctors to return to school. Self-conscious about his hair loss and the baseball cap he had to wear as a result, Yehuda was nervous about coming back. R' Chanina told him enigmatically, "Don't worry. When you return to yeshiva, you'll feel comfortable."

Upon his return, Yehuda was pleasantly surprised to see that his entire class was wearing baseball caps! For the rest of the school year, the boys in his class were given special permission to "break" the dress code and wear caps to yeshiva, in order to help their classmate feel comfortable.

R' Chanina put his mind to helping his *talmid* ease back into school, came up with a solution, and saw it to fruition.

One morning in the early 1980's, R' Stern* was teaching his class at Yeshiva Toras Chaim, when there was an unexpected knock at the door. There stood the *gadol hador,* R' Moshe Feinstein, flanked by R' Binyamin Kamenetzky and R' Herzberg. R' Stern, along with his class, stood there in shock and awe. No one knew what to do, how to respond. R' Binyamin shared a few words, welcoming the *gadol* on his visit to the yeshiva and they left the room. Afterward, the other rebbeim found out who was in their midst and lined up their *talmidim* to give *shalom aleichem* and shake R' Moshe's hand.

R' Moshe had davened in the Young Israel of Woodmere that morning. R' Binyamin Kamenetzky, who was there, as well, had asked R' Moshe to stop by the yeshiva on his way back home.

After R' Moshe left the school, R' Stern complained to R' Chanina,

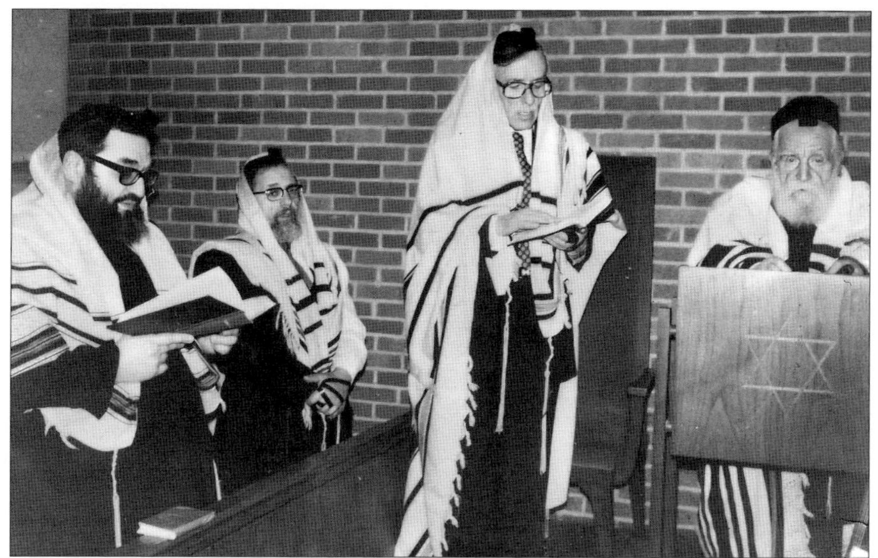

That morning, at the Young Israel of Woodmere (l-r): R' Reuven Feinstein, R' Binyamin Kamenetzky, R' Shaya Lebor (rav of the shul), R' Moshe Feinstein

"We were the first class that R' Moshe visited. However, we were so surprised that we did not know how to react, and we failed to line up and shake his hand. R' Herzberg, as you know, this year Alex,* who recently transferred to yeshiva from public school, is in my class. Most of the boys in the school got to shake R' Moshe's hand, but Alex didn't. He would have gained so much from shaking the *gadol hador*'s hand. It would have given him so much *chizuk* to come face-to-face with R' Moshe. Such a pity that this opportunity was lost."

Around a year later, R' Chanina heard that R' Moshe was visiting the area again. This was R' Chanina's chance to make it up to Alex. R' Chanina approached R' Binyamin, who would be at the same event that R' Moshe was attending, and convinced him to once again ask R' Moshe to stop by the yeshiva.

The moment arrived. A car pulled up to Yeshiva Toras Chaim, with R' Moshe Feinstein in the front passenger seat. R' Chanina brought out Alex, who had moved up to the next grade, to the passenger side window, where Alex shook the hand of the *gadol hador* and said *shalom aleichem*. The remainder of his class followed, and only then did the rest of the yeshiva line up to shake R' Moshe's hand.

With everything on R' Chanina's mind, he kept Alex at the forefront, never forgetting about his missed opportunity, and when an opportunity came again, he did all within his power to make the meeting happen.

R' Avraham Fridman, former general studies principal at Yeshiva Toras Chaim, discussed how R' Chanina would take phone calls at all times, as late as 12:00 at night and as early as 5:00 in the morning. "At times," R' Fridman recalled, "he would leave me a message at 1:00 a.m., 'R' Avraham, I'm thinking about this *talmid* and I can't sleep. Please call me back as soon as you hear this message.' And I would call him back at 6:00 in the morning as soon as I heard the message, because I knew he wanted to hear from me. One time, after receiving such a message, I waited until I saw him at 9:00 a.m. in yeshiva to discuss the matter. He *muhned* me, 'Why did you wait so long? Please don't do that again.'

"His overall view was: How can you rest as menahel?"

There were times in which R' Chanina called R' Yehuda Kelemer, rav of Young Israel of West Hempstead, at 2:00 a.m. about a child whose family davened in Young Israel, as per the rav's instructions. R' Chanina had great respect for the rav's *mesiras nefesh* on behalf of his *kehillah,* and he mirrored that level of *mesiras nefesh* on behalf of Yeshiva Toras Chaim.

R' Chanina made himself accessible to the parents of his *talmidim.* Whether someone called his work, home, or cell phone, he answered the call whenever feasible. If he missed a call, he was careful to return messages, usually the same day, or at the very least within 24 hours.

In the middle of August, 2006 (5766), as R' Chanina was busy preparing for the new school year, he suffered a heart attack. As he lay there in the intensive care unit, not yet knowing the extent of the damage to his heart, R' Chanina called parents regarding class placement or their concerns for their children for the coming year.

R' Chanina didn't just think into the big issues; he would pinpoint the seemingly minor issues affecting a child and try to help him. He knew that too often, the "small problem" is merely a symptom of a larger one. He would tell his children, "If you treat a small child's problem like a big one, then when the child himself grows bigger, he will only have small problems."

As he described it, a child should be viewed like a skyscraper, a building designed with structural foundations that go deep into the ground. After the structure is complete, passersby may not realize that the entire support for the weight of the building is beneath the surface, where it is not seen. Yet the slightest fault in the foundation can have catastrophic results.

"Parents and teachers are best advised to build up children, slowly, methodically, and with patience," R' Chanina advised. "Do not put undue pressure on a youngster, but build him naturally, brick upon brick, level by level. Until one day you'll see a vibrant individual, a productive member of Klal Yisrael."

After R' Chanina's *petirah,* his son Moshe recounted the anecdote in the Gemara (*Bava Metzia* 85b) about Rabbi Chiya's undertaking to ensure that Torah study would not be forgotten within Klal Yisrael. He began by planting flax, from which he constructed nets to capture deer. Then he slaughtered the deer and used the hides for parchment, upon which he wrote the *Chamishah Chumshei Torah*. He traveled from town to town, teaching Torah to five boys in each town. He taught each of the five boys one Book of Chumash, then instructed all of them to teach the other boys the Books each one had just learned. He did the same with the six *sedarim* of the Mishnah and six boys, teaching each young man one *seder* and instructing them to teach the others.

As Moshe explained, Rabbi Chiya taught us a fundamental concept in regard to the *achrayus* a rebbi must feel toward his *talmidim*. A rebbi's job is to calculate, to conceive every strategy in the book to ensure his *talmidim*'s success, and to spend his time and resources toward reaching his goal.

When R' Chanina visited Eretz Yisrael for the first time, arrangements were made for him to meet with R' Chaim Kanievsky. R' Chanina helped raise thousands of dollars each year for Kollel Chazon Ish,

R' Chanina visiting *gedolim* in Eretz Yisrael

Greeting R' Yosef Shalom Elyashiv

Asking R' Michel Yehudah Lefkowitz for chinuch guidance

Asking R' Chaim Kanievsky for chinuch guidance

where R' Chaim had learned, and the Herzberg family and friends looked forward to the special visit, eager to see what R' Chanina would glean from it.

When R' Chanina arrived at R' Chaim's home, he spent a significant amount of time deep in private discussion with the *gadol*. After they left, R' Chanina's family members asked what he and R' Chaim were speaking about so intently. "I was dealing with a difficult issue in regard to two *talmidim*, a problem that had been bothering me for the past few weeks," he responded. "I discussed with R' Chaim the various angles, in order to obtain a clear understanding of how to proceed."

"But what about your personal requests and *berachos*?" the family asked.

R' Chanina was taken aback. "What do I need for myself? I have everything I need! I have a beautiful family, grandchildren, *parnassah*. All is good!"

This scene repeated itself when visiting R' Michel Yehudah Lefkowitz.

His mind was on his *talmidim* and how to help them, how to bring out the best in them. Why would he think of himself?

R' Aaron Schechter commented to Yitzchok Herzberg regarding R' Freifeld, "He learned from the rosh yeshiva (R' Hutner) the *sod*, the secret, of *oiftzutohn mitt menschen*, of accomplishing with people. Accompanying this secret came the interest and concern that *yenem* should *vox*, that others should develop and grow."

R' Shlomo transmitted this *sod* to R' Chanina. When a *mechanech* feels the responsibility and drive to make sure that his *talmid* accomplishes and grows in his *avodas Hashem*, he will never stop thinking of ways to help that student grow even more. He realizes that he's on a 24/7 mission to accomplish with every one of his *talmidim*.

At times, R' Chanina took the concept of 24/7 literally. At a weekend bar mitzvah of a *talmid* from Yeshiva Toras Chaim, the eighth-grade *talmidim* were mistakenly placed on the same floor of the hotel as the adult guests. R' Chanina understood that this could spell a recipe for disaster. As boys will be boys, the chances were very high that they would keep the adults up most of the night.

Not to worry. R' Chanina simply stayed up the entire night, sitting in the hallway with a *sefer* in hand, ensuring that quiet reigned.

WHEN R' CHANINA ASKED POTENTIAL REBBEIM, "WHAT ARE YOU learning?" he didn't want to hear that the prospective rebbi was focusing only on his learning. He wanted to know that the rebbi was working on the balance between his personal growth and the growth of his *talmidim,* a harmony not easily achieved but very necessary for a *mechanech.* On one hand, the rebbi feels a responsibility to be there for his *talmidim* in every way possible, but on the other hand a voice inside of him calls out, "What about your own growth? You need to learn Shas; you need to learn *sugyos b'iyun*!"

Achieving Harmony

In an address to menahalim (see *Moreh Tzedek*, p. 115), R' Avraham Pam discussed this conflict. "Many *melamdim* ask me, 'When am I going to be able to do my own learning?' I always give them the same answer: I also have this problem. When I began my career in *chinuch,* I tried to have *sedarim* in other topics that I was interested in learning, aside from those I was teaching. However, within a short time I began to realize that this is not the proper way. My responsibility is to my *talmidim."*

R' Pam brought a *vort* to prove his point. In *Malachi* (2:7), we are taught: *"Ki sifsei Kohen yishmeru daas veTorah yevakshu mi'pihu, ki malach Hashem Tzevakos hu* — For the lips of the Kohen should safeguard knowledge, and people should seek teaching from his mouth; for he is a *malach* of Hashem, Master of Legions." Based on this verse, the Gemara (*Chagigah* 15b; *Moed Katan* 17a) tells us that if a rebbi is *"domeh l'malach Hashem,"* similar to an angel of G-d, we should learn Torah from him. If not, we should not.

R' Avraham Pam

How is a rebbi expected to be similar to a *malach Elokim*? R' Pam then cited the *sefer Panim Yafos* (*Parashas Vayeira* 18:2), which explains that *malachim* are *omdim,* stationary beings, always staying the same, unable to rise to another level. Human beings, however, are *mehalchim,* always moving, growing, evolving (see *Zechariah* 3:7). A rebbi must be like a *malach,* who is not focused on his personal growth and development, but rather on the growth and development of his *talmidim*.

R' Pam continued: Yes, there was a time, before he took his position as a rebbi, that this individual had a *she'ifah* to learn all of Shas or to be an expert in a certain area of Torah, but now that he has accepted the responsibility of taking care of his *talmidim*, his job is to dedicate himself to them 100 percent.

A rebbi in Yeshiva Toras Chaim heard about an early morning kollel that was opening in the neighborhood, and he considered joining. However, he recognized that enrolling in the kollel would impact his sleep. Unsure whether or not to sign up, the rebbi asked R' Chanina for his thoughts. R' Chanina knew that every minute of sleep or lack thereof could affect this rebbi's performance in the classroom, and therefore advised against it.

R' Chanina could have taken the "selfish" or "lazy" approach, and just looked for peace and quiet, while wishing away all the issues he dealt with on a daily basis. Yet he embraced his mission in life, knowing that this is what the *Eibishter* wanted from him. He once remarked to his son, "Do you know how many times I could have finished Shas had I not been busy with the *tzibbur*? Yet my *tafkid* is to dedicate myself to my *talmidim*, to the yeshiva, to the *tzibbur*. And I am enjoying every moment, knowing that I am fulfilling my purpose through this *avodas hakodesh*."

Enjoying every moment

This is not to say that a rebbi is completely absolved from learning on his own or working on himself. Eli Herzberg once asked his father, "What does it take to be a great rebbi?" With a smile on his face and a twinkle in his eye, R' Chanina replied, "Well, he has to master Chumash with Rashi, Ramban, and *Midrash Rabbah*, plus Shas, *Shulchan Aruch, Mesillas Yesharim*, and *Sefer Chofetz Chaim*, and then hopefully he'll be okay!"

The Dubno Maggid once asked the Vilna Gaon, "How is a luminary of a given generation able to impact the masses?"

"This is analogous to a large vessel surrounded by smaller ones," the Gaon responded. "If one were to pour liquid into the large one, once it is completely full, it will begin to spill into the vessels encircling it. Likewise, if one is overflowing in *yiras Shamayim*, his fear of Heaven will inevitably spill over to those around him."

This was R' Chanina's motto. "If you're continuously growing, then your *talmidim* will continue to grow!"

R' Chanina exhorted his rebbeim to keep their positions as rebbeim in the forefront of their minds at all times. "You are a *melamed* first, and that thought must impact every decision you make." Of course, the *melamed* must continue to grow, but it's all in order to be a better *melamed*, to be *mashpia* on his *talmidim*.

Grabbing a few minutes to learn during a visit to Eretz Yisrael

When a rebbi lives his life with this in mind, he'll be able to achieve harmony between his growth and his *talmidim*'s growth.

Someone Who Cares

PARENTS ONCE CAME FOR AN INTERVIEW WITH THEIR CHILD TO Yeshiva Toras Chaim and mentioned to R' Chanina, "We have a very sensitive child."

R' Chanina didn't hesitate. "Don't worry, I have 450 sensitive children."

He would quote the Midrash (*Shemos Rabbah* 1:27), which tells us how Moshe would leave Pharaoh's palace (*Shemos* 2:11), where he was residing at the time since his adoption by Bas Pharaoh, to feel the *tzaar* of his Jewish brethren and to assist them in their back-breaking labor. Despite his elevated standing in society, Moshe was able to connect to those on a "lower social status."

Similarly, the Midrash (*Shemos Rabbah* 2:2) praises Dovid HaMelech and Moshe Rabbeinu for the sensitivity they demonstrated to the animals in their care. When Hashem saw how Dovid divided the flock according to age, feeding each group of sheep the grass that best suited it, He stated, "The one who knows how to feed the sheep, each according to its strength, should come and feed My sheep." Moshe Rabbeinu also showed extreme care and concern for the sheep under his watch. While he was tending Yisro's sheep, one lamb ran and ran, until it reached a pool where it stopped to drink. Moshe said to the lamb, "I had no idea that you ran away because you were thirsty. You must be tired." With that, he lifted the animal on his back and brought it back to the rest of the flock. Hashem declared, "You have such mercy to care for the sheep belonging to a man of flesh and blood, so will you care for My sheep, Klal Yisrael!"

R' Chanina said, "You see from here that no matter how great you are, you must always remain attentive to the basic and individual needs of the masses."

R' Avraham Fridman described the responsibility R' Chanina took upon himself on snow days. "He used to drive around in his car at around 4:00 or 5:00 a.m. to check if the streets were safe before making a decision whether or not to close yeshiva. When he grew older, sometimes he asked me to do the checking for him. Even if the bus company decided not to offer busing, if he thought driving could still be safe, he would check it out to see if we could have car pools."

R' Yitzie Ross, rebbi in Yeshiva Toras Chaim, reminisced, "Many

R' Chanina and *talmidim* getting ready to board the coach buses for a school trip

years ago, the eighth grade was going on a graduation trip, and all the boys excitedly lined up to board the coach bus. And there was R' Herzberg, examining the tires. When it came to the safety of others, there was no compromising." He was constantly thinking about every aspect of the lives of the *talmidim* under his jurisdiction, in and out of school. R' Chanina frequently raised money for *talmidim* who couldn't afford the full price of the school trips, so they would not be deprived.

A *talmid* of Yeshiva Toras Chaim was once involved in a tragic accident and was hospitalized for a period of time. R' Chanina made sure that the entire class went on a trip to the hospital in the city to visit the injured boy. He also ensured that the boy's rebbi called or visited and learned with him every day, so he would not fall behind in his learning.

Joey,* who transferred from public school to yeshiva in fifth grade, was understandably apprehensive. Noticing his nervousness, R' Chanina told him, "Stick with me and I'll take care of you," which he did, not letting go. When Joey had trouble finding a *shidduch,* he called R' Chanina and reminded him of his promise to take care of him. R' Chanina put his wife on the case. Before long, Joey was engaged, with Mrs. Herzberg serving as the *shadchan.*

R' Aaron Schechter was asked: What makes someone a great menahel?

His answer sums up R' Chanina: Someone who cares.

R' Chanina giving *shalom aleichem* to R' Aaron Schechter, with R' Shmuel Kamenetsky looking on

Daven, Fast, and Cry

ONE SUMMER IN THE 1980'S, R' CHANINA AND A REBBI FROM YESHIVA Toras Chaim made their way to Camp Ohr Shraga, where R' Yaakov Kamenetsky was spending time, seeking guidance on an important *chinuch* matter.

A boy in Yeshiva Toras Chaim was constantly playing tricks, acting spiteful toward his classmates, and speaking disrespectfully to his rebbeim. The rebbi accompanying R' Chanina was set to have this boy in his class for the coming school year and was apprehensive. He was concerned that the boy would disrupt the flow of the learning and cause irreparable damage. R' Chanina asked R' Yaakov if the boy should be asked to leave the yeshiva.

R' Yaakov shelved the concept of expelling the boy, instead giving R' Chanina and the rebbi suggestions on how to keep a firm hand on the boy and regulate his behavior, for example, with private tutors. If they were to follow through, the boy could be saved without wreaking havoc in the classroom.

As R' Chanina and the rebbi were preparing to leave, they were called back by R' Yaakov. When they returned, R' Yaakov looked at R' Chanina and asked, "Were you *mispallel* for the boy? Did you daven for him?"

Thrown off by the question, R' Chanina softly replied, "No."

R' Yaakov then turned to the rebbi and inquired, "Throughout your time as a *mechanech*, have you been davening for your *talmidim*? Do you have them in mind in your *tefillos*?"

The rebbi was also uncomfortable. "No, I don't."

R' Yaakov looked at both of them gravely and stated, "Fifty percent of the job of a *mechanech* is davening for his *talmidim*. One must always have them in mind during *tefillah*, and daven for their success!"

This incident took place early in R' Chanina's career as a menahel. For the next 35 years, he made an effort to daven for his *talmidim*'s success and improvement, as he took R' Yaakov's "*tochachah*" seriously: One must never forget to daven to the *Eibishter* for his *talmidim*.

But he did more than daven.

There was a child in the yeshiva with an acute problem, and R' Chanina found himself at a loss. He presented the situation to R' Shlomo, expecting a detailed response on how to help the child, but that wasn't what he received.

"R' Chanina," R' Shlomo posed, "have you tried fasting for him yet?"

"No," was the answer.

"Go fast for the boy and if that doesn't work, come back to me and we'll talk," R' Shlomo instructed.

R' Chanina with *talmidim*

R' Chanina revealed to his children that after this incident, his sense of responsibility rose to a new level. R' Shlomo made him realize that not only must we daven for our *talmidim*, but we must fast for them, as well.

One of R' Chanina's children once noticed that their father was not himself. For the past few days, he had not been eating, and he had been pacing the floors. After being asked for the reason behind his uncharacteristic behavior, R' Chanina explained, "For various reasons, a boy in our yeshiva had to be asked to leave. It pains me greatly, and it's not a simple matter. But I had to do it. This week, I received a phone call from a rav, berating me for my decision. Does he know that I spent three days agonizing over it? Does he know that I secured a place in another yeshiva for this boy? Does he know that I fasted before asking the boy to leave?"

On another occasion, R' Chanina's nephew, R' Yehuda Spiegel, who was a *bachur* at the time, came into the house and overheard R' Chanina raising his voice on the phone. "Don't start questioning me about the decision! Do you have any idea how much R' Binyamin Kamenetzky and I agonized over this decision before asking the boy to leave? Do you know that we both fasted that the situation should improve so that he should be able to stay in the yeshiva?"

Although there were a few times in which R' Chanina had no choice but to ask a *talmid* to leave, it was only after exhausting all possible means, davening intensely, accepting a fast upon himself, and making sure the child had proper placement in another yeshiva.

Mr. Richard Altabe, lower school principal at HALB Elementary School in Woodmere, served as dean of general studies at Yeshiva Darchei Torah in Far Rockaway, from 1988 (5748) to 2006 (5766). He described how R' Herzberg and R' Yaakov Bender, rosh yeshiva of Yeshiva Darchei Torah, worked together closely to benefit the children and the community. If either one had a *talmid* who needed a fresh start, he would send the boy to the other yeshiva.

"Frequently, a child from Yeshiva Toras Chaim needed Darchei, and a child from Darchei needed Yeshiva Toras Chaim," explained Mr. Altabe. "Both R' Herzberg and R' Bender were very big about making sure that every boy had a place, and they were not afraid to say that if a boy didn't fit in their yeshiva, perhaps he would fit better in the other one. It was really beautiful to watch how these *gedolei chinuch* worked together."

At a meeting in HALB for CAHAL (Communities Acting to Heighten Awareness and Learning), with *hanhalah* members and administrators from the Five Towns community R' Bender is speaking (center), and Mr. Altabe is next to him (left); R' Chanina is at the far right.

R' Chanina was so pleased with this arrangement that he mentioned this brainchild at a Torah Umesorah meeting of menahalim.

But R' Chanina did more than daven and fast and make sure every child had a place.

A young man was facing serious issues, and his mother was at her wit's end. People advised her to speak to R' Shneur Kotler, rosh yeshiva of Beth Medrash Govoha in Lakewood. Since R' Chanina knew her family and was familiar with the background, he called R' Shneur to arrange a meeting and accompanied her on the appointed day.

As the woman told her story, R' Shneur started to cry, the tears coming rapidly. He was able to feel her *tzaar*, her distress, and what she was going through.

R' Chanina repeated this story many times, because it taught him that not only does he have to daven for others, not only does he have to fast for them, but he also has to cry for them!

An eighth-grader in Yeshiva Toras Chaim had his heart set on a certain high school. But it was easier said than done. Not one to give up easily, R' Chanina spent an inordinate amount of time advocating on the boy's behalf, through tireless work and many phone calls. As he saw it, this high school was the best choice for this particular *talmid,* and he was determined to make it happen. One day, R' Chanina's son Eli walked into his father's office and saw him on the phone with the boy's mother. "Mrs. Rothberg,*" he began, "Aryeh* was accepted into the high school of his choice. I just received the phone call from the rosh yeshiva. He's in!"

As R' Chanina transmitted the news, he began to cry tears of happiness.

R' Chanina would frequently cry over serious situations relating to his *talmidim* and others he was dealing with. At times, his family members even heard him crying in his sleep, while muttering the names of *talmidim* and the issues they or their families were enduring. Their pain was his pain, their struggles his struggles, their triumphs his triumphs. R' Chanina did his utmost for every *talmid,* never giving up on a single one.

Such was the love and concern he had for them.

His mind was on them, day and night, 24 hours a day, seven days a week.

Chapter 9

Recognizing Potential: The Outlook of a Mechanech

DURING THE *SHIVAH* FOR R' CHANINA, A MAN IN HIS UPPER 30'S walked into the Herzberg house to be *menachem avel*. This individual

What You Will Become

had undergone his share of challenges, and for some time had strayed from the path of Torah. As it was wintertime, the man came in wearing a heavy coat. After a few minutes, he tentatively began to remove it, stopped for a moment, rethought his decision, and then shared, "You know, I have tattoos all over my arms. In any other home, I'd be embarrassed to take off my coat. But in this house — in R' Herzberg's house — I'm not uncomfortable, because your father was the only person who, when speaking to me, didn't speak to who I was, but spoke to my potential!"

The man who was not embarrassed to remove his coat in R' Chanina's home is *menachem avel* the family after taking it off

R' Chanina was able to see the potential, even if it was hidden, in each and every person. This is one of the many skills he gleaned from R' Freifeld.

Soon after Hersh Leib Gefen joined Yeshiva Sh'or Yoshuv, he was given the honor of *maftir* on Shabbos Shuvah. The *bachur* was perplexed. It is customary to grant *maftir* of Shabbos Shuvah to an *adam chashuv,* someone of stature. *What did I do to deserve this honor?* he wondered. After davening, Hersh Leib voiced his question to R' Shlomo.

"You're making a big mistake," R' Shlomo set the record straight. "In this yeshiva, we don't judge you by what you are; we judge you by your potential, by what you will become."

To this day, R' Hersh Leib gets the chills every year during *maftir* of Shabbos Shuvah, as he relives the scene and hears R' Shlomo's battle cry: A person must continuously work to bring out his potential, the strengths that lie within.

This was ingrained in R' Chanina, as well, from his own experience as a 6-year-old, when R' Yitzchak Schmidman brought him to yeshiva and changed the course of his life. He always looked at what he became *with* R' Schmidman in his life, and compared it to what he would have become *without* R' Schmidman in his life. These side-by-side visions, the vision of Charlie juxtaposed with that of Chanina, or rather, metamorphosing into Chanina, empowered R' Chanina to realize the potential in others.

Daniel,* a boy who gave his rebbeim and teachers in Yeshiva Toras Chaim a run for their money, recalls how R' Chanina often called him Charlie. "No, it wasn't my name, but I think it was his way of telling me, 'Hey, look at me! I was once Charlie and look how I grew, look at what I became. Great things lie ahead for you, too. Fulfill your potential!'"

In a *hesped* delivered at the Torah Umesorah convention following R' Chanina's *petirah,* his son Yitzchok revealed the key to R' Chanina's success in *chinuch.* "He took note of the potential of every child who entered the yeshiva. Using his keen insight, he envisioned what the child could be as a 40-year-old grown man. He saw the totality of the mensch from beginning to end, and every interaction he had with his *talmidim* was with the objective of how to get this child to reach his potential, to become the person he envisioned him becoming. When we deal with a child in that way, it's a different world. In that world, it's '*Chanoch l'naar al pi darko* — Train the youth according to his way' (*Mishlei* 22:6), in its purest form. We're not doing something because that's the protocol, because that's what's done in such-and-such situation. We're doing something because that's what *this* child needs in order to get to the next step, to reach his potential. We're not confined to

Inscribing a *sefer* for a *talmid*

a box, or even multiple boxes. In fact, there is no box. That's what made my father the masterful *mechanech* he was."

While still a seventh-grade rebbi in Yeshiva Tiferes Moshe, R' Chanina penned an end-of-the-year letter to a *talmid* who needed *chizuk*. "Yossi,* you have so much potential! You need to believe in yourself! Great things lie ahead." That *talmid* kept that note and still cherishes it.

At the *levayah*, Yudi Herzberg recounted how he once came home with a 55 on a math test. Crying nervously, he showed it to his father. Noticing his son's disappointment and distress, R' Chanina turned the moment into a teaching one. "55%? If you were playing for the Mets, you would be batting 550! That's amazing! You would be an MVP, an all-star. There's nothing to cry about!" R' Chanina believed in every boy, including his own children, and encouraged them to keep trying.

R' Chanina discussed how, when Hashem first appeared to Moshe and appointed him to go to Egypt to redeem the Jewish people, Moshe asked (see Rashi: *Shemos* 3:11-12; *Shemos Rabbah* 3:4), "What merit do the Jews have that entitles them to miracles? Haven't they fallen too far from the legacy of Avraham, Yitzchak, and Yaakov, making them not redeemable?"

Hashem responded, "When you take the Jews out of Egypt, you will serve Hashem on this mountain," meaning that they would accept the Torah on Har Sinai. True, they were lacking in merit, but they had the potential to be great, to become Hashem's chosen people — and because of that they deserved to be redeemed.

In addition, when Moshe asked Hashem what Divine Name he should use when telling the Jewish people they will be freed, Hashem told him, "*E-heyeh asher E-heyeh* — I shall be as I shall be." Why was this Name of Hashem, *E-heyeh,* the Name with which Hashem would take the Jews out of Egypt?

The Chozeh of Lublin explains that *E-heyeh* is in the future tense, to symbolize to the Jews that in order to be taken out of Egypt, they had to recognize, "*E-heyeh,* I will be." The key to Yiddishkeit is growth. It is not what you are today; it is what you will become tomorrow.

Years before stepping into Yeshiva Toras Chaim, R' Menachem Bernstein, now a rebbi there, learned a foundation of life and *chinuch* from R' Chanina. "R' Herzberg called me one evening to ask about someone I knew, as a possible *shidduch* for one of his children. As I was describing the person, R' Herzberg asserted, 'We are not looking for a finished product, as long as there is the raw material.' Those words left a strong impression on me. He wasn't interested in a complete person. He knew that was not the current goal. R' Herzberg looked for the person's potential, the yearning and possibility for growth."

Removing the Rock

R' SHLOMO ONCE CONVEYED TO R' CHANINA, "I SEE PEOPLE *KLAPPING 'al cheit'* on Yom Kippur, and they look so down and depressed! I say, *'Sur mei'ra'* (*Tehillim* 34:15), turn away from the bad; don't focus on it! Rather, *'asei tov'* (ibid.), do good; focus on your potential! Look at all the good you can do!"

By the time he was 15, Eliyahu* had gone through a lot. A child at risk, he unfortunately became involved with the wrong crowd — until his life was unexpectedly cut short. R' Chanina was tasked with the impossible job of speaking at Eliyahu's *levayah.* The night before the *levayah,* he admitted to his son how overwhelmed he was by this charge. "What can I say? How can I possibly bring comfort to the tormented *mishpachah?*"

Nonetheless, he came through as always, dispensing *chizuk* to the assembled with his words of wisdom. Yirmiyahu HaNavi (31:19) communicates Hashem's love for Bnei Yisrael. "*Havein yakir li Ephraim im yeled shaashuim, ki midei dabri bo zachor ezkerenu od* — Is Ephraim My favorite son or a delightful child that whenever I speak of him I remember him more and more..." R' Meir Shapiro, the rosh yeshiva of Yeshivas Chachmei Lublin, had an exceptional *talmid* named Ephraim who was *niftar* while still a *bachur*. At his *levayah*, R' Meir Shapiro paraphrased the *pasuk* and wailed, "Ephraim! I'll always remember the *od*, the more! I'll always remember how much more you could have been, what you were destined to become!"

"Eliyahu," R' Chanina addressed the *niftar*, "I will always remember the *od*! I'll always remember the potential that lay within you, waiting to come out!"

R' Chanina now turned to the assembled. "That is how we need to remember Eliyahu. We need to remember the potential!"

The message made its way into the hearts of Eliyahu's family, bringing them much-needed comfort.

Following the *levayah*, R' Chanina remarked to his son, "If only we could view all children in this light, it would make such a difference in their lives."

In a similar vein, R' Chanina used to quote R' Freifeld, who cited the *pasuk* (*Tehillim* 84:5), "*Ashrei yoshvei veisecha od yehallelucha selah* — Praiseworthy are those who dwell in Your house, may they always praise You, *selah*," and explained it homiletically:

"*Ashrei yoshvei veisecha*," who's the lucky one, the one who dwells in Hashem's house?

"*Od*," the one who pushes himself and puts in a little more effort.

He is the one who will merit: "*yehallelucha selah*," to always praise Hashem.

Once again, it is the *od*, the additional effort, which is emphasized. It is our job to uncover it and bring it out in our children and in our students.

One Shabbos, during the week of *Parashas Vayeitzei*, R' Chanina stood in front of a packed crowd in Bais Medrash of Harborview/ Bais Pinchas of Lawrence (R' Kalish's shul), to make an appeal for CAHAL (Communities Acting to Heighten Awareness and Learning), which serves students with learning challenges in yeshivos throughout the Five Towns, Far Rockaway, and beyond.

"Let me tell you just one story about just one girl in CAHAL." R' Chanina began. "Esther* first attended a mainstream school, yet she felt worthless, sapped of all her self-esteem. Then she was transferred to

CAHAL, where she participated in a choir as part of a concert, and was given the role of star soloist. As the auditorium filled up with women and girls for the event, those who knew Esther were anxious, desperately hoping she wouldn't make a fool of herself. Her turn came and she opened her mouth to sing. And boy, did she sing! As she stood there, singing like a pro, tears flowed freely down the faces of the women in the audience. Esther finally had her moment, her moment of success. This one experience changed her life. After tasting the flavor of success, she began leading a successful life.

"In this week's *parashah,*" R' Chanina continued, "we learn about a large rock that covered the well. The only way for the shepherds to remove the rock was by coming together, in unity, focused on one purpose — to remove the rock and gain access to the effervescent well that lay beneath it.

"Every person has an effervescent well within him. However, some of us have a rock covering that well, covering our untapped potential. Sometimes, the only way to uncover the well is by coming together to remove the blockage. So let us come together and support CAHAL. Let us help uncover the potential that lies within each child!"

Chaim, a sixth-grade student in Yeshiva Toras Chaim, wasn't doing well in school, to put it mildly. He was acting out in class and failing miserably. When his parents came to parent-teacher conferences, while the rebbi and teachers all mentioned that Chaim was extremely capable, they also delineated their concerns regarding his overall performance.

The parents recounted the details of the conferences to R' Chanina, who had one point to add. "One thing I'll tell you. If I had to leave the school for a day, I would feel comfortable leaving Chaim in charge until I got back." Chaim's parents now understood clearly that though their son had issues that needed to be addressed, he possessed great potential, as well.

R' Chanina would mention the Midrash (*Bereishis Rabbah* 8:5), which teaches that the word אדם (man) is comprised of the same letters as the word מאד (very). R' Hutner explained this in a profound manner. The word "very" cannot be specifically defined. Is it a mile, a kilometer, an acre? In truth, it has no defined limit. Similarly, man's capabilities are unlimited; he can keep on growing, without boundaries. Mankind possesses unlimited potential.

R' Chanina recognized the potential in every *talmid*

The Alter of Slabodka, who constantly stressed the *gadlus ha'adam,* the greatness of man, encouraged his students to accomplish as much as they could by planting within them a strong awareness of their potential. It was this *mesorah* that R' Chanina received from R' Shlomo, who received it from R' Hutner, who received it from the Alter of Slabodka.

Inside Out

WHEN HE FIRST ACCEPTED THE POSITION IN YESHIVA TORAS CHAIM, R' Chanina was informed that R' Yaakov Kamenetsky wanted to speak to him. R' Chanina drove to Monsey to R' Yaakov's home, where R' Yaakov told R' Chanina how he felt the yeshiva should be led, emphasizing over and over, "People think that a yeshiva should be made up of children from families who are all very similar in their *hashkafas hachaim,* dress, yarmulkes, etc... I disagree. A yeshiva needs to be a microcosm of Klal Yisrael. It is important for children to be taught to judge their fellow Jew by their character, and not just by their outward dress and mannerisms. Our children need to be taught that you can be an *ehrliche Yid* if you have a beard or no beard, a big yarmulke or a small yarmulke. Yidden need to love each other and tolerate each other. And we need to teach this to our children when they are young. Where is it better to teach such things than in yeshiva?" That was R' Yaakov's take on *chinuch*. He told R' Chanina very clearly, "A yeshiva is not a factory. No two children need to be the same, nor should they be expected to be the same."

A man who had recently moved to the Five Towns was seeking the right yeshiva for his son, a place that was real and would accept him for who he was. Before walking into the interview at Yeshiva Toras Chaim, the man, looking to challenge R' Chanina, hung a gold chain around his neck and opened the top button of his shirt. R' Chanina had no way of knowing this man had once been a student in an illustrious yeshiva; he certainly didn't look the part.

But that didn't matter to R' Chanina.

When the man entered R' Chanina's office, R' Chanina hugged him, chatted with him, and treated him as if he had come in with a long beard and *peyos*. That's when the man knew this was the place for his children.

Because R' Chanina didn't look at an individual's *chitzoniyus*. He saw through all that, to the potential. What was inside, ready to come out.

This, too, was learned from his rebbi. R' Shlomo once turned to R' Amos Bunim, who had come to see him in the *beis midrash* of Yeshiva Sh'or Yoshuv, and waved his hand in the direction of a young man seated nearby.

R' Naftali Jaeger being *maspid* R' Chanina at a *sheloshim* gathering in Yeshiva Sh'or Yoshuv

"Do you see that boy?" he inquired.

R' Amos nodded his head.

But it was as if R' Shlomo had not heard the response. "Do you *see* him?"

R' Amos once more indicated that yes, he did see the boy.

Finally, R' Shlomo got to the point. "You see a long ponytail and a torn T-shirt. But you're not seeing the boy's *neshamah*!"

R' Naftali Jaeger said in a *hesped*, "R' Chanina always looked at the *yachid*. He looked at the individual. He looked at what was right for that person, not what was right for him, not what was

(l-r): R' Yehuda Kelemer and R' Chanina at the *hanachas tefillin* of Dovie Hirsch in Yeshiva Toras Chaim

right for the yeshiva. He wanted to know, 'How do we make this person reach his potential? How do we make this person into a *ben Torah*?'"

That's all that mattered.

R' Chanina would advise others, "Be very tolerant of parents and their *hashkafah*. Not everyone is like you, nor are they obligated to be like you." Yoel Judowitz, a Toras Chaim alumnus, wrote, "We were encouraged to explore creativity, to befriend children of all backgrounds..."

At his *levayah,* R' Chanina's approach was clear for all to see. His *yedid nefesh,* R' Yehuda Kelemer, stated that it was an eclectic *levayah.* All kinds of Jews, in all manner of dress, were in attendance, many of whom had learned in Yeshiva Toras Chaim or were parents of students or alumni.

R' Chanina didn't classify people. Rather, R' Kelemer stated, he was like Shevet Dan, the *"me'asef l'chol hamachanos* — the rear guard of all the camps" (*Bamidbar* 10:25). Like Dan, the tribe that traveled in the back and gathered all the remnants from the rest of Klal Yisrael, R' Chanina was the one who took everyone in.

Our Very Own Treasure

AT THE PURIM *SEUDAH* FOLLOWING R' CHANINA'S *PETIRAH,* HIS CHILdren opened their father's *Chiddushei Harim,* one of his favorite *sefarim,* and saw that he'd underlined a thought on the topic of Purim (*Chiddushei Harim al haTorah, Inyanei Purim*). The Gemara (*Megillah* 5b) teaches, *"Rebbi netiah shel simchah nata,"* Rabbi Yehudah HaNasi planted a sapling on Purim; it was a planting of joy.

The Chiddushei Harim expounds upon the Gemara. Every person in Klal Yisrael has his unique potential, his specific planting, which is different from the next person. This planting should be done with pride, with joy, knowing that this is his mission. It should be a *netiah shel simchah.*

After reading the words of the Chiddushei Harim again and again, R' Chanina's children all voiced the same thought. "Abba embodied these words. Like his rebbi, his life's mission was to help his *talmidim* fulfill their unique potential, their specific planting."

To underscore this point, R' Chanina would retell a well-known story he heard from R' Shlomo about R' Isaac of Cracow.

Before it was destroyed in World War II, there was an old shul called R' Isaac's R' Yekel's shul, named after Isaac, the son of Yekel (Yaakov). How did this shul come into existence?

> *Legend has it that one night, Isaac, a poor yet pious man, dreams of a bridge in Prague, with a treasure chest beneath it, right by the river's edge. He has never been to Prague and doesn't even know if there are any bridges in the city. Even so, the images are still vivid in his mind when he awakens. He tells his wife about the dream, and they both have a good laugh. Silly dreams.*
>
> *The next night, he has the same dream. The same city, the same river, the same bridge, the same spot where the treasure is supposedly buried. The next morning, he tells his wife about the dream. "Two nights in a row, the same dream. The same Prague. The same bridge. The same treasure. Something is going on." This time they don't laugh too much about it. But his wife says, "Who knows? Maybe it's something you ate before you went to sleep that's causing these strange dreams."*
>
> *The third night, he has the same dream, with exactly the same picture, to the last detail. He wakes up in a sweat, certain that the Al-mighty is sending him a message. "I'm going to Prague," he tells his wife. "I'm going to look for that bridge." His wife, a*

good, sincere woman, does not object. She packs some food for him, and he is off.

Not having any money for coach fare, Isaac has to go by foot to Prague. It takes him weeks and weeks, until finally he arrives in Prague. Which looks exactly like the city in his dreams. He asks people in the street if there is a river with a bridge, and he describes the bridge of his dreams. They direct him to a particular bridge, and to his amazement, it is exactly the bridge of his dreams. The river, the riverbank, everything is exactly the same.

Just one thing is different. In his dream, the spot on the riverbank where the treasure is buried is deserted, but now, there is a fly in the ointment. An army sits directly on the spot. There are tents everywhere, and sentries are patrolling the perimeter. The situation seems hopeless. How can he dig for the treasure with an army camp right on the spot? What can he do? He is not prepared to turn around and return to Cracow empty-handed. So he sits in the distance and stares at the army camp. Perhaps they'll eventually break camp and move on to another place, and he'll be able to dig for his treasure.

One day passes. Two days. Three. Four. It dawns on the soldiers that the Polish Jew with the long caftan and long peyos is sitting and watching them. He must be a spy. They arrest him and bring him to the commandant.

The commandant looks at the hapless Isaac and realizes that this is no spy. "Tell me, my good fellow," he asks, "what are you doing here? You know that you are facing very serious charges. Spies are executed. So it would be wise to tell me the truth."

Terrified, Isaac tells him the story exactly as it happened. The commandant laughs. "You foolish bumpkin! You walk all the way from Cracow to check out a dream? But you know what? I believe you. You are free to go." R' Isaac breathes a sigh of relief and turns to leave.

"By the way," adds the commandant, "before you go, let me tell you a strange coincidence. I've had a similar, recurring dream for the last week. I've been dreaming about such-and-such an address in Cracow — I don't even know if such a place exists — and that there is a treasure buried under the oven. Isn't that a funny thing?"

Isaac nods in agreement and leaves as quickly as he can. He can't contain himself. The address in Cracow does exist. In fact, it is his own house. He can't wait to get out of Prague and return home.

Back in Cracow, he digs under the oven and finds the buried treasure, a box full of gold coins, just as he had dreamed. He had to walk all the way to Prague to discover that the treasure is right there in his own house!

According to the legend, Isaac used some of his money to build the shul that carried his name. They say that the Rebbe Reb Bunim of P'shis'cha used to tell this story to his new *talmidim*."[2]

Each of us must recognize the treasure and potential lying within, and not look over our shoulders at the strengths and talents others possess.

R' Shlomo once excitedly called over R' Chanina. "R' Chanina, last night I was sitting with a bunch of my *chaverim* at a *simchah* and I had an eye-opening moment, as I looked around the table and recognized the different strengths of each one of my friends. This one is a *gadol* in halachah, that one is a *gadol* in *chesed*, and another one is a *gadol* at understanding *Aggadeta*. This made me realize that I have unique strengths, as well!"

Identifying the unique potential within each child is one of the keys

R' Shlomo Freifeld at R' Chanina's *chasunah*

2. Based on *R' Freifeld Speaks*, ArtScroll Publications, pp. 81-84, R' Yaakov Yosef Reinman.

to *chinuch habanim*. As R' Simcha Wasserman expressed, "Too often, people look at themselves as the first edition of a book, and their children as the second edition — an improved version of themselves. That's a mistake. Each person is a unique individual, and each person must write his own life story." People are allowed to make their own mistakes, and then to grow from them. With this perspective, parents, rebbeim, and *moros* are able to be more patient in their dealings with children.

Following R' Chanina's *petirah*, R' Mordechai Kamenetzky spoke of how that week's *parashah, Vayechi,* highlights the *Birchos Yaakov,* the blessings and observations Yaakov imparted to each of his children. The Torah sums up the blessings with the words (*Bereishis* 49:28), "*Kol eileh shivtei Yisrael shneim asar, v'zos asher diber la'hem avihem vayevareich osam, ish asher k'virchaso beirach osam* — All these are the twelve tribes of Yisrael, and this is what their father spoke to them and blessed them; each man, according to his blessing, he blessed them."

If the Torah is telling us about the personalized blessings for each individual, shouldn't it have employed a singular expression, ending its sentence, "Each man, according to his blessing, he blessed *him* ("*beirach oso*"), not he blessed *them* ("*beirach osam*")?

Reflecting upon the loss of R' Chanina, R' Kamenetzky pointed out how R' Chanina possessed the ability to see every child's blessing as an individual, for each child brings his own brand of *berachah* to the table. "However," R' Kamenetzky posited, "he realized and appreciated that the diversity of blessing is exactly what made Klal Yisrael so special. Each man, according to his blessing, '*beirach osam,*' he blessed them. The fact that everyone was different, dressed differently, acted differently, had different abilities and aspirations, was the blessing for all of us as a Klal."

Sizing Each One Up

R' CHANINA WOULD FREQUENTLY REFER TO AN INCIDENT THAT HAPpened with him and his rebbi, to demonstrate that *chinuch* advice must be dispensed on a case-by-case basis. During his years in Yeshiva Sh'or Yoshuv, Chanina took courses in college at night, mostly to satisfy his mother, who wanted him to have a college degree under his belt. At a certain point, though, Chanina began to second-guess his decision to finish college. He and his friend, who was also enrolled in college and was also having doubts about his choice, went to R' Shlomo to ask his advice. R' Shlomo told Chanina's friend to finish the semester in college and thereafter to remain in yeshiva full-time. Chanina expected to be given the same directive, but R' Shlomo didn't operate that way.

R' Chanina with his mother at his *chasunah*

"Your mother is an *almanah,*" he reminded Chanina. "She so badly wants you to finish school, to get an education. To that end, she's been putting aside money so she can have a son with a college degree. Finish all your coursework, and do it for the sake of your mother. I'm telling you, one day this degree will help you out." (In those days, college was more commonplace among yeshiva *bachurim.*)

Ever the obedient *talmid,* Chanina completed his bachelor's degree. When R' Binyamin Kamenetzky was looking for a menahel for Yeshiva Toras Chaim, R' Shlomo recommended R' Chanina for the position. After hearing what R' Shlomo said about his *talmid,* R' Binyamin Kamenetzky very much wanted to give the job to R' Chanina. However, the board of directors of the yeshiva was hesitant. They wanted someone with a college education, and they weren't sure R' Chanina fit the bill. Then they discovered R' Chanina possessed a bachelor's degree, and the deal was sealed.

As soon as he received the good news, R' Chanina made his way over to his rebbi. Excited for his dear *talmid,* R' Shlomo gave him a huge hug. From his cabinet, he removed a bottle of schnapps and some *mezonos* to make a *l'chaim,* but then he remembered something. "Wait a minute," he said. He picked up his phone and called R' Chanina's mother. As soon as Mrs. Herzberg answered the phone, R' Shlomo congratulated her on her son's new position, and then credited it all to her. "This is thanks to your vision and hard work. You were the one who encouraged your son to complete his degree, and you were the one who helped fund it. You have what to be proud of." Now, R' Shlomo was ready to make a *l'chaim* with R' Chanina.

R' Shlomo could have easily decided that R' Chanina, a budding *talmid chacham,* should leave college immediately and immerse himself full-time in learning. However, after viewing the situation from all angles, R' Shlomo determined that Chanina should remain in college. This experience impacted how R' Chanina related to his *talmidim,* his *baalei batim,* or anyone who came to him for advice. There were no generic answers to any specific question, because although the question may have been the same, each person was different and each situation was different, and therefore the answer was different. It was in large part due to this approach that people gravitated to R' Chanina and sought his counsel.

A 3-year-old boy, Nesanel Meisels,* had hearing issues, which led to speech difficulties. Worried that Nesanel may have learning challenges, his parents brought their concern to R' Chanina. R' Chanina offered an unconventional suggestion, that they send the boy to public school.

Mr. Meisels was aghast. "R' Herzberg," he exclaimed, "how can you sit behind your desk with a beard and *peyos* and advise me to send my son to public school?"

"Don't worry," R' Chanina countered with his usual calm. "You'll see, everything will be okay."

Still not pacified, Mr. Meisels approached two of his rabbanim. "There is a man with a beard and *peyos* telling me to send my child to public school. Should I listen to him?"

When they learned the identity of the "man with a beard and *peyos,*" both rabbanim responded, "If R' Chanina says to send your child to public school, you send him. No questions asked."

Nesanel went to public school, a school that was able to offer the necessary resources to properly develop his speech. A year or two later, he was enrolled in yeshiva. He was not just up to par; he even skipped a grade a while later. Today, Nesanel is a true *ben Torah.*

But there was no one-size-fits-all.

Soon after R' Chanina's *petirah,* a *talmid* conveyed, "We moved to Woodmere nearly 20 years ago. Due to my special education needs and our dire financial situation, my mother felt that public school would be the best option for me. Yet we still looked into area yeshivos. Upon checking out Yeshiva Toras Chaim, my mother mentioned to R' Herzberg that she was considering placing me in the public school system. R' Herzberg made it clear to my mother that a Jewish child does not belong in public school and assured her that both concerns of hers could be worked out.

"What surprised my mother even more was that he strongly discouraged her from giving me additional time in the *limudei kodesh* resource room, explaining that I should just be a child. He was 100 percent right. All the district services I received were taking their toll on me socially. Whatever free time I was offered was thus cherished, enabling me to create lifelong friendships in yeshiva."

R' Chanina knew people. He knew children. For one child, public school was the answer; for the other, he wouldn't hear of it. And for a third, something else entirely was the called-for resolution.

Zevi,* a seventh-grader who couldn't sit still, found trouble before it found him and constantly disrupted the class. So much so that the rebbi could barely teach with Zevi around. But that was only during *limudei kodesh*. For some reason, during general studies he conformed, behaving and participating nicely.

Everything the rebbi and parents tried to get Zevi's behavior to improve during *limudei kodesh* seemed to backfire. It reached a point in which the parents were thinking seriously of transferring him to public school, where he wouldn't need to deal with the issues that kept coming up in *limudei kodesh*.

R' Chanina couldn't bear seeing a Jewish child placed in public school, and he resolved to work on it. After some time, he came upon a solution. R' Chanina paid a visit to a local jewelry store that sold and repaired watches and asked to speak to the owner. "Hi, my name is Chanina Herzberg. I am the principal of an elementary school not far from here. I was wondering if you had any use for a talented 13-year-old, who could learn from you how to fix watches. He could be your apprentice. It wouldn't cost you anything and he could be a big help to you." The owner thought about it and said, "Sure, no problem. I'm willing to try it out."

Every morning, Zevi went to yeshiva for davening and breakfast, after which R' Chanina would unobtrusively drive him to his "job" as "watch apprentice." During lunch, R' Chanina would slip out of yeshiva to pick up Zevi and drive him back to yeshiva. Zevi felt accomplished, and his self-esteem was slowly built up. He continued to grow, eventually "mensching out" and becoming an *ehrliche Yid.*

Many years later, after R' Chanina had already passed away, his wife was traveling from Eretz Yisrael to America when she bumped into Zevi's sister. "Mrs. Herzberg, you know, your husband saved my brother's life!"

It Boils Down to Ratzon

TOWARD THE END OF EIGHTH GRADE, SIMCHA* WAS HEADED DOWN A slippery slope. His eighth-grade rebbi got wind of his situation and told the menahel about it. R' Chanina called Simcha into his office one morning and stated without preamble, "Simcha, I hear you're up to no good." Simcha responded with a mischievous smile and an impish yes.

R' Chanina could have easily criticized, reprimanded, and scolded him for his actions. But he knew, with his innate ability, that such an approach wouldn't help. Instead, he turned to the boy and asserted, "Simcha, you can do better," and then reiterated, "Simcha, you're better than that."

Within a month or two, Simcha realized that the menahel was right. "I *can* do better," he would tell himself, and he stopped misbehaving. Later that year, Simcha was ready to choose a high school. As he made his decision, R' Chanina's words, "Simcha, you can do better…Simcha, you're better than that," kept playing in his ears. And he knew he had to select the high school that brought out the best in him.

During the *shivah,* Simcha recounted his story, maintaining that R' Chanina had saved his life and that he was forever grateful to him.

"Had I continued down that dark path, I'm afraid to think where I would have ended up. Throughout our conversation, he said these lines over and over, imbuing me with the assurance that I really could do better, that I could overcome whatever I was struggling with, that I must strive to do better."

While R' Hutner, R' Shlomo's rebbi, never met the Chazon Ish, R' Avraham Yeshayah Karelitz, he had a special reverence for him, a reverence passed down to R' Shlomo. R' Shlomo merited meeting the Chazon Ish and spending several hours in conversation with him.

R' Shlomo would recap the Chazon Ish's take on achieving greatness. True *gadlus,* he averred, has nothing to do with natural *kishron,* mental acuity, but diligence and determination. The Chazon Ish then listed three *gedolim* who developed into bright stars in the annals of our history, through sheer perseverance and grit.

When repeating the details of this encounter, R' Chanina summed it up with a bang. "By the way, my rebbi revealed the names of those *gedolim*. It will blow you away. The Netziv, R' Naftali Tzvi Yehudah Berlin; the Kovno Rav, R' Yitzchak Elchanan Spector; and the Ketzos HaChoshen, R' Aryeh Leib HaKohen Heller.

"In *lashon hakodesh,*" he went on, still quoting his rebbi, "the word רצון, *desire,* has the same letters as the word צנור, *pipeline.* If a person has the desire to do, to succeed, to perform, he creates a special pipeline between him and *Hakadosh Baruch Hu,* through which *siyata d'Shmaya* comes pouring down."

The Chazon Ish

He continued (in the name of R' Meir Shapiro), "Hashem told Avraham (*Bereishis* 15:5), 'Look, please, at the sky and count the stars, if it is possible to count them.' And then Hashem said, 'So will your children be.' Of course, Avraham followed the command of Hashem and went outside and started counting the stars. But Hashem told him in the same sentence that doing so was impossible. So why did He tell Avraham to count them in the first place?

"Hashem was teaching Avraham an invaluable lesson. Even though, *b'derech hateva*, it is impossible to count all the stars, He still said, 'I want you to begin, I want you to try. You do your share and I'll help you with the rest. It doesn't matter if it's possible or not, because with *siyata d'Shmaya*, anything is possible.'

"Hashem explained to Avraham, 'The same will apply to your children. I want them to know this lesson, as well.' Whenever something needs to be done, if it is the right thing to do, don't worry whether it is possible or not. You have to do what you can, and then Hashem will help with the rest."

If we have the *ratzon* and apply our determination and grit to learn and to grow in our learning, anything can happen. The potential is there; it is up to us to bring it out.

Chapter 10

Al Pi Darko: The Role of a Mechanech

IN DISCUSSING THE GOAL OF A YESHIVA, R' SHLOMO QUOTED A STORY he heard from R' Leizer Platchinsky, the grandson of the Alter of Slabodka. When the Alter prepared to establish a yeshiva in Slabodka, he davened and fasted that all should go well, and then proceeded methodically.

Building Up Talmidim

First, he asked R' Yisrael Salanter, "What is a yeshiva? In other words, what philosophy must a yeshiva follow?"

R' Shlomo Freifeld speaking at an Agudah Convention

Based on the *pasuk* (*Yeshayah* 57:15), "*Ki koh amar ram v'nisa shochein ad v'kadosh Shemo, marom v'kadosh eshkon v'es daka u'shefal ruach l'hachayos ruach shefalim u'l'hachayos lev nidka'im* — So says the exalted and uplifted One, Who abides forever and Whose Name is holy: 'I abide in exaltedness and holiness, but I am with the despondent and lowly of spirit, to revive the spirit of the lowly and to revive the heart of the despondent,'" R' Yisrael

R' Chanina uplifting the spirits of his *talmidim*; to the left is R' Yitzy Bald

simply stated, *"L'hachayos ruach shefalim u'l'hachayos lev nidka'im,"* the purpose of a yeshiva is to revive the spirit of the lowly and to revive the heart of the despondent. In R' Shlomo's words, "We have to give *chizuk* to broken *keilim*; we have to fill *keilim* of big *baalei kishron*." A yeshiva's purpose is *l'hachayos,* to revive and give life!

R' Chanina would cite the *pasuk* and then, like his rebbi, and like the Alter and R' Yisrael Salanter, exhort his listeners to follow in the ways of Hashem, Who, despite His sanctity and grandeur, revives and encourages the lowly and despondent. "A yeshiva is there to BUILD UP PEOPLE! Of course, we need to educate the children with a formal curriculum, but never forget the true motto: Build! Build! Build!"

R' Yisroel Besser, author of *Reb Shlomo,* who spent time with R' Chanina when writing the book about R' Chanina's rebbi, relayed, "R' Chanina, a *talmid muvhak* of R' Shlomo Freifeld, absorbed his rebbi's ability to use words like an artist uses ink. He was able to create happiness and uplift spirits in any situation."

R' Chanina was always looking to build people up, and this was most apparent in his role as *mechanech.* One of his seventh-grade *talmidim* from his Tiferes Moshe days reflected on his ability to pinpoint the positive attributes of each *talmid.* "He looked for every possible way to build up the *talmidim*. If a *talmid* knew how to *teitch* a Gemara well but had difficulty with *havanah,* he focused on what the *talmid* was good at. He gave the *talmid* the feeling that *teitch* was the most important thing

R' Chanina connecting with *talmidim*

in the world. And if there was a *talmid* who excelled at *havanah* and not *teitch,* he gave the *talmid* the feeling that *havanah* was the most important thing in the world. The *talmidim* felt successful, and success bred success. Somehow, he managed to bring out the best in every *talmid*." As R' Shlomo said in the name of his rebbi, "Nothing builds confidence like a little bit of success."

As menahel, R' Chanina read through every report card, the grades and the comments, and gave feedback to the rebbeim when necessary. He urged the rebbeim not to include negative comments or to give a *gimmel* or *dalet*. "If you have something negative to say about a *talmid,* don't put it in writing. Rather, call the parent and express it verbally. A child may come across the report card three years later and say to himself, 'This is what my rebbi thought of me,' which will leave a negative taste in his mouth."

By the end of third grade, Shimon,* a *talmid* in Yeshiva Toras Chaim, had defined himself as a troublemaker. Shimon and another boy, Yaakov,* would plan when and how they were going to misbehave and then carry through, disrupting the class and influencing other boys to join.

One day, R' Chanina called Shimon and Yaakov into his office. "I have a special prize for both of you, an electronic organizer."

"Why are you giving this prize to us?" they asked in confusion.

"I'm giving it to you because you two are 'organizers,' and as 'student activists,' your help is needed to push the class in the right direction. You are both leaders and the boys in the class will listen to you. I'm giving the electric organizer to you so you can recognize your potential."

Looking back at that moment, Shimon said, "R' Herzberg didn't say one negative word, not that we were in a bad place, not that we had behavior issues, not that we were wise guys. Rather, he focused on the positive. That moment completely changed our behavior. We stopped looking at ourselves as staging an uprising, and instead we started looking at ourselves positively, as skilled boys who could be positive leaders. That confidence and outlook — of a leader — stayed with me until today. It made me who I am!"

R' Chanina's door was always wide open to his "activists"; they came to discuss different issues they had in the yeshiva, and R' Chanina took them seriously. They also helped R' Chanina decide which trips would work for their class and which prizes they would like. In addition, R' Chanina counted on them for feedback from the other boys in the class about the school's special programs and activities. Once, before a trip, he called in the cook in front of Shimon and Yaakov, asking him to please order certain food items because his "student activists" recommended them for the trip.

His door was always open to his *talmidim*

R' Chanina with *talmidim* during a Lag BaOmer trip

This didn't continue for just a week, a month, or a year. When the two of them were in sixth grade, three years after the original "deal," R' Chanina announced that no roller blades would be allowed on the Lag BaOmer trip to the park. Shimon approached R' Chanina and asked if he could please change his mind and explained why. The next day, R' Chanina came into Shimon's class and retracted his initial announcement, stating that he would be allowing roller blades on the trip. He even made a point of saying that he changed his mind because Shimon asked. That day, R' Chanina demonstrated to his students, *My door is always open to you. If you have a request, come and ask and you'll see, I'm a reasonable person.*

Shimon's story doesn't end there. Every year from third grade and on, he got the feeling that his rebbeim, as well as the rebbeim from the parallel class, were going out of their way to shower him with extra attention. When Shimon was in seventh grade, his rebbi said to him, "Shimon, I heard that last year you occasionally presented *divrei Torah* to your class on Fridays, and you did a great job. We're going to institute a new program in our class. Every week, two boys will share *divrei Torah,* and I want you to be part of the rotation." As Shimon's confidence grew, he began speaking at other venues within the yeshiva, as well, such as in shul after davening. His eighth-grade rebbi told Shimon that any time he shares *divrei Torah* on Fridays, he would receive extra credit toward his Gemara grade. Additionally, he was chosen as *gabbai sheini* at the daily *minyan.*

It was only in eighth grade that Shimon's rebbi disclosed to him that it was R' Chanina who had orchestrated the entire "build up Shimon campaign," telling the rebbeim to do whatever it took to boost Shimon's confidence and give him *chizuk*; he wanted to assure he remained on the straight and narrow, to channel his *kochos* toward appropriate pursuits. This, too, was based on a teaching of R' Shlomo: No child left behind!

On the way to R' Chanina's mother's *levayah,* R' Chanina and his son passed a billboard that read, "No man is so tall as when he stoops to help a child." R' Chanina jotted down the aphorism, mumbling to himself, "That is so true, so true..." He was going to bury his mother, yet he still had the presence of mind to focus on growing and showing respect to others.

R' Chanina's *talmid* was extremely tall, already standing at 6'5" in eighth grade. R' Chanina would tell him, "Hey, buddy, your height is really based on how high you can lift someone else, not on how many times you look down on him." At an opening meeting for his staff, R' Chanina declared, "In our yeshiva, the underdog will be celebrated just like the top boys in the yeshiva. The underdogs are the most vulnerable and therefore need extra *chizuk*."

One day during dismissal, a bunch of boys were standing together when Yechiel,* a boy from a well-to-do family who was beginning to display bullying tendencies, noticed that Shaya,* who came from a poor family, was wearing cheap sneakers. In front of the crowd, Yechiel shouted disparagingly, "Hey, look at the sneakers you're wearing, from Payless! I'm wearing Nikes!"

"No man is so tall as when he stoops to help a child."

Shaya was broken and didn't know what to respond. Little did he know that his savior was in earshot. At that moment, R' Chanina happened to be passing by and heard the comment. "Everyone here shops at Payless!" he belted out.

R' Chanina proceeded to give

an impromptu *mussar shmuess.* "Boys, you're going to learn in time that the sneakers you wear make no difference. It's where you will walk and talk in those sneakers that will make a difference. It's about what's on the inside that counts. It's not about the money you have, it's about what you do with it. As you grow older, you're going to ask yourselves: *Where did these sneakers take me?"*

Just warming up, R' Chanina gave Yechiel an assignment. "Tomorrow, come back and tell me what you are going to achieve in life with these sneakers. What great things are you going to accomplish with everything you have?"

Yoni* witnessed the scene and related that at that moment R' Chanina was successful on two fronts: lifting Shaya's spirits and overturning Yechiel's attitude regarding what's important in life.

Mr. Daniel Winkler, principal of general studies in Yeshiva Toras Chaim, noted, "One of the first things R' Herzberg told me was, 'Mr. Winkler, you can catch a lot more flies with honey than with vinegar.' That line resonated with me through all these years. His sweetness, love, understanding, and warmth toward each boy in the yeshiva were contagious, and each rebbi, teacher, and member of the administration emulated that vision. This kindness was, and continues to be, the foundation of each child becoming a true mensch and *ben Torah.*"

R' Chanina would walk through the hallways, building up *talmidim* with compliments about their learning, manner of dress, and even haircuts. If a boy was wearing new sneakers, a new coat, or new glasses, R' Chanina was sure to notice and compliment the child. "Your rebbi told me you're learning up a storm; keep on *shteiging,*" or "You're looking handsome!" was often heard in the corridors, as the menahel walked by.

A highly successful menahel was looking for a yeshiva for his children, so he and his wife brought their son for an interview at Yeshiva Toras Chaim. After meeting with the parents and their son in his office, R' Chanina showed them around the school. Many years later, the menahel told R' Chanina's son that in those few minutes of observing R' Chanina's interactions with the *talmidim,* he learned more about *chinuch* than he learned in all his years in college. "The way he knew each boy's name, the way he found ways to compliment them and build them up as he walked by, it was something special."

The kind words were not made up. He made sure to find the good in each *talmid*. As R' Moshe Monczyk, a former *talmid,* pointed out, even the way he waved at his *talmidim* — with his right hand significantly above his head — showed a higher level of recognition.

In turn, the *talmidim* would do anything for him. One *talmid* articulated, "If R' Herzberg said, 'Jump,' we asked, 'How high?'" Dr. Jason Ostreicher, a Yeshiva Toras Chaim alumnus, elaborated. "In school, R' Herzberg was the person we were trying to impress; he was the person we were trying to avoid causing any trouble to. We all strove for his approval...we wanted to be his focus. And he made us feel like his focus. He would make every *talmid* feel like he was the only person in the room. He made the parents feel like he made the *talmidim* feel, like they were the only people who were important. And when you feel special, you want to do more to impress that person. It makes you want to do more to become worthy of that focus."

When Shua* was in fifth grade at Yeshiva Toras Chaim, he found a five-dollar bill on the floor in school. He gave it to R' Chanina so he could help find the owner. R' Chanina took the bill, and Shua left his office. The next morning after davening, with all the students from fifth through eighth grade present, R' Chanina stood up at the *bimah* to make an announcement. He proceeded to tell the story of a boy in yeshiva who had found five dollars the previous day, and instead of putting it in his pocket, took the time to try and find the true owner.

Shua, who was sitting in his seat, was taken by surprise; he had almost forgotten about his find by then. While R' Chanina was making the announcement to try to locate the owner of the money, it was clear that he was also trying to make his *talmid* feel special.

A rebbi in Yeshiva Toras Chaim would invite R' Chanina to return big *bechinos* to the *talmidim*. The tests had two parts: Part I and Part II. When R' Chanina passed out the tests, he would zero in on the part of the test with the higher mark, always focusing on the positive.

R' Chanina had no interest in publicity, for himself or for the school.

It was unusual to see his picture in the paper, and that was exactly how he wanted it. However, if placing a picture of a *talmid* in the newspaper would build up the *talmid* and make him happy, he was all for it.

R' Chanina would pop into classes for a short, impromptu discussion with the boys and their rebbi, kibbitzing with the children in a *geshmak* and fun way. His visits to the classroom were exciting for everyone, "events" they all looked forward to. Inevitably, the conversation would shift toward how the *talmidim* were *shteiging* and maturing in their *avodas Hashem.* R' Chanina always made sure to build up the *talmidim* in the eyes of their rebbi, as well as the rebbi in the eyes of the *talmidim*.

R' Shlomo Pfeiffer, who taught sixth grade in Yeshiva Toras Chaim, recalls how R' Chanina taught the rebbeim to look at each boy in a positive light while simultaneously bringing *simchah* into the classroom. From time to time, R' Chanina would open the door of R' Pfeiffer's classroom, and with outstretched hands and a huge smile, exclaim, "Oh, my favorite class! How's it going?" A young *talmid* remembered, "One time when I was in third grade, R' Herzberg came in while we were learning. He said we're a super-duper-luper-wuper class!" As a rebbi in Yeshiva Tiferes Moshe, he would say to his class, "I'm going to go buy a crowd pleaser, a two-liter bottle of Coke, because you are learning so well!"

With a *talmid*

Mrs. Elana Fertig, who was fortunate to watch R' Chanina in action on a daily basis, summed it up, "From R' Herzberg, I learned the concept of 'hugging with words.'"

Those compliments and "word hugs" kept coming. Though Yissachar* was a force to be reckoned with throughout elementary school, he eventually shaped up, becoming a true *ben Torah* and going into *chinuch*. In time, he landed a job in a prestigious yeshiva as principal. The summer before his job was to begin, R' Yissachar met R' Chanina at a *bris*. R' Yissachar greeted R' Chanina and then made sure to share the wonderful news with his former menahel.

R' Chanina pulled R' Yissachar close by his lapel and while shaking his finger at him, proclaimed, "Yissachar, I knew you would be great! I never lost hope in you! I'm so proud of you!"

Those few words of *chizuk* meant the world to R' Yissachar, an interaction etched in his memory. "I still can't bring myself to erase his number from my phone because he still lives on inside of me," R' Yissachar admitted.

Years later, R' Chanina was still building his *talmidim*.

It wasn't always easy to keep building up the boys, to keep up the positive atmosphere, especially at the end of his life. Yet to R' Chanina, this was a number-one priority. While undergoing treatment for cancer, R' Chanina's hair started to fall out, and he was told that within several weeks he would lose his beard.

R' Chanina was distraught. Though he wanted so badly to be in yeshiva, to him, being around *talmidim* without a beard wasn't an option, for two reasons: First, he was concerned that since most of the children weren't capable of understanding the circumstances, they would be scared and uncomfortable. Second, his life's mission was to build up *talmidim*, to create a *ruach* in the yeshiva of positivity and warmth. Being there without a beard would create a negative, unsettling atmosphere and would constitute a contradiction to what he was trying to accomplish. If he couldn't do what he was supposed to do, it would be better for him not to be there at all.

Knowing how much this meant to her husband, Mrs. Herzberg researched fake beards used in professional plays and theaters and

R′ Chanina (back row, third from right), continuing in yeshiva with his fake beard, with his dear *talmidim* as they celebrate receiving their first *siddur*

ordered them. Every morning, she would paste a beard on her husband's face using a special glue and each evening she would take it off. Besides being a very time-consuming process, a few hours each day, it was also a very painful one. At times, R′ Chanina would cry out in pain from the tugging and plucking and stickiness on his delicate skin.

But R′ and Mrs. Herzberg soldiered on. The two of them would awaken every morning at around 4:00 a.m. and begin the process, so R′ Chanina could be ready to go to yeshiva by 7:00. There was nothing R′ Chanina and his extraordinarily dedicated wife wouldn't do or go through for his *talmidim*.

When R′ Chanina was very sick, R′ Zev Davidowitz visited him. At that time, R′ Chanina spoke openly about the challenges involved in wearing the fake beard. "I feel the worst for my wife," he said, "because of all she has to do in regard to my beard. You have no idea what she does for me."

"This made a big impact on me," R′ Davidowitz later shared. "It was the first time he let his guard down in front of me; it was so real."

Whenever R′ Chanina underwent a health issue, such as the saga of his final illness or the time period in which he had problems with his legs, he would go out of his way to make sure his *talmidim* did not sense that he was uncomfortable. He could be walking slowly through the halls of the yeshiva, clearly in pain, yet when he saw a *talmid*, he would stop, stand up tall, put a smile on his face, and greet the *talmid* joyfully and with a kind word, as if everything was fine.

All part of creating an atmosphere of building, of *simchah.*

Good Morning

R' CHANINA PRIDED HIMSELF ON THE FRIENDLY, WARM, LOVING atmosphere in Yeshiva Toras Chaim, and he worked hard to hire rebbeim and *moros* who projected that friendliness, warmth, and love. Because, as he put it, "That's what Yiddishkeit is all about — that love that one person gives to another person... That's what the yeshiva is built upon: *middos,* smiling, saying hello to someone else, giving someone a *shalom aleichem.* And I believe that when you walk into the building, you feel that spirit, you feel that *ruach* in the yeshiva."

When R' Chanina'a son became a menahel, he imparted a piece of priceless advice. "Over the course of your day as menahel, it's very likely that the most important thing you will do is stand outside and greet the *talmidim.* Not everyone understands the importance of it, but I'm telling you, it's a game changer."

R' Chanina made it a point to say a personal good morning to the *talmidim* as they entered the yeshiva. The good morning was more than a cordial gesture; it was an *avodah gedolah,* a call to the *talmid* of "You can do it!"

If a boy could use some extra *chizuk,* R' Chanina would dispense a quick dose of encouragement along with his good morning. To one *talmid,* he would say, "Keep it up!" to another, "Good luck on the test today; I'm sure you'll do great!" and to yet another, "Make me proud today!"

While greeting the *talmidim,* R' Chanina got to hear about the mazel tov's in each *talmid*'s family, along with other tidbits that warranted a quick response that could make a child's day. It was his opportunity as menahel to connect to every *talmid,* to get to know him in a real way.

R' Marty Katz, a parent of Yeshiva Toras Chaim *talmidim,* reminisced how his children

would come home from yeshiva with comments such as "R' Herzberg shook my hand today as I came into yeshiva!" or "R' Herzberg said hello to me this morning!" or "R' Herzberg asked me how I'm doing!" Through those seemingly small interactions, R' Chanina made them feel special.

Following R' Chanina's *petirah,* an elementary school *talmid* wrote, "R' Herzberg did a lot for this yeshiva and for me. When I saw his smile, it made me want to smile just as much as he did. He gave off this warm feeling, like Hashem was next to him, which felt great." Many other *talmidim,* young and old, described the positive vibes R' Chanina exuded through his smile and his warm and personal greetings.

Moshe* was in second grade when his family moved to the Five Towns. They planned to check out several yeshivos for Moshe, beginning with Yeshiva Toras Chaim. R' Chanina met with Moshe and his father, and then proceeded to show them around the yeshiva.

As they were walking out, Moshe's father informed him, "Moshe, this is the yeshiva you're going to attend."

"But Abba," Moshe inquired, "aren't we going to check out other yeshivos?"

"No, this is the place where you belong. You know why? Because as we walked through the school, the principal greeted every student by name, often with a personal comment to go along with the greeting. This is the type of person I want to entrust with my children's *chinuch.*"

AS A *TALMID* IN YESHIVA TORAS CHAIM, CHARLIE WAS *FARHERED* SEVeral times by R' Nissen Telushkin. Many years later, he recollected,

The Purpose of the Farher

"When I was a *talmid* in Yeshiva Toras Chaim, there were two types of *farhers*. One was given by a certain *talmid chacham,* who *farhered* the class to show each boy how much he *should have known*. After those *farhers,* I walked out feeling terrible, as I never did well. Then there was the 'R' Telushkin *farher.'* He *farhered* to show you how much you *knew*. When I walked out of the 'R' Telushkin *farher,'* I felt like a million dollars. When I *farher* a class," R' Chanina concluded, "I give the 'R' Telushkin *farher*.'"

R' Scharhon related that when R' Chanina would come to give his class a *farher,* he and R' Chanina had a secret code: "R' Telushkin." If R' Scharhon noticed that a particular *talmid,* who generally didn't know the material that well, was able to answer a specific question that R' Chanina had just posed, R' Scharhon would interject, "'R' Telushkin,' you didn't call on this boy yet," or "'R' Telushkin,' I think this boy has an answer to this question." After hearing the code, R' Chanina would call on the boy and praise him to the sky when he got the answer right. And if there was still a boy who hadn't done well on the *farher,* R' Chanina would ask R' Scharhon to send the boy to R' Chanina's office, so the *talmid* could say a piece of Gemara that he knew well and receive his share of praise.

As R' Chanina saw it, the purpose of a *bechinah* is to show the *talmid*

R' Chanina visiting R' Scharhon's class

The Chazon ish (between R' Yaakov Halpern and R' Eliyahu Dessler) *farhering talmidim* in Bnei Brak

how much he knows and how good he is, to demonstrate to him what he can be and what he can do. It is *not* for the rebbi to see how much the *talmid* knows; he should already know how his *talmidim* are faring without the *bechinah.*

The *sefer Maaseh Ish* (Vol. 7, p. 61) describes a *farher* given by the Chazon Ish. "We received many *farhers* from the Chazon Ish," recalled a *talmid* who grew up in Bnei Brak, "and each time we were certain that he did everything he could to make each boy feel good about how he did on the *bechinah,* that the boy would experience *seva ratzon* and walk away with a renewed *cheishek* to continue learning."

That was the purpose of the Chazon Ish's *farher.*

And R' Telushkin's.

And R' Chanina's.

Levi,* an eighth-grader, was struggling in Gemara. Before a *farher* with R' Chanina, he was extremely nervous and uncomfortable. Sensing his discomfort, R' Chanina made sure to ask him an easy question.

"I walked away feeling so proud," recalled Levi.

R' Gershon Greenberg shared a tip he learned from R' Chanina: to give extra points on tests to reward *talmidim.* Most boys take their grades seriously and extra points will make them excited. And if the rebbi already knows where his *talmid* is holding, then additional points will not give him a false impression. Moreover, since the objective of the test is to build up *talmidim,* additional points will only build them up more.

IN THE LAST *CHINUCH* CONVERSATION THAT YITZCHOK HERZBERG had with his father, he asked R' Chanina to share a piece of *chinuch* advice from R' Shlomo. R' Chanina thought for a moment and said, "My rebbi told me, 'Always remember, everything you say or don't say to a *talmid* could change your *talmid*'s life forever.'"

The Right Words at the Right Time

Through his words, R' Chanina was careful to change his *talmidim*'s lives for the better. R' Hershel Billet, rabbi of the Young Israel of Woodmere, wrote about R' Chanina following his *petirah*, "With skilled phrases, he built each boy in a way that made the child feel like a king."

R' Moshe Greenspan, an eighth-grade rebbi in Yeshiva Ketana of Long Island, related a vignette that took place when he was a student in Yeshiva Toras Chaim. "I'll never forget the time R' Herzberg gave me a compliment in front of the other boys. It made me feel special and gave me a boost of self-confidence, which I didn't even realize I needed. R' Herzberg knew exactly what each child needed, and he was there to give it at the right time and in the most appropriate way. I always think of him when I try to find a nice word or make a nice gesture to a friend or *talmid*. What can I say to be *mechazek* him? How can I change his day? How can I put a smile on his face? What would R' Herzberg have said or done?"

R' Chanina advised rebbeim not to let children go home in a bad mood, and he himself worked to make sure that didn't happen. A student in R' Chanina's class in Yeshiva Tiferes Moshe, Nati Sternberg,* was going through an emotionally challenging experience at home. One day as he was teaching, R' Chanina noticed Nati's despondent mood. As R' Chanina walked around the class, he dropped a note on Nati's desk. Nati looked at the note, smiled, and put it in his pocket.

With a *talmid* at his *hanachas tefillin*

Over 20 years later, when R' Chanina was a menahel, a middle-aged man walked into his office to enroll his son in Yeshiva Toras Chaim. It was Nati. After exchanging pleasantries and reminiscing about the good old days in his class in Tiferes Moshe, Mr. Sternberg proceeded to take an old, creased piece of paper from his wallet. "R' Herzberg, take a look at this piece of paper. Does it look familiar?" R' Chanina recognized his handwriting but had no recollection of writing the note.

Nati went on to remind R' Chanina about the story behind that little note. "R' Herzberg, this piece of paper has stayed with me all these years, and has served as an unlimited source of *chizuk* from that very day until today."

On the paper was a smiley face with the saying, "When you smile, the world smiles with you!"

An older English teacher in Yeshiva Toras Chaim passed away suddenly from a heart attack. A professional was called in to speak to the teacher's class, to discuss what happened and how to deal with it. R' Chanina stood in the back of the room as the professional spoke to the class.

A boy raised his hand with a question. "Could it be that our teacher had a heart attack because we didn't behave in his class?"

A tough question.

R' Chanina spoke up from the back. "Don't worry! I guarantee you that when I was your age, I was much worse!"

Many years later, that same professional was giving a lecture on the topic of trauma. He repeated this story as an example of how one wise comment defused a stressful situation, lifting the burden of guilt from the boys and enabling them to still feel good about themselves.

In the early 1980's, a family wanted to enroll their children in Yeshiva Toras Chaim and made an appointment with R' Chanina. Since it was during the summer, the interview took place in the Sh'or Yoshuv bungalow colony, where the Herzbergs were staying. "I'll never forget that first meeting," the father recalled. "We arrived at the bungalow colony and started walking toward R' Herzberg's bungalow. R' Herzberg saw us coming and walked out of his bungalow, a huge presence of a man, to greet us. My children were looking at him, mouths open. He went right up to my children and asked, 'So what are you? Mets fans or Yankees fans?' My children fell in love with him right away."

He sensed the children's discomfort and knew just what to say.

Ephraim,* an eighth-grader, had an issue. The major event of the year, the eighth-grade graduation trip to Washington D.C., was rapidly approaching, and Ephraim was anything but excited. Hampered by a fear of sleeping away from home, he had never gone to sleepaway camp. How was he going to go on the trip and sleep in the hotel?

"The only thing that gave me comfort," Ephraim recounted, "was the fact that my mother was going to call R' Herzberg and ask him to keep an eye on me."

The big day arrived and the boys loaded the buses. Throughout the day, R' Chanina didn't say a word to Ephraim, but as he got off the bus to enter the hotel, R' Chanina pulled him over and whispered, "Ephraim, are you doing okay?"

That was all he said. No long speeches to make Ephraim feel uncomfortable, just a few calculated words at exactly the right time to make sure everything would work out, and work out it did.

Another eighth-grader, Chaim,* also had an issue with the eighth-grade graduation trip to Washington D.C., but for a different reason. Chaim frequently wet his bed at night, making it complicated for him to sleep with his classmates. Chaim's mother called R' Chanina for advice.

R' Chanina's response? "Don't worry, I'll be going around in the morning to wake up the boys. Just tell Chaim that if he happens to have an accident, he should signal to me at that time, and I'll 'shoot up the room' with a Super Soaker!"

Sometimes, R' Chanina's ability to say the right words at the right time seemed uncanny. Sam Davies, former president of Yeshiva Toras Chaim, described this ability. "At times, I would inform R' Herzberg of a particular issue and he would tell me, 'Don't worry about it. I'm going to take care of it, and things will change.' And that's what happened. He would get involved with boys who were having issues or with classes that were having issues — and things did change. He was like a magician, an illusionist."

There are times in which the right word at the right time means… no words at all. During the annual eighth-grade Shabbaton at Camp JEP in Upstate New York, Motti* totally lost himself, to the point of becoming physical. Called to the rescue, R' Chanina quietly approached Motti, sat down next to him, and calmly put his arms around his shoulder, holding him in place until he settled down and the other boys were out of danger. R' Chanina did not utter a single word throughout the process. When he was finally back to himself, Motti opened up to R' Chanina, detailing what had taken place, and then rejoined the activities.

Without saying a word, R' Chanina communicated to Motti, *I'm right here with you. Everything will be all right.*

To Know Every Child

IN ORDER TO BUILD A BUILDING, A PERSON MUST FAMILIARIZE HIMself with the property and all the strengths and weaknesses within its infrastructure, as well as exactly what kind of materials he will be using and what kind of structure he plans to build; only then can he proceed to actualize his plan. So, too, in *chinuch*. To build a child, one must get to know where the child comes from — his background, his roots, his upbringing — as well as who he is — his nature and *kochos hanefesh* — and what he wants to become. Only then can he be *mechanech* him properly.

The *pasuk* (*Mishlei* 22:6) teaches, "*Chanoch la'naar al pi darko gam ki yazkin lo yasur mimenah* — Train a child according to his way; even when he grows old, he will not turn away from it."

In a *chinuch derashah*, R' Chanina explained the *pasuk* in the name of the Gra (ad loc.).

When educating a child, a parent has to pay attention to the unique *mazel* and nature of the child. Only once he familiarizes himself with these aspects of his child can he proceed to be *mechanech* him. If he is *mechanech* his child in this way, he will achieve the desired result and the *chinuch* will endure into old age!

However, if one doesn't educate his child according to his *mazel* and nature, the child may listen to his parent for the time being, out of fear. But once the yoke of his parent is no longer on the child's neck, he will no longer follow his parents' ways. This is because it is not possible for a person to break his *mazel*.

R' Chanina quoted R' Michel Yehudah Lefkowitz (*Imrei Daas*), who bolsters this with a *pasuk* from *Parashas Pinchas* (*Bamidbar* 27:16): "May Hashem, G-d of the spirits of all flesh, appoint a man over the assembly." Rashi elaborates: Moshe requested of Hashem, Who knows every person's personality, to appoint a leader with the capacity to put up with each individual, *l'fi daato,* according to his personality.

R' Michel Yehudah then cites the Netziv (*Ha'amek Davar* ad loc.), who takes it one step further. The only one able to lead Bnei Yisrael with perfect integrity is the one who understands their needs, without thinking about his personal desires or benefits. This is extremely difficult, conceded R' Chanina, because it's only natural that when a student disobeys his rebbi, his rebbi's personal bias and feelings kick in, which can cause him to deal with the student in a way that is not necessarily in line with the child's personality and tendencies. A *mechanech* needs to overcome this tendency and relate to the student, as Rashi states, *l'fi daato.*

During R' Zvi Soroka's first year of teaching eighth grade at Yeshiva Darchei Torah, he found the adjustment challenging. When he turned to R' Chanina for guidance, R' Chanina admitted, "I also had a difficult time during my first year of teaching, and I asked R' Shlomo Freifeld for advice. R' Shlomo advised me, 'Buy a notebook and on the top of each page write the name of each *talmid,* and underneath write all his strengths and weaknesses. Each day, review the entire notebook, and from time to time come to me with the notebook, and we'll review it together.'

"I did just that," R' Chanina concluded, "and I had incredible *hatzlachah* with that first class."

R' Zvi did as R' Chanina suggested. "After following R' Herzberg's advice," he related, "I was *zocheh* to astounding *hatzlachah* with that class, forging an extremely close bond with those *talmidim*. Many years later, some of those *talmidim* invited me to their *chasunos,* even

R' Chanina with a *talmid* at a succah fair

honoring me with a *berachah* under the *chuppah*. That's how close a bond it was."

R' Chanina stressed another point, as well. "A rebbi has to get to know the *whole* child. *Somehow, someway*, a rebbi needs to get to know his *talmidim* out of the classroom, as well. He is responsible for the whole child."

For this reason, R' Chanina insisted that each rebbi in Yeshiva Toras Chaim remain with his class during recess, instead of having a rotation where one rebbi watches many classes at a time. Although this precluded the rebbeim from taking a break, R' Chanina felt that spending recess with their classes was just too important. To R' Chanina, recess duty is not a duty, but an opportunity. "Recess is the perfect time to get to know the *talmidim* out of the classroom. There are other advantages, as well. It's a great time to build up your *talmidim*, as well as to show them you care... *Hakadosh Baruch Hu* doesn't want us to learn during those times; He wants us to get involved: to make sure that all the boys are included in the game, to break up a fight before it gets out of control... *not* to finish up our personal *sedarim*."

When the idea of a comfortable teachers' room for rebbeim in Yeshiva Toras Chaim was broached, R' Chanina agreed, on one condition. "The room has to be near my office. I want the rebbeim to have to walk past my office as they walk to and from the teachers' room. This will serve as a reminder that as soon as he takes care of his needs, a rebbi returns to his *talmidim*."

His *talmidim* from Yeshiva Tiferes Moshe reminisced how R' Chanina wasn't just concerned about their learning; he was concerned about every aspect of their life. They remember how their rebbi enjoyed watching them play punchball, basketball, and football during recess. He was their biggest fan as he cheered them on. When a *talmid* made a catch or scored a point, he would scream, "Great catch!" or "Way to go!" It wasn't an act to get on the *talmid*'s good side; he genuinely enjoyed every one of his *talmidim*'s successes, whether in learning or in other areas, and the *talmidim* felt it.

R' Chanina also helped the *talmidim* organize their games, ensured they were running properly, and made sure all the boys were included. At times, he would join the games, as well, knowing that this was what particular *talmidim* needed to help them grow. The reasoning was simple. If their rebbi genuinely cared about what was important to *them*, they would care about what was important to *him*. Though R' Chanina played ball with his students, it didn't diminish the respect they had for him. On the contrary, they respected him more. R' Chanina would take a shot and inevitably his shirt would become untucked. Before continuing the game, he would quickly tuck himself in. This sent a subliminal message to his *talmidim* that although he was playing with them, he was their rebbi and needed to act as such.

In his capacity as menahel, R' Chanina made sure to get to know the boys, as well. Mrs. Fertig stated plainly, "R' Herzberg wasn't into data. He knew every child." Mr. Sam Davies mentioned how R' Chanina was unique in the amount of time he spent getting to know each of the hundreds of *talmidim*, and on a personal level.

He did this purposefully, talking to the *talmidim* about their interests, their hobbies, or whatever was on their mind. This helped him

R' Chanina getting to know *talmidim* on a personal level

understand what made each *talmid* tick, his *techunos hanefesh,* his unique *mazel* and nature, so he could educate each one *l'fi daato*. By so doing, he was better able to help each child maximize his growth, helping him reach his own potential, *al pi darko*. Mrs. Elana Fertig observed, "R' Herzberg connected with children at their age level."

As R' Chanina once said, a menahel is not an administrator, he is a *mechanech*! A *mechanech* in every sense of the word. A menahel needs to know every boy in the yeshiva by name, along with his personality, his strengths and weaknesses, and his social standing among his classmates. He needs to understand the child's family dynamics, as well.

If a parent called R' Chanina to discuss an issue with their child, he was able to conduct the initial conversation with the parents without having to tell them, "I need to speak to the rebbi and teacher first to see how he's doing, and I will get back to you." That's not to say that he took a course of action to help the child without checking first with the rebbi and teacher. But he didn't have to depend on their assessment; he knew each child that well.

R' Yaacov Lewis recalled, "Over 20 years ago, when my eldest son was in first grade, I came to school one day to bring him something. It was one of my first times visiting the yeshiva, and I did not know R' Herzberg well. He stopped me in the hall. He knew who I was, knew

R' Chanina and R' Yisroel Kaminetsky greeting each other; on the left is Mrs. Naomi Herzberg.

who my son was, and proceeded to tell me that my son had a good day in the classroom and answered a few questions from his rebbi properly. But he had an altercation on the playground.

"I was amazed that not only did he know both me and my son, but knew exactly everything he had done that day, both in the classroom and during recess. There were over 450 boys in the yeshiva at that time, and he knew each boy's strengths and weaknesses, and even knew their daily routines."

Mesivta menahalim would marvel at how deeply R' Chanina understood each boy, and how honestly he conveyed this knowledge. Following R' Chanina's *petirah,* R' Yisroel Kaminetsky, menahel of DRS High School in Woodmere, wrote, "R' Herzberg was first and foremost an *ish emes*... We spoke often about hundreds of boys over the years, and not once did he ever try to 'sell me a bridge.' He was always honest and on the mark in his description of the boys and their families. I totally trusted him about the boys. While he, of course, wanted me to accept every boy, he also would not lie for them, nor stretch the truth." This, despite the fact that he spent a lot of time and energy making sure that his *talmidim* were accepted into the high schools that fit them best.

R' Chaim Aryeh Zev Ginzberg communicated, "Whenever I called R' Chanina to discuss a boy in the yeshiva whose family I was involved with, R' Chanina's incredible depth and clarity in understanding the inner dynamics of both the boy and his family were unlike anything I'd ever seen before."

R' Shmuel Katz, who served as executive director of Yeshiva Toras Chaim, worked closely with R' Chanina for several years and had his share of stories. He recalled that when deciding which class would have which rebbi for the upcoming school year, R' Chanina spent hours estimating which personalities and educational styles fit the needs of the *talmidim* in the class.

R' Chanina knew about the little things, as well. In R' Shmuel's words, "When talking about R' Herzberg to parents and prospective parents, I would often extol one of his greatest talents. He really got into the *kishkes* of the vast majority of the students in the yeshiva. I used to say that R' Herzberg not only knew why a specific student went to sleep late the night before, but he also knew what the student ate for breakfast and why he skipped lunch." A young couple was looking for a yeshiva for their eldest son, and they were told to send to Yeshiva Toras Chaim. Why? "R' Herzberg knows which children like chocolate milk!"

Knowing each child was very important to R' Chanina. This became apparent when the neighborhood began growing exponentially, and there was a large influx of boys who wanted to attend the yeshiva. The classes were bursting, and the school was no longer able to accommodate the number of families trying to send their boys to Yeshiva Toras Chaim.

At one point, R' Chanina resisted efforts to add an additional class per grade. Since he had his finger on the pulse and knew every boy, his main concern was that if the yeshiva grew too large, the *hanhalah* would no longer be able to know and interact with every boy, and the individual care and warmth of the yeshiva would dissipate. Eventually, the yeshiva needed to expand and R' Chanina doubled down, keeping his finger on the pulse and making sure the yeshiva never lost its personal touch.

Mendy Silber, a parent in Yeshiva Toras Chaim, related how he once received a phone call from R' Chanina in middle of the school day.

"Mendy, is everything all right at home?" R' Chanina asked.

"No," Mendy responded. "My father-in-law was recently hospitalized. Why do you ask?"

"I noticed that your two boys weren't themselves, so I figured something was going on at home."

R' Chanina dancing with a *Sefer Torah* donated by Mr. and Mrs. Mendy Silber

After sharing the story, Mendy added, "This story took place when the yeshiva had three classes per grade, and yet he still knew every child!"

And he didn't forget his *talmidim* later. Avi,* an alumnus of Yeshiva Toras Chaim who had become a *chassan,* was in the supermarket with his *kallah.* Seeing R' Chanina a little farther down the aisle, he said to her, "Come, let's go say hi to my elementary school menahel."

"There's no way he's going to remember your name," his *kallah* insisted.

As they were walking toward R' Chanina, before they had a chance to open their mouths, R' Chanina noticed his *talmid* and called, "*Shalom aleichem,* Avi!"

With Menachem Butler

Menachem Butler relayed, "After we graduated from Yeshiva Toras Chaim, R' Chanina always wanted to know what we were up to. He was interested in connecting with the *talmidim* and their experiences. He not only remembered the *talmidim,* but their friends and *chevrah,* as well.

Keeping up the connection with *talmidim*

As the *mesader kiddushin* at a *talmid's chasunah*

Reciting a *berachah* under a *talmid's chuppah*

With R' Moshe Monczyk

With the Slansky brothers

He was a *mechanech* who happened to teach elementary school students, but viewed himself as a rebbi for life."

Lifelong Impact

A *TALMID* ARTICULATED, "SOMETIMES A TEACHER CHANGES THE LIFE of a student with a particular lesson, sometimes with a decisive action or intervention. R' Herzberg changed my life by being R' Herzberg."

During the *shivah*, Dr. David Pelcovitz, noted psychologist in the Five Towns community, told the family, "Your father turned around lives on a regular basis. I always knew that if a boy had to change things around, I could send him to South Shore."

This was because throughout R' Chanina's career, he connected to his *talmidim*. It was only after his *petirah* that it became clear to how many and to what extent. As R' Chanina's *levayah* drew to a close, R' Tzvi Schechter, a *talmid* at Tiferes Moshe from over four decades earlier, made his way to the front of the *beis midrash*. Tapping one of R' Chanina's children on the shoulder, he pleaded to share a few words of *hesped*. "Please! I feel that I need to speak. If I don't convey my thoughts

R' Tzvi Schechter speaking at the *levayah*

about Rebbi, I will regret it for the rest of my life. I must express my *hakaras hatov* to my rebbi for changing my life."

After being granted permission, R' Tzvi addressed the assemblage. "It's very unusual to ask to speak at a *levayah*. But after having a rebbi who left an impression on me and my class, I think it's incumbent on me to speak now, 42 years later. R' Herzberg's first year in *chinuch* was not easy for him, and it surely wasn't easy for us. It was the first year that the yeshiva decided to make a second class. You see, there was the *aleph* class, and then there was our class; I don't know if you could even call us *beis*, maybe *gimmel*. They put R' Herzberg in charge of us, about fifteen boys, and he had some difficult times, we had some difficult times, but it was a year of growth for all of us. I am up here because I have *hakaras hatov* to Rebbi. I think it would be very good for him to know that 42 years later, a lot of these boys, whom people would have given up on, became *ehrliche Yidden*. One is even a rosh yeshiva today. That first year turned out unbelievable fruit."

As the family arrived home following the *levayah* and *kevurah*, there was a knock at the door. A man in his 50's hurriedly entered the house, apologizing for coming to pay a *shivah* call so soon. "I couldn't make it to the *levayah*," he explained, "but I had to come at the first moment possible. Your father was my seventh-grade rebbi over 40 years ago, and he changed my life."

His declaration was far from unique. During the *shivah*, scores of *talmidim* — from Tiferes Moshe and Toras Chaim — came from far and near to pay their respects. Some hadn't seen their rebbi since their elementary school days, but they all brought similar messages. "I felt I had to come to express *hakaras hatov* to R' Herzberg for the life-changing impact he had on my life. He cared for me, understood me, and took me to a whole new level."

Caring, understanding, taking to a whole new level — that's what it was all about. Aryeh was a really wild boy in Pre-1a. One day, he was told that R' Chanina wanted to see him. When he came to the office, R' Chanina greeted him warmly. "Aryeh, I have a present for you, a hat with your name on it!" Upon seeing the hat, Aryeh figured that R' Chanina had probably found it somewhere and was giving it to him because it had his name on it. When Aryeh voiced his thoughts, R' Chanina replied, "No, I really had this made just for you!" Aryeh took that hat and cherished it for many years.

The hat Aryeh still had 35 years later

After telling the story at the *shivah,* Aryeh reached into his pocket and withdrew a red, white, and blue hat, with a pom-pom on top and the name Aryeh appearing again and again. "Here it is," he exclaimed. "I still have it, 35 years later!"

Indeed, one of the main takeaways from the *shivah* for R' Chanina was the lifelong impact a *mechanech* is capable of having on his *talmidim.*

A few days into the school year, a preschool boy switched from another yeshiva to Yeshiva Toras Chaim. After the interview was over and the boy was accepted, R' Chanina had one more order of business to see to. Noting how difficult the transition was for the young child, he asked permission to give the little boy a kiss on his yarmulke.

Permission granted, R' Chanina planted a kiss on the boy's yarmulke. A kiss the boy still felt decades later, along with the comfort it gave him, knowing that he was coming to a yeshiva where the menahel cared so deeply for him.

R' Chanina was a magnet. Not because he was charismatic, but because he was real. The connection was real, as well. You had to meet R' Chanina only once to connect with him and feel as if you knew him for years. A few months following R' Chanina's *petirah,* his son Yitzchok met a Yeshiva Toras Chaim parent, who gave Yitzchok a big hug and told him, "Your father was someone really special. What made him unique was that every *talmid* felt that he had a special relationship with him."

When R' Aryeh Lebowitz was in eighth grade, he and his friends "planned" their future together, down to the children they would send to Yeshiva Toras Chaim, so that they, too, could benefit from having R' Herzberg as their menahel. "Who ever heard of such a thing," R' Lebowitz wondered after R' Chanina's *petirah,* "that an elementary school menahel should be loved so much that eighth-graders are expressing this wish? But that's how beloved R' Herzberg was to the *talmidim.*"

R' Yaakov Bender pointed out that as an elementary school menahel, R' Chanina connected to his *talmidim* in such a way that many of them viewed him as a rebbi for life. A mother of a former Yeshiva Toras Chaim student noticed that the "wallpaper" on her teenage son's phone screen was a photograph of R' Chanina davening. When she commented on this, her son responded, "Mommy, all my friends have R' Herzberg's picture as the background on their phones!" And this was many years after these boys had graduated!

Additionally, many of his *talmidim* from Yeshiva Tiferes Moshe reminisced about their days in R' Chanina's class and agreed that though he had been their rebbi years ago in seventh grade, they still considered him their *rebbi muvhak.* And he was in his 20's when he taught them! Until this day, when his seventh-grade *talmidim* hear the name R' Chanina Herzberg, they can't help but smile.

Such was the connection R' Chanina forged with his *talmidim.* He remained the one who brought out the best in them, the one who made them smile, no matter how much time had passed.

Mrs. Naomi Nadata is the program director of CAHAL, providing smaller classes for children with learning differences in local yeshivos in the Five Towns area. She had the *zechus* of seeing R' Chanina in action. Mrs. Nadata wrote: "R' Herzberg understood so well that children learn differently. He had the wisdom to recognize that the students who could not learn in the larger mainstream classes could flourish in smaller, more individualized settings. From CAHAL's inception, R' Herzberg was a role model and mentor for all of us. He did not just know each of our CAHAL students, he made it his business to connect with their parents and be there for guidance and *chizuk.* We became part of the Yeshiva Toras Chaim family, and were swept up in the inclusive atmosphere established by our revered menahel… R' Herzberg was welcoming and loving to all our CAHAL *talmidim* over the years. Many came back to visit him after they graduated and moved on."

Happy to be with their menahel: R' Chanina on a visit to Camp Dora Golding; Eli Herzberg is on the left in the back.

Nor was R' Chanina's influence on *talmidim* confined to school. Over the years, he served as rebbi or learning director in several camps. He felt that the camp experience is a unique time for growth, as it affords each child the opportunity to shine in a different way. Especially for boys who don't excel academically, camp helps build confidence by

Learning with campers in camp

allowing them to shine in other areas, such as sports and performances.

In addition, he would say, "The summer is a time when children can take all the 'book smarts' they acquired during the school year and put them into action." He would advise rebbeim, "Make sure your *talmidim* are going to the right summer camp!"

At the *shivah*, a man in his late 40's made a brief but meaningful statement about R' Chanina and camp. "R' Herzberg was my rebbi for three weeks in camp. I consider him my rebbi for life!"

On Their Level...

SO MANY YEARS LATER, A *TALMID* FROM R' CHANINA'S CLASS FROM the 1970's still recalled his rebbi's warmth and caring, as well as the short story or joke with which R' Chanina began the class each morning. He knew how to connect on their level, how "to warm us up before starting the *shiur*."

R' Aaron Schechter praised a particular rebbi for his ability "to teach a whole class, yet each *talmid* feels as if his rebbi is connecting to him personally." Whether as a rebbi teaching a class, or as a menahel speaking to tens of *talmidim*, R' Chanina, too, had the unique ability to make every *talmid* feel like he was connecting to him on his level, enabling R' Chanina to exert the best possible influence on each *talmid*.

Shragi Portal, a Yeshiva Toras Chaim parent and alumnus, remembered, "When my son was in first grade and we attended his Chumash party at the yeshiva, I couldn't help but think back to my own Chumash party. What struck me was not the bagels or the songs, but the genuine smile and happiness that R' Herzberg had when he presented the Chumash to each individual boy. I remember feeling that this must be an important moment in our lives — because it was clearly an important moment in his. He handed out thousands of Chumashim during his career as menahel, yet he was never simply smiling for the photo op. He was genuinely thrilled to be bringing another Jewish boy into the world of Chumash and Torah, and that joy and excitement of his has stuck with me throughout my life."

"As menahel, R' Chanina defined the words 'personal attention,'" R' Shalom Rosner, rav in Ramat Bet Shemesh, noted Daf Yomi *maggid shiur*, and Toras Chaim alumnus, maintained. "He was never too busy for any *talmid*, no matter his age or background."

When Shmully* was in first grade, he was quite the character and he would regularly compliment R' Chanina on his ties. At times, R'

"He was genuinely thrilled to be bringing another Jewish boy into the world of Chumash and Torah."

Chanina would approach Shmully and ask him what he thought of his tie. Shmully felt like he was on top of the world.

In general, R' Chanina was approachable. Any *talmid,* no matter his grade, felt comfortable walking over to him in the hallway or into his office to ask a question, to discuss an issue he was having with a friend, to tell him that he wasn't feeling well, or simply to request assistance in tying his shoelaces.

R' Chanina was their menahel, but he was their father, as well. Or, in later years, their grandfather. Mrs. Elana Fertig commented, "R' Herzberg treated every child like a grandson."

R' Chanina's son-in-law, Shua Nachman, related, "Obviously, my father-in-law would check in on my children who attended Yeshiva Toras Chaim, asking me, 'How does Nesanel like learning Gemara? I told you he was going to love his rebbi! And how is Yehuda doing in yeshiva?' But it wasn't because they were my children. I am convinced he did the same for everyone's children. He really, really cared about all his *talmidim* equally.

"Once, when parents came to look at the yeshiva and my father-in-law was showing them around, my Yehuda, who was about 5 years old at the time, called out, "Hi, Zeidy!" before running off. The parents were

With his grandchildren at Yeshiva Toras Chaim

so impressed that the children in the yeshiva call the menahel Zeidy, but Abba set the record straight. 'No, that was my grandson!'

"But I really think he had that sort of *kesher* with all his *talmidim*. He made every child feel special."

Avner* was never the biggest fan of school. He always dreamed of having school for two months a year and then vacation for the rest. Alas, his dream did not come true. When he was in sixth and seventh grade, Avner used to count the days until the end of the school year, beginning in November.

R' Chanina heard about Avner's count and frequently stopped him in the hall to inquire, "Avner, how many days are left?" When a momentous day, such as 100, then 75, then 50, then day 25 rolled around, R' Chanina would dance with Avner in the hallways, singing, "The summer is coming! The summer is coming!"

Avner summed it up. "I'm sure R' Herzberg enjoyed the summer months, but he had no need to count down the days with a sixth-grader. Yet he wanted to connect to this sixth-grader and show him: *I know what you're feeling. I was also in school; we'll get through this together.*"

When Mordechai* was in first grade, he suffered from anxiety, causing him to miss several days of school. The absenteeism finally stopped when R' Chanina paid a special visit to his house, bearing a gift. "Mordechai, I bought you a vehicle that will help 'bring' you to yeshiva: a toy army truck." Almost 40 years later, the warmth of that moment still lingers with R' Mordechai, now an accomplished *mechanech*.

A *talmid* of R' Chanina who was teaching seventh grade had an issue with Gavi,* a boy in his Navi class. Gavi had no interest in learning; he would sit and draw all day. One night, the rebbi thought to himself, *What would R' Herzberg do? How would he connect to this child?* After thinking about it for a while, he came up with an idea.

The next day, he called Gavi over. "You know, I have a problem I think you can help me with. Some boys in the class don't understand the Navi. I was thinking that it would be great if I could give the boys drawings for each *perek*, like they have in comic books. But there's one problem. I don't know how to draw. I noticed that you enjoy drawing — and that you're good at it. Can you please help me with this? Each day as I teach the Navi, you can draw the scenes and we'll put them together to give to the class. I'll even give you extra credit for your efforts."

Gavi happily agreed, and he went on to become one of the better *talmidim* in the class. After a few weeks, the rebbi called R' Chanina to tell him how he'd dealt with the boy. R' Chanina's response has not left the rebbi. "Ahh, brilliant! For that I give you *semichah*!"

R' Chanina viewed the connection between rebbi and *talmid* as crucial to the success of the *talmid.* A rebbi came to R' Chanina, complaining that a boy in his class belonged in the other track. R' Chanina made the switch immediately.

"Do you agree with me?" he asked another staff member, who happened to be in his office at the time, after the rebbi left the room.

"Why not get the boy extra help before switching him?" the staff member asked.

"The boy would have been fine in this class," R' Chanina replied. "However, the rebbi didn't want him in the class, and it's not good for a *talmid* to be in a class if the rebbi doesn't want him."

R' Chanina was not quick to switch children from one class or track to another, but if there was no bond between teacher and student, he felt there was no alternative.

R' Dovid Bashevkin described a memorable experience for many Yeshiva Toras Chaim *talmidim.* Every morning, when R' Chanina removed his Rashi *tefillin* to put on his Rabbeinu Tam *tefillin*, he would give his Rashi set to a "privileged" *talmid* to wrap. As R' Bashevkin expressed, he took off his *tefillin* to a crowd of outstretched sixth-grade hands that looked like a flock of seagulls waiting to be thrown bread. He would pick a different boy every day and in R' Bashevkin's words, "When you got chosen, it felt like you won an Olympic gold medal."

This was something preteen and teen boys could appreciate, and R' Chanina understood that. As Menachem Butler reflected, "We wanted

In his *tallis* and *tefillin* at Yeshiva Toras Chaim

to have a *cheilek* in his mitzvah. It was an incredible *chinuch* moment."

R' Chanina frequently stopped by a classroom in Yeshiva Toras Chaim where they sang after davening. Many of those *talmidim* nostalgically recall how he would join them for the high part of *Bilvavi*. (This song had special meaning to R' Chanina; the words were written by R' Hutner, based on a line in the *Sefer Chareidim* by R' Elazar Azikri, and sung to a melody composed by R' Chanina's *yedid* and fellow *talmid* of R' Shlomo Freifeld, R' Shmuel Brazil.) His powerful voice took over as

(l- r): R' Shmuel Brazil, R' Yehoshua Kurland (partially hidden), and R' Chanina singing at a *chasunah*

he became completely engrossed in the song, and the boys just stared at him mesmerized as he gave it his all.

R' Gershon Greenberg, rebbi at Yeshiva Toras Chaim, used to invite R' Chanina to come into his classroom and speak to the boys about life. He spoke about his own life, his trials and tribulations, his ups and downs, how he was looking for direction and how he met R' Freifeld.

Connecting at its best.

Yosef* recalled the first time he met R' Chanina. "My family had just moved to Far Rockaway and my parents took me to R' Herzberg for an interview. R' Herzberg asked me, 'Are you a Mets fan or a Yankees fan?'

"'I'm a Yankees fan,' I informed him.

"R' Herzberg came back with 'I guess we'll take you anyway.'"

Comments like these gave the *talmidim* the feeling that their menahel understood where they were coming from, forging a special connection.

... Taking Them to the Next One

YET EVEN WITH ALL THE CONNECTING, AND THOUGH HE MET THEM on their level, R' Chanina demonstrated that sports *cannot* take over one's life, that ball players should *not* become our role models.

Every morning after davening in a camp where he served as learning director, R' Chanina, still in *tallis* and *tefillin*, would relate a short story and a lesson to kick off the day.

On the morning of August 14th, 1995, the day after the iconic baseball player, Mickey Mantle, passed away, just about everyone was talking about him: his outstanding career, his MVP awards, the seven championships he won.

After davening, the campers and counselors noticed something different. Before R' Chanina spoke, he removed his *tallis* and *tefillin*, carefully extracted a newspaper from a bag, and only then did he approach the *shtender* in front of the camp shul. Lifting up the paper in clear vision to the crowd, R' Chanina began to shout, "Sixteen pages about Mickey Mantle! The Mick is dead! The Mick is dead! The Mick is dead! *Ah menuval*! *Ah sheigetz*! An alcoholic! This is who we talk about, this is who we look up to, this is our role model?!

"Our role models are our rebbeim, roshei yeshiva, Rebbes, *gedolei Yisrael*; those are the people we need to talk about, the people we need to look up to, the people who will make us 'big Jews.'"

Decades later, when they came to be *menachem avel* R' Chanina's family, various campers mentioned that those few timely words constituted the most powerful *mussar shmuess* they ever heard.

One of the crucial strategies of combat is knowing your enemy. A good general, i.e., menahel, must know what he is up against. This was brought home to R' Chanina by R' Aaron Schechter. One morning in the 1990's, R' Schechter attended a *bris* in Mesivta Ateres Yaakov, which at the time was located across the street from Yeshiva Toras Chaim. When the *bris* was over, R' Chanina escorted the rosh yeshiva through Yeshiva Toras Chaim and R' Schechter, an alumnus of the yeshiva from its days in East New York, was duly impressed.

Then, as R' Chanina later described, "R' Aaron grabbed me by the arm and said, 'R' Chanina, you'll see that there may come a time, very, very soon, where it will be very difficult to teach children a *blatt Gemara* or even a line of Gemara. Because their minds are going to be so *farshtupt*, so inundated, with garbage.'"

Those words came true before R' Chanina's eyes, and he did what he could to combat the challenges of the day. Every Friday, R' Chanina gave an Erev Shabbos *shmuess* to the *talmidim* in fifth through eighth grade, where he masterfully intertwined that week's *parashah* with what the *talmidim* needed to hear. From sports to politics to so many other subjects on the boys' minds, R' Chanina always put things into perspective, meeting the boys on their level, while helping them move to the next one. R' Chanina understood what the *talmidim* were exposed to, and the need to drive home what's important and what's not.

R' Zev Davidowitz described the makeup of the *shmuessen*. Each *shmuess* consisted of a short *vort*, a *maaseh* about *gedolim*, and a charge — a call to action. The two topics he usually spoke about were being a mensch and being a "big Jew." He emphasized how each one of us can become a "big Jew," for every person in this world is capable of living above the daily grind, of serving the *Eibishter* without getting stuck on the insignificant things.

"The way he did it was special,"

pointed out R' Davidowitz. "The *shmuess* wasn't said in a condescending way, causing the *talmidim* to put up a defense shield. Just the opposite, it was done in a way that built them up. He lifted the *talmidim,* inspiring them that this is a level that they are *shayach* to. He showed he believed in them, that they should never underestimate their ability to achieve the goal of becoming a 'big Jew.' He took a lofty concept and explained it on their level."

R' Moshe Scharhon added that many times when speaking to the *talmidim* about important topics such as *yiras Shamayim,* R' Chanina would become choked up. Not only was he comfortable showing his emotions, but this was an important piece of his being *mechanech* the *talmidim.* In addition, this was where R' Chanina "introduced" the *talmidim* to R' Shlomo and R' Hutner. As Menachem Butler expressed, "R' Herzberg wasn't just the bridge to R' Shlomo and R' Hutner; he brought their teachings down to the *talmidim*'s level."

Even though the *talmidim* heard these *shmuessen* when they were 10 to 14 years old, many were still able to repeat the lessons they derived from those talks decades later, after R' Chanina was *niftar* — when a number of them were well into their 40's. In the words of R' Yehoshua Meltzer, sixth-grade rebbi in Yeshiva Toras Chaim, these *shmuessen* were legendary. R' Shalom Rosner, one of R' Chanina's *talmidim* in the early 1980's, distinctly recalled the excitement the *shmuessen* engendered, how even then the *talmidim* appreciated the opportunity to hear them, and how the talks helped shape their *hashkafas hachaim.*

An example of a memorable talk was what became known as the "Michael Jordan *shmuess.*" Before the annual eighth-grade trip to Hershey Park, R' Chanina stressed that as Yidden, *talmidim* must always wear their yarmulkes and *tzitzis,* even in an amusement park. "Imagine," he said, "if Michael Jordan, the best player in the NBA, was traded to the New York Knicks, but on one condition. When he plays, he wears his Chicago Bulls uniform. What would happen? Even the fact that he's the best player on the planet wouldn't help him. He wouldn't be allowed to play. Boys, as Yidden, we also have our uniform, a yarmulke and *tzitzis,* which must be worn at all times!"

R' Aryeh Lebowitz reminisced about his graduation trip to Hershey Park, where a concert was taking place in the park's amphitheater. The parking lot was swarming with all types of people, most of the least desirable variety.

The Yeshiva Toras Chaim group boarded the buses. Then, capitalizing on a *chinuch* moment — for he was always on the lookout for just such moments — R' Chanina instructed the *talmidim,* "Look out the windows! There are Yidden in that crowd. Can you identify them?"

After the students realized that there was, unfortunately, no way to identify the Jews among the lower echelons of society, he delivered the clincher. "The difference between a Jew who has a Torah education and one without is the difference between you and those in the parking lot." R' Chanina showed the eighth-graders in the simplest terms what Torah does to a Jew — and what a life devoid of Torah can lead to.

Nor has R' Aryeh forgotten a speech based on *Parashas Kedoshim,* which he heard when he was 10, in fifth grade. That was when R' Chanina discussed the concept of *naval birshus haTorah* (a lowly individual within the confines of Torah law; see Ramban, *Vayikra* 19:2), and how hanging out in pizza shops on Motza'ei Shabbos may not entail doing anything wrong, but can border on, or lead to, becoming a *naval birshus haTorah.* R' Aryeh, who had never heard of this concept before that speech, later revealed, "It became a formative concept in terms of developing my own *hashkafas hachaim,* my own understanding of what the Torah *hashkafah* is. That it's not only about the words of the Torah, it's about the *retzon haTorah.* It's about what *Hakadosh Baruch Hu* really wants from us. That was probably the most memorable *mussar shmuess* I ever heard."

In another one of these *shmuessen,* R' Chanina expounded on the damage caused by movies. "Going to a movie theater is like going into a newly painted room that hasn't dried yet. Everything looks so nice and

R' Chanina toward the end of his life, giving his weekly *shmuess* to *talmidim*

glamorous, but after spending time there you come out all soiled." One *talmid* still recalled the speech decades later, along with the impression it made.

The power to connect on the level of a *talmid,* and use that connection to bring the *talmid* up a level, was also absorbed from R' Shlomo.

Jack,* who grew up Orthodox in Brooklyn, needed his freedom, seeking what to him were greener pastures. In time, he landed on an Indian reservation where he plowed the soil, ate his own produce, and lived off the land. Yet he yearned for more. After hearing of a woman who purportedly possessed phenomenal insight, he traveled to her, only to be told, "You are not one of us. Go back to your roots; that's where you belong." Arriving back in New York, Jack somehow made his way to Sh'or Yoshuv, to R' Shlomo's office. Sensing Jack's need for connection, R' Shlomo met him on his turf and conversed with him about the great outdoors — deer and elk, hunting, reservations, Indian culture — for hours at a time.

But how did R' Shlomo know all this information?

At one point, Jack discovered the secret. R' Shlomo had amassed a small collection of books on these topics, all so he could properly understand the mindset of his new disciple, and to connect with him.

"It was then," Jack stated, "that I realized how much my rebbi really loved me."

Jack went on to study at Sh'or Yoshuv for years, becoming a *talmid chacham* and a true *talmid* of R' Shlomo.

Living the Churban

R' MOSHE SCHARHON INSTITUTED A PROGRAM IN YESHIVA TORAS Chaim known as "Chevra Tehillim," in which *talmidim* from fifth grade and up volunteer to say one *perek* of *Tehillim* a day, every day of the year. In this manner, the entire *Sefer Tehillim* is completed daily. When the program was introduced, R' Chanina, in an uncharacteristic fashion, insisted that he be able to join and that he recite Chapter 137, the *perek* of *Al Naharos Bavel,* which discusses the destruction of the *Beis HaMikdash.*

R' Scharhon recollected, "It was clear that R' Chanina had a strong connection to that *perek* and its message. There were times in which I would walk into R' Chanina's office and he would motion to me to wait as he recited his daily *perek.* I would stand there and watch as he said the words, '*Al naharos Bavel, sham yashavnu gam bachinu b'zachreinu es Tzion* — By the rivers of Bavel, there we sat and also wept when we remembered Tzion.' Tears would form in his eyes, tears that came from his *kishkes,* from the depths of his being. It was then that I understood that he was especially connected to this *perek* because of his connection to the *Churban Beis HaMikdash* and the fact that *Shechinta b'galusa,* that the Divine Presence is in exile."

R' Scharhon explained that R' Chanina's genuine pain over the loss of the *Beis HaMikdash* and the accompanying suffering of the *Shechinah,* which distances us from *Hakadosh Baruch Hu,* formed the basis of his lifelong mission to be *mechanech Yiddishe kinder.* "His whole life was about bringing the *Eibishter*'s children closer to *Avihem she'ba'Shamayim.* And that's what *chinuch* is all about."

The Client Is the Child

R' CHANINA WAS WONT TO SAY, "NEVER FORGET THAT AT THE END OF the day the client is the child!" He would explain to *mechanchim,* "Many times as *mechanchim,* we deal with situations where other variables may affect our decision-making ability. It may be the opinion of others who work with us, the opinion of the board of directors, or the fact that the child's parents think they know best and are being extremely difficult to deal with. Whatever the reason, we need to remember Who our Boss is — the *Ribbono shel Olam* — and who our client is — the child. Only then can we make the correct decision."

A rebbi was dealing with a troubled child, whose parents did not see eye-to-eye with the yeshiva on how to handle him. At the end of one meeting with the rebbi and the parents, R' Chanina turned to the parents and stated, "All your plans sound well and good, but what will be with your child's *neshamah*?" That comment stopped the parents in their tracks and made them rethink their approach.

It was their child's *neshamah* at stake.

Mr. and Mrs. Applebaum* discussed their son Aharon's* class placement for the upcoming year, explaining to R' Chanina why they felt strongly that for Aharon to excel, he needed to switch classes. R' Chanina heard them out, but then respectfully disagreed, maintaining that Aharon would do better if he stayed put. Surprised at R' Chanina's reaction, Mr. and Mrs. Applebaum tried one last-ditch effort to change R' Chanina's mind.

"But R' Herzberg, you have such a wonderful reputation of working with the parents."

"True," R' Chanina countered, "I work 'with' the parents but I work 'for' the child, and I can't do something that I feel isn't good for your son."

"Early on in my career," R' Shlomo Pfeiffer recounted, "I approached R' Herzberg for advice regarding a boy in my class. The boy unfortunately came from a broken home, had a difficult life, and was a *tzubrochene* child.

"'What should my goal be this year for this child?' I asked.

"'I want this boy to be around *Yiddishe* boys, and to come to yeshiva happy and leave yeshiva happy,' R' Chanina replied.

"He gave this advice close to 30 years ago," R' Shlomo emphasized. "It wasn't necessarily what was being done then. He was 'holding' then where we are 'holding' today."

R' Yaakov Bender communicated, "I had the *zechus* of working alongside R' Chanina for many years. Even though we worked for different yeshivos, I felt that he cared about only one thing: the *talmidim*. Whatever was best for a *talmid* he would do, and nothing else got in the way of that."

Yudi Herzberg, who was making the transition from kollel *yungerman* to nursing home administrator, asked his father for advice as he headed into the workforce. At first, R' Chanina insisted he knew nothing about healthcare, but after giving it a little more thought, he offered, "Never forget who your client is. In my line of work, the client is the child and I need to do what's best for the child. In your work, the client is the resident and you need to do what's best for the resident. Not what's best for the owner, board of directors, or the healthcare workers, but what's best for the resident!"

Partnering With Parents

IN A JOURNAL AD IN MEMORY OF R' CHANINA, ONE COUPLE WROTE, "R' Herzberg had a unique ability to empower parents in a way that made us feel like the yeshiva was a real partner in our son's *chinuch*. We sent our son to South Shore because of our initial meeting with R' Herzberg and the way he communicated the mutual trust he had with the parent body in bringing up all his students. Once we met with him, we didn't need to look elsewhere."

R' Chanina gave parents confidence in their abilities to be *mechanech* their children and make proper decisions. He once told a parent, "*Chinuch* is 90 percent parents and 10 percent the yeshiva."

One parent conveyed, "We went to Yeshiva Toras Chaim for an interview. Everything was going well when we asked R' Herzberg a controversial question. 'What is your *shitah* in regard to rules for the parents? Can we send our child to a coed school or coed camp?' We had no intention of doing so, but the answer would tell something about the yeshiva.

"R' Herzberg looked at us, made a face, and kind of laughed. But his response was incredibly powerful. 'You trust us with your children for eight hours a day, and we're not going to trust you with your own children at home?!'"

The parents walked out of that interview empowered and confident in their role as parents. As one would expect, they decided to send their child to Yeshiva Toras Chaim.

Just as R' Chanina knew his *talmidim,* he knew their parents. How did he know the parents so well? To R' Chanina, it wasn't a question. That was his "job" as a menahel. He gave several reasons for this. First, to fully understand each *talmid,* one must first understand his parents. In

With a parent, Mendy Silber

addition, when the menahel forms a personal connection with his parent body, and the parents genuinely feel that he cares about them, he earns their trust. Then, when he suggests to the parents that their son needs additional assistance, in the form of a resource room rebbi, tutor, or social worker, they will follow through on the suggestion. This is because they already trust the menahel and know he has their son's best interests at heart. They will also acquiesce to his decisions, even if those decisions include painful pills to swallow. Finally, when a true connection exists, the parents feel comfortable calling the menahel for *chinuch* advice.

One Yeshiva Toras Chaim parent summed up R' Chanina in one word: normal. "You could speak to him about anything, and he related to you."

R' Chanina was a master at dealing with parents in varied circumstances and situations. At times, parents would ask R' Chanina for a meeting to voice an issue they were having with the yeshiva, with the same scenario repeating itself again and again, to the marvel of those who witnessed the "before" and "after." In R' Dovid Kramer's words, "There was a line everyone would say about R' Herzberg, 'Parents come into yeshiva upset and when they leave R' Herzberg's office, they come out smiling.'" Not because he gave in to them, but because he had a unique *koach* to calm people down.

R' Mordechai Kamenetzky had the opportunity to sit in on some of those parent-*hanhalah* meetings and he explained how R' Chanina was able to accomplish this. "He listened, listened, and listened some more, until the parents got everything out of their system. The whole time, he didn't say a word, he didn't defend himself, he didn't try to deflect — he just listened. Only once he was sure that the parents said everything they wanted to say did he start talking."

R' Chanina was no pushover. And many a time he would hold his ground, but it was the process that helped him make parents happy no matter their mood when they first entered his office. "He dealt with contentious situations without budging, but without fighting," R' Kamenetzky articulated.

R' Yaakov Bender expounded, "R' Chanina would never dream of saying to a parent, 'If you don't like it here, go someplace else.' He would hear the parents out and validate them. However, at the end of the conversation, if he disagreed with the parents, he would tell them, 'I hear where you're coming from. Even so, taking the whole picture into consideration, this is what I need to do.' Then he followed through with what he felt was the right approach… He set the tone in the community that you don't have to be afraid of the menahel. *I'm a good person, but I can't always do what you want me to do."*

R' Chanina counseled his rebbeim in how to deal with contentious situations, as well, at times with unconventional solutions. Though R' Landman* did his best to demonstrate love and give attention to Nachum Kleiner,* it seemed like Mr. and Mrs. Kleiner had something against him from the first day of school. No matter what he tried, he couldn't get them on his team.

Turning to R' Chanina for advice, he was surprised at the menahel's suggestion. "Make a *melaveh malkah* in the Kleiners' home."

"But how is that going to help?" protested R' Landman. "The parents feel only animosity toward me."

"Just try it," R' Chanina insisted. "What do you have to lose?"

With trepidation, R' Landman called up the Kleiners and asked if they could host a *melaveh malkah.* For some reason, they agreed and welcomed Nachum's class and their rebbi into their home. Believe it or not, after the *melaveh malkah,* Mrs. Kleiner expressed how impressed she was by how R' Landman interacted with the *talmidim.* And just like that, the hostility fell away.

R' Chanina demonstrated *pikchus,* not only in how he handled parents but also in how he advised his rebbeim.

Just as he made himself approachable with regard to the *talmidim,* R' Chanina made himself approachable with regard to their parents. In R' Bender's words, "R' Chanina was *mechadesh* a very big *yesod.* Parents aren't crazy. They are talking about their child. Listen to them..." When R' Binyamin Jacobi, second-grade rebbi in Yeshiva Toras Chaim, came to R' Chanina to discuss the idea of going into *chinuch,* one of the first *yesodos* R' Chanina transmitted was: "Believe in the parents; they want what's best for their children, and many times they have invaluable insights that help us in being *mechanech* their children. Take what they say seriously and don't brush them off."

R' Chanina took mothers' words and emotions seriously, as well. Mrs. Rookie Billet (wife of R' Hershel Billet, rabbi of the Young Israel of Woodmere), whose children attended Yeshiva Toras Chaim, remembers the genuine respect R' Chanina demonstrated for a mother's intelligence and her desire regarding the *chinuch* of her children. And mothers felt it.

Mrs. Elana Fertig, who gleaned from R' Chanina's expertise in regard to her own family, as well, shared, "R' Herzberg taught us that davening for our children is part of our *hishtadlus*." If a mother broke down crying at a meeting with the *hanhalah* regarding a difficulty with her child, R' Chanina would later remark to the other attendees, "Never underestimate the power of a mother's tears." R' Yitzie Ross was once in R' Chanina's office when a mother came in crying that her son wasn't happy. He told R' Ross, "Any time a mother cries over her children, you need to take her seriously."

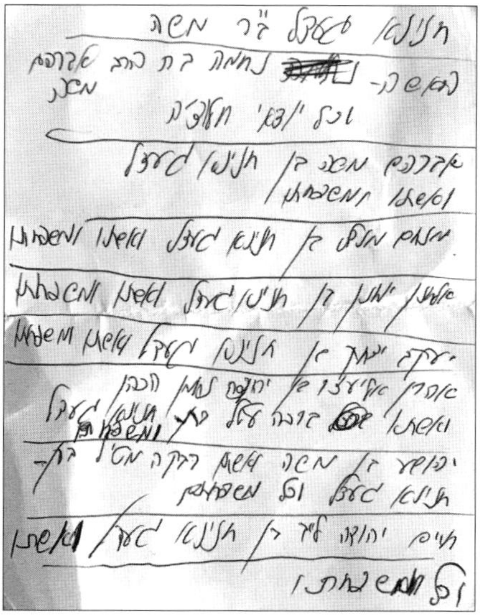

Paper found in R' Chanina's siddur listing all his children's names, so he could daven for them on a daily basis

He took the parents seriously and helped them handle the challenges they were facing. One parent pointed out that one of R' Chanina's most outstanding *maalos* as a principal was his self-confidence, his sense of calm. "When you spoke to him, you felt that everything would be okay. He didn't tell you he knew what he was doing, but the self-confidence and calmness were transmitted to the parent."

At times, R' Chanina apologized to a parent even though he was really right and there was no reason for an apology. To him, it was all about making sure the child succeeded, and if he had to apologize to make that happen, so be it. After all, when parents are happy, the menahel can better take care of their children, and that was all that mattered.

R' Bender elaborated on this theme. "His *koach* was that he was a nice person, and his idea was not to win the fight. His idea was that at the end of the day, the child should be successful."

R' Chanina was the first to admit if he was wrong. One Erev Yom Kippur during the *seudah hamafsekes*, R' Chanina disappeared from the table and was nowhere to be found. A half-hour later, the front door opened and in he walked, finally shedding light on his mysterious disappearance.

"This summer, I received a call from the Bergsteins* requesting a class switch for their third-grader. After discussing it with them and hearing them out, I decided that it's best for the boy to remain in his class. However, now that we are a few weeks into the new school year, I realized that I made a mistake. This was causing me *agmas nefesh*, and I wanted to ask the Bergsteins *mechilah* before Yom Kippur. So I went to their home to tell them I made a mistake and to ask them to forgive me. I also let them know that right after Yom Tov, I am going to fix my mistake and switch his class."

R' Chanina, who was not tech-savvy, used to say, "*Baruch Hashem*, I don't know how to use a computer and send emails, because now before I respond to someone, I can think. Then I can call and speak to them on the phone. Because of technology, many people respond without thinking and inevitably make mistakes." He may not have had a smartphone but communicate he did — and smartly.

A *talmid* of his accepted a *hanhalah* position in an institution in which email was the accepted mode of communication with parents. R' Chanina gave him an important piece of advice, which served him well in his career. "If a parent texts or emails you regarding their child, don't have the discussion via text or email. Just say to them, 'Your child is too important to discuss via text or email. Please, let's talk over the phone.'"

The Nachas Call

IN *MOREH TZEDEK* (P. 116), R' AVRAHAM PAM POINTS OUT THE IMPORtance of a rebbi or menahel communicating with parents just to share some *nachas*: "Your son is progressing in his learning," or "Your son is excelling in a particular character trait," or "Your son learned well today," and the like. This elevates the child in the eyes of his parents. As a result, the relationship between child and his parents improves, as the parents look at their child in a more positive manner. As R' Pam stated, doing this creates "*mofsim, mamash mofsim*."

R' Chanina added other benefits to making *nachas* calls. "Giving *nachas* is a big *yesod* in earning the parent's respect and trust. When a *mechanech* reaches out to a parent for nothing else but to give them *nachas* about their child, it shows the parent that the *mechanech* really cares about the child, thereby changing the whole relationship between the *mechanech* and parent, as well.

"There is another benefit. Whenever you have the ability to pump up a child and lift him, grab the opportunity. That *nachas* call makes the

R' Chanina with a *talmid*

talmid feel so special. This causes the *talmid* to believe in his ability, to strive to be even better."

R' Marty Katz remembers vividly, "I received a phone call one winter night from R' Herzberg, and I braced myself, expecting a negative report about one of my children. Why else would I be receiving a night call from the menahel?"

This is what happened. "R' Marty," R' Herzberg boomed over the phone, "your son did something beautiful today! The bar mitzvah boys gathered for Maariv immediately following yeshiva and I saw your son there, as well. I told him to hurry, since his bus to Queens would be leaving any minute and if he would stay for Maariv he would miss it.

"You should hear what he responded," R' Chanina continued. "He told me, 'Don't worry, R' Herzberg. I'm just staying to hear *Borchu* and then I'll get on the bus.' I was so impressed! You should have continued *nachas*!"

R' Marty was most pleased but also taken aback. "R' Herzberg, you didn't have to call me at night on your own time just to tell me this," he said.

"Yes, I did," R' Chanina answered. "A menahel can't just call home for negative things; he has to call home for positive things, as well. Whenever possible, he must stress the positive, not the negative. These *nachas* calls have incredible results on so many levels."

Visiting *talmidim* in Camp Dora Golding

It's over 25 years later, and R' Marty still remembers the moment he got the call and R' Chanina's tone. And he still shares the story often.

One summer, during a visit to Camp Dora Golding, R' Chanina took out his phone to call his yeshiva's preschool director, Mrs. Elana Fertig, whose son attended the camp. Mrs. Fertig didn't pick up the phone so R' Chanina left a message. "Mrs. Fertig, I'm standing here next to your son. Wow, look how much he grew! You should have continued *nachas*!"

"That message was very meaningful to me," Mrs. Fertig remembers. "It gave me so much *chizuk* that I still have it saved on my phone."

R' Chanina not only gave *nachas* to parents about their children, but he gave *nachas* to children about their parents, as well. It was common practice for R' Chanina to tell a *talmid*, "You know, your father is a big *talmid chacham*," or "Your father is a big *baal chesed*," or "Your father is a *chashuve Yid*."

To paraphrase R' Pam, by telling children positive things about their parents, one lifts the parent in the eyes of the child, causing the relationship between parent and child to improve. The child looks at his parents more positively, and therefore respects them more.

All part of the role of a *mechanech*.

"How Can I Not Go?"

WHEN R' CHANINA BECAME A SEVENTH GRADE REBBI, R' SHLOMO Freifeld gave him a mandate. "You must go to every bar mitzvah!" He explained, "Your *talmidim* may not remember what you taught them, but they'll always remember that you came to their bar mitzvah."

And so it was. R' Chanina never missed a *talmid*'s bar mitzvah. It didn't make a difference how far, it didn't make a difference how difficult, R' Chanina was there. Many years later, the *talmidim* would reminisce about R' Chanina's presence at their *simchah*. For R' Chanina, going to a bar mitzvah wasn't a burden; it was another opportunity to connect with the *talmid*, and the *talmidim* felt that connection.

This continued when he was menahel. During his tenure, Yeshiva Toras Chaim grew from one class per grade to two, and then three, which came to many bar mitzvahs per year. And he went to every single one.

With a *talmid* at his bar mitzvah

A parent of a boy in the yeshiva asked R' Chanina why he made himself so crazy to go to every *talmid*'s bar mitzvah. He looked at the parent with a baffled expression and asked, "How can I *not* go to every *talmid*'s bar mitzvah? I need to go and show how important that *talmid* is to me. I must go and deliver words of *chizuk*, not only for the strongest *talmidim*, but also for the weaker ones. What would one of them think if, *chas v'shalom*, I didn't come to his bar mitzvah for no reason?"

During R' Chanina's son's *vort*, R' Chanina was suddenly MIA, returning after about a half-hour. When asked where he had disappeared to, he answered, "I went to a *talmid's* bar mitzvah, which is taking place nearby. The *talmid* wanted me to speak, so I had the parents call me five minutes before my slot. I made it there right on time, spoke, and now I am back." He concluded with his refrain, "But how could I *not* go?"

R' Chanina with his *talmidim* at a bar mitzvah

R' Chanina didn't just attend every weekday bar mitzvah, but every Shabbos bar mitzvah, as well. If it was humanly possible to walk to a Shabbos Kiddush, R' Chanina was there. As long as his health still allowed, he would even walk over four miles each way, just to attend a Kiddush. Until he had his

Dancing at a bar mitzvah

own shul, he didn't attend only the Kiddush, but davened at the bar mitzvah, too, for two reasons: to hear the boy *lein* his *parashah,* and to further enhance the *simchah* with his presence.

One Shabbos, a *talmid*'s bar mitzvah was to take place at the Jackson Hotel in Long Beach; R' Chanina and his wife were slated to attend. Toward the end of the week, Mrs. Herzberg, who had given birth weeks earlier wasn't feeling so well. R' Chanina called the parents and explained the situation, and that it would not be feasible for him to attend.

On Thursday night, R' Chanina received a phone call from the bar mitzvah boy himself, who was in tears. "Rabbi Herzberg, if you don't come to my bar mitzvah, I'm not going. I cannot have my bar mitzvah without you!" After hearing the boy's feelings, R' Chanina discussed the situation with his wife, who agreed with him that he must attend. After all, how could he *not* go? As for his wife, despite not feeling well, she — as always — happily stood behind her husband in his *avodas hakodesh.*

R' Chanina spoke at every bar mitzvah of his *talmidim*. During the *shivah,* many rabbanim voiced the same sentiment, how they were

Speaking at a bar mitzvah

amazed at the way R' Chanina spoke about the *talmidim*. Each *derashah* was different, because each *talmid* was different. He would brilliantly zero in on the special qualities of each and every *talmid* and his unique potential, capturing the essence of the *talmid,* while connecting his thoughts to a *vort* from the *parashah*.

A number of sons of the *mispallelim* of R' Chaim Aryeh Zev Ginzberg, rabbi of the Chofetz Chaim Torah Center, attended Yeshiva Toras Chaim. R' Ginzberg attended their bar mitzvahs, and saw for himself how R' Chanina perfectly described the nature of every boy, how his speeches were tailor-made to each *bachur*, always spot-on. He knew and deeply understood every child under his care.

R' Moshe Teitelbaum, rabbi of Young Israel of Lawrence-Cedarhurst, which also has sons of congregants in Yeshiva Toras Chaim, pointed out that as R' Chanina spoke about what made every bar mitzvah boy special, he truly meant it, and the *talmidim* felt it, as well.

He wasn't above a well-placed joke either. If a boy was known as a troublemaker, R' Chanina might say something like, "I know Akiva* well; the two of us share an office!"

R' Chanina made it a point to also mention the bar mitzvah boys' parents, both the father and the mother. For example, "Your father works hard, but after a long day, he goes to the *beis midrash* at night to learn with his *chavrusa*," or "Your parents are *moser nefesh* for your *chinuch*. And they bring all their *chinuch* questions to their rav," or "Your mother is a superb *baalas chesed,* always helping others." Speeches including lines like these were the norm.

In fact, after hearing R' Chanina speak at a bar mitzvah, some parents in the Five Towns area decided then and there to send their children to Yeshiva Toras Chaim.

It wasn't just the speech. For R' Chanina, dancing at a bar mitzvah was an *avodah* unto itself. A young couple was basically satisfied with their community, but they weren't happy with the choice of yeshivos for their son. They were looking to move to a community with a more suitable yeshiva. While they were still on the lookout for the community that fit the bill, they attended a bar mitzvah of a *talmid* of Yeshiva Toras Chaim. After watching R' Chanina dance with the *talmidim,* their decision was made. Five Towns it would be, and their son, of course, would attend Yeshiva Toras Chaim.

R' Chanina was once at a *talmid*'s bar mitzvah in which the decorum was not proper and there was mixed dancing, something he had not expected. R' Chanina didn't know what to do. On one hand, if he were to leave, the bar mitzvah boy would be devastated. On the other hand, how could he and his *talmidim* remain at a bar mitzvah where there was mixed dancing?

Dancing with a bar-mitzvah boy, an *avodah* unto itself

He quickly ran to the nearest pay phone to call his rebbi, hoping he would pick up the phone and tell him how to proceed. Thankfully, R' Shlomo answered and, with his unmatched *pikchus,* advised, "Here's what you should do. Take all the *talmidim* and form your own circle and dance with *geshmak.* You'll see, the other men will join, and before long, the dancing will become separate."

R' Chanina followed his rebbi's

Linked arm-in-arm with *talmidim* at a bar mitzvah

advice, and that's exactly what happened! R' Shlomo demonstrated to his *talmid* that Yidden have a tendency to seek *kedushah* and *taharah.* Show them the beauty of Torah and they will follow.

These experiences remained with the boys. After R' Chanina's *petirah,* Yoel Judowitz communicated, "The image of R' Herzberg linked arm-in-arm with a circle of young bar mitzvah boys singing *HaMalach HaGoel* will stay with me. Another spark in the heart of a young boy, giving hope and strength for the road ahead."

Another *talmid* penned a letter to the family, "Obviously, as menahel, your father had to go to a ton of bar mitzvahs, even those a little farther away. Though that interrupted his regular Shabbos morning routine, it can be considered a necessary part of the job of every menahel. However, your father went above and beyond in this regard.

"For my friend's bar mitzvah, the family arranged a special *minyan* in the basement of Beth Sholom (which is over two miles from your parents' house). One boy from Queens slept at my house for Shabbos so he could attend the bar mitzvah *minyan* and lunch. We woke up Shabbos morning to 18 inches of snow, with more coming down. We trudged down the middle of Broadway (the middle of the street, with absolutely no cars) for the mile from my parents to Beth Sholom. I was sure there would be a sparse crowd and not that many boys.

"Lo and behold, when we finally got there and went downstairs to the *minyan,* not only were a lot of boys there, but your father was standing there in his *tallis* and davening. Aside from attending the *minyan,* he made sure to arrive on time, too. The bar mitzvah boy's mother was so appreciative that your father made it there. It really made a *roshem* on us."

As R' Chanina saw it, notwithstanding a two-mile walk in each direction in a blizzard, if it meant so much to the *talmid* and his family, how could he *not* go?

Chapter 11
Eye on the Goal: A Well-Balanced Chinuch Approach

The Right Hand Draws Close

"THE LEFT HAND SHOULD ALWAYS PUSH AWAY, WHILE THE RIGHT hand draws the person close" (*Sotah* 47a). This methodology, a foundation in *chinuch*, was one in which R' Chanina was an expert. In a *shiur* given in 1983 (5743), he shed light on his approach to discipline. "I remember when I was in middle school and got a smack from my rebbi. Here's what happened. Every day, we used to daven Minchah in the classroom. One day at the end of Minchah, I was in a good mood and I started singing *Aleinu* out loud. My rebbi looked at me with fire in his eyes, called me over to him, and told me, 'I don't like that *niggun* for *Aleinu*,' and... *wham*! — he slapped me across the face! He slapped me so hard that when I came home five hours later, I still had marks on my face. Believe me, I never sang *Aleinu* during Minchah again."

R' Chanina analyzed what happened here through the words of R' Eliyahu Dessler (*Michtav MeEliyahu* 3: pp. 16-17). R' Dessler explains the difference between doing something out of *yirah,* fear, and doing something out of *ahavah,* love. When you do something out of fear, you become distanced from that entity. But when you do something out of love, you become closer to that entity. If a rebbi tells a *talmid* who's misbehaving in class, "You better behave or I am going to call your mother

or father," essentially the rebbi is distancing the *talmid* from whatever it is he wants the *talmid* to do.

R' Chanina bemoaned the fact that unfortunately, many people today have no connection to Yiddishkeit. Each person has his own story and reason, but one of the reasons could be, in R' Chanina's estimation, that as children, they were imbued with such fear: "You have to learn — or else…" And yes, they learned while still in yeshiva, but since the learning stemmed from fear, they and the Torah did not become one. On the contrary, they and the Torah became disconnected, and as soon as they had the chance to leave the Torah behind completely, they did.

In contrast, we see that those who succeeded in being *mekarev* others did so through an outpouring of love that infused the recipients with a good feeling, until they said to themselves, "Yes, I want to learn. I don't know yet what learning is all about, but I see that there is something pleasant about Yiddishkeit, something positive about Yiddishkeit, something pleasant and positive about Torah." As they learned *aleph beis,* and then Chumash, followed by Mishnah and then Gemara, they felt closer and closer to Torah — until they and the Torah became inseparable.

"When my rebbi slapped me for singing *Aleinu* out loud," R' Chanina concluded, "he didn't bring me closer to davening; he distanced me from it! Yes, of course, there are times in which we have to discipline our children, but we must always remember the goal, that the child should become closer to that which we want him to do, not farther from it. If we train ourselves to think this way, our whole approach will be different."

R' Shlomo Wolbe[3] discusses the concept of punishment. There are parents and rebbeim who think that the main way to be *mechanech* children is through punishment. In truth, punishment needs to be a last resort. If a parent or a rebbi feels that when he has the ability to punish, he has control, this is the wrong approach, one that takes away from healthy *chinuch*.

R' Wolbe continues. Shlomo HaMelech teaches (*Mishlei* 13:24), "*Choseich shivto sonei beno* — One who withholds his stick hates his child," since the child will grow up without proper guidance. R' Wolbe explains that the word *shivto*, his stick, doesn't necessarily mean to hit. The *pasuk* (*Zechariah* 11:7) states, "*Va'ereh es tzon hahareigah lachein aniyei hatzon va'ekach li shnei maklos l'achad karasi Noam u'l'achad karasi Chovelim va'ereh es hatzon* — I had tended the flock meant to be slain, because they were the meekest of the flock. I took for Myself two staffs — one I called Pleasantness and the other I called Destroyers; and I tended the flock." We see there are two types of staffs, or sticks. There is a stick called *Noam*, Pleasantness, and the stick of *Chovelim*, Destroyers. It is important to be aware that a stick of pleasantness is also a stick. If a child does something good and his parent gives him a piece of chocolate, that's also a stick, a pleasant stick.

It is impossible to measure how much damage is caused by striking a child. Moreover, R' Wolbe points out that equal to hitting, and perhaps even worse, is screaming at a child. The author of *sefer Minchas Shmuel* quotes his rebbi, R' Chaim of Volozhin, who said (many years ago), "*Bizman hazeh kashos einam nishma'in* — Nowadays, people don't listen to harsh words."

R' Chanina counseled rebbeim, "Don't scream in your class. It's your responsibility to maintain your presence of mind and spirit, even in the most trying circumstances." He once called over a rebbi because there was too much yelling in his class. "If you need assistance with classroom management, I can work with you," he explained. "However, we can't have screaming in the classroom."

Chazal relate (*Bereishis Rabbah* 10:6) that every blade of grass has a *malach* that hits it, telling it, "*Gedal* — Grow!" This doesn't mean that

---

3. Based on *Zeriah U'Vinyan B'Chinuch*, pp. 23-26.

every blade of grass has an angel standing over it and striking it. Rather, there is a *koach* that causes the grass to grow, and this *koach* is referred to as "hitting." According to R' Wolbe, this is what Shlomo HaMelech is telling us when he says that the one who spares the rod hates his child. There are many ways far more preferable to corporal punishment when it comes to being *mechanech* children.

To R' Chanina, the goal of discipline was simply to get the child to grow. He was careful to keep that goal at the forefront of his mind, judging each situation from all possible angles to help each child develop, based on his nature and the circumstances.

He kept his eye on the goal: "*Gedal!* Grow!"

R' Avraham Fridman conveyed, "As soft, warm, and approachable as R' Herzberg was, he was an embodiment of *yirah*. Not because lightning would strike you if you crossed him, but because he had so much love for you, you were afraid of disappointing him. He had this effect on everyone."

R' Chanina did not *demand* respect; his very essence *commanded* it.

R' Moshe Teitelbaum offered an apt description. "R' Herzberg's facial expression, really every movement, was steeped in and spoke of his desire to raise *bnei Torah* for the sake of *Shamayim*. He wasn't driven by a pedagogic approach. Of course, all he did was pedagogically and educationally correct, but more importantly, it was infused with the overarching question of: *How can these kinderlach become ovdei Hashem*? He didn't have to say it; you felt it. Everything in his demeanor spoke dignity, not his own dignity, but *kvod Shamayim*."

In the 1980's, a *yungerman* whom we'll call R' Yaakov* was contemplating going into *chinuch* and becoming a rebbi. He asked R' Shlomo Freifeld if he thought he was suited for the profession. R' Shlomo questioned him, "Do you remember throwing rocks into the lake when you were young?"

R' Yaakov nodded his head.

R' Shlomo continued, "What did you enjoy more, the splash of the rock hitting the water, or watching the ripples moving outward along the surface?"

R' Yaakov thought for a moment and answered, "I liked watching the ripples."

R' Shlomo smiled. "You will make a good rebbi!"

R' Chanina learned this concept from his rebbi; he understood that it's not about the now, about the immediate results, but about reaching the ultimate goal, the ripples. About planting seeds that will take root properly, in the proper time. He used this concept to encourage rebbeim with challenging classes. "Remember, you're planting seeds!" He would repeat the famous proverb, which was also displayed in his home, "All the flowers of tomorrow are in the seeds of today."

Getting the Point Across

FOLLOWING R' CHANINA'S *PETIRAH,* R' DOVID BASHEVKIN WROTE,[4] "There were two types of moments you could have with R' Herzberg, one in his office and one after winning a raffle. The former was terrifying, the latter exhilarating. When R' Herzberg officiated, and there is no other appropriate term to describe the way he conducted a raffle, it was like he was the *mesader kiddushin* at a wedding. There was gravitas and anticipation as he picked out the lucky name who would win a few dollars or a soda. R' Herzberg used his own black hat as the receptacle for the tickets, and as he pulled out the name, it's how I imagined it looked when Abraham Lincoln pulled out the Gettysburg Address from his top hat. But before pulling out a name, he would mix up the tickets and always say the same line: 'The *lokshen* is always at the bottom.' He reminded us that, like with a hearty bowl of chicken soup, the good stuff was at the bottom of the hat.

"That, however, was not the only place he used the phrase. Walking into R' Herzberg's office was nothing short of harrowing. He would sit behind his desk, with his imposing elbows planted on his desk. But once the door shut, R' Herzberg balanced rebuke with warmth. It was always clear, to me at least, that he enjoyed the students who were a little wilder and jumpier. A student who was sincere and struggling was not a problem or an issue — it was the *lokshen* at the bottom, waiting to be discovered."

Discipline to R' Chanina was all about reaching the desired goal. It

4. *Top 5: Lists of Jewish Character and Characters,* R' Dovid Bashevkin, Israel Bookshop, p. 104.

was not about punishing the child; it was about teaching the child the right way to behave. About helping the child discover the *lokshen* at the bottom. And he used various means to get his point across. His discipline approach was different for each child, because each child is different.

R' Avraham Fridman related, "When people tried to institute rule-books in Yeshiva Toras Chaim, dictating the consequences for each infraction, R' Herzberg had no interest. One *talmid* did something minor and R' Herzberg gave it to him, while another *talmid* could do something severe and R' Herzberg responded lightly, sitting and talking with him."

A prominent menahel was faced with a dilemma. A group of 12- and 13-year-old boys attended their friend's weekend bar mitzvah at a hotel, leaving the televisions on over Shabbos so they could watch a sports playoff game on Friday night after the *seudah*. Hearing what happened, the menahel wasn't sure how to react.

It was only after discussing the issue with R' Chanina that he felt a sense of direction in dealing with the matter. R' Chanina instructed him to think about each boy individually — analyze his background, his parents, his neighborhood — and only then sit with each child and talk about *kedushas Shabbos*. He underscored that each *talmid* had to be spoken to on his own level.

The menahel followed R' Chanina's advice and dealt with each child differently. Many years later, those *talmidim* still remembered how their menahel handled the situation, dealing with each one differently — and successfully.

Naftali,* an alumnus of Yeshiva Toras Chaim, shared what he referred to as "a golden story." When he was in seventh grade, Naftali's class joined the eighth-graders for Minchah in their classroom. Every day, when Naftali came into the eighth-grade classroom for Minchah, he and an eighth-grader would get into an altercation during Minchah, disrupting the *minyan*. Word reached R' Chanina about the daily battle, and he decided to finally put an end to the chaos.

And so it was, the day arrived. R' Chanina came to the classroom to take a look. Arriving on the scene, he stood and stared as Naftali and the eighth-grader went head to head, knocking over a desk in the process. Suddenly, everyone realized R' Chanina was standing there, and they all froze in fear.

"It's come to my attention," R' Chanina began, "that there's a problem in this class between two boys. Don't you see," he continued, directing his words at Naftali and his nemesis, "that you would make great friends, if only both of you would realize what you have in common? You know why you two keep fighting? Because you want to have fun and do something together, because you want to make a show for your friends. Well, congratulations! You passed the auditions, and everyone has been thoroughly entertained. Now, the show is over!"

R' Chanina began to applaud, and everyone else joined in.

"The show is over," he repeated. "And one more thing. From now on, if two boys have a problem, come to me and we'll work it out. I'm not a movie director and I'm not a policeman."

With those words, R' Chanina walked away.

As for those two boys, they became good friends and never clashed during Minchah again.

"In fact," Naftali appended, "R' Herzberg actually made us look pretty cool, and we became popular from the story. Little me, a seventh-grader, earned the respect of the eighth-graders."

Technically speaking, R' Chanina may not have handed out any consequences that day, but with his thought-out approach, he achieved his goal. Not only did the fighting stop but the former adversaries became friends, as well. Had he merely reacted with a consequence, perhaps the brawls would have stopped, but chances are the boys would not have become friends.

The story doesn't end there.

A year later, Naftali, now an eighth-grader, was at it again. This time, he was sneaking into the Mesivta Ateres Yaakov building next door. The high school boys used to sell bagels every morning. Naftali went there to buy bagels for breakfast, something strictly prohibited to the eighth-graders. Eventually, the tenth-graders grew upset that Naftali was buying their bagels and another tussle broke out, with tables flipping over in the process.

Suddenly, out of nowhere, R' Chanina appeared. "Act Two has begun!"

R' Chanina asked Naftali for the captain hat that he happened to be wearing at the time, and said, "You're not the captain, I am!"

Turning to the high school boys, he announced, "By the way, you have to give Naftali credit for having the guts to come into the mesivta and hang out with the older boys."

Naftali's old enemy and new buddy, who was now in ninth grade, was there at the time and piped up, "That boy's all right. I already went through this with him last year when I was in eighth grade."

R' Chanina then censured Naftali for his behavior, warning him not to sneak in to buy bagels again.

After describing both scenarios, Naftali stated, "In both situations, R' Herzberg understood what needed to be said in order to get me to change. To R' Herzberg, it wasn't about the action of disciplining, it was about the *talmid* getting the point."

Throughout elementary school, Meir* was a typical boy, toeing the line and doing well in yeshiva. In seventh grade, however, he became wild, making it difficult for the rebbi to teach. One day, Meir took it too far, cracking an irreverent joke in class. The rebbi felt he had no choice but to give him a consequence and place him in another class. After Meir spent part of the day in the "new class," R' Chanina walked into the classroom and told Meir to meet him outside.

"I was walking down the hallway with R' Herzberg, side by side," Meir remembers. "Then in the sincerest way possible, he said to me, 'Meir, I know you're a good boy.' That was it. No speeches, no lectures, just those few poignant words. R' Herzberg didn't even tell me to stop misbehaving and go back to class. All he said were those few words before he walked me back to my classroom.

"At that moment," Meir later determined, "R' Herzberg gave me the *chizuk* to realize who I really am!"

Now a grown man, Meir still thinks about those few words, "Meir, I know you're a good boy," and they continue to give him *chizuk*.

Once, when several boys threw smoke bombs in school, causing the fire alarm to go off and the firefighters to come, R' Chanina was strict with the perpetrators as he meted out punishment. At the same time, he made it clear that their action did not define them.

They were good boys, who happened to have done something foolish.

Then there was Avigdor,* whom R' Chanina caught climbing in the air conditioner vents. "Hey, Spiderman," R' Chanina called to him, "next time let me know so I can have you fix the vents."

"I stopped misbehaving after that," Avigdor shared, "It just wasn't worth it anymore." Avigdor had been seeking attention, albeit negative, but R' Chanina had reacted so indifferently that he was no longer achieving his goal. Hence, it was no longer worthwhile.

R' Chanina was creative in his methods of discipline. There were times in which R' Chanina and a rebbi would stage a conversation in order to temper the rebuke a child had coming to him. For example, R' Scharhon related, "If a child was misbehaving, R' Chanina would plan with me that I would stand near the boy while R' Chanina read him the riot act, and then I would 'calm' R' Chanina down and stick up for the *talmid.*"

Getting the point across, while reminding the child how much his rebbi loved him, how far he would go to defend him.

Like many elementary school children, Chesky* remembers finishing a juice or chocolate milk box, blowing it up, and then jumping on it to hear the infamous pop. One Sunday morning, when he was in second grade, Chesky saw a chocolate milk box on the floor. He jumped on it, expecting it to make a pop, which would make everyone laugh. Little did he know, the chocolate milk box was full! When he jumped on it, a significant portion of its contents splattered on Chesky's rebbi. The rebbi did not find this particularly funny and sent Chesky to R' Chanina's office.

R' Chanina asked Chesky to clean up the mess, and then called his father to come down to yeshiva immediately to discuss what happened. R' Chanina tried to explain to Chesky what he had done wrong. But since he'd thought the box was empty, Chesky could not comprehend what was improper about his action. R' Chanina tried a few more times to explain it to him, but for some reason, his message was not penetrating. In the end, R' Chanina turned to Chesky's father and said, "Just forget about it. Go home and enjoy the rest of your afternoon."

Chesky mentioned this story to R' Chanina's son Eli during *shivah*. Eli explained to Chesky R' Chanina's reasoning. "Of course he let you off scot-free. You didn't understand what you did wrong, and if he would have punished you, he would have caused you to feel animosity toward the rebbi, without understanding the wrongdoing involved. That would have been pointless. He saw there was no *chinuch* lesson to be learned, so he just sent you on your way."

R' Chanina walked into a first-grade classroom and noticed a boy playing with a calculator with bells and whistles, producing a variety of sounds. Not wanting the boy to disturb the class, R' Chanina confiscated the calculator. Soon after, he noticed another boy in the hallway, crying. When asked the reason for his tears, the boy explained that the calculator belonged to him and he had just lent it to the boy who had been playing with it. Ever the one to own up to his mistakes, and also to only discipline if there was a point, R' Chanina immediately returned the calculator to its owner.

In an ad journal in memory of R' Chanina, one mother penned a beautiful memory. "When we joined Yeshiva Toras Chaim almost 17 years ago, a decision we are still extremely thrilled with, we noticed a very kind and gentle side to R' Herzberg. I thought he had a special affinity for my boys, when he let my boys get away with all kinds of nonsense. It was only with the passage of time that I realized he picked his battles carefully, selecting only those in which all sides will emerge victorious: the yeshiva and my boys.

"That was wisdom that is ahead of our time. I will be forever grateful for that foresight, and I am sure that as my boys get older and realize this, they, too, will have endless appreciation for him."

R' Chanina was fond of telling a story in which he was involved. A 16-year-old boy desecrated Shabbos multiple times and was sent away from his yeshiva. The boy began to feel dejected, like no one cared about him and no yeshiva wanted him. R' Chanina, who was asked to help out, took the boy to R' Avraham Pam.

At first, R' Pam spoke to the boy by himself, and he gave the boy strong *mussar* for 10 minutes. After a break to daven Minchah, R' Pam continued to speak to the boy, this time with R' Chanina in the room. As R' Pam discussed *kedushas Shabbos,* he was crying the whole time!

"You know what?" R' Chanina testified. "It worked! The boy resolved to change his ways. R' Pam sized up the child and dealt with him in a way that would bring about the desired outcome."

R' Chanina added, "We have to be *mechazek* others. We can't just brush others off. This is Yiddishkeit — to feel for another Yid."

Mastering the "How"

NO MATTER HOW WELL A TEACHER KNOWS HOW TO CONTROL A classroom in theory, he will not be able to get past first base if he doesn't know how to present the material.

R' Shmuel Rozovsky, rosh yeshiva of Yeshivas Ponevezh in Bnei Brak, was world-renowned for his *shiurim*, each of which was presented with absolute clarity. R' Shmuel expended an inordinate amount of time and effort preparing those *shiurim*. He had already mastered the material — that was not what took time. Rather, as he delineated to those who asked, there were three steps to preparing his *shiur*. First, he prepared *what* to say. Next, he prepared what *not* to say. Finally, there was the actual presentation of the *shiur* itself: *how* to say it.

R' Chanina, a master of the "how," taught others how to do the same.

In his words, "How the material is transmitted is as important, if not more important, than the actual material being transmitted. 'How' includes several components: the order of the material being transmitted; the excitement and *geshmak* that you display when giving over the material; appropriate examples to help the *talmidim* understand and internalize the material; and proper emphasis on important words and concepts. Children need clear messaging, nothing convoluted. When talking to *talmidim*, make sure the words you use are simple and on their level. This could make all the difference in whether or not they absorb the material properly. This requires preparation, but is very necessary." R' Chanina had another practical reason for being well-prepared. "Because if you're not prepared, the *talmidim* will pick up on it and eat you up alive!"

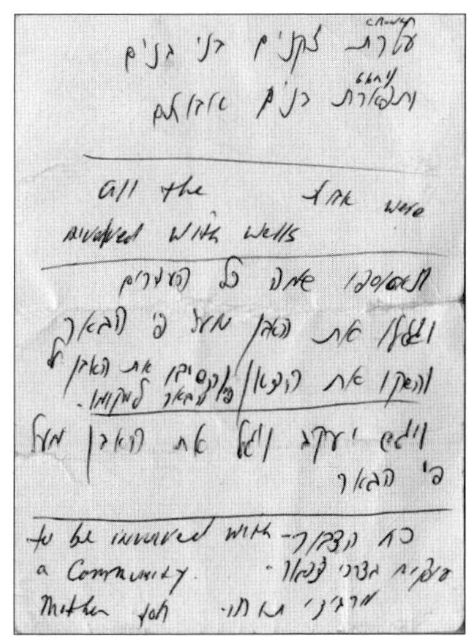

Pointers jotted down on the inside of a place card in preparation for a bar mitzvah speech

When preparing to speak in public, in his shul or at a bar mitzvah, R' Chanina always made sure to jot down what he planned to say, along with the sequence of his speech.

As a seventh-grade rebbi, as well, he was meticulous about preparing each day's lesson. After his *petirah*,

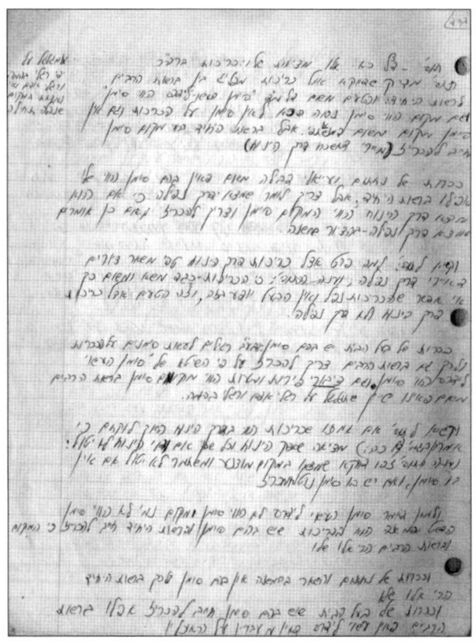

R' Chanina's notes in preparation for teaching Gemara

the family found his notes on the various *perakim* of Gemara that R' Chanina taught, with the *shakla v'tarya* (give and take) of each Gemara clearly and meticulously written out, along with the relevant *mefarshim.* This was in line with the instructions of R' Shlomo, who explained the words of *Pirkei Avos* (1:6), *"U'knei lecha chaver* — And acquire for yourself a friend," homiletically. The word קנה can also be translated as a reed, or a writing implement. In other words, make your pen your good friend and write down what you are learning and what you are planning to teach. R' Shlomo cited R' Isser Zalman Meltzer, who would write down the Gemara as he prepared the *shiur* for Yeshivas Etz Chaim.

When he came into class, R' Chanina delivered the *shiurim* with excitement and *geshmak.* R' Mordechai Respler, rosh yeshiva of Mesivta of Long Beach, was in R' Chanina's class as a seventh-grader in Yeshiva Tiferes Moshe in Queens. Remembering those days, R' Respler described how his rebbi would come in to teach the daily Gemara. "He was alive, he was *geshmak,* he was on fire, and it was contagious." Another *talmid,* R' Eliakim Koenigsberg, rosh yeshiva in RIETS, described R' Chanina as "a *gavra,* whom you wanted as your leader, to march to his drumbeat... He never sat; it was like he was dancing around the room." After observing R' Chanina in action in his classroom, R' Yussie Lieber noted, "R' Chanina had his students mesmerized with the typical 'R' Herzberg *kedushah* with a sense of humor.'"

One day, R' Chanina paused in the middle of teaching a piece of Gemara and intercepted in a booming voice. "Do you hear the symphony? The Gemara, the Rashi, the Tosafos — it is *mamash* a symphony! Ahh, what could be better?"

His seventh-grade *talmidim* remember how the Gemara itself became relevant in R' Chanina's classroom, through practical, relatable *meshalim*. Once, when teaching the *sugya* of "*haba b'machteres*," which speaks about digging a tunnel to enter someone else's house, R' Chanina could see that his *talmidim* were struggling to understand the concept. "It's like when the Jets run through the tunnel to enter the field," R' Chanina illustrated. The *talmidim* smiled, grasped the concept, and were ready to learn.

The final component of the "how," emphasis on the appropriate words and concepts, can be understood through a story R' Shlomo used to share regarding the Kotzker Rebbe, R' Menachem Mendel Morgenstern. The Kotzker Rebbe once came to a *cheder* to test the students. The boys had just finished learning *Parashas Bereishis*, and a boy was asked to recite some verses near the end of the *parashah*, which detail the genealogy of the generations from Adam to Noach.

The wording of the verses (*Bereishis* 5:3-32) is identical. "*Vayechi Adam…vayamos… Vayechi Sheis…vayamos…* — Adam lived… and he died… Sheis lived… and he died," and so on. The boy was translating the verses fluently and confidently into Yiddish: "*Vayechi* — *Un ehr hut gelebt* (and he lived); *vayamos* — *un ehr is geshturben* (and he died)." Then again for the next descendant, "*Vayechi* — *Un ehr hut gelebt* (and he lived); *vayamos* — *un ehr is geshturben* (and he died)."

The Kotzker Rebbe stopped the boy and said, "That's not how you say those verses. Recite them again."

The boy was surprised; he was repeating them exactly as he had heard from his rebbi, but he obeyed. Once again, he recited, "*Vayechi* — *Un ehr hut gelebt; vayamos* — *un ehr is geshturben*." The boy was sure that he said it right this time.

However, the Kotzker Rebbe corrected him. "No, that's not how these *pesukim* are said. This is how you say them," and he called out in a bellowing voice, "*VAYECHI* — *UN EHR HUT GELEBT*! (AND HE LIVED!)" And then in a barely audible voice, "*Vayamos* — *Un ehr is geshturben* (and he died)." The Rebbe exclaimed again, "*VAYECHI* — *UN EHR HUT GELEBT*! (AND HE LIVED!)" and in a soft, low voice, "*Vayamos* — *Un ehr is geshturben* (and he died)."

After finishing the story, R' Shlomo smiled. The Kotzker's lesson was obvious. One must live with verve and vibrancy.[5]

R' Shlomo's lesson was obvious, as well. Proper emphasis on specific words can make all the difference.

---

5. Based on *Reflections of the Maggid*, ArtScroll Publications, p. 255, R' Paysach J. Krohn.

From a Wellspring of Love

"GROWING UP, WHEN WE SAW OUR PRINCIPALS, WE RAN FOR COVER. We were afraid of them," reminisced R' Yaakov Bender. "R' Chanina was one of the main people in the Five Towns community who eradicated that." This was an important facet of R' Chanina's outlook. He once remarked to his son, "The day that the *talmidim* run away from me out of fear is the day I retire from *chinuch*."

Even so, when R' Chanina had to react strongly, react strongly he did. He was uncompromising in his desired goal to change the child, no matter what it took. R' Shalom Rosner remembers, "R' Herzberg had a tangible love for his *talmidim*, but at the same time he was *'chareid lidvar Hashem,'* determined to keep the word of Hashem. If something had to be said, if the *talmidim* needed to hear it, he said it and didn't mince words." But it came from a place of love.

R' Shmuel Kamenetzky, director of advancement at Yeshiva Toras Chaim, wrote following R' Chanina's *petirah*, "As a menahel, there were many times when he had to discipline a child. But he did it in the most loving way. He was tough, and he would not back down on what he believed was true or proper. He would look at a *talmid* with a sincere look, penetrating to the *talmid's* very essence, but there was so much love in that look. His *talmidim* understood everything from that look, and even before he gave his rebuke — and sometimes the consequence, which he dutifully carried out — the *talmid* understood that it came along with genuine love."

Throughout elementary school, Menashe* misbehaved; he was a recurrent "guest" in R' Chanina's office. Menashe shared a "tough love"

moment he had with R' Chanina when he was in eighth grade. Menashe was up to no good, spending time with inappropriate company in the neighborhood, and R' Chanina found out about it. This was a critical issue and needed to be addressed immediately.

The next morning during breakfast, R' Chanina called Menashe over in the lunchroom for a serious conversation. "Menashe, I hear you're hanging out with the wrong crowd. But just know, if I'm driving in the neighborhood and I see you hanging out, I will stop my car in the middle of the street, get out of the car" — here R' Chanina delivered the clincher with a slight grin — "and with a big smile on my face, I will smack you in the middle of the street in a way that you'll never forget!"

That conversation was a turning point for Menashe.

As a *chassan,* when Menashe was planning the *kibbudim* for his *chasunah* along with his father, he requested that R' Chanina receive a *berachah,* and explained why. "For all the *'Gehinnom'* I put him through. Through it all, he never gave up on me, loving and caring for me all along."

Eventually, R' Menashe became a successful *mechanech.* Reflecting on that far-reaching moment in the lunchroom with his "*mechanech* eyes," he realized that everything about that conversation was calculated. R' Chanina chose to have the discussion in the lunchroom and not in the typical place, his office, and he did it with a smile. "It was as if he was telling me," inferred R' Menashe, "that the rebuke he was giving me came from love, because he cared about me. Not just because as a menahel he couldn't have boys acting in this manner. My takeaway from that moment is: When administering rebuke, you have to make sure you say it the right way, at the right time, and in the right place."

Even at the beginning of his career, as a rebbi in Yeshiva Tiferes Moshe, R' Chanina's goal was not to instill fear in his *talmidim*'s hearts. He believed that if *talmidim* see that their rebbi loves them, they will respect him, and everything else will come. When he had to discipline a child in his class, he did it in a way that the child understood that it was not personal, but because he cared about the *talmid*'s growth.

As menahel, if a child was sent to the principal's office for disciplinary reasons, and R' Chanina had to be firm and strict to achieve his objective, the *talmid* still knew that it stemmed from a wellspring of love. Since the *talmidim* realized how much he cared about them, R' Chanina's words of *mussar* were not rejected, but allowed to penetrate their hearts.

At times, a child could be seen leaving the office with a huge smile on his face. When asked why, the child would often reply, "R' Herzberg made me feel good about myself. He even gave me a treat!" The whole approach emanated from a source of deep love, care, and concern. As R' Chanina's son Yudi said, "The more you misbehaved, the more you loved my father!" They felt the love — and reciprocated.

Bentzion* was what many would call "the biggest troublemaker who ever walked the halls of Yeshiva Toras Chaim," and on many occasions he had to be dealt with severely, even being suspended numerous times. Eventually, he turned his life around, becoming a *ben Torah.* When he was interviewed for the book, he had only one description for R' Chanina's interactions with him: "It was just love!"

Another *talmid* communicated, "I can personally attest to this love. From my earliest days, I had frequent flyer miles piling up from being sent to R' Herzberg's office. I felt like I had a menahel in the front office who truly understood me and just wanted me to be able to reach my potential, although over the years he did rebuke me many times. Every time I walked out of his office, he made sure I walked out with a smile, yet at the same time instilled in me an appreciation of what I did wrong. He had the understanding that many times children enjoy having fun and are sometimes *chutzpah'dik* as a result. They do not specifically intend to be disrespectful; it simply turns out that way."

One day, when R' Chanina was teaching seventh grade, he noticed a boy playing with a toy gun in class. R' Chanina immediately confiscated the gun and placed it on his desk. After waiting a short while for the message to penetrate, R' Chanina lifted the gun, pointed it at the boy, and with a grin on his face, "shot" him. The *talmid* later related that this was R' Chanina's way of telling him, "I had to confiscate the gun, but I also know you are a boy. And boys will be boys."

When Nachi* and Zechariah* were in third grade, dismissal was at 4:15 p.m. Since they lived in Queens and there was only one bus from school to Queens, they had to wait in yeshiva for the 5:15 bus. The waiting game did not always bring out the best in them.

One day, Nachi and Zechariah were in the middle of an intense fake shootout in the lunchroom/*beis midrash*, using their hands as fake guns. Suddenly, R' Chanina walked into the room, and everything came to a stop. R' Chanina looked at them with an unsmiling face, shook his head from side to side in disappointment, and kept on walking.

After walking a few feet, R' Chanina spun around without warning. He pretended to take a gun out of the inside of his jacket pocket and proceeded to "shoot" both of them with his hand/gun. Then he picked up his hand, i.e., the fake gun, blew the "smoke" off the top of his finger, and walked away.

Three decades later, Nachi described the experience as "an awesome moment," one that "made a huge impression on me. R' Herzberg made his point, but with love and *geshmak*."

Later, when Nachi was in eighth grade, he was selling firecrackers with another friend, Yair.* One day, Yair was caught with the contraband and spilled the beans about his partner, Nachi, who was sick and at home. Soon after, the phone rang in Nachi's house, and his mother answered. It was R' Chanina calling for Nachi. Very slowly and nervously, Nachi took the phone. "Naaaachi," R' Chanina said in a singsong tone, "I want some firecrackers. Do you know where I can buy some firecrackers?" Nachi's blood ran cold.

Though he ended up suspended from yeshiva for a day or two, in Nachi's view, this story, too, demonstrated R' Chanina's love. "He had the uncanny ability to put true fear into you. On one hand, he was very strong and serious when our actions were wrong. On the other hand, his discipline was completely surrounded by warmth and love.

"Both these stories," Nachi averred, "capture one aspect of the greatness of R' Herzberg. Regarding many people in *chinuch*, if people love

them, it's because they act very *geshmak* in an overly exuberant way. But R' Herzberg was not like that at all. He was a very serious person because he had a very serious job as a menahel, as a *mechanech*. He treated us seriously, as *bnei Torah*, even like men sometimes. I was definitely scared of him because he was serious. You were supposed to do certain things and you weren't supposed to do other things. And that was the most amazing thing, because it was so real and genuine. But of course, that was backed up by much more serious love and care, and not taking himself too seriously.

"That is how, at least for me, he made such a great impression. I have an unbelievable love for him. I still think about him a lot. I even have a picture of him in my office. As a social worker, I try to keep in mind what he taught me and ask myself what he would do in specific situations."

Balancing Act

R' CHANINA WAS UNCOMPROMISING, BUT WELL-BALANCED. A YESHIVA Toras Chaim alumnus conveyed, "In seventh grade, I was the first boy in my class to become a bar mitzvah. The yeshiva had a rule that every bar mitzvah *bachur* must wear a hat and jacket during davening. I remember complaining bitterly to R' Herzberg about being the only one who had to wear a hat and jacket; I wanted to wait until the next boy in my class became a bar mitzvah to start wearing them. But R' Herzberg held his position firmly and explained to me that a *ben Torah* always wears a hat and jacket when davening before Hashem, even if it involves social discomfort. His persistence made a huge impact on me, as this important message of wearing a hat and jacket during davening was implanted within me at a young age.

"R' Herzberg wasn't just a school principal. He was a man of principle, who saw what was best for his *talmidim* and never wavered from what he believed to be truly right."

In a similar vein, a parent shared, "Our son was the oldest in his class, and he became a bar mitzvah in sixth grade. He was proud to wear a hat and jacket during davening, but a problem arose. There were no empty hooks or cubbies downstairs upon which to hang his brand-new hat and jacket. There was space allotted for the seventh- and eighth-graders, but those hooks and cubbies were full. My son asked R' Herzberg what to do.

"Instead of telling my son to bring his hat and jacket back to his classroom, which may have led to ruining his hat, or even worse, caused him embarrassment, R' Herzberg came up with a simple solution. 'Keep your hat and jacket in my office,' he suggested. 'I have an extra hook just for you.' My son agreed, but was still worried what would happen if R' Herzberg was not there one day, or if he was in a meeting before Minchah and his office door was locked. R' Herzberg told him not to worry. He instructed his secretary, Mrs. Monika Weinberg, that any time my son needed his hat and jacket, she should open the door for him!"

While R' Chanina was *makpid* that boys should wear a hat and jacket under all circumstances, he also understood the challenges involved, and came up with an out-of-the-box approach to solve the issue.

Accentuating the Positive

YOEL,* A PARTICULARLY ROWDY FIFTH-GRADER, WAS HAVING A TOUGH day. After a scuffle with a friend in the yard during recess, Yoel raced back into the building and bolted down the hallway, through the *beis midrash*, and toward the classroom. As he was nearing the safe haven of his classroom, he crashed right into the menahel, R' Chanina. R' Chanina had been observing Yoel's mini-marathon from afar and held out his arm to stop the sprinter in his tracks.

After the initial shock of being caught running in the halls, Yoel followed R' Chanina to his office to hear his consequence. R' Chanina sat

Yoel down, looked the boy in the eye, and asked, "Do you know what I saw you do?"

Yoel fought to find words with which to respond. He finally answered sheepishly, "I was running in the hallways."

R' Chanina went on. "But do you know what else I saw?"

Yoel shrugged his shoulders.

"I saw that as you ran through the door of the *beis midrash,* you slowed down a bit to kiss the *mezuzah.*" R' Chanina smiled. "You have such a good heart, and you have a real feeling for mitzvos. I want you to focus on that, and that will be your path to becoming a better person."

Shlomo HaMelech teaches (*Mishlei* 9:8), "*Al tochach leitz pen yisna'eka hochach l'chacham v'ye'ehaveka* — Do not rebuke a scoffer, lest he hate you; rebuke a wise man, and he will love you." The Shelah explains that Shlomo is referring to one person; the scoffer and wise man can be one and the same. By calling a person a derogatory name, i.e., a *leitz,* a scoffer, we are addressing his evil side and causing him to hate us rather than listen to us. However, if we tell him that he is a *chacham,* that he is wise, and that it is shameful for someone like him to conduct himself improperly, we are addressing his virtuous side. Then he will love us and will be willing to accept our words.

The Shelah is teaching us a very simple concept: A person acts according to the way he is treated. Call him a fool and he will act like a fool. Call him a *chacham* and he will do his best to live up to that designation.

R' Chanina sought the positive qualities of his *talmidim* and they responded accordingly.

Gershon,* a *talmid* in Yeshiva Toras Chaim, was a fair student. However, when he was in the upper elementary grades, his mode of dress and behavior shifted toward the rebellious side. He grew his hair longer and wore clothing that was less refined than that of the other boys. As time passed, his behavior also bordered on the disrespectful, and his rebbeim grew concerned. One day, he came to yeshiva with the top two buttons of his shirt open and a gold chain around his neck.

A *hanhalah* member took note of him and approached R' Chanina, suggesting that Gershon had crossed a line and a strong reaction was warranted. With his keen understanding of youth, coupled with the loving and accepting philosophy he received from his rebbi, R' Chanina asked the *hanhalah* member, "Did you ever watch Gershon daven?"

Surprised by the question, he responded in the negative.

"Watch how he davens," R' Chanina said. "Watch how he stands and says *Shemoneh Esrei,* eyes closed, with deep concentration."

At the next opportunity, the *hanhalah* member observed Gershon in prayer. He truly davened with intense concentration, his *Shemoneh Esrei* lasting almost 20 minutes.

"A boy who davens like this," R' Chanina maintained, "will come into his own if left alone."

R' Chanina's patience and tolerance paid off. Gershon kept growing. Today, he is a fine *ben Torah*... and his davening is still exemplary.

Eli Herzberg, who spent many years working with his father, conveyed an important *yesod* he heard from R' Chanina. A menahel should make his office open and accessible to the students. This will give them a place to walk into and vent on any issue affecting them, preventing a very high percentage of incidents from occurring in the first place. Additionally, if the children have plans that could negatively impact the yeshiva, the menahel will most likely hear about it from a class goody-goody, allowing him to solve the problem before it even happens.

R' Chanina's office was a haven for the children with behavioral issues. They would just walk in, sit down opposite his desk, and begin discussing the issue "du jour." Furthermore, R' Chanina solved many children's problems just by giving them a little bit of extra attention. Numerous *talmidim* remember how R' Chanina would take them to the pizza store for a quick lunch treat. This individual time gave them terrific *chizuk* and the impetus to settle down. R' Chanina also made the troublemakers his helpers, getting them to run little errands around the

yeshiva in order to keep them out of trouble and give them a sense of accomplishment.

The Full Picture

ONE SHABBOS MORNING, R' CHANINA EXCITEDLY CALLED OVER HIS son and showed him a story about R' Elazar Menachem Man Shach, rosh yeshiva of Yeshivas Ponevezh, which encapsulates the mindset necessary when disciplining a child.

A yeshiva *bachur* was caught a number of times being *mechallel Shabbos* in his dormitory. His roshei yeshiva went to ask R' Shach for permission to expel the *bachur* from the yeshiva. Very weak and frail due to advanced age, R' Shach rarely saw people at that point. Because of the severity of the situation, though, the roshei yeshiva were permitted entry. After hearing them out, R' Shach sat deep in thought for several minutes. Finally, in a feeble voice, he asked, "What is the financial situation in the boy's home? Do his parents have *shalom bayis*?"

The roshei yeshiva were surprised by these questions. "How should we know what is happening in his house?" they wondered.

R' Shach became visibly agitated. With great difficulty, he strengthened himself, grasped the table, and pushed himself up. With tears in his eyes, he yelled, "*Rodfim, gei avek fuhn mein shtub*! Pursuers (a *rodef* is the terminology used for a person chasing someone for the purpose

R' Elazar Menachem Man Shach

of killing him), get out of my house! I don't want to speak to you. You don't know the boy's home situation, you don't delve into his personal life, and all you know is how to throw him into the street!"

They hastened to investigate and discovered that the family suffered from extreme poverty and the parents had recently divorced.

Years ago, a relative of R' Chanina was dropping off her child at his yeshiva, and she noticed a peculiar sight: a bareheaded man walking his son into school. Several days later, R' Chanina was visiting this relative, and she mentioned how strange it was to see a father walking into a yeshiva with no head covering. It bothered her that this person wasn't more sensitive to the *kedushah* of the yeshiva, and she expected R' Chanina to agree with her.

However, the opposite happened! Uncharacteristically, R' Chanina raised his voice. "Do you know where this person is holding in life that you're able to judge him? Do you know everything he's going through?" He continued softly, "Listen, every person goes through things in their lifetime. Maybe this man is going through a spiritual crisis, or maybe not. Maybe he was on his way to work and forgot that his head was uncovered. The main thing is to never judge a person hastily."

R' Chanina was always willing to find a side of *zechus* in any situation. The remarkable thing was that so often he was correct! Either way, by thinking a bit more into what another person may be going through, he was able to pinpoint and "diagnose" the issue and then find a workable solution when needed.

He applied this approach to *chinuch* situations.

R' Chanina emphasized, "When disciplining a *talmid*, a *mechanech* has to stand back and view the full picture. Why is he behaving this way? Is it because there is an issue at home? Is it because he hangs out with the wrong people? Is it because he does not see *hatzlachah* in his learning and therefore has low self-esteem? Maybe he has some other underlying issue that needs to be addressed? Only by dissecting the issue can one properly approach the situation and deal with it appropriately."

"Since I worked as a rebbi under my father for so many years," Eli Herzberg confided, "I was fortunate to sit in his office many, many times. He would open a conversation and say, '*Nu*, Eli, what would you do in such a situation? The *talmid* is like this, something is happening, so what would you do?' I would listen and I'd offer my opinion.

"Then my father would say, 'Okay, now what would you say if I told you that the family situation was such-and-such? Would that change your opinion?' I would say, 'Yes, of course,' and he would continue, 'And what if I told you that the mother or father came from such-and-such background, and that affected what's going on in their lives?' Again, I would have to change my answer. "He would look at every single situation in a unique way and from every single possible angle, approaches you couldn't even imagine, until he would formulate his opinion."

R' Chanina enjoyed quoting George Bernard Shaw on the topic. "Few people think more than two or three times a year; I have made an international reputation for myself by thinking once or twice a week."

R' Avraham Robinson also gleaned this from his many conversations with R' Chanina. "I learned to take time to think, in order to gain a deeper understanding of a given situation and to see it from as many angles as possible, before coming to any kind of conclusion." Multiple times, R' Robinson would walk into R' Chanina's office and find him sitting there, with his arms crossed and staring into space. Eventually, R' Robinson learned that whenever he had to make a decision, R' Chanina would tear through the issue "like a *talmid chacham* 'learning up' the *sugya* from all possible angles."

In R' Zev Davidowitz's words, "R' Herzberg was a master chess player. He saw the big picture, and he saw the small picture. He knew when he needed to sit and plan. When others saw confusion, he saw the clear pathway to execute his plan. He had an overarching control and clarity."

R' Chanina with his son Eli
at a Yeshiva Toras Chaim dinner

A rebbi in Yeshiva Toras Chaim caught a *talmid* playing Hangman in class. The rebbi handed the paper back to the boy and sent him to the menahel. "Go show R' Herzberg what you were doing in class!"

The boy entered the menahel's office, sheepishly gave him the paper, and explained that he was there to show his "work." Taking in the whole picture and knowing that this boy could use some *chizuk*, R' Chanina glanced at the paper, locked eyes with the boy, and with a twinkle in his eye, said, "Oh, you're playing hangman? Give me a 'K'!" He then rebuked the boy softly, offered him *chizuk*, and sent him back to class.

While contemplating going into school administration, R' Yussie Lieber visited R' Chanina in Yeshiva Toras Chaim to observe how the master operated.

A rebbi walked into R' Chanina's office with a *talmid*. "This boy is ruining the class," the rebbi stated, leaving the boy in the office and returning to his classroom.

R' Chanina arose from his chair, walked to the other side of the desk where the boy was seated, and sat down next to him. "Are you really interested in ruining the class?" he asked.

"No," the boy replied. "It's just hard for me to sit still."

"Okay, I'm punishing you for what you did, for exactly one minute." After a minute passed, R' Chanina told the boy, "Now that you've been punished, we're going to have a meeting with your rebbi." R' Chanina asked the rebbi to come back to his office and told him in front of the boy, "To me, it seems that ____ wants to be the best boy in the class. Please let him walk around the class when he needs to."

The rebbi agreed.

When sharing this story, R' Yussie concluded, "You should have seen the smile on the boy's face. He was so *b'simchah*. It was as if he were saying, 'Someone cares about me.' At that moment, I had the feeling that R' Chanina saved his life."

In fifth grade, Elchanan* was involved in so much mischief that he practically shared an office with R' Chanina. Every time he was sent to R' Chanina's office, Mrs. Weinberg, R' Chanina's secretary, would announce, "It's him again!" Elchanan would enter the office and R' Chanina would be sitting back in his chair. In a friendly and animated voice, R' Chanina would yell, "Chuni!"

"We'd talk, he'd give me a cold can of Fresca, and then he'd send me back to class," Elchanan/ Chuni recalled. With his infinite wisdom and long-range vision, R' Chanina understood that this was the approach Elchanan needed.

R' Robinson pointed out that at times, R' Chanina would address a discipline problem head-on, yet at times he would hear about an issue and ostensibly leave it unaddressed. At times like these, others may have thought that R' Chanina was sweeping the issue under the rug, but nothing could be farther from the truth. Every action, and inaction, was thought out and calculated. Sometimes not addressing the problem at all, or at least for the time being, was the proper method in attaining the ultimate goal.

Before disciplining a child, R' Chanina asked himself, *Is the time and place appropriate to say something to him? Perhaps in a different setting or a different time he would be more receptive?*

This was imbued in him through an incident with his rebbi. R' Chanina was once called into R' Shlomo's office, and R' Shlomo got right to the point. "A few years ago, you didn't speak to me with the proper respect. You should be more careful in the future."

Perplexed, R' Chanina inquired, "But Rebbi, why didn't you tell me when it happened?"

"Because then," R' Shlomo stated, "you weren't ready to accept the rebuke, and now you are ready!"

"I remember a time," R' Shmuel Katz related, "when a student thought he had done something very inappropriate. Thankfully, after checking into it, it turned out that there was nothing to worry about and the student had misinterpreted the situation. I, as well as other administrators involved, were quite relieved with the results of the 'investigation.' We said so to R' Herzberg. I will never forget his reaction.

"'Yes, it's a relief that this boy was not involved in what he thought, but what about his mental state? He thought he did something wrong and is still agonized over it! Our job is not done until we heal his mental injuries and make sure he can successfully move past this.'"

That's called seeing the full picture.

R' Chanina highlighted the importance of not reacting out of anger, but taking time to study the ins and outs of each scenario. Shlomo HaMelech (*Koheles* 7:9) teaches, "*Al tevahel b'ruchacha lichos, ki chaas b'cheik kesilim yanuach* — Do not be hastily upset, for anger lingers in the bosom of fools." The wise person takes his time evaluating a situation and allows himself the time and introspection to reflect on a proper response.

R' Chanina (center) with his sons (l-r): Yitzchok and Eli, on a Chol HaMoed trip

Citing this *pasuk*, R' Chanina would caution his son Eli, "Don't react right away to any *talmid* who is acting up in class. Evaluate the situation and look deeper into the real reason the student is acting this way. There is always an underlying reason for a person's actions. If you respond to a *talmid*'s actions out of anger, the damage is twofold. One, you won't be assessing the situation correctly. Two, the *talmid* won't even listen to you! What are you accomplishing then?!"

When Eli and Yitzchok, both of whom are in *chinuch*, would ask their father for advice about how to react to a disciplinary issue, R' Chanina would tell them, "Sleep on it and you'll see, in the morning you will have clarity." This is based on the *Sefer Chassidim* (Chapters 83, 655), which tells of a man on his deathbed who begged his son to honor him after death by agreeing to never react hastily when he feels anger overcoming him. He requested, "Always allow yourself to 'sleep on it,' so you should never respond out of anger."

Despite his capabilities, Tuvia,* an eighth-grader in Yeshiva Toras Chaim, was not interested in learning in *limudei kodesh*. His rebbi, R' Isaacson,* tried every trick in the book but Tuvia remained unmotivated. At the end of the year, R' Chanina informed R' Isaacson that Tuvia was slated as salutatorian in general studies. To R' Isaacson's protests that Tuvia did not deserve to speak if he had underperformed in *limudei kodesh*, R' Chanina replied, "It's important to look at the big picture over here. Knowing Tuvia and his personal situation, if he deserves to be salutatorian in general studies and is not awarded the honor, he may have a *taanah* against us. We must take into account how our decision will affect this specific child and how he will react, along with the ultimate result."

On one occasion, a boy who had skipped eighth grade and was already in ninth grade in mesivta was invited by R' Chanina to join his friends on the graduation trip, because, as he expressed, "You only graduate once."

But that wasn't the only time R' Chanina invited a boy who was officially out of school to come along on the long-awaited trip. When a Yeshivas Toras Chaim *talmid* got into mischief in eighth grade and endangered the entire school — students and staff alike — with his antics, he was, understandably, asked to stay home until the end of the school year, for about six weeks.

But R' Chanina was still concerned about the graduation trip. If this young man would not be permitted to go on the trip, he would not forget the affront for the rest of his life, and R' Chanina could not allow that to happen. So though the boy deserved to be punished and was not allowed back to school, R' Chanina showed his care and concern by inviting the *talmid* on the graduation trip.

Everything was calculated just so.

When Eli was 18, he awoke early one Shabbos morning, expecting to see his father learning *Midrash Rabbah* in his study as he usually did. Instead, he found R' Chanina crying.

"Abba, what happened?" Eli asked.

"A teenager from a local yeshiva was found smoking last night, and someone just came to ask me for the proper response, how to handle the situation. Tell me, Eli," R' Chanina continued, "aren't you learning *Maseches Sanhedrin*? Do you know the definition of *dinei nefashos*? This is *dinei nefashos*!"

And he treated it as such.

R' Chanina also knew when a *chinuch* question was out of his domain and it was time to ask a *gadol*. At a meeting of menahalim from various yeshivos, the discussion arose regarding when it's warranted to send a boy away from a yeshiva. The dialogue went on for a few minutes, until R' Chanina asserted, "That's why we have *gedolei Yisrael*. You have to go to a *gadol* and ask him what to do."

Every year, R' Aharon Rogoznitzky and R' Pinchas Segal, of Tashbar Chazon Ish in Bnei Brak, would stay at the Herzberg home during their

R' Aharon Rogoznitzky (center) with R' Chanina in R' Michel Yehudah Lefkowitz's house, being shown a *sefer* R' Chaim Kanievsky inscribed for his rebbi, R' Michel Yehudah

fundraising missions in America. They told R' Chanina a story, one that reinforces what he said to the menahalim.

Feivel Atlas* was thrown out of a New York *cheder* for being *chutzpah'dik* to his rebbi in public. Despite his best efforts, Mr. Atlas was unable to get his son reinstated. Several days later, R' Shlomo Kanievsky, son of R' Chaim Kanievsky, was in Brooklyn. Mr. Atlas met with him and unloaded. Upon hearing Mr. Atlas's tale of woe, R' Shlomo shared a story that he had heard from his father.

A *bachur* in Eretz Yisrael was expelled from yeshiva by his rebbi for smoking a cigarette on Shabbos. Distressed, the father went to the Chazon Ish, who called the rebbi in and told him, "For *dinei mamonos,* money matters, you need a *beis din* of three. For *dinei nefashos,* life-and-death matters, you need a *beis din* of 23. So how can you *pasken* this on your own?"

The rebbi, however, wouldn't budge and did not want to allow the *bachur* reentry.

With the confidence of a *gadol,* the Chazon Ish said to him, "I'm a *ne'eman* and I can *pasken* the *shailah* — and I say you must take him back."

The rebbi stubbornly stuck to his position. "It's him or me!"

To which the Chazon Ish replied, "It's you." The rebbi was out.

But the problem wasn't completely solved just yet. The next day, the menahel of the yeshiva complained to the Chazon Ish, "Now, I have no one to say the *shiur*!" The Chazon Ish, in his humility, offered to say the *shiur* instead. Hearing what was taking place, the rebbi apologized and came back to the yeshiva, where he continued teaching the *bachur*.

The *bachur* eventually became a *gadol baTorah*.

Coming Clean

ONE DAY, WHEN R' CHANINA'S SON WAS IN EIGHTH GRADE AT YESHIVA Toras Chaim, he was walking in the hallway with his friend Binyamin.* Binyamin decided to take the fire extinguisher off the wall and spray it all over the hallway, a severe offense. Later that day, R' Chanina called his son into the office.

"Listen, I know who did it, but here is the problem. Now that I know about it, I have to deal with the issue and I can't ignore it. If I 'find out myself,' then I am going to have to call in Binyamin and give him a severe consequence. However, if he comes clean, admits his mistake, and shows real remorse, I can turn it into a positive moment and praise him for admitting his error and doing *teshuvah*. Then there will be no need for a consequence, because he will have learned his lesson. It could also serve as a lesson for the rest of the class that if a person makes a mistake, he should own up to it. Please talk to Binyamin and convince him to confess.

"One more thing," R' Chanina added. "Make sure not to tell him I sent you."

And that is exactly what happened.

The same son related another incident. "I was at a weekend bar mitzvah in a hotel, celebrating the *simchah* of a classmate. We were playing catch in the lobby of the hotel on Friday night after the *seudah*. Unfortunately, one of my throws went awry and smacked into a vase, cracking it in the process. I quickly ran over to the vase and turned it around, so that the crack was facing the wall and not the lobby area.

"On Shabbos morning, I was discussing the incident in passing with my parents, who were also there for the weekend. My father and mother immediately walked over to the vase to see the extent of the damage. After giving the vase a look-over, my parents explained that I need to go over to the owner and apologize for the damage. I was very embarrassed, but I did, and she said, 'No problem, don't worry.'

"Sunday morning, my mother told me that we were going to buy another vase for the hotel lobby. I protested, 'Mommy, the hotel owner said it's all right! Why do we have to buy her a new vase?' My mother replied firmly, 'It's the right thing to do.'

"We went to T.J. Maxx, bought a vase, and brought it home. My mother, who is a floral designer, put together a beautiful centerpiece. We then drove back to the hotel to hand-deliver the vase."

That son concluded, "I learned from my parents the importance of owning up to one's mistakes. Until this day, I have no issue admitting when I am wrong — thanks to that incident."

One morning, Eitan* and some of his seventh-grade friends decided that instead of coming to davening on time, they would play basketball in the classroom, using the trash can as the basketball hoop. R' Chanina found out and gathered all the culprits in the shul, calling upon each boy, one by one, to explain himself. At first, the boys gave one ridiculous excuse after another and then sat down to await their "sentencing."

Until it was Eitan's turn. "I realized that what everyone else was trying wasn't working," Eitan explained later. "So I got up and said, 'R' Herzberg, I have no excuse. I made a mistake and recognize it was the wrong thing to do, and I'm ready to accept whatever punishment you have in mind for me.'

"R' Herzberg told me, 'Say it louder so everyone can hear what you just said!'

"I said it louder and then R' Herzberg said, 'Eitan, go back to class. You are excused and nothing is going to happen to you!'"

Eitan, now a well-known rav, relayed, "It's been many years and I've made many mistakes since then, but I've never had a problem apologizing and taking responsibility for my mistake, though I see that other people do have trouble in this area. Why is it that I don't have a problem? Because at an early age, R' Herzberg taught me that admitting your mistake is the right thing to do."

While grading a yeshiva-wide test, the administration realized that several boys in one class had cheated. R' Chanina went into the classroom and said, "If you admit that you cheated, you won't get into trouble." Three boys raised their hands. R' Chanina gave a short *shmuess* about stealing, and that was the end. He never brought it up again.

R' Dovid Bashevkin also remembered that R' Chanina was very big on honesty. "R' Herzberg would prefer that a *talmid* did a big infraction and came clean than if he did a small infraction and did not come clean."

From time to time, Sholom* hung out in the classroom instead of attending Shacharis. R' Chanina would come upstairs in his *tallis* and *tefillin* looking for him. As soon as Sholom heard the menahel coming, he would scurry away and return to the yeshiva's *beis midrash* before R' Chanina could catch him. One time as Sholom ran away, R' Chanina made a quick move, took a shortcut, and was waiting for Sholom at the bottom of the stairs. All he had to say was, "Sholom, it's not about the davening, it's about the honesty! What are you playing games for? Come on!"

Point well taken.

They'll Outgrow It!

R' CHANINA WOULD QUOTE A *PASUK* (*YESHAYAH* 1:18), "*LECHU NA v'nivachechah yomar Hashem, im yiheyu chata'eichem ka'shanim ka'sheleg yalbinu* — Come now, let us reason together, says Hashem. If your sins are like scarlet, they will become white as snow," along with R' Yaakov Kamenetsky's explanation, based on the *Yerushalmi* (*Yoma* 6:5).

If your sins are "*ka'shanim,*" which can also be translated as "like the years," then they will become white as snow. If a 10-year-old child is sinning in an age-appropriate manner, like his years, then there is no need to worry. Eventually, he will outgrow his behavior, which is simply a "*maaseh naarus* — action associated with youth" (see Rashi, *Bereishis* 37:2), and his record will be white as snow.

A *talmid* came into yeshiva with a magazine that was inappropriate for a Torah institution. After R' Chanina dealt with the boy, someone questioned him, wondering if perhaps he should have reacted more strongly.

"Don't worry," R' Chanina responded, "I know the boy well. He'll be fine. This was "*maaseh naarus.*"

Today, that boy is a kollel *yungerman*.

R' Chanina understood boys and the challenges they faced. One morning, Ovadiah* shmoozed his way through Shacharis in yeshiva, and not with his Creator. Despite numerous warnings from his rebbi, he simply could not control himself. He was therefore not surprised when

R' Binyamin Kamenetzky and R' Chanina in the Yeshiva Toras Chaim shul following Shacharis

R' Chanina came over to him during breakfast and said, "Ovadiah, please go to my office. We need to talk."

R' Chanina entered the office soon after and spoke very firmly. "Ovadiah, I must call your parents regarding the disrespect you're displaying toward *tefillah*. It is simply unacceptable! Would you prefer if I call your father or your mother?" He placed his hand on the phone, as if to call.

However, before punching in the numbers, he turned to Ovadiah and inquired, "Can you at least tell me what was so important that you shmoozed the entire davening?"

Ovadiah, a huge sports fan, admitted, "I wanted to find out all the sports scores from yesterday's games."

R' Chanina put the phone down. "Oh, why didn't you say so?" He reached into his briefcase and handed Ovadiah the daily newspaper. "Here, will this help? Find out what you need and go to *shiur*. I am going to be asking your rebbi how your day went. I expect to hear great things!"

At the *shivah* for R' Chanina, Ovadiah described how the care and concern from R' Chanina still reverberated, nearly 40 years later!

Zero Tolerance Policy

R' CHANINA HAD ZERO TOLERANCE FOR BULLYING. THERE WAS NOTHing that elicited stronger intervention from him than students bullying one another, and he made it his business to eradicate the problem as soon as he found out about it.

Following R' Chanina's *petirah*, as the stories poured in about his zero-tolerance policy in regard to bullying, his children couldn't help but wonder, *What was it about bullying that struck such a chord with our father?*

A few years later, they found their answer. As R' Chanina's family members were going through old belongings in their childhood home, they came across their father's eighth-grade graduation autograph book, in which his classmates had written him notes and penned their best wishes. R' Chanina's children read through the book and were astonished by some of the autographs in the book, which mocked the fact that he was overweight.

Looking at each other in disbelief, it suddenly dawned upon his children why their father had taken bullying so seriously. As a child in elementary school, Chanina was overweight and he himself was bullied.

R' Chanina did not have a specific methodology when it came to dealing with bullying, just as he did not have a specific method in dealing with other issues. Each child is different and therefore each child was dealt with differently. Since R' Chanina knew every child, he was able to choose the best approach for each one. For one type of bully, the optimum approach was just discussing the issue with the child in a calm way, while for another it was raising his voice and instilling within the bully true fear. For another, it meant talking to the bully and making it his business to check up on the situation daily for days or even weeks, until the issue was completely resolved. Yet for a different type, it meant calling the bully and his victim out of class and talking to the two of them every few days, until they became good friends.

Mr. Robbins* recalled that soon after he enrolled his eldest son, Elisha,* in Yeshiva Toras Chaim, Elisha found himself not only having to contend with his newbie status, but also being severely bullied on the school bus. R' Chanina was apprised of the problem and immediately hatched a plan. One day, as the buses were pulling away from school, he jumped into his car and followed Elisha's bus. When the bus was within walking distance of the bully's house, R' Chanina told the bus driver to stop the bus, walked up the steps, and walked onto the bus.

Looking the bully in the eye, R' Chanina told him, "If you bully a boy on this bus, you have no permission to remain. So please get off and walk home." Seeing he had no choice, the boy stepped off the bus and began walking home, while R' Chanina drove slowly alongside him to make sure he made it home safely. The boy never bothered Elisha again, and they even became good friends.

When relating the anecdote, Mr. Robbins added, "R' Herzberg never told me what he did. It was only five years later that I heard the story."

A different parent mentioned another approach. "My son was in third grade and was being bullied by another boy. One day, he refused to leave the car in the morning, and my wife was exasperated. R' Herzberg came out to the car, took my son by the hand, and let him remain in his office with R' Herzberg for a few hours until my son felt ready to go back into his classroom."

A Yeshiva Toras Chaim alumnus recalled, "When I was in fourth grade, my friends and I were involved in a big dispute. R' Herzberg called us out of class, sat us down in his office, and talked to us for a while. He continued to do this every few days, until we became best friends. I am over 40 years old, and one of those boys is still one of my closest friends. It's all because of R' Herzberg, and his incredible *pikchus* and foresight in dealing with the issue."

In most cases, if R' Chanina noticed that a class was having *bein adam la'chaveiro* issues, he would pay them a visit and tell them a personal story. "I was once walking along the boardwalk in Far Rockaway, when I passed a man who looked familiar. It was clear he was not frum and was going through a difficult time.

"He looked at me and I looked at him.

"'Charlie?' the man finally asked. 'Is that you?'

"I couldn't believe it; it was an old classmate of mine from elementary school! 'Avraham,* it's so nice to see you,' I said. 'We haven't seen each other since our days in elementary school in Yeshiva Toras Chaim. How are you?'

"'I'm not great,' Avraham replied, 'I've lived a difficult life.' Then Avraham told me something that shook me to the core. 'Charlie, you're probably wondering what happened to me. I was a regular frum boy in elementary school, and now I'm not frum and look like a bum. I'll tell you what happened. I don't know if you remember, but when we were in elementary school, I was overweight and the class gave me a nickname.'

"'Sure, I remember,' I told him. 'They called you Blimpie, and you seemed to enjoy the name.'

"'Well, Charlie, let me tell you the real story. I hated the name! Yes, I smiled when boys called me Blimpie, but that was just to cover up how hurt I was. I would cry myself to sleep at night, I couldn't take it, but the boys thought it was funny and they wouldn't stop. This went on for years. Finally, we were in eighth grade, and I had to choose a high school. I told my parents there was no way in the world that I was going to mesivta with my friends. My parents tried to convince me, but I just wouldn't listen; I was too hurt inside.

"'To make a long story short, I refused to go to mesivta and ended up going to public school. When I was in public school, I fell in with the wrong friends and as they say, the rest is history. One thing led to another and before I knew it, I wasn't frum and got involved in no good. I am who I am today because of our elementary school class!'

"It was at that point," R' Chanina would tell the students, "that I realized the power of our words, how they can change people's lives. It's a life lesson I always carry with me. What he told me gave me an extra sensitivity toward boys being bothered or bullied."

After R' Chanina was *niftar* and the family sat *shivah*, the alumni came, one after the other, and acknowledged that they would never forget the "Blimpie" story, and the powerful lesson it carried.

Chapter 12

Chinuch by Example: "Do as I Do, Not as I Say!"

"CHILDREN PICK UP ON EVERYTHING. THEY ARE CONSTANTLY WATCHING us, evaluating, observing, and most importantly, learning from our actions. They have an uncanny ability to notice inconsistencies, to see when we are sincere and when we are not completely one with what we're doing. One of the main tricks in raising a healthy family is to be consistent, to be real."

Show, Not Tell

This was R' Chanina's take on *chinuch.*

R' Chanina in a moment of *dveikus;* with his children at his daughter Rivky's *chasunah*

R' Chanina and his wife ran a home steeped in Torah and *yiras Hashem*. In their phenomenal approach to raising children, they implanted within their children a deep appreciation for Torah ideals, a yearning for greatness in *avodas Hashem*, and for the boys, a desire to become *talmidei chachamim*.

But there was so much more.

Growing up in the Herzberg home was a unique experience, and the children intuited that they were part of a special upbringing. Their parents projected a subtle undercurrent, a silent missive calling out to their children to grow, that there is more to life than the mundane.

What was their secret? How did they transmit this message?

As can be expected, R' Chanina was *mekabel* his *derech* in *chinuch habanim* from his rebbi, R' Shlomo Freifeld, who was *mekabel* from his rebbi, R' Yitzchak Hutner.

R' Shlomo described how R' Hutner enlightened him. "When my first child was born, I was very perplexed. I was suddenly faced with the task of being *mechanech* a child. I noticed that people did it in different ways. I did not know what to do. I went to my rebbi and I told him I'm suddenly tasked with this awesome responsibility of bringing up a child. Every person wants his child to go *b'darchei haTorah* and *b'darchei hayirah*, to have *ahavas Torah* and *ahavas haYahadus*.

"I told him I see people who constantly talk to their children, preach to their children, criticize their children — they are constantly watching their children — people who pinch their children to get them to daven. And I know myself; I can't do any of these things, so I felt at a loss.

"I said to my rebbi, 'Please teach me what to do. How is it done? What's the recipe?'

"He laughed at me and told me, 'It's a very simple recipe. Whatever you want your child to do, you do. You want your child to make *berachos*, you make *berachos* properly. You want your child to *bentch* with *kavanah*, you *bentch* with *kavanah*. You want your child to daven with *kavanah*, you daven with *kavanah*. You want your child to learn, let your child absorb and see that you learn. That is the recipe; there's no other recipe!'"

R' Chanina recapped the "recipe" R' Shlomo received from R' Hutner, adding other "ingredients" as examples of how children mimic their parents. "The foundation of good *chinuch* is the personal example parents set for their children. This idea is repeated over and over in the *sefarim* of 'big Jews,' and I have personally witnessed this myself. You want your children to be *baalei chesed* and sensitive Jews, you need to be the paradigm of *gemilus chasadim.* You want them to have *middos tovos*, you need to have *middos tovos*. If a father and mother are committed to developing their own character traits, then the children, by osmosis, absorb their behavior into their own personalities.

"Numerous times over the last 40 years, I have seen children of 'regular, simple Jews' who became the heads of beautiful families, vibrant members of communities, and fine, outstanding ambassadors of our nation. It was not because their parents forced them to learn or daven. Rather, it was their own humble approach to *avodas Hashem*, and their constant, subliminal message that they provided for their children. A message of *middos, chesed, ahavas Yisrael, ahavas Torah*, and concern for what was important. We must set good examples for our children. If we do, we stand a very good chance of having *doros yesharim mevorach*, blessed generations following the straightforward way of the Torah."

Though R' Chanina believed in this method of *chinuch habanim* from the moment he had his first child, it took time until he managed to master the methodology and make it a part of him. And it was R' Shlomo who helped him get there, all but knocking it into him. One Shabbos morning, soon after R' Chanina had been hired as menahel of Yeshiva Toras Chaim, he was davening in Yeshiva Sh'or Yoshuv with his eldest son. He was trying to coerce his son, all of 9 years old, to daven Shacharis. After all, how would it look if the menahel's own son is not davening?

After davening, R' Shlomo summoned R' Chanina for a quick "conference."

"R' Chanina, what were you doing to your son during davening?"

Slightly flustered, R' Chanina replied, "I was trying to get him to daven."

"No!" R' Shlomo asserted. "Do not preach. Let him see that you take it seriously, that it's real to you. Then he will daven.

"And one more thing," R' Shlomo added with his usual dose of humor, "if I ever see you poking your son again, trying to get him to daven, I'll hit you over the head with a stick!"

That one incident helped formulate a path in *chinuch* that has impacted thousands of children. It was the catalyst to mastering the method of practicing, not preaching. For close to 40 years, R' Chanina related this story to young parents who came to him for advice; it became his refrain: "*Rabbosai*, I'm telling you, if you want your children

R' Chanina's *dveikus b'mitzvos*

to do something, then make sure you are doing it yourself!" Those few words of advice helped numerous parents lay the proper framework for excellence in *chinuch habanim.*

R' Chanina would often say, "Children learn more from looks than from books." In many ways, parents and teachers teach more through action, by what the children see them doing, than through book-teaching. He often repeated what R' Binyamin Kamenetzky, rosh yeshiva of Yeshiva Toras Chaim, told him. As a young boy, he learned how to *bentch* by observing his own parents, R' Yaakov and Rebbetzin Ettil, reciting the words of *Bircas HaMazon* out loud. "Our parents never *told* us how to *bentch,*" R' Binyamin punctuated. "They *showed* us how to *bentch*!"

R' Chanina's children don't recall their father telling them to wash *netilas yadayim* in the morning or to make a *berachah.* In fact, it was uncommon for their father to *tell* them what to do at all.

He *showed* them what to do.

Tefillah

ONE OF THE MANY QUESTIONS PARENTS GRAPPLE WITH IS IN REGARD to davening in shul: *At what age should I start taking my children to shul? Should I force them?*

R' Chanina never forced his sons to come with him to shul on Shabbos. He never even brought up the topic. If his boys asked to come to shul to daven with him, they were more than welcome, but on one condition: that they sit in shul like menschen without talking. If R' Chanina felt they were not mature enough to sit in shul and refrain from disturbing, he discouraged them from coming.

He believed that a child should not be coerced to daven in shul when he is not yet ready to behave appropriately. If he is, then improper conduct during davening, along with negative feelings toward *tefillah* in general, become embedded within him, hindering him for life. R' Chanina much preferred that his boys begin davening in shul at an older age, but that they do so properly.

R' Shlomo Wolbe[6] concurs with this method. "A person should be careful not to take his children to shul with him at too young an age. A child doesn't have any idea what is happening in shul. He doesn't understand the order of davening and the child doesn't daven. Therefore, besides the fact that ultimately the child will inevitably disturb others, the main problem is the *chinuch* of the child himself. A child needs to know from the first moment that he steps foot into a shul that this is a special place. Here there needs to be *mora mikdash* (awe of the holy place). A child must be given the feeling that here we don't play around. If a child is too young and therefore can't be expected to behave properly in shul, then a parent shouldn't bring him to shul. The more a person postpones starting to bring the child to shul, and the child understands better what is happening in shul, the better his *chinuch* will be, as will his *yachas* to shul in the long run. If the child is brought when he is too young and the shul becomes a place to play, this will stick with him, and it will be very hard to change."

Chazal (*Taanis* 2a) teach us that *tefillah* is *avodah she'b'lev,* service of the heart, and R' Chanina would give it his all, every single day, every single moment. Hence, when the time came for his children to come to shul, they saw in their father a living example of how a Yid davens to the *Eibishter* — word by word, with full concentration, in conversation with his Father in Heaven, and nobody else. An expert in the *nusach hatefillah,* R' Chanina knew the different *niggunim* and *minhagim,* and enjoyed davening for the *amud.*

One of the first *mispallelim* to arrive in shul on Shabbos morning, R' Chanina would sit by his *shtender* in his *tallis,* davening *Pesukei DeZimrah* carefully and slowly. Aharon Kaplan, his son-in-law, attested, "He never came late to a *minyan.* Never." To ensure this, he always insisted on leaving to the *minyan* with plenty of time to spare. At times, Aharon would assure his father-in-law that there was no need to rush. "It's fine. We will go soon and we will get there in time." But no, they had to leave right then. He was not taking any chances.

On the Yamim Noraim, there was even more to learn. For example,

---

6. Based on *Zeriah U'Vinyan B'Chinuch,* pp. 43-44.

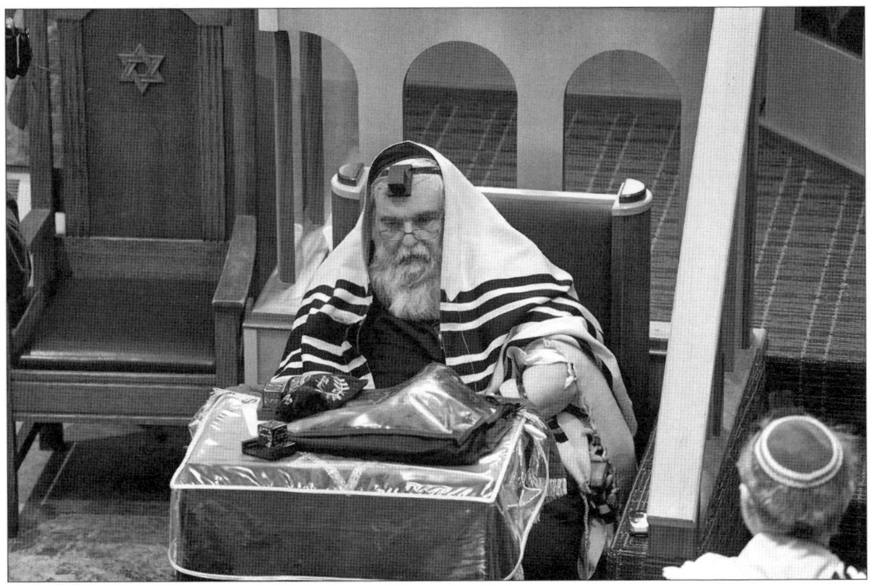

Davening in Yeshiva Toras Chaim

on Yom Kippur, when reciting the *piyutim* of the *Asarah Harugei Malchus* — one of the emotional parts of the Yom Kippur davening — R' Chanina would start slowly, in a low voice. As he delved deeper into the words, his *tefillah* would reach a crescendo as tears rolled down his cheeks, a reflection of his pure *neshamah.*

During the week, R' Chanina davened with the *talmidim* in yeshiva. He recited the entire *tefillah* out loud, one word at a time. Simultaneously, he would look out over the entire room filled with *talmidim,* making eye contact and encouraging them, with his warm gaze, to daven properly. His enthusiasm was contagious, and the *talmidim* would join wholeheartedly.

R' Chanina's own davening had a profound effect on the *talmidim,* just as it did on his children. "As R' Herzberg davened the entire davening word for word out loud," Reuven Davies, an alumnus, articulated, "he burned the words of davening into my brain, especially the way he *leined Krias Shema* with the *trop*. Even now as an adult, every day as I say *Krias Shema,* I picture R' Herzberg in my mind. I see his eyes looking at me, and I think to myself, *I hope I can live up to his expectations*. I feel like he's still watching me today as he was watching me then, making sure I say *Krias Shema* properly."

R' Yussie Lieber observed R' Chanina not only in the classroom

Presenting siddurim to first-graders

and in the office, but also in the yeshiva's shul, to see how he ran the school's *minyan*. "For a large part of the davening," R' Yussie recalled, "R' Chanina didn't leave his *shtender.* He stood there davening while looking at every boy with a smile. Later on, he walked around and again smiled at every boy. At the end of davening, he complimented the *talmidim,* 'It's such a pleasure to daven with this *minyan,* all *bnei Torah* who want to be close to the *Eibishter.*'"

R' Yussie summed it up, "He ran everything so well, and with such positivity."

To impress upon *talmidim* the true essence of *kavanah* in *tefillah,* R' Chanina told them an amusing but true story. "There was a *pashute Yid* in the shul in East New York, where I grew up. He was davening with so much enthusiasm that his pants fell down — and nobody in the shul laughed! Now, boys, why would nobody laugh? Wouldn't that be a funny sight? The answer is that because every single one of them was looking in his siddur, trying to daven with *kavanah* and say the words properly... they simply didn't notice. That's what it means to daven with *kavanah*!"

Along with his special love and appreciation for *tefillah,* R' Chanina also demonstrated an awe for prayer, which he gleaned from his rebbi. "What is our *avodah* in *tefillah*?" asked R' Shlomo (*Nitzavim-Vayeilech* 5750). In answer, he told the story of a *talmid chacham* who

became incapacitated as he aged. When he sat outside, even on hot days, he was careful to wear his hat and *kapota*. To the question, "Why doesn't the rav take off his hat and his *kapota*? It's much more comfortable without them in this heat," he replied, "I'm older already and I don't have the strength to really daven and learn. At least let me sit *b'eimah u'v'yirah* before the *Ribbono shel Olam*."

"That's what our davening has to be like," said R' Shlomo. "We may not know what *tefillah* is, but at least we can sit *b'eimah u'v'yirah* before the *Ribbono shel Olam*."

Naturally, R' Chanina did not tolerate talking during davening. This continued even after his children were married. If their father noticed them talking in shul, he would let them know that such behavior was not acceptable.

At times, though, he didn't have to rebuke others not to talk in shul to get his point across; his obvious *ahavas Yisrael* did the job for him. It was the first time R' Chanina davened *Kabbalas Shabbos* at a bungalow colony near his summer home in Woodridge. Settling himself at the back table, he opened his siddur and began to daven. Yet his *kavanah* was compromised, because one row over sat a *chevrah* of young men who chattered through the entire davening.

About 30 years later, one of those men depicted the scene. "R' Herzberg was an imposing figure, with a long beard, a *kapota,* and an up-hat, and we were expecting to be blasted by him for talking throughout davening. To our surprise, immediately following davening, R' Herzberg came over to us and said *shalom aleichem* and talked to us.

"We were so taken by the fact that instead of giving us *mussar,* he befriended us, that from then on we wouldn't talk in shul when R' Herzberg davened with us — because we were embarrassed to talk in front of him."

AT THE *SHELOSHIM* GATHERING FOR R' CHANINA, HIS SON ELI described how his father inspired a love of learning within his children.

Limud Torah

First, he prefaced by saying that R' Chanina's method was unique and not necessarily the only way. However, since R' Chanina was an expert *mechanech,* Eli felt it worthwhile to publicize his approach.

"Our father never learned with us. Never. Now, let me explain. He never formally opened a *sefer* and sat down with us to learn Gemara, halachah, Chumash... anything. He did not take us to Motza'ei Shabbos learning programs. He did not take us to Yeshivas Mordechai HaTzaddik on Purim. He did not encourage us to spend Chol HaMoed in the *beis midrash*. He did not force us. He did not tell us. He did not make it the centerpiece of his relationship with us.

"Yet he and Mommy are *zocheh* to have children who all make *avodas Hashem* the focal point of their lives. Their children are *mesayem masechtos* and *sedarim* in Mishnayos, make *siyumei haShas*, and complete multiple sets of *sefarim*.

"How is that possible? Doesn't your father need to learn with you to make this happen?

"Here is what our father did.

"He learned.

"And learned.

R' Chanina (third from right) at a son's *siyum* in Yeshiva Sh'or Yoshuv; to his right are R' Binyamin Kamenetzky and R' Naftali Jaeger

"And learned.

"Early in the morning. Shabbos morning and Shabbos afternoon. Chol HaMoed. Days off from work. He sat in his chair in the living room for hours on end with his *sefarim*. He sat in front of his summer home in Woodridge for hours on end learning, with an iced coffee by the side of the Gemara.

"Our father never told any of his children to learn. He did not need to do that to instill *ahavas Torah* in us. We knew that we should love Torah, because why would our father be spending all his extra time learning if it wasn't *geshmak*?

"He did not *make* his children into *ovdei Hashem*. He *showed* us how an *eved Hashem* lives and conducts his life!

"And by the way, if we did decide to learn on Motza'ei Shabbos, or go on Chol HaMoed to the *beis midrash* for a little while, or if we wanted to buy a *sefer*, or to be *mesayem* Shas and complete multiple sets of *sefarim*, we knew how proud he was of us. His twinkle, which was always there in his beautiful blue eyes, would light up just a little brighter, and he would say, 'I'm very proud of you,' and that meant the world to us. He would then grin mischievously and add, 'But don't be too good. That might kill your reputation... be careful...'"

Rabban Yochanan ben Zakkai had five *talmidim*, each one of whom he praised in a different manner (*Pirkei Avos* 2:10-11). Regarding Rabbi Yehoshua ben Chanania, Rabban Yochanan stated, "*Ashrei yoladeto* — Fortunate is the one who gave birth to him!" What was special about Rabbi Yehoshua ben Chanania that this was said about him?

The Bartenura informs us that it was thanks to Rabbi Yehoshua's mother that he became who he became. When she was expecting him, his mother went from one yeshiva to another, asking the *talmidim* to daven that her son should become a *talmid chacham*. And from the day he was born, she kept his crib in the *beis midrash* so he should hear only words of Torah.

R' Moshe Aharon Stern, renowned mashgiach of the Kamenitz Yeshiva, wondered: What difference does it make if a baby sees the sights and sounds of the *beis midrash*? What does he understand?

The answer is that it leaves an impression on the child, and the child grows up differently. The mashgiach then told a story of a *gadol* who was presented with a question from a very sincere father. "What can I do?" the man wanted to know. "I want my son to be like Rabbi Yehoshua ben Chanania. I want to bring him to the *beis midrash* to hear

Learning in his beloved study

the sounds of learning, but no *beis midrash* will permit me to bring in a crib or carriage!"

The *gadol* answered, "If you can't bring your child into the *beis midrash*, bring the *beis midrash* to your child! See to it that your home is a home of Yiddishkeit, with *berachos* and *tefillos*. Your son should see you sitting and learning. Having a lot of *sefarim* is not enough; he must see his father learning."

R' Moshe Aharon elaborated. "I asked children of *gedolei Yisrael* and roshei yeshiva, who became *talmidei chachamim* in their own right, if they recall their childhood. They said that they remember that if they woke up in the middle of the night, they would always witness their fathers sitting and learning near a small lamp, with such pleasantness, that it penetrated their bones. They took it all in and went back to sleep."[7]

R' Chanina constantly implored fathers to make sure their children see them learning; the children have to take note of the supremacy of Torah in the home. "If you want to imbue within your children what *ahavas Torah* is, have a set *seder* every night at your dining room table, so your children will see you learning. It could be for a whole hour or

7. Based on *With Wisdom and Warmth,* Israel Bookshop, pp. 366-370, with permission from the copyright holder, Moshe Sauer/The Sarah Sauer Foundation.

R' Chanina's children spending time with him in his study

for as little as 15 minutes. If someone calls during that special learning time, instruct your children to tell the caller that their father is learning now and could he please call back later."

R' Chanina had a beautiful study packed with *sefarim*. After a long day of work at the yeshiva, he did not run out to the *beis midrash* to learn. Instead, he spent his free time learning at home in his beloved study.

This study was not hidden away in the basement or attic; it was on the main floor, smack in the middle of the hustle and bustle. This was not by accident; it was calculated. R' Chanina felt that learning at home should be done in a way that the children "feel it," as this helps infuse the house with *ahavas Torah*. Although having seven young children made for a hectic home, he always left his study door open, so his children could see and hear him learn. Some of the fondest memories of R' Chanina's children involve sitting in "Abba's study," playing with their toys or reading a book while taking in the scene of their father learning Torah.

On Leil Shabbos, whenever R' Chanina's boys went to learn in Sh'or Yoshuv after the *seudah*, they came home to see their father dozing over a *sefer*. And on Chol HaMoed, R' Chanina's children knew that the best relaxation for their father was to sit and learn undisturbed. He accompanied them on their Chol HaMoed trips, yet he managed to make the children feel he was actively involved in the trip and spending time with them, while learning from a *sefer* whenever he could.

Catching up on his learning while on vacation

About three years after R' Chanina was *niftar,* his son Yudi dedicated a *Sefer Torah* in his memory and addressed the assembled. "If Abba was alive today," Yudi stated in his remarks, "he would roll his eyes at me and say, 'Very nice, but now you have to learn more! Easy to buy a *Sefer Torah*, harder to live a *Sefer Torah*!'"

R' Chanina did his best to live it, to show his children how to live it.

Yudi Herzberg dancing with the *Sefer Torah* he donated to Khal Zichron Chanina Getzel, May 2022

R' YITZCHAK HUTNER STATED, "YOU DON'T BECOME A *GADOL* FROM learning; you become a *gadol* from *chazering*." At a *siyum* on a *masechta* held in 5749, R' Freifeld elaborated on this theme. "You just made a *siyum* on *Maseches Megillah*. I want to tell you how foolish it would be to put this *masechta* away now that you've learned it. Just the opposite, now that you've learned it, you have to *chazer* it. The Gemara (*Chagigah* 15a) says that Torah is hard to come by, like gold, but once you have it, it is easy to break, like glass. You acquire the *emes* that is in Torah through *chazarah*.

Chazarah, the Key to Success

"An *adam gadol* used to spend two-thirds of his learning doing *chazarah* and the other third learning new *inyanim*. You have to *chazer* without any *cheshbon* of how many times you've already *chazered*. *Chazarah* creates a *dveikus* between you and the *masechta* you learn. If you will *chazer*, you'll see that you won't be — you'll excuse me — a baby anymore. Your relationship to Torah will become totally different, with a *penimiyus*."

R' Shlomo hammered home the importance of reviewing again and again, until the learning becomes part and parcel of a person's thinking, until the words of the Gemara flow from his mouth like the words of *tefillah*. In fact, he posited, *chazarah* can actually make the words of the Gemara as powerful as davening. "And with this '*tefillah*,'" he maintained, *"kehn men altz oispoilen*, one can accomplish everything."

Along these lines, he would cite R' Aharon of Belz, who revealed a tried and tested *segulah* for retaining one's learning: *chazarah.* R' Shlomo wondered: We generally think of a *segulah* as an unnatural phenomenon, which works in ways we cannot understand. So how can a basic formula — review leads to wisdom — be termed a *segulah*?

In actuality, R' Shlomo answered, being able to understand Hashem's Torah, the infinite Divine wisdom, is a supernatural phenomenon. If not for His mercy, and the fact that He allows us to comprehend His holy words, we would not be able to comprehend even one word of Torah. To the degree that we exhibit a true desire to learn, He will open the floodgates of wisdom for us. Each time we review, we indicate how much we want to learn His holy Torah. As such, He sends comprehension our way, raining it down upon us.

Yes, it is a *segulah*, concluded R' Shlomo. It is Hashem's response to our unspoken entreaty for enlightenment.

R' Chanina imbibed this lesson from his rebbi. Throughout his life, he chose to learn *masechtos* of Gemara very slowly, with constant *chazarah* of the *shakla v'tarya*. For years, he expended great effort *chazering* and mastering Mishnayos. He also regularly reviewed *Midrash Rabbah* and *Ein Yaakov*, stressing that the only way to have true *hatzlachah* in Torah is through constant review.

He further drilled in the importance of review by citing a *vort* based on *Parashas Haazinu* (*Iturei Torah*). Moshe Rabbeinu impresses upon us, *"Ki lo davar reik hu mikem* — For it (the Torah) is not an empty thing from you" (*Devarim* 32:47). The Talmud Yerushalmi (*Pe'ah* 1:1) punctuates the *pasuk* differently, yielding a different interpretation. *"Ki lo davar reik hu* — For it is not an empty thing." And it it is, then, "*mikem hu* — it is from you!" You are to blame, for not spending enough time toiling in Torah.

R' Chanina holding his baby with one hand and his cherished *Ein Yaakov* in the other

In addition, the Gemara states (*Chagigah* 9b), "One cannot compare the one who reviews his learning 100 times to the one who reviews 101 times." The word מכם has the numerical value of 100. Based on this, we can explain the *pasuk* further. *"Ki lo davar reik hu* — For it is not an empty thing." And if it is, it is because of מכם, because you did not review enough. You should have reviewed 101 times, not just 100!

R' Chanina bolstered this with a *pasuk* (*Shir HaShirim* 1:2): *"Yishakeini mi'neshikos pihu* — Let Him kiss me with the kisses of His mouth." Why does the *pasuk* use the word *pihu* to refer to His mouth, instead of the usual *piv*? The *gematria* of פיהו is 101. Thus, the *pasuk* is letting us know that the ultimate kiss from the mouth of Hashem will come only if one reviews as he is supposed to: 101 times.

Furthermore, the Gemara (*Bava Basra* 10b) states, *"Ashrei mi she'ba l'kan v'talmudo b'yado* — Fortunate is the one who arrives here (in the Next World) with his learning in his hand." The word לכאן also has the numerical value of 101. If a person reviews 101 (לכאן) times, then *"talmudo b'yado,"* his learning will remain with him.

Whenever one of the Herzberg boys finished a *masechta* and excitedly told his father about his accomplishment, R' Chanina's first response was always, "Did you start *chazering* yet?" Only then did he wish him mazel tov on completing the *masechta*. This made an indelible impact on his sons.

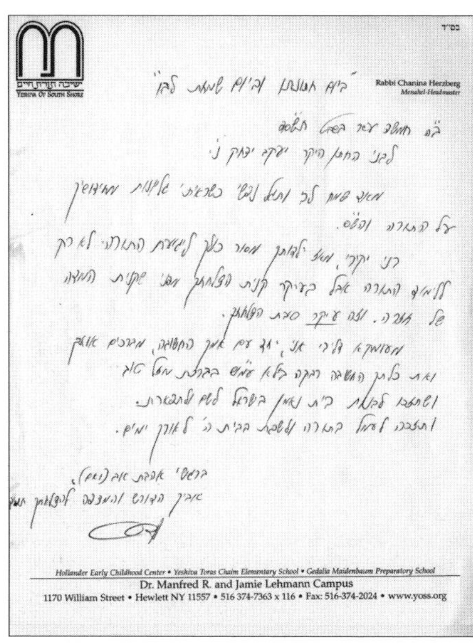
בס"ד

ישיבה תורת חיים
Yeshiva of South Shore

Rabbi Chanina Herzberg
Menahel-Headmaster

"ביום חתונתו וביום שמחת לבו"

Hollander Early Childhood Center • Yeshiva Toras Chaim Elementary School • Gedalia Maidenbaum Preparatory School

Dr. Manfred R. and Jamie Lehmann Campus

1170 William Street • Hewlett NY 11557 • 516 374-7363 x 116 • Fax: 516-374-2024 • www.yoss.org

Letter written by R' Chanina for his son's *kuntres*, which was published in celebration of his *chasunah*

When one of his sons published a *kuntres* upon the occasion of his *chasunah*, his father penned a special letter, in which he reminded his son that his success in learning came from *chazarah*. "You always loved learning from a very young age. However, you need to remember that you attained such a level of scholarship because you acquired the desire to always review your learning. This is the main reason for your success."

As R' Hutner expressed it, "You don't become a *gadol* from learning; you become a *gadol* from *chazering*."

In the late 1970's, the Herzbergs' bungalow was next door to that of R' Feivel Cohen, prominent *posek* and author of *Badei HaShulchan*, and his family. With awe in his voice, R' Chanina later reminisced, "I would get up early just to watch R' Feivel learn. It made such an impression on me! He sat outside his bungalow, from very early in the morning, reviewing from a little Gemara, turning page after page after page. It's no wonder he became such a *gadol baTorah*!"

And R' Chanina's children watched their father review and drew lessons of their own.

The Gift of Shabbos

THE GEMARA (*SHABBOS* 10B) TEACHES THAT HASHEM SAID TO MOSHE, "I have a good present in My treasure house and its name is Shabbos, and I want to give it to the Jewish people. Go and let them know." R' Shlomo Wolbe (*Alei Shur*: Vol. 2, p. 384) explains that part of the gift of Shabbos is the ability to attain the *menuchas hanefesh*, the peace of mind, which Shabbos affords.

R' Chanina had a special love for Shabbos. Though by nature a private person who kept his *ruchniyus* out of view, at the time of *Kabbalas Shabbos*, R' Chanina underwent an obvious transformation. He would sing *Lechah Dodi* with his eyes closed and a look of serenity on his face, as he entered into Shabbos with *menuchas hanefesh*.

Several years before his *petirah*, R' Chanina was asked to speak at a gathering about *kedushas Shabbos*. Among the attendees were teenagers, who, R' Chanina was told, were struggling with an unfortunate phenomenon. They were texting on Shabbos and leaving their phones on through Shabbos to receive updates regarding their favorite sports teams. R' Chanina, who was asked to address the gathering, related a well-known story about the Chofetz Chaim.

Speaking to a large crowd, a rabbi once told the story about a student in the Chofetz Chaim's yeshiva who used to smoke on Shabbos. For months, the other *bachurim* pleaded with him to stop, to no avail. One day, the boy received a message that the Chofetz Chaim wanted to see him. There was a big commotion in the yeshiva: The Chofetz Chaim had found out that he was smoking on Shabbos! The student went into the Chofetz Chaim's room and emerged a few minutes later. After that, he never touched a cigarette on Shabbos again. No one knew what the Chofetz Chaim had told him, but in those few minutes he accomplished what no one else had been able to, despite their untiring efforts.

After the rabbi finished speaking, an elderly man walked up to him. "I was the boy in the story."

His curiosity aroused along with his surprise, the rabbi asked, "So what did the Chofetz Chaim tell you?"

"When I was called into the office, I started to tremble; I didn't know what to say. The Chofetz Chaim motioned for me to come around the table, and he held onto my hand, without speaking a word. He then looked at me and uttered two words, slowly: 'Shabbos... Shabbos...' As he spoke, two tears dripped from his eyes onto my hand, piercing a hole right through my heart. He wasn't just telling me off like I felt everyone else was doing. I could see he really cared about me and the honor of Shabbos. I decided right then and there to never smoke on Shabbos again!"

After R' Chanina finished retelling the story, he closed his eyes and with emotion and passion, he called out, "Shabbooos! Shabbooos! Shabbooos! Shabbooos! Shabbooos! Shabbooos! Shabbooos!"

It was a powerful moment, a moment with a lasting effect, a moment that also spoke to R' Chanina's personal love for Shabbos.

Chazal (*Shabbos* 119a) demonstrate how various Amoraim prepared for Shabbos, each in his own special way: twining wicks for the lamps, roasting and salting delicacies, performing household duties. These leaders set the precedent for all generations to follow, and the lesson was not lost on R' Chanina, who took responsibility and helped prepare for Shabbos, whether it was grocery shopping, cooking, or running errands.

Shabbos was most important to R' Chanina and his wife, because it afforded them special time with their children. It was vital that their children be fortified with a love for Shabbos and the accompanying spirit of relaxation. The *seudos* were not about what the children had covered in school during the week. Rather, the Shabbos table was a venue in which to discuss whatever was on the children's minds. It was during these gatherings that R' Chanina transmitted his opinions on significant matters and shared stories and the accompanying *hashkafos* from Torah giants he knew, met, or learned about.

To R' Chanina, the Shabbos table was an oasis in a crazy world. "The Shabbos table is an opportunity to shmooze with your family; to ask your children how their week was; to talk about current events through the lens of Torah; to tell stories of *gedolim* that instill in your children *emunah* in the *Eibishter*, a love for learning, and proper *middos*. When you run your Shabbos table in this fashion, the table becomes an enjoyable place to be. What could be better than shmoozing about life over great food and singing? It's these moments at the Shabbos table that implant in our children a deep-rooted love for Yiddishkeit, strengthening their bond with the *Eibishter*!"

R' Chanina did not conduct his Shabbos table in a rigid manner. He felt that in so doing, one was taking the enjoyment out of the Shabbos table. As such, he was gratified to hear a quote from R' Mattisyahu Salomon.[8] "The rebbeim and *moros* think that by sending home piles of sheets with questions and *divrei Torah*, they are enhancing the Shabbos table for the children and their families. And that is a mistake… All too often, one of the children will run off in tears because he didn't know the answers well enough. For him, the Shabbos table has turned into a Tishah B'Av table."

As menahel, R' Chanina allowed rebbeim to send home *parashah* sheets, while reminding them that the handouts should not be overwhelming for their *talmidim*. He wanted the children to look forward to Shabbos and feel that their home is a place where they can relax and be comfortable. "The home is not meant to be a classroom."

On Friday afternoons, R' Chanina frequently drove his children to the library to select books to read over Shabbos. As his children "disappeared" from the Shabbos table to read their favorite books on the couch, he would look on with pride. When questioned regarding this "practice," he countered, "Ah, they're enjoying Shabbos! Does it get better than that?"

R' Chanina understood that demanding that small children sit at the table for the whole *seudah* without a break is not practical. Here, too, his view was in line with R' Wolbe (*Zeriah U'Vinyan B'Chinuch*, p. 16). "Expecting a young child to sit through an entire Shabbos *seudah* is impossible. Asking a child to do more than he is capable of has a damaging result."

Shabbos morning was a special time for learning Torah. It was then that R' Chanina would sit for hours with his coffee, reviewing *Midrash Rabbah* on the weekly *parashah*, studying *Ein Yaakov*, mastering Mishnayos, and perusing his favorite contemporary *sefarim*. To him, that was relaxation, part of the gift of Shabbos.

---

8. *With Hearts Full of Love*, R' Yaakov Yosef Reinman, ArtScroll, pp. 82-83.

YAMIM TOVIM IN THE HERZBERG HOME WERE SPECIAL, BEGINNING from the days leading up to each Yom Tov. R' Chanina went out of his way to set an example and ensure that his wife would have as easy a time as possible in regard to Yom Tov preparations; all the shopping and shlepping (in his younger years) were on him.

Yamim Tovim

Before Pesach, R' Chanina ground the *maror*, selected matzos for the Seder, and ensured that the wine was ready. He prepared the *charoses* along with his children, sharing his "secret" recipe and making the preparation enjoyable and exciting. While adding ginger to the mix, he stressed that this was an ingredient his grandmother had always included. To him, all this was basic *chinuch*. "There is so much that parents can give over to their children just preparing for Pesach!"

He especially loved when his mother, Mrs. Florence Herzberg, came for Yom Tov and prepared her Pesach "bagels" for the grandchildren. To R' Chanina, having someone from the previous generation in the family's midst added a priceless dimension to Yom Tov. He had pleasure watching his mother sit with his children, peeling potatoes and sharing special Pesach memories from her childhood. From one generation to the next.

Baking matzos with his sons

For over 20 years, the Herzberg family traveled to Woodridge to their summer home for the entire Pesach. Several weeks before Yom Tov, R' Chanina would take his children with him to *kasher* the kitchen. The children all looked forward to these trips, as they involved stopping off at Kiryas Yoel (in Monroe, New York) for delicious food, spending quality time with each other, and hearing numerous stories, thoughts, and ideas from their father. Additionally, R' Chanina trained his children in how to properly *kasher* a kitchen. To him, this experience was part of the *mesorah* of *chinuch habanim* and fit into the grand plan of what he and his wife were trying to impart to their offspring: a vibrant and pulsing love and appreciation for Yiddishkeit and mitzvos.

After weeks of feverish preparation, it was finally time for the Seder, that unique time of the year when parents are singularly commanded, "And you shall tell your son" (*Shemos* 13:8). R' Chanina would chant the Haggadah in a melodious tune, making sure to say each word carefully. He was always very emotional during the Seder, especially during the last few years of his life, when he was experiencing health challenges. He would inevitably break down during the *berachah* of *Shehecheyanu* at Kiddush, expressing *hakaras hatov* to Hashem for allowing him the opportunity to see another Yom Tov, with all the beauty it encompasses.

Every year, R' Chanina would retell a *vort* regarding the mitzvah of *sippur Yetzias Mitzrayim.* The word סיפור comes from the same root as ספיר, *sapphire.* A parent must shine like a sapphire when telling the story of *Yetzias Mitzrayim*. Only then will he leave his children with a lasting impression. Sitting at a royal table, bedecked in his white *kittel,* and surrounded by his loving family, R' Chanina certainly shone on Seder night — and that image remains in his children's minds and hearts.

The Herzberg family's Seder progressed quickly, without additional *divrei Torah.* Here and there, R' Chanina shared a brief recollection from his rebbeim. For the most part, the *divrei Torah* at the Herzberg Seder were reserved for the *Shulchan Orech* portion of the Haggadah. It was then that children showed off their school projects.

He explained to his children that on the first night of Pesach, he specifically moved the Seder along. "It bothers me to shlep out the Seder when I see that Mommy is so wiped out from the enormous preparations involved in preparing for Pesach. Tomorrow night, *im yirtzeh Hashem,* we'll go a little slower."

R' Chanina saw a thought on this topic in *Haggadah shel Pesach Mareh*

Kohen.[9] "According to many Rishonim, the *afikoman* must be eaten before *chatzos*. However, sometimes, in an effort to perform *mitzvos bein adam la'Makom* with various *hiddurim*, people commit serious violations of *mitzvos bein adam la'chaveiro*. One place that this frequently occurs is with regard to the *afikoman*. In the rush to eat the *afikoman* before *chatzos*, one may be hurtful to another person, namely the *baalas habayis* who worked so hard to prepare and serve the *seudas Yom Tov*...This is after the *nashim tzidkaniyos* have labored for weeks in preparing for Yom Tov... Even if she does not express it, this causes her pain.

"*Lo zu ha'derech*, this is not the right approach. If a person wants to be stringent about eating the *afikoman* before *chatzos*, there are two options: First, he may rely on the well-known condition of the Avnei Nezer (2:381:5). Second, if someone does not wish to follow the Avnei Nezer's opinion, he can shorten the *Maggid* section by allowing fewer interruptions for added *divrei Torah*, thereby leaving sufficient time for *Shulchan Orech*, as well...*Mehn darf gut shokel zein vuss mehn tut*, one must carefully weigh whatever he does."

The main focus of the Herzberg Seder was on the powerful words of the Haggadah itself. R' Chanina would impress upon his children the importance of the night with his genuine behavior and heartfelt recitations. Of course, all the children and grandchildren were given the opportunity to say the *Mah Nishtanah*, with as many as 10 to 15 children reciting it and being granted their time in the limelight.

Chol HaMoed was a special time for R' Chanina. He was *makpid* to wear *bigdei Shabbos*, and he looked forward to a slower davening than on the regular workdays. When the Herzbergs were in Far Rockaway for Yom Tov (before R' Chanina was a rav), he always went to Sh'or Yoshuv,

Chol HaMoed outings with his family

9. R' Avraham Pam, pp. 129-130.

Chol HaMoed Pesach *seudah*, in the Woodridge house

so he could enjoy a slow yeshiva davening. Everything slowed down, as it was a true *moed* for him. Aside from making extra time to learn, he was careful to wash at all the *seudos*, and to eat meat and drink wine, as well.

Chol HaMoed was also family time. R' and Mrs. Herzberg would take the family to amusement parks, the zoo, golfing, and boating. They enjoyed the time together immensely, and as grandchildren came into the picture, Chol HaMoed took on a whole new level of pleasure for R' Chanina and his wife.

R' Chanina had a great-aunt, Aunt Lilly, who spent Yom Tov at a hotel in the Catskills for many years. An *almanah*, she had never been blessed with children. R' Chanina told his children, "Everyone goes to hotels with their *nachas*, their children and grandchildren. Can you imagine how Aunt Lilly feels in the hotel, all by herself? Yes, I know she has friends there, but we need to bring some *simchah* to her!" Every Chol HaMoed Pesach, the Herzbergs would spend a day with Aunt Lilly. She was always waiting for her great-nephew and his children, and the *nachas* those visits brought her was apparent on her face as soon as they arrived.

To Be an Ehrliche Yid

R' CHANINA OFTEN EXPRESSED THE SPECIAL LOVE AND APPRECIATION he had for old-time, *pashute Yidden*. His children sensed that as great as their father would become, his life's mission was to never forget the importance of being a *pashute Yid*, because this guaranteed he would remain true to himself. This was yet another concept he gleaned from R'

Shlomo, who, in turn, gleaned it from R' Hutner. It was also a concept he passed on to his children through his actions.

As R' Hutner explained (cited in *Olos Yitzchak*), "The opposite of *gadlus*, greatness, isn't *pashtus*, simplicity; the opposite of *gadlus* is *katnus*, smallness." In a similar vein, R' Shlomo Wolbe wrote in a letter (*Igros U'Kesavim* 2:351), "The mainstay of a person's life is to be a *pashtan*, and as deep as he becomes, to never abandon the *pashtus*."

When R' Chanina's childhood friend heard that a book was being written about R' Chanina, he said to R' Chanina's son, "But he was just a regular guy!" Yet that's precisely the point. As much as he accomplished, as big as he became, R' Chanina always managed to remain a "regular guy."

A *talmid* shared, "My last conversation with R' Herzberg was about being a *pashute Yid*. I told him, 'Oh, being a *pashute Yid* — that's simple,' to which he replied, 'No, being a *pashute Yid* is not simple at all.'" R' Chanina had a sincere appreciation for the *ehrliche, pashute Yid* and transmitted it to his children. "Oh, how much we can learn from observing a *pashute Yid*'s *avodas Hashem*! No fanfare, just a Yid serving the *Ribbono shel Olam*! Look at the way he davens, the way he learns, the way he's *mechanech* his children!" He would draw attention to one Yid's *mesiras nefesh* in waking up early during the week to go to a morning kollel, and marvel when another Yid in the neighborhood made a *siyum haShas* after 28 years of consistent learning, day after day after day.

R' Chanina cautioned his children, "Do not think for a moment that the only people who know how to raise children are *mechanchim* or rabbanim! It's not so! Go look at So-and-So's children, how special they are. You know why he has such wonderful children? Because he is the real deal. He gets up early in the morning to learn, then puts in a hard day's work, and at night he learns a little bit, as well." It was the consistency and constancy of these comments that taught his children to respect and appreciate all types of Jews from all different circles.

One of R' Chanina's children came to their father for advice regarding *chinuch habanim*. The response he got was not what he was expecting. "Go to Mr. and Mrs. So-and-So and ask them what they think."

The son respectfully objected. "But Abba, these people are like everyone else in the neighborhood. There's nothing special about them! What could they know?"

R' Chanina's rejoinder was sharp. "What could they know?! They raised a beautiful *mishpachah,* with healthy, well-adjusted children. You think it happened by accident?"

It was 1986 (5746) and R' Chanina saw an ad in the paper advertising a home in the Catskills: "HOUSE FOR SALE ON BLOCK OF YESHIVA." R' Chanina was intrigued. Whereas until that point he and his family had vacationed in the Sh'or Yoshuv bungalow colony, R' Chanina was ready for a change. He had recently discussed with his rebbi that as a menahel, he felt he would benefit from a winterized home upstate, a place where he could unwind when yeshiva was not in session. What R' Chanina was looking for was not commonplace in those days. He wanted a winterized home, which was close to a year-round *minyan.* Perhaps this house could work.

R' Chanina answered the ad and made an appointment to see the house. As he and his family pulled into Tuttle Avenue in Woodridge, New York, they were happy to see that it was a *Chassidishe* yeshiva that had recently relocated to that neighborhood.

It turned out that the owner of the house was also a Yid. A survivor who was no longer observant, the man had a strong dislike for frum Yidden. He had gone to Florida for the winter and when he returned, he was most surprised to see that a yeshiva had moved onto the block. He began causing a lot of anguish to the yeshiva by calling the building department and creating zoning issues.

So what made him decide to sell the house now? "Recently, I visited my elderly mother in Israel," he disclosed to R' Chanina. "She also survived the war, yet she remained Orthodox. I told her the whole story, including my complaints and the problems I had caused the yeshiva to coerce them to move out. After hearing my rant, she called me close and smacked me across the face, admonishing me, '*Mein zuhn, tcheppeh zich nisht mit ah yeshiva* — My son, don't ever start up with a yeshiva.' As soon as I came home, I put the house up for sale."

R' Chanina repeated this story many times to his children, and his son Mendy can still conjure up the passion in his father's eyes. "Children, there's so much we could learn from *pashute Yidden.* We just have to open our eyes to it! This woman was a *pashute Yid,* but her understanding of Yiddishkeit was so deep! *Halevai* our Yiddishkeit should be so deep!"

He also retold the story of a *talmid chacham* who was perturbed that his children, although frum, did not live up to his expectations, while the children of his neighbor, a *pashute Yid* and certainly not a *talmid chacham*, were all *talmidei chachamim*. He asked R' Shlomo Zalman Auerbach about this oddity, and R' Auerbach explained it to him.

"At the Shabbos table, both you and your neighbor relayed the same *dvar Torah,* which the rav had said in shul. However, that's where the similarity ended. While you questioned the rav's explanation and showed your children that the rav didn't know what he was talking about, your neighbor, who wasn't learned enough to argue, repeated the *dvar Torah* to his children and showed them what an amazing explanation the rav had given. The children raised in the simple man's house grew up hearing how great *talmidei chachamim* are. The children raised in your home grew up hearing how inept they are. So why would they want to become *talmidei chachamim*?"

Kvod Talmidei Chachamim

R' CHANINA DISPLAYED AN EXCEPTIONAL MEASURE OF *KAVOD* FOR *talmidei chachamim*. It did not matter if the learned person was a rosh yeshiva or a businessman, older than him or younger; respect for Torah, and a person's accomplishments in that realm, was uppermost in his eyes.

When he taught in Yeshiva Tiferes Moshe in Queens, R' Chanina had the opportunity to discuss *chinuch* matters with the rosh yeshiva of Yeshivas Chofetz Chaim, R' Henoch Leibowitz.

R' Henoch Leibowitz with *talmidim*

After joining Yeshiva Toras Chaim, R' Chanina spoke to R' Yaakov Kamenetsky, R' Binyamin's father, about all the important matters of the yeshiva. Whether it was in person in R' Yaakov's home in Monsey, or on the telephone, R' Chanina gained tremendously from R' Yaakov's perspectives and insights.

R' Chanina would speak in awe about the different *masmidim* and *talmidei chachamim* who live in the Far Rockaway-Five Towns area, many of them his age or even much younger than him. And he encouraged his children to get to know them all.

For many years, the Herzberg family traveled upstate to their house in Woodridge for the first days of Succos. During the summer, Woodridge is a pulsating community with numerous *minyanim*. But on Chol HaMoed, the options for Shacharis consisted of the 6:45 "town shul" *minyan* and the 9:00 *Chassidishe minyan*. However, 15 minutes away by car, in Yeshiva Gedolah Zichron Moshe of South Fallsburg, there was a *minyan* at 8:00 a.m.

R' Chanina with R' Elya Ber Wachtfogel on a visit to Yeshiva Toras Chaim

R' Chanina would say to his children, "We need to daven one morning in South Fallsburg with the rosh yeshiva, R' Elya Ber Wachtfogel; it is worthwhile to daven there just to see his face. But once we are there, we must go over to him and give him *shalom aleichem,* because you never felt such a *shalom aleichem*. You should know that though R' Elya Ber is one of the *gedolei hador,* he sits up here, in Upstate New York, hidden away!" R' Chanina's face would light up with genuine *simchah* at the prospect of seeing R' Elya Ber, and he would treat his children to stories about R' Elya Ber and his father, R' Nosson Meir, the mashgiach of Beth Medrash Govoha.

After spending the first days of Succos in Woodridge for over two decades, the Herzberg family spent the first days of the Yom Tov in a camp upstate. They did this for several years and it proved enjoyable and uplifting. Joining them was R' Elya Meir Sorotzkin, rosh yeshiva of Yeshiva Tiferes Boruch in Springfield, New Jersey, along with his family. R' Chanina and his entire family were mesmerized by the *avodas hatefillah, hasmadah,* and *middos* of R' Elya Meir. At the end of the first days of Succos, the Herzbergs, the Sorotzkins, and the other families joined for a *simchas beis hasho'eivah.* They sat together for hours, singing and exchanging *divrei Torah.* One year after Yom Tov, R' Chanina, in his unique manner, shared a few words about R' Elya Meir, who was almost 10 years younger than him, "He's a real Jew!"

The Herzberg family with R' Elya Meir Sorotzkin and family, singing in the succah

It was through these calculated comments about the *maalos* of rabbanim and *talmidei chachamim* that R' Chanina inculcated within his children those oh, so important *chinuch* lessons and ideas he wanted to leave them with.

R' Chanina internalized many of the messages and stories of *gedolim* he shared, making them part of his own persona. R' Chanina liked to tell the story of R' Yonasan Shteif, rav and rosh yeshiva of the Viener Kehillah in Williamsburg, and the *kvod haTorah* he displayed. Once, at a *chasunah*, Rebbetzin Shteif walked over to her husband's *gabbai* and asked, "Is R' Moshe Feinstein here tonight?"

"Yes, he is."

"Can you please point him out to me?"

The rebbetzin walked over to the *mechitzah* and looked at R' Moshe for a short while, before turning to go back to her seat.

Unable to resist, the *gabbai* asked, "Rebbetzin, why did you want to see R' Moshe?"

Her answer was telling. "I wanted to see the rav who is so important that whenever my husband speaks to him over the phone, he stands the entire time!"

R' Chanina didn't just tell stories, he lived them. His son once walked into his parents' home to a peculiar sight. His father was walking out of the guest room, taking off his suit jacket, and hanging it up on a hook. He was holding a phone in his hand, and it appeared as if he had just finished a conversation.

His son asked him, "Abba, what just happened? Why were you wearing your suit jacket in the middle of the day, inside the house? You aren't going anywhere."

R' Chanina tried to evade the question, but his son persisted. "Ah," he finally replied, "I just finished a conversation with R' Hillel David. I cannot talk to him, even over the phone, without wearing a suit jacket. It's proper *kvod haTorah*!"

Wherever R' Chanina davened, whether during the week or on Shabbos, he made sure to approach the rav of the shul and say *shalom aleichem* or *gut Shabbos*. He felt it was basic *menschlichkeit*: *I am in his territory now; he's the rav of the shul and he deserves my respect.* This taught his children about the concept of authority and the proper respect one must show to those in authority.

When R' Chanina was in his 50's, he underwent a serious heart procedure. Moments before he was taken into surgery, with the breathing

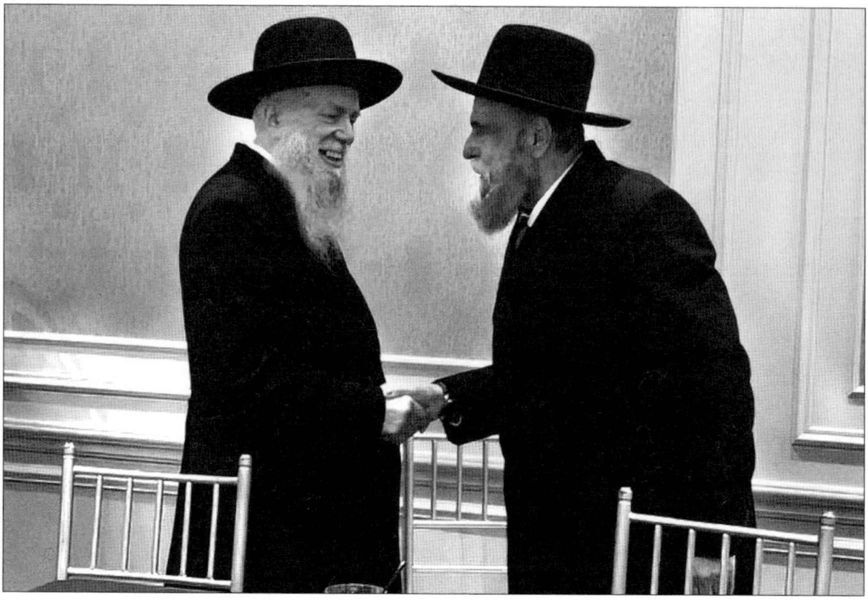

R' Hillel David and R' Chanina at R' Chanina's grandson's bar mitzvah

mask already covering his mouth, he motioned to one of his children that he would like a piece of paper and a pen. He hastily wrote, "Call R'______ and tell him I'm having a serious procedure today. He should please be *mispallel* for *Chanina Getzel ben Chana Fradel,* and not have any *taanos*!"

Several months earlier, word had gotten back to R' Chanina that this rav, a *talmid chacham,* had a grievance against him regarding a community matter. Even though this rabbi was younger than him, it bothered R' Chanina to no end. "My whole life, I'm always chasing *shalom*!" His respect for *talmidei chachamim* was so strong that here, moments before his procedure, this was what was on his mind.

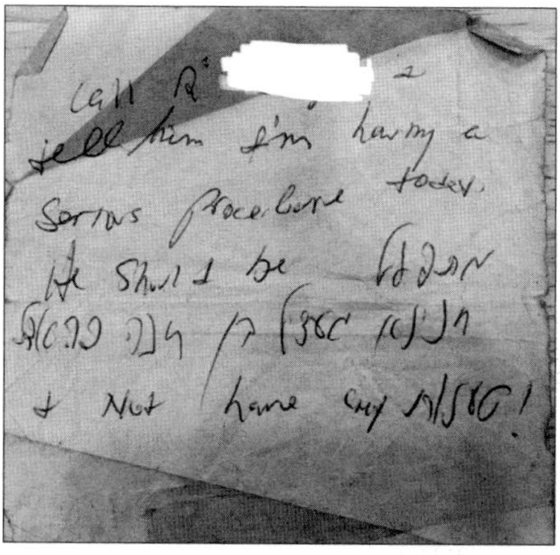

Call R' [redacted] &
tell him I'm having a
serious procedure today.
He should be מתפלל
חנינא געצל בן חנה פריידל
& Not have any תענות!

Note written by R' Chanina before surgery

He would tell his children about a person who had shown disrespect to a *talmid chacham* in East New York nearly 60 years earlier, and had suffered terribly afterward. R' Chanina warned his family, "Never start up with *talmidei chachamim*!"

R' CHANINA HAD AN INCREDIBLE LOVE FOR EVERY JEW. HE HELPED foster this love in his children by taking them on special trips. Several times a year, on the way up to the mountains, the entire Herzberg family would stop in Kiryas Yoel in Monroe, New York, for shopping and pizza. R' Chanina regaled his children with stories about the Satmar Rebbe, R' Yoel Teitelbaum, especially his *gadlus* in Torah and his *ahavas chesed*. When the family drove to the Williamsburg area, there was always a stop at Gottlieb's Delicatessen. R' Chanina marveled at the numerous institutions and the sheer population explosion in Williamsburg. "Do you think the Satmar Rebbe ever imagined this? He came after the war with nothing and rebuilt a *malchus*!" The natural exposure to other communities fostered in R' Chanina's children a similarly natural appreciation for the people there.

To Love Every Jew

The Herzberg summer home in Woodridge was on a block with only *Chassidishe* families. To R' Chanina, all Jews were one and the same. "It's very healthy spending the summers surrounded by Chassidim," R' Chanina told his children. "It teaches you to appreciate all different types of Yidden."

R' Chanina derived special *nachas* from davening in the Woodridge town shul, Ohave Shalom. Under R' Irving Goodman and later R' Hillel Grossman, different types of Yidden congregate there. Every summer, the shul had a rotation of speakers for *shalosh seudos,* and each year R' Chanina was asked to give the *shalosh seudos* speech for Shabbos Nachamu. He always opened with the same thought. "I don't know if there exists another shul like this one. There are Yidden with hats, no hats, *shtreimlach,* black yarmulkes, colored yarmulkes...all getting along and davening *b'achdus*. I believe that when Mashiach comes, the Woodridge town shul will be his first stop!"

R' Dovid Sitnick, menahel of Talmud Torah Siach Yitzchok in Far Rockaway, was a close *chaver* of R' Chanina. R' Chanina held R' Dovid in high esteem and would praise him to his children, especially in regard to R' Dovid's *avodas hatefillah.* Following R' Chanina's *petirah,* one of R' Chanina's sons shared with R' Dovid some of the words of praise R' Chanina had said about him. R' Dovid told R' Chanina's son that this *middah* of an *ayin tovah,* of seeing the good in everyone, was

At a Talmud Torah Siach Yitzchok dinner: R' Dovid Sitnick presenting R' Chanina with the Shalsheles HaTorah - R' Shlomo Freifeld Memorial Award

nurtured by R' Shlomo. R' Shlomo used to speak of the importance of having an *ayin tovah,* not only when it comes to viewing others but also in hoping for their success. R' Shlomo shared with his *talmidim* that he used to daven for his friends that they should become great *talmidei chachamim* and Torah leaders.

By observing R' Chanina and seeing how he praised his *chaverim* and their *avodas Hashem*, this *middah* was fostered within his children, as well.

Derech Eretz

THE *SHULCHAN ARUCH* (*O.C.* 170) DEVOTES A FULL CHAPTER TO HOW a Yid should conduct himself while eating. R' Chanina would tell his children that you can tell a lot about an individual from the way he eats. R' Chanina himself had a special "set of rules" that he kept in regard to eating.

He was once sitting at a *chasunah* with his son. The waiter came around with the food and placed a portion before some of the people at the table, including R' Chanina and his son. Noticing that R' Chanina had not touched his portion, his son asked, "Abba, why aren't you eating?"

R' Chanina replied, "How can I start eating when other people at the table didn't receive their food yet?"

When children witness such behavior, treating others with *derech eretz* automatically becomes part of their very being. R' Chanina would also tell his children, "It's easy to be strict with yourself in regard to *bein adam la'Makom*. However, the moment it involves another person's feelings, *bein adam la'chaveiro,* it's time to reevaluate."

In *Moreh Tzedek* (pp. 161-162), R' Avraham Pam answers a query regarding how to deal with a lack of *derech eretz* at home and in yeshiva. R' Chanina underlined the response in his *sefer.* If one wants to inspire children to act with *derech eretz,* R' Pam contended, they need to see this behavior from their parents. Parents must "honor" their children when they speak to them and when they ask them for help. "This is what I saw from my mother," stated R' Pam, "how grateful she was when we cleared the table on Leil Shabbos after the *seudah.* She would thank us profusely and *bentch* us for helping her. On Erev Shabbos, the mother of the house is generally very busy and tired, too, yet whatever our mother asked us to do was in a respectful manner... She never insulted any of us at all. We never heard a single word from her that wasn't the purest of the pure." If a child observes this type of behavior in his father and mother, R' Pam went on, this will have more of an influence on him than anything else. The general rule is to educate with *nachas,* with gentleness.

R' Pam made clear that this concept applies equally to a *melamed* in the classroom. If a *melamed* honors his student, and the child sees and hears only respectful and kind language, never any form of anger or disdain, this is called *"chinuch l'derech eretz,"* teaching proper decorum. This is the best and most effective way to be *mechanech* children to act with *derech eretz.*

R' Pam concluded by quoting the Gemara (*Succah* 56b), "What a child says in the marketplace is either from his father or his mother." A child speaks in the street in the same manner his parents speak in the house.

Mrs. Naomi Herzberg recalled how R' Chanina was wont to say, "When being *mechanech* our children, we need to remember that children are also people. Children need to be treated with the same dignity and respect given to adults."

The Gemara (*Nazir* 23b) teaches that Hashem does not withhold reward for "pleasant speech." In reference to this Chazal, R' Shlomo would bemoan how people have forgotten the proper way of speaking to one another. He stated, "Talking and having a conversation are also parts of *avodas Hashem*! A conversation is much more than just words. It's actual *binyan olam,* building of the world. You can elevate and build up people with a good word or compliment."

R' Chanina incorporated the concept of "pleasant speech" into his life, to young and old alike. A prominent rav once mentioned to R' Chanina's son that he always looked forward to speaking to R' Chanina. "Your father could sit with me for hours talking about the most serious topics, at the same time expressing sincere interest in my personal life, complimenting me on my *derashos*. His pleasant demeanor made me feel so good, and I gained so much from merely spending time with him."

His children watched, listened, and learned.

Kibbud Av Va'eim

R' CHANINA'S CHILDREN KNEW THAT IF MORE THAN A DAY PASSED without a call to their parents, they would receive a phone call from their father, reminding them that a child needs to call his parents daily. They accepted this *mussar* easily because here, too, their father practiced what he preached. He called his mother daily and never went to sleep without first calling her and saying good night, and he did this until her *petirah*.

Every Sunday afternoon after yeshiva, the young Herzberg family piled into the car and headed to R' Chanina's mother's house in Canarsie. An *almanah* for several decades, she looked forward to these visits. They would spend the afternoon with her, eat supper, and then return home.

As bubbies love to do, she would often buy treats for the young children, including chocolate, ice cream, and other goodies labeled OU-D,

A visit to Bubby's house

non-*chalav Yisrael*. Since R' Chanina and his wife served only *chalav Yisrael* in their home, their daughter Rivky once asked R' Chanina if it was okay to eat the OU-D products her grandmother served. R' Chanina's response taught Rivky an unforgettable lesson.

"Rivky, you know that Bubby has been living alone for all these years. Do you know how much *nachas* she has when we come over? Not only should you eat the products and enjoy them, but you must also make sure that Bubby sees you enjoying them! This is *kibbud av va'eim* on many levels!"

His daughter Brochie shared a memory, as well. When R' Chanina's mother was in her early 70's, she moved from Canarsie to Far Rockaway. On Shabbos morning, after davening in the White Shul, she frequently joined R' Chanina and his family for the *seudah*. Whenever she did, R' Chanina instructed Brochie to meet his mother at the shul and escort her to their home. He didn't want his mother to walk on her own.

When R' Chanina's mother passed away, R' Chanina's wife asked him how is it she never sees him cry. He answered, "I have nothing to cry about. I gave my mother tremendous *kavod* and *nachas* while she was alive. Now that Hashem has taken back His gift, I have nothing to cry about. No guilt."

Shalom Bayis

R' CHANINA'S CHILDREN SAW FIRSTHAND HOW TO ACT TOWARD A wife, how to run a home. R' Yaakov Bender observed, "With all his overwhelming responsibilities, R' Chanina never forgot his responsibility to his children and to his wife. What a great father and husband he was!" In an interview, R' Bender expanded, "R' Chanina had an incredible *derech eretz* for his wife. A menahel is a *dugma*, an example, to everyone of how a person should act. Everyone in the community saw the special way R' Chanina treated his wife. And because of it, his *talmidim* felt comfortable coming back to him years later for advice."

Despite his busy schedule in and out of school, R' Chanina took care of all the grocery shopping, including the main shopping *lichvod Shabbos*. Every

Thursday night, for decades, he would be pushing the cart along the aisles of Gourmet Glatt. (He was so well-known there that one of the long-time cashiers mentioned to a Herzberg child that their father was one of the kindest people she ever met.) He could also be counted on in the kitchen, cooking the chicken soup and adding special spices, condiments, or delicacies to the cholent every week. It was not uncommon for R' Chanina to place kishke, salami, franks, or choice cuts of meat into the cholent pot, with the express purpose of surprising and delighting his family members during the Shabbos *seudah*. In addition, he was happy to assist with errands, such as dropping off and picking up the clothes from the dry cleaners every week.

His son-in-law, Aharon Kaplan, recalled the *shalom bayis* in the home. R' Chanina was constantly wondering, "What does Mommy want? Is Mommy okay? Does she have what she needs?"

While saying a *shiur* for Yeshiva Toras Chaim alumni in Eretz Yisrael, R' Chanina's cell phone rang. Apologizing to the crowd, he checked his phone. "It could be my wife; I left her shopping." After ascertaining that it was not his wife, he told his audience, "If it would be my wife, I would answer." A vital lesson to impressionable boys on the cusp of marriage.

As a *bachur,* Shaya Novak spent a lot of time in the Herzberg home. He later shared that already as a young man, he learned the *kavod* a man should accord his wife just by observing R' Chanina and how he regarded his wife.

While R' Chanina evinced how to treat a wife, Mrs. Herzberg certainly was a role model on how to treat a husband, how to stand by his side, how to support him in his role as *marbitz Torah,* how to run the household so he can focus on his *avodah*, and how to assist him in that *avodah.* A few months before R' Chanina was *niftar*, his son-in-law Shua Nachman was sitting next to R' Chanina's close *chaver,* who said to him, "You know, your mother-in-law deserves a medal for helping your father-in-law all these years. He relied on her for everything." Shua nodded in agreement, but later he said, "I think I should have said that they don't make medals big enough."

After R' Chanina's *petirah*, his son Eli directed his words to his mother in a *hesped.* "Mommy, Abba told me, especially over the last six months, that he owes everything to you. He said it to me multiple times and not just to me — to all of my siblings also. You were his rock."

As Rabbi Akiva said about his wife, "*Sheli v'shelachem shelah hu* — What is mine and what is yours is hers" (*Kesubos* 63a).

WHENEVER R' CHANINA HAD THE OPPORTUNITY, HE MADE SURE TO include his children in the *tzedakah* projects in which he was involved.

Tzedakah and Chesed

On Purim, R' Chanina collected hundreds of dollars for *matanos la'evyonim* to distribute in the Far Rockaway-Five Towns area. Instead of distributing the monies himself, he would send his teenage children to clandestinely deliver the envelopes to various families. R' Chanina would purchase hundreds of dollars of gift cards from his own money and give them to *almanos* before Chanukah, enabling these women to give gifts to their children. Here, too, he had his children take care of the distribution.

For many years, R' Chanina was an integral part of the fundraising for the prestigious Tashbar Chazon Ish in Bnei Brak. Twice a year, R' Aharon Rogoznitzky and R' Pinchas Segal made the Herzberg home their base for a week at a time. Over the years, R' Chanina helped them raise tens of thousands of dollars, and at different points in time, all the Herzberg boys were recruited to drive these *chashuve* rabbanim around the neighborhood.

THE HERZBERG HOME WAS RUN IN A LAID-BACK MANNER, GIVING each of the children their own space. However, when it came to helping

Responsibility

in the house, every child was expected to fulfill his or her responsibility. Each child had an Erev Shabbos job, to help prepare the house for Shabbos. On Thursday nights, the main shopping night, all the children were required to help carry the packages into the house and help put the purchases away.

Later, when the older children were married and only two boys remained at home, they were expected to come home from yeshiva (which was local), bring up the packages, and head straight back to yeshiva to learn. This was not enforced out of laziness on their parents' part, but to teach the boys the importance of responsibility. This would make them better people, and, of course, better husbands.

This concept impacted R' Chanina's advice to parents when asked whether or not to send their sons away for yeshiva. R' Chanina would say in the name of R' Yaakov Kamenetsky that unless there is a specific reason for a high school boy to go away for mesivta, it's better that he stay home and attend a local yeshiva. The main *chinuch,* R' Yaakov emphasized, takes place at home, and during the teenage years a child begins to develop his ability to understand what is taking place around him. It is during this critical stage that parents need to imbue their sons with what it means to be part of a family, to see how a husband treats a wife and what it takes to run a home.

Learning From His Parents

MUCH OF WHAT R' CHANINA TRANSMITTED TO HIS CHILDREN — IN the spheres of *kibbud av va'eim,* family life, *menschlichkeit,* and honesty — were passed down to him by his own parents. Mrs. Florence Herzberg once communicated, "The reason I merited to remain frum was in the merit of the mitzvah of *kibbud av va'eim.* While my siblings moved to Long Island, I decided to stay close to home, to help my parents. That's the only way I remained strong against the tides of the time."

R' Chanina's sister Sharon conveyed, "My brother learned how to be a father from his father. Our father was devoted and loving and always put his family first."

But that wasn't the extent of it. Moish Herzberg, R' Chanina's father, owned a fish store in East New York. One day, he came home and said to his wife, "Florence, the neighborhood is changing. Because of the change in demographics, we have no choice but to close the store. But somehow, someway, I will figure out how to pay up all the employees."

He was not a wealthy man by any stretch of the imagination, but he was certainly a mensch, and an *ehrliche Yid.*

R' Chanina and his sister Sharon with their mother

Many years later, Sharon met a former employee of Mr. Herzberg, who used to deliver the smoked fish and now augmented the story. "Your father was beyond a mensch," he told her. "When the store closed, he paid me out every penny."

And their son, too, taught by example. In all areas of *avodas Hashem — bein adam la'Makom* and *bein adam la'chaveiro* — R' Chanina served as a model for his children, for his *talmidim,* and for all those who were privileged to observe him, in how to do it right.

Chapter 13
Navigation System: Raising Healthy Children

SHLOMO HAMELECH TEACHES (*MISHLEI* 24:6), "FOR THROUGH STRATEGIES you can wage war for your benefit, and salvation is with an abundant of counsel." After quoting this *pasuk,* the *Midrash Rabbah* (*Vayikra* 21:5) recommends a strategy to counteract the *yetzer hara*: to make oneself like a captain of a ship when it comes to performing mitzvos.

Strategizing

R' Chanina would frequently quote this *pasuk* and the Midrash, explaining, "You have to be like a captain of a ship facing an onslaught of waves and dangerous conditions. In order to escape the danger, you can't steer into the waves head-on, or the ship will capsize. Rather, you must study the angles of the waves and try to navigate the boat based on that knowledge." When advising parents, he would explain the connection to bringing up children. "What greater mitzvah is there than raising emotionally healthy children, who want to serve Hashem properly? But to do it right, you must strategize how you want to raise your children, what to make a big deal out of, and what to ignore."

R' Chanina discussed how parents these days are so preoccupied with work, *simchos,* their phones… that they hardly have time to get to know their children, let alone speak to each other about how their children are doing and how to be *mechanech* them. R' Chanina would decry the fact that many people are busy asking their rabbanim all different types of halachic *shailos*, except when it comes to *chinuch habanim.* In

Spending time with his children

this arena, they believe they have all the answers, and don't even think of asking their rav.

Many important *chinuch shailos* come up in regard to exposure to outside influences, such as "My son's friends are going to a baseball game. Should I let him go?" and "Should we let our children read books from the public library? If so, what types of books?" and similar inquiries. "Many factors play a role in answering these questions," R' Chanina pointed out. "Where you live, who your children's friends are, and the long-term effects of these exposures. If a couple chooses to live in a community that is more exposed to external culture, then it is natural that their family will be more exposed to a myriad of values and cultural schisms. Extreme strictness under these circumstances may lead children to rebel against their parents. Sometimes it's unclear where to draw the line. These are critical questions in *chinuch habanim,* and you need someone who is familiar with you and your situation, a rav or rebbi who knows you well, to answer your questions."

R' Chanina's aunt and uncle would send clothing to the Herzberg children from time to time. They once sent them a short brown leather jacket, and one of R' Chanina's teenage sons wore it to yeshiva. A rebbi in the yeshiva took note and approached R' Chanina to voice his bewilderment, how the picture just didn't add up. "Your son is wearing a white shirt, has his *tzitzis* hanging out and *peyos* behind his ears — and he's wearing a leather jacket?"

R' Chanina responded calmly, "Just leave him. He'll come to the realization himself that the leather jacket is not who he is, and he'll stop wearing it." And so it was. A few weeks later, the "fad" wore off, as R' Chanina had predicted, and his son never wore the jacket again.

Mrs. Herzberg reflected on the leather jacket incident. "My husband and I knew that some of our son's friends had similar jackets, and he was just testing the waters, to try and be cool and fit in with the other boys. We felt that if we told him not to wear it, it might make him want to wear it more. We knew, based on where he was holding as a *ben Torah,* that it would only be a matter of time before he came to the realization himself and felt silly putting it on. As a matter of fact, we believed that because he came to the realization on his own, it gave him a stronger identity as a *ben Torah.*"

One of the children weighed in. "Our parents didn't care that others would question, 'How can a menahel's son wear that?' If that's what was right for that child, then what other people thought didn't make a difference to them."

Peer Pressure

R' CHANINA WOULD OFTEN SPEAK TO HIS FAMILY ABOUT NOT FALLING prey to pressure from others. He would say, "Just because everyone is doing something doesn't guarantee that it's right. Do your own investigations. Then make a rational decision."

R' Herzberg and his son were once sitting at a *chasunah* when someone at their table wrongfully riled the others with an unsubstantiated rumor about the caterer's kashrus standards, and a commotion ensued.

When the waiter came around to take orders, everyone declined except R' Chanina. His son asked him, "If everyone else is not eating, why are you? Aren't you concerned?"

R' Chanina provided a telling response. "The time to investigate the trustworthiness of a caterer is *before* you come to the *simchah.* Once you respond that you are coming and that they should save you a seat, you are essentially saying to the *baal simchah,* 'I trust you and the caterer you chose for the event.' I heard these rumors and checked into them weeks ago, when I received the invitation. There's nothing to worry about. Everyone here is just reacting to peer pressure."

Toward the end of his life, R' Chanina spoke to his children, expressing his frustration regarding the tendency to worry what others will think. "Young parents ask advice about how to handle a particular challenge, I tell them what to do, and they answer, 'How will it look to my friends if I do that?'" R' Chanina turned to his children and said, "I'm telling them how to save their children, and they care about such silliness! In 20 years from now, *maybe* they'll realize their 'friends' were not even thinking about them!"

Ever R' Shlomo's *talmid,* R' Chanina went on. "I'm not making up the answers as I go along! I had a rebbi, and he taught me exactly what to do in each situation. It's like someone going to a doctor with 40 years of experience and proclaiming that he knows better than the doctor."

Giving Children Space

ONE OF THE CHALLENGES OF *CHINUCH HABANIM* IS WALKING THE tightrope between being on top of one's children and their actions, ensuring they grow and progress properly in their Yiddishkeit, while also giving them space. R' Chanina and his wife seldom told their children what to do, instead relying on the example they set for them. Yet they kept their eyes on each child, ensuring that each one developed properly, becoming a true *ben Torah* or *bas Yisrael.*

In R' Chanina's words, "The Torah ideals we all strive to transmit to our families need to be displayed in a delicate, thoughtful, and natural way. The Torah lifestyle is not, *chas v'shalom,* 'overbearing.' On the contrary, it is filled with light and everlasting love. A sensitive parent will watch over his children, looking to inspire them to grow in *avodas*

R' Chanina and his sons dancing at a niece's *chasunah*

R′ Chanina and his sons dancing at his son Yitzchok's *chasunah*

Hashem, and then ever so carefully give them the necessary space to come into their own and mature in their relationship with Hashem."

R′ Chanina reminded parents not to pressure their children. In this manner, their development is more natural and real, enabling each child to develop according to his unique *kochos hanefesh* and potential. In contrast, along with pressure comes the danger of creating an environment of cookie-cutter *chinuch*, where children become what their parents want them to become, and not what their unique *kochos hanefesh* require them to become.

"Just give your children space," R′ Chanina used to tell parents. "Then strategically water your precious sapling from time to time, and watch from afar as that sapling sprouts and grows with confidence, strength, and vigor."

While conversing with Mr. Cooperman,* R′ Chanina realized that Mr. Cooperman was pressuring his children too much; he wasn't maintaining the proper balance in their *chinuch*. R′ Chanina gave him straightforward and simple advice. "Leave the *chinuch* to your wife. She's fully capable and has it all under control!" Mr. Cooperman followed R′ Chanina's advice. Many years later, he tearfully confided in R′ Chanina's son that handing over the *chinuch* to his wife was the best thing he ever did. Thanks to R′ Chanina (and Mrs. Cooperman), his children grew into healthy, well-balanced *bnei Torah*.

If R' Chanina saw that one of his children could use a break from yeshiva, he would tell him to take a day off and stay home to recharge himself. Likewise, he encouraged parents to take their children out of yeshiva on random school days and spend quality time with them. This has a twofold benefit. It affords the parents the ability to get to know their children and connect with them. In addition, for the children, having their parent all to themselves leaves lasting memories and impressions, affecting their emotional growth in a positive way. He told parents, "Take your child for a walk and go out for lunch, and you will see how much *chizuk* he will receive!" A small action with huge dividends.

Sometimes, parents would ask if they could take their child on a vacation with them during the school year. R' Chanina frequently granted permission, along with his best wishes. "Have a great time, and make sure to enjoy your *nachas* (the children)." He explained to his son, "Nowadays, I see many households where both parents are working full-time jobs, just to pay the basic bills. The children don't see their parents enough. For these families, it could be wonderful for the children to go on vacations with their parents. For many children, it is the highlight of the year. I'm not talking about the destination, but the quality time spent with their parents."

Different Strokes...

AFTER R' CHANINA'S *PETIRAH,* MRS. ELANA FERTIG WROTE, "R' Herzberg taught us: BE NORMAL and laugh! Many times, I found myself asking R' Herzberg questions in regard to my own children and my own life. His messages were clear: Educate with love, don't add on extra for the sake of rules, care about your children, and understand what they need and that different children need different things."

In the Herzberg home, what was expected of one child wasn't necessarily expected of another. Each child was different and was dealt with accordingly. Not all the Herzberg boys attended the same yeshiva for mesivta or for *beis midrash*; there was a special calculation each time. When one of R' Chanina's children finished mesivta and had serious thoughts of attending a yeshiva that his friends would be attending, R' Chanina sat him down and discussed the issue at length, explaining to his son why he felt Sh'or Yoshuv was the place for him.

Yet his son wasn't entirely convinced. "Most of the *talmidim* in Sh'or Yoshuv are older than me and I'll feel out of place," he reasoned.

"But R' Naftali Jaeger is a world-class *talmid chacham,*" R' Chanina countered, "and I really feel that being around him will help you reach your potential."

Based on his father's input, the son reconsidered and went to Sh'or Yoshuv. He developed an extremely strong bond with R' Jaeger, and he has his father to thank for that.

R' Chanina's method of dealing with each child according to his personality was also apparent when deciding whether to send the boys to Eretz Yisrael for yeshiva after a few years in *beis midrash*. To one son, R' Chanina instructed, "You're learning really well here, and you're making for yourself a rebbi. You're better off staying in America, learning where you are." Another child was advised, "Go learn in Eretz Yisrael for a year or two," while a third received a completely different recommendation. "Go to Eretz Yisrael for just a summer *zman*, and then return to your yeshiva."

Most of the Herzberg teenagers received their driving permits in eleventh or twelfth grade. However, one son was allowed to begin driving a bit earlier, in tenth grade. A parent of a classmate of this son complained to R' Chanina, "Your son was the first one in the class to receive his permit, and now the other boys are also asking for their permits. They're saying that if R' Herzberg's son received his permit, they can, too."

R' Chanina explained, "I have my *cheshbonos*. It's true, in most cases, I would wait another year. But for this son, I felt the right thing was to allow him to drive a year earlier. But one thing I'll tell you, he may be the first one to drive, but he'll be the last one to drive on the highway."

Some decades prior, when R' Yehuda Frankel (dean of Yeshiva of Spring Valley) was menahel at Yeshiva Darchei Torah in Far Rockaway, he spoke to R' Chanina (who was a member of the board of education) about a family that was too hard on their children in regard to grades. R' Chanina commented to R' Frankel, "I don't care what my son does in life to make a living, as long as he is happy."

Whether in kollel, in *chinuch,* or in the workforce, each son and son-in-law attests that he felt equally special in the eyes of R' Chanina and his wife, who transmitted the feeling that they were equally proud of each of their children and children-in-law; each one is serving the *Eibishter* in his own way, with the goal of becoming the ultimate *eved Hashem.* This was the tone set in the house from childhood, creating a healthy, refreshing, and enjoyable upbringing.

R' Chanina frequently praised his children. And he had no problem complimenting one child in front of the other about various

R' Chanina with his sons and sons-in-law at his youngest son's *chasunah*

accomplishments each one achieved. This ingrained in the children the concept that each child has different talents and will shine in different areas. Instead of being jealous, they were, and are, proud of each other. This, too, contributed to a healthy upbringing, where children are encouraged to be themselves, tapping into their talents and creating their own path in *avodas Hashem*.

Instilling Confidence

IN A *HESPED*, ELI HERZBERG SPOKE TO BOTH OF HIS PARENTS. "MOMMY and Abba, you instilled in all of your children the belief that we could do anything, that nothing is impossible."

Every morning on the way to yeshiva, R' Chanina stopped at the bagel shop for a coffee. His children who attended Yeshiva Toras Chaim came along and enjoyed bagels and hot cocoa and other treats. At one point, one of his sons, who was 11 at the time, was tasked with going into the store and buying whatever was on the list that morning. Many times, that son would forget something on the list, yet R' Chanina never complained nor said a word about it. What's more, he kept sending him, day after day, until eventually the boy matured and stopped forgetting the items on the list.

Years later, that son mused, "The fact that my father never said a word to me and didn't stop sending me to the bagel store helped build my confidence in a very big way."

Though it sounds counterintuitive, R' Chanina recommended that if a child has a bad day, his parents should not coddle him too much. Life happens and a child needs to learn how to deal with difficulties and challenges, and move on. If this skill is already acquired as a child, he will be better equipped to handle adversity later in life. Children will inevitably have *yeridos* as they cope with the vicissitudes of life. Yet if they are fortified with self-confidence and a sense of perseverance, they will overcome the downs of life and come out on top.

Even as adults, if one of his sons called R' Chanina to discuss an issue that R' Chanina deemed insignificant, he'd say, "Why are you wasting your time thinking about this silliness? Go learn a *blatt Gemara*!" One of his children called to vent about a troubling encounter he had experienced. R' Chanina countered, "I'm surprised that you let something like that bother you!"

All part of R' and Mrs. Herzberg's thought-out approach to educate their children to be healthy and well-adjusted.

Part of the Experience

R' CHANINA WOULD TELL HIS CHILDREN, "THE LOVE I HAVE FOR YOU can stretch to others, because I feel I have a mission to take care of all of Hashem's children. And Hashem takes special care of *my* children, because I take care of *His* children." Although R' Chanina spent a lot of time out of the house with the yeshiva in general and bar mitzvahs in particular, his children didn't feel ignored or abandoned. On the contrary, they felt part of their father's mission.

Furthermore, R' Chanina used his *chochmah* to involve his children in his *chinuch* experiences. Any time there was a special trip or get-together, his children were invited to come along. One of the highlights of the year was joining their father on the eighth-grade graduation trip to Washington D.C.

As menahel of the yeshiva his children attended, R' Chanina kept his door open to his children. Even if he was in the middle of an important meeting, his children knew they could walk in and speak to their father, even just to say hi. As R' Chanina said, "If they can't see me so much out of school, at least let them see me in school!" In addition, as his son Yudi related in a *hesped*, "Whenever we called our father, even if he was in the middle of the most important meeting with rabbanim, menahalim,

R' and Mrs. Herzberg at their son's birthday party in Yeshiva Toras Chaim

roshei yeshiva, and board members, he would pick up the phone. He would say simply, 'Everything okay? Okay, I'll call you back in a little while.' But he never ignored the phone call; he always wanted to make sure everything was okay with his children."

Yudi added, "When I was in yeshiva, people often asked me, 'Isn't it hard having your father as a menahel? It must be tough. Your father is your father, but you know, he has to be your menahel, and he has to discipline you, and he has to punish you when you do things wrong.' And I said no, my father didn't do that. My father had a choice. Either he could be a menahel to his son, or he could be a father to the rest of his *talmidim,* and that's what my father was. My father was a father to the rest of the *talmidim.*"

Bringing his son to yeshiva for his *upsheren*

His son Mendy expounded, "His *talmidim* and his children were one, and we never felt deprived. This was part of his *pikchus.* On a more personal level, as busy as he always was, he was always available for his family. We spoke every day, and if I didn't call him, he would call me. He was an outstanding *baal eitzah*. I would ask for advice about *chinuch*-related matters, really about anything, and he was always on target with his *eitzos*. If I didn't listen to him, that's when I got in trouble!"

Bonding with his grandson

In a *hesped*, Eli addressed his words to his father, "A remarkable thing about you, Abba, was that you never carried your work home with you. One would think that in our home, *chinuch* would be the daily conversation, but no. You kept it all inside."

Eli had more to say to his parents in regard to the lessons they taught their children in terms of family. "Mommy and Abba, you exhibited a relationship based on caring, growth, and family. Family, family, family. You can rest assured that we all got the message because you displayed the importance of our family all the time."

The love and involvement carried over into the next generation. R' Chanina's eldest grandson, Aaron Herzberg, spoke at an *azkarah* in Eretz Yisrael. "I would sit in Zeidy's house and he would ask me, '*Nu*, Aaron, what do you think I should do in the following situation?' He knew how to make me feel so good! He didn't need my input, but he would ask me to build me up."

R' Chanina made up cute nicknames for many of his grandchildren. He would make each one feel so good, kibbitzing with them, and often feigning shock if they did well in school, saying, "Are you sure that you are from our family? It must be Bubby's D.N.A.!" He played with the grandchildren, shmoozed with them about their daily lives, and was altogether connected to them.

Family was everything to R' Chanina, extended family included. In December 2016 (5777), at a family Chanukah *mesibah*, R' Chanina addressed the assembled. Grateful as he was for the recovery of a relative, Shira,* from a recent illness, he had tears in his eyes as he shared a heartfelt message about the power of family.

R' Chanina spending time with his grandchildren

"Besides being a celebration of the Yom Tov of Chanukah, this is also a *seudas hoda'ah*, a *seudah* of thanks to the *Ribbono shel Olam*. I believe that a family has unusual spiritual strength. *Baruch Hashem*, we are here together celebrating that Shira is well. And I believe a lot has to do with the *tefillos* of everybody in this room and outside this room... The *Ribbono shel Olam* was very kind and answered everyone's *tefillos* and *bakashos l'tovah*. It's a very special moment.

"...We should share in only good tidings for many years to come in good health, and we should be *zocheh* to share in many *simchos*... and always be *b'simchah*."

A Safe Haven

THE REALITY IS THAT CHILDREN FACE SPIRITUAL *NISYONOS*, AND IT falls upon parents to help them overcome those challenges. R' Chanina imparted the importance of creating a *ruach* in the home, whereby children look forward to coming home at the end of the day: a happy, loving, and caring home, a home that is a "safe haven," where children feel that all their problems will be solved by their "omnipotent" parents. When a child feels this way, he will be open to sharing his challenges with his parents, opening a window into his life and enabling them to help him. Even if he chooses not to open up to his parents, this feeling of protection will, in and of itself, help him pull through his challenges.

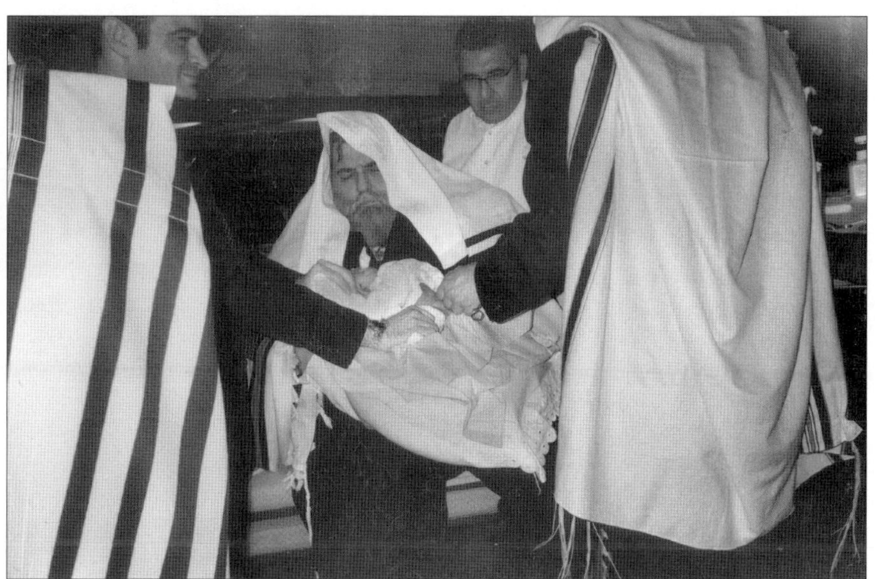

R' Chanina serving as *sandak* at his grandson's *bris*

R′ Chanina and his wife worked on creating this kind of atmosphere in their home. Not only would R′ Chanina not retire to his room for the night until all his children were home, but he also made a point to talk with each of his children about their day. He and his wife, who is also a positive, upbeat person, infused the house with a warm and reassuring feeling. The ultimate goal for R′ and Mrs. Herzberg was to create a healthy relationship with their children, so much so that even after they married and left the house, they would still call to check in, share the goings-on in their lives, and ask advice.

A goal they achieved, thanks to *chinuch* with *chochmah.*

Chapter 14
Serving His Creator: "It's Not About Me."

A FEW MONTHS AFTER R' CHANINA WAS *NIFTAR*, R' ARYEH LEBOWITZ published a Haggadah along with his *mispallelim* in Beis HaKnesses of North Woodmere, with a dedication to R' Chanina, part of which read,

Signposts

"R' Herzberg taught us how fortunate we are to be Jews, and how proud we should be to be true servants of Hashem."

The *Mesillas Yesharim* (Chapter 1) writes, "*Yesod hachassidus v'shoresh ha'avodah hatemimah hu she'yisbarer v'yisameis eitzel ha'adam mah chovaso ba'olamo* — The foundation of piety and the root of impeccable service are to clarify and validate what is his obligation in his world." R' Chanina constantly asked himself: "What is my obligation in this world? What does Hashem want from me now?" He had no "self"; he was here only to serve his Creator.

R' Chanina would constantly share stories of *gedolim* with his *talmidim* and his children, believing that through these stories, a person can glean *hadrachah* and *hashkafah*. At various junctures, R' Chanina served as learning director in several camps. In one of these camps, the camp director asked him to deliver a message immediately following davening, before the campers were dismissed to breakfast. Each morning, R' Chanina would share a short thought and a story about a *gadol*, always with a lesson that the campers could apply to their own lives.

A few days into camp, the director approached R' Chanina. "That

Davening at Me'aras HaMachpeilah

wasn't what I had in mind. I think a daily halachah is more appropriate, not stories about *gedolim*."

R' Chanina disagreed. "Children need to hear stories about *gedolim* Of course, a daily halachah has a time and place. However, after davening and immediately before breakfast, young campers won't be able to absorb a daily halachah. But they *will* listen to stories, and they *will* remember them." R' Chanina continued with his daily *gadol* story and takeaway.

About 20 years later, a former camper told R' Chanina's son, "I still remember many of the stories and *shmuessen* from your father, which I heard when I was all of 10 years old. From time to time, I think about them and they give me *chizuk*."

R' Dovid Kramer added, "It was clear that R' Herzberg picked up things from stories and his own personal experiences. I learned from him to learn from your experiences and make yourself a better person and better Yid. He saw the lessons in life that Hashem sent his way and grew from them, and that's why he became the person he became."

Those stories and life experiences were his signposts, which led him to grow and reach the destinations he yearned for. To become a "big Jew," and to help others do the same.

Proper Mindset

IN A *SHIUR* GIVEN TO YOUNG MEN LEARNING IN YESHIVA SH'OR Yoshuv in the 1970's, R' Chanina shared his perspective on the adjustment of a *yungerman* who leaves kollel and goes out to work, and the mindset he should maintain. "For many people, there comes a time when one must leave the *beis midrash*. Not everyone is *zocheh* to sit in the *dalet amos shel halachah* his whole life; a man has to go out into the world. It's very interesting; sometimes there is a man, who, as a *bachur* or *yungerman,* learned during the *sidrei hayeshiva,* but was not necessarily as connected to *Hakadosh Baruch Hu* as he should have been. And then you see him a few years after he went out to work, and he's truly connected, continuously growing in his *avodah*. How did this happen?

"I'll tell you how it happened. When he was in kollel, he may have learned a lot but perhaps he didn't put in the effort he was capable of. But when he goes out to work, he is wise enough to make sure that no matter what, he learns every day, and that requires immense effort. While the quantity of his learning is certainly decreased, the quality of his learning is increased. He is living a life of *yegiah*. He davens with *yegiah* and he learns with *yegiah,* and through that he is connected and a bigger person.

"I want to add one important point," R' Chanina continued. "I once heard someone speaking to *yungerleit* who left kollel and were now working. He was explaining to them that their *achrayus* toward the Torah has now changed. Until now, their main responsibility was to learn Torah, and now that they went to work their main responsibility is to support Torah, to support yeshivos.

"I believe that person missed the boat. That's the working man's *achrayus*?! To go break his back so others can learn? What about himself — he's not a *metziyus,* he's not a person? He's not a unique thing, he's not a star? The *Ribbono shel Olam* gave the Torah only to the fortunate people who sit and learn in the *beis midrash* 16 hours a day?!

"You know what his *achrayus* is? To learn, to continue growing in his *avodas Hashem*! And if he is *zocheh* to make money, of course his responsibility is to support *mosdos haTorah,* but that's not his whole purpose, it's secondary. Everybody has to build himself. Everybody has to learn. True, he can't put in as much time learning as when he was in kollel. Maybe he can't learn every Tosafos and every R' Akiva Eiger, but he has to learn as much as he can!

R' Chanina's life revolved around Torah

"A person's goal in life doesn't change depending on whether he is learning in kollel or working. The goal remains the same, to be the ultimate *eved Hashem* that one can be.

"Don't fool yourself. I'm telling you that you can be an *amel baTorah* by learning five minutes a day. How do you think the old Jews in shul when I was a boy lived their lives? Most of them didn't know how to learn and they were *Torah'dike* Jews in their own simplistic way. Where did they get their *kochos* from?

"Aside from the fact that they were European and they saw Jews we'll never see again, it's very simple. A man went to shul in the morning and the rav said a *shiur* before davening. He went to shul in the evening, and the rav said a *shiur* between Minchah and Maariv. On Shabbos morning, the rav said a *shiur* on Chumash/ Rashi before davening. On Shabbos afternoon, the rav gave a *shiur* on a *blatt Gemara*. During *shalosh seudos*, the Yid heard a good *vort* from the rav. This was his schedule for his entire life. His life revolved around Torah."

The ultimate *eved Hashem,* whose life revolves around Torah. That's what R' Chanina spoke about, and that is what he strove to be.

Yehuda Bakst, who was in R' Chanina's seventh-grade class in Yeshiva Tiferes Moshe, still remembered a dialogue that took place in R' Chanina's class decades earlier. R' Chanina said to the class, "If there's one thing you should remember, it's that no matter what you're going to do in life, you have to learn."

A boy raised his hand. "I want to go into my father's business."

"Okay," R' Chanina said, but then punctuated, "but you still have to learn. Not only roshei yeshiva have to learn; *baalei batim* also have to learn."

R' Chanina also emphasized the importance of learning Torah in order to improve. In a *chinuch vaad* given in 1998 (5758), he told a story to bring out this point:

R' Simcha Zissel, the Alter of Kelm, was a "big Jew," who constantly worked on himself to refine his character. His teenage son was far away in yeshiva. After six months, R' Simcha Zissel set out to visit him. In those days, before the advent of frequent air travel, travel was arduous and time-consuming.

At long last, R' Simcha Zissel arrived at the yeshiva and asked one of the *bachurim,* "Do you know where my son is?"

The *bachur* replied, "Yes, he is in *shiur* now. Should I call him out?"

The Alter wouldn't hear of it. "Absolutely not. Please just direct me to his bedroom."

When R' Simcha Zissel arrived in his son's room, he looked around, saw the bed was neatly made, the clothes in an orderly row in the closet, and the Shabbos shoes tidily arranged. Turning to the *bachur,* he said, "Please tell my son I was here and returned home. There is no need to bother him; I can see he is doing well!"

After finishing the story, R' Chanina continued, "The point of learning Torah is that you allow the Torah to change you!"

Constant, Steady Growth

WHEN DESCRIBING THE WORLD BEFORE CREATION, THE *PASUK* RELATES (*Bereishis* 1:2-3), *"V'haaretz hayesah sohu va'vohu v'choshech al pnei sehom ...Vayehi ohr* — The earth was astonishingly empty, with darkness upon the surface of the deep... And there was light."

The question is, R' Chanina pointed out in a *derashah* to mesivta boys, why do we have to know what existed before Creation? What difference does it make to us?

R' Chanina offered an answer from the Putiker Rav, an answer providing the key to success in *avodas Hashem.* "Every person is an *olam katan,* a small world unto himself. We go through tough times, we get down on ourselves, we want to do more, we want to grow, but we don't know how. The Torah comes to teach us not to give up. If we put in the effort, then in a split second, *boom*! We can experience *'vayehi ohr,'* an illuminating light!"

We must make sure not to rest on our laurels, but to keep growing. Within this context, R' Chanina related a story to his children about the famed mashgiach, R' Chatzkel Levenstein. After World War II, R' Chatzkel resided in the United States for a brief period, and then moved to Eretz Yisrael with his family, where he accepted the position of mashgiach in Yeshivas Mir in Yerushalayim. What is not well-known is the reason he left America.

R' Chatzkel was walking down the street on his first Shabbos in America when he saw Jewish people desecrating Shabbos. He let out a groan of dismay and deep sorrow over their actions. After some time passed, however, he noticed that he wasn't as sensitive to the desecration anymore. He had become used to it. It was then that he decided he had to move.

R' Chanina turned to his children and proclaimed, "A secret in *avodas Hashem* is not to become too comfortable in your situation. A Yid must always have the desire to do more! You can't allow yourself to stagnate!"

In a *shiur* on *Michtav MeEliyahu* (3: p. 18), R' Chanina conveyed an important *yesod* in *avodas Hashem*. R' Dessler writes that the more responsibility a person accepts upon himself in terms of Torah and *avodah*, the more *kochos* Hashem gives him. Then he gave an example, one he had just witnessed, which portrays how an individual can continue to *shteig*, even in old age.

"Today, R' Yaakov Kamenetsky visited Yeshiva Toras Chaim. He's 93 — and he's so vibrant. I saw the way the little children came to give him *shalom aleichem*, and he was like a young person, like a 35-year-old. You see it in his smile and how he conducts himself with people.

"His son R' Binyamin told me that when R' Yaakov was approaching his mid-80's, the doctor told him he should slow down. At first, he listened, but he became very unhappy. Then he was *mekabel* on himself to go all over, wherever they invited him, to visit. Today, he's younger at 93

R' Yaakov on a visit to Yeshiva Toras Chaim; also seen:
R' Binyamin Kamenetzky (next to his father), and R' Chanina (far left)

than he was at 85. You have to see it to believe it; I can't explain it in words. It's *ahyom v'nora.* He's a young man.

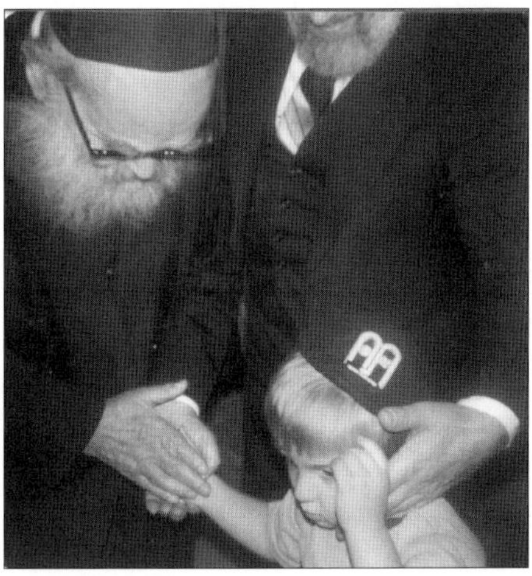

R' Yaakov giving a *berachah* to Eli Herzberg

"You know where it comes from? It comes from an *achrayus* for the *tzibbur*. The more *achrayus* R' Yaakov took on himself, the younger he became. When you look at his face, he may look like he's in his 90's, but when you look at his smile and his interactions, you see a young person. Why? Because the more responsibility you accept on yourself, the more *kochos* you are granted…and you're a different person. The more you *shvitz* over the *tzibbur,* the bigger the person you become."

As with everything their father taught them, R' Chanina's children were able to take in their father's lessons about constant *aliyah* and new *kabbalos*, because he didn't just preach. He was a living example of consistent development. His sterling character and his own aspirations for continued healthy growth were self-evident. Step by step, a little bit each day.

R' Chanina would cite the Midrash (*Devarim Rabbah* 8:3), which compares a fool to a wise man. The fool wonders, "How will I learn all of the Torah? It's so big!" while the wise man resolves, "Today, I will learn one chapter and tomorrow another chapter. Eventually, I will learn the entire Torah!"

His son Moshe stated in a *hesped* that R' Chanina, like his rebbi, had an appreciation for the small things. R' Chanina understood that this is how a person grows, through the seemingly less significant actions. He mentioned to Moshe that since he was 18, he had not missed *zman Krias Shema shel Shacharis.*

"Yes, it is a relatively small detail," Moshe reiterated, "but it's something that speaks volumes about my father's *avodas Hashem.*"

Another seemingly small detail: When R' Chanina was a *bachur* in Yeshiva Sh'or Yoshuv, his 18-year-old friend, Shmuel Tzvi Davis, was tragically killed in a car accident. As a *zechus l'ilui nishmaso,* R' Shlomo advised the bachur's *chaverim* to accept upon themselves to always *bentch* from a *bentcher*. R' Chanina kept this *kabbalah* for the rest of his life.

A Daily Dose

IN ORDER TO ACHIEVE THIS STEP-BY-STEP GROWTH, R' CHANINA — AS taught by R' Shlomo — believed that learning from a specific *sefer* on a daily basis is crucial. "Everyone has to have a *sefer*, which he looks into every day," R' Shlomo asserted (*Parashas Beha'aloscha* 5746/ *Parashas Devarim* 5743). "A *sefer* that speaks to his *seichel*. Learning a *sefer* in such a way can help us to hear. After all, if we're deaf to the *chesronos* that we have, how are we ever going to work on them?

"I have the letters from the Divrei Chaim, R' Chaim of Sanz. In one of the letters, he mentions that every night before Maariv for 30 years, they used to bring him a specific *sefer*. He would look at the same place in that *sefer* and think about it for a few minutes, until the pages of the *sefer* were black from use.

"So I always think about this; he had to make contact with that *emes* every day. I don't know what *sefer* it was or where in the *sefer* he was looking. Can you imagine what that is, for 30 years to ask the *Ribbono shel Olam* every day, '*Ribbono shel Olam*, show me the *emes*,' to continually knock on the door begging, '*Eibishter*, please let me in'? The Divrei Chaim, with all his *geonus*, understood that for his own *ruchniyus'dike* growth, he had to make contact with a certain *emes* every day."

In a *derashah* to mesivta boys, R' Chanina said, "I was thinking, what can I tell you? Then I thought to myself that the greatest gift I can give you is to tell you to go to the *sefarim* store and buy the book on R' Shlomo Freifeld called *Reb Shlomo,* and read a couple of pages every day.

"The world today is very difficult; it's difficult to be a good Jew. It's a tough world out there. We waste so much time with all these gadgets. I'm *mispallel* every day for my children and grandchildren that they should be *ehrliche Yidden*! R' Binyamin Kamenetzky told me that when he became bar mitzvah, his father, R' Yaakov, gave him a watch and told him, 'Time is precious; don't waste it!'

"To overcome the obstacles of this world, we need a medication. The medication is to pick a *sefer* and learn a few lines every day. This is the key to growth, and I believe that for mesivta *bachurim,* the *sefer* to read is the *Reb Shlomo* book. It's a *sefer* that you don't need a rebbi to learn with; you can read it yourself and it will change your life.

"I want to share a story. If you walk away with it in the back of your head and the front of your heart, it will help you become 'big people.' Two weeks ago, R' Benjie Brecher, the man behind the *Reb Shlomo* book, received a call from a man who identified himself by the last name Brayer. He went on to tell R' Benjie that he reads the *Reb Shlomo* book often.

The Boyaner Rebbe,
R' Nachum Dov Brayer

"R' Benjie recognized the name Brayer and asked the caller if he's the Boyaner Rebbe. He responded yes. The Boyaner Rebbe asked him if he plans on coming out with the *Reb Shlomo* book in *lashon hakodesh.*

"'Why?' asked R' Benjie.

"The Rebbe replied, 'It is a big mitzvah to translate the book into *lashon hakodesh,* because it is a *mussar sefer* for *mechanchim* and *marbitzei Torah* on how to draw *bachurim* close.'

"If the Boyaner Rebbe,"

R' Chanina's worn-out *Reb Shlomo* book

concluded R' Chanina, "a *gadol b'Yisrael,* gains from reading the *Reb Shlomo* book, we will, as well."

Here, too, R' Chanina didn't just talk the talk, but also walked the walk. After his *petirah,* his children came across his copy of the biography on R' Shlomo. It was significantly worn out from constant use. Though R' Chanina had been extremely helpful in the printing of the biography, contributed many stories to its pages, and read the manuscript before it went to print until he was very familiar with its contents, he still referred to it on a constant basis.

R' Chanina had a special affinity for the *sefarim* of Ger, especially those of the Chiddushei Harim and the Sfas Emes. He was proficient in these works and frequently quoted from them. He believed they captured the heartbeat of Klal Yisrael, accentuating the positivity in *avodas Hashem.* This fit with the *mesorah* in *chinuch* he received from his rebbeim, rooted in the teachings of the Alter of Slabodka, focusing on finding the positive attributes in an individual and elevating him further.

As a young *bachur,* R' Yehuda Goldfeder sat behind R' Chanina on Shabbos. R' Chanina was constantly looking into the *Chiddushei Harim,* and turning around every so often (during times when one is permitted to speak) to exclaim, "You've gotta see this *shtickel.*"

"By listening to the bar mitzvah *derashos* of R' Chanina, I became familiar with the teachings of the Sfas Emes," related R' Chaim Aryeh Zev Ginzberg. "A few years ago at a bar mitzvah in Woodmere, he actually stood at the podium and said that he wanted to apologize to R' Ginzberg for not quoting a Sfas Emes for me. He then went on to quote the Alexander Rebbe. For the last 10 years or so, every time we would be together, I asked him either for an 'Alexander *vort*' or a 'Sfas Emes *vort.*'"

It came to a point where R' Ginzberg affectionately referred to R' Chanina as "the Gerrer Rebbe of the Five Towns."

No Mechitzah

QUOTING WHAT HE HEARD FROM A *TALMID CHACHAM,* R' SHLOMO advised in a Shabbos *derashah* (*Korach* 5743), "You know what is the first thing you should think of when you open your eyes in the morning? That this world is not the *ikar,* and there will be a World to Come. We're only visitors here; it's not ours. It doesn't belong to us."

This is how R' Chanina conducted his life. As R' Naftali Jaeger articulated at the *levayah,* "R' Chanina lived *'Olam Haba'dik.'* For him, there was no *mechitzah.* He knew what this world was about."

R' Chanina felt the pain of the *Shechinah* in *galus.* He quoted a *vort* from his rebbi on this theme. We read in *Megillas Eichah* (2:13), "*Ki gadol ka'yam shivreich mi yirpa lach* — Your ruin is as vast as the sea; who can heal you?"

The *pasuk* can be understood on a deeper level, as well. The struggle we have in mourning the loss of the *Beis HaMikdash* is not only because it happened a long time ago. It's more than that. It's as if it never happened at all. We are so comfortable in our daily lives, we don't even realize we are in *galus* and are missing the *Beis HaMikdash.* The *pasuk* is telling us, "Your ruin is as vast as the sea," because just as the sea swallows a ship and leaves no trace that it was ever there, so, too, the *Beis HaMikdash* is gone, and we don't even realize we ever had it.

R' Chanina continued: The Levush (*O.C.* 559:1) writes that the *minhag* is not to write *Megillas Eichah* in a permanent way, i.e., a hardcover book, rather in a pamphlet or softcover edition, as if it is temporary. This is to instill in us the belief that we may not need it next year, and to impress upon us the fact that we must never forget that we are in *galus.* We must always yearn for the coming of Mashiach, when we will once again have the *Beis HaMikdash.*

In the beginning of the *Shulchan Aruch* (*O.C.* 1:3), the Beis Yosef teaches that aside from our obligation to mourn the *Churban* on Tishah B'Av, we must, on a daily basis, feel pain and anguish over the fact that the *Beis HaMikdash* has not yet been rebuilt.

R' Chanina lived with this pain and anguish.

IN A *DERASHAH* TO MESIVTA *TALMIDIM,* R' CHANINA TOLD A STORY about the Sfas Emes. One Rosh Chodesh, the Sfas Emes revealed to his

One Goal

Chassidim that a Jew can obtain anything he needs if he intensifies his *kavanah* when he recites the words, "*Ana Hashem* — Please, Hashem," in *Hallel.* Thereafter, whenever the Chassidim recited *Hallel*, they screamed (*Tehillim* 118:25), "*Ana Hashem hoshia na! Ana Hashem hatzlichah na* — Please, Hashem, save now! Please, Hashem, bring success now!" with exceptional *kavanah.*

After the Sfas Emes was *niftar* and his son, the Imrei Emes, became the Rebbe, one of the Chassidim expressed that some people felt that their *bakashos* weren't being answered, causing them to question the words of the Sfas Emes. The Imrei Emes explained, "The Chassidim are making a mistake. There's another '*Anah Hashem*' in *Hallel*: '*Anah Hashem ki ani avdecha* — Please, Hashem, for I am Your servant' (ibid. 116:16). That's the '*Anah Hashem*' the Sfas Emes was referring to." The Chassidim began saying the words, "*Anah Hashem ki ani avdecha,*" with great *kavanah* and they felt that their *tefillos* were answered.

"In *avodas Hashem,*" R' Chanina concluded, "it's all about the desire to serve Hashem with all your abilities — to be the quintessential *eved.*" R' Chanina was a living example of "*Anah Hashem ki ani avdecha.*"

In his *hesped,* Moshe Herzberg stated, "As children, we knew our

With his children: Yitzchok (left) and Mendy

father in so many facets. We knew him as a father, as a son, as a husband, as a brother, as a *talmid,* as a rebbi, and as an *oveid Hashem.* There are so many traits within each of these relationships. But one common thread in all his dealings was that he embodied the concept of *hatzne'a leches.* He did it all quietly. He despised publicity and pomp. He was real and genuine, with no airs about him. That was the way he ran his life, the way he taught us."

R' Chanina remarked to another son, "My personal goal in life is to do the right thing at all times. Then, when my time comes and I pass on from this world, it should be as if I never existed." He then reiterated, "You hear me? This is what a person's mindset in life needs to be!" A person should not believe that he exists for his own *kavod,* but only to fulfill his obligation in this world.

A short while after R' Chanina's *petirah,* one of his children was reading the biography of the Tosher Rebbe and was excited to see that the book ends with a similar quote from the Rebbe. "Our job is to do, and to do, and to do some more, but in the end, it's as if we don't really exist."[10]

Likewise, R' Chatzkel Levenstein proclaimed, "Someone who cannot make himself at home in this world — someone who enters quietly (*shayeif ayeil*) and who leaves quietly (*shayeif nafeik*) — is a guest in this world; he is just passing through. When you feel like this, you are a *ben Olam Haba.*"[11]

R' Chanina's *avodah* was performed in a quiet, unassuming manner. His son Yitzchok said in his *hesped,* "The *pasuk* teaches us, '*V'hatzne'a leches im Elokecha* — Walk humbly with your G-d' (*Michah* 6:8). I heard from R' Hillel David in the name of R' Schwab that every Yid should have one mitzvah that only Hashem knows about; not his son, not his father, and not his wife. Only Hashem. My father's entire life was one of '*V'hatzne'a leches im Elokecha.*'"

R' Chanina wore a *kapota* on Shabbos, per his rebbi's recommendation. "A menahel has to hold himself on a different level," he told him. "He has to be *derhoiben.*" It was for this reason that R' Shlomo told him to wear Rabbeinu Tam *tefillin.* Yet none of this — the *kapota,* the Rabbeinu Tam *tefillin,* the long beard, the *gartel* — made a difference in terms of R' Chanina's humility. As much as he accomplished in his capacity as menahel and rav, he never let it go to his head. In a certain

---

10. *The Tosher Rebbe,* R' Yisroel Besser, ArtScroll, p. 326.

11. *Reb Chatzkel,* R' Yitzchok Kasnett, ArtScroll, p. 200.

way, he was always a *pashute Yid* from East New York, striving to serve Hashem in the best way possible.

Because it was never about him.

R' Chanina once asked his seventh-grade class a thought-provoking question: "If you could be granted one wish, what would it be?"

After the last boy gave his response, his *talmidim* turned the question back to R' Chanina. He thought for a moment and then stated, "I would wish that my children would be greater than me."

R' Chanina was teaching his *talmidim* what is important in life: to do *retzon Hashem,* to ensure the continuity of Klal Yisrael, and to take yourself out of the picture.

After going for an interview in another yeshiva, a young couple decided to visit Yeshiva Toras Chaim to see the yeshiva. They were open with R' Chanina, telling him that they had already interviewed elsewhere. R' Chanina was unflappable. "If you send to the other yeshiva and decide at some point to switch to Yeshiva Toras Chaim, I'll always have a spot for your sons; they are wonderful children."

After they left the yeshiva, the woman turned to her husband and said, "We're sending to Yeshiva Toras Chaim. If R' Herzberg could say that to us, then he's the person I want educating our children!"

As a *mechanech,* R' Chanina cared about one thing, and that was to do what was right for each child. A *talmid* did not succeed in Yeshiva Toras Chaim, and needed to switch to another *mosad.* There he finally tasted success, and matured and grew into a healthy and productive *ben Torah.* Years later, R' Chanina was asked if it bothered him that this *talmid* had been *matzliach* in another yeshiva, not his. "You think I care about my *kavod*? I wanted the boy to succeed, that's it! You do what's best for the *talmid*!"

At the *shivah*, a sentiment voiced by many *talmidim* was, "Your father loved me! I knew that he always wanted what was best for me, and nothing else. That's why we loved him!"

The Chazon Ish (*Emunah U'Bitachon*: Ch. 13) tells the story of a man who invited a guest to eat in his home on Shabbos. The members of his household were already looking forward to greeting the guest, for they loved hosting guests. Unfortunately, there was a mix-up and the guest ended up in another family's home for the *seudah*. When the first family realized they would have no guest, they were sad and disappointed.

Their father, however, saw it differently. "My only concern is that the guest has his needs taken care of and receives a Shabbos meal. It makes no difference if he receives all this from me or from someone else."

Even so, the Chazon Ish acknowledges, "This is not the way of ordinary people. If a person likes to do good deeds, he may become jealous or unhappy when others perform the good deed instead of him."

But R' Chanina was not like ordinary people. Thus, the ability to be happy with the result, while not caring for his own pride or ego, was one of his trademark attributes.

Speaking to the Crowd

AT A *SHALOSH SEUDOS* IN YESHIVA SH'OR YOSHUV (5743), R' SHLOMO touched upon the concept of "less is more" in regard to public speaking. "It takes clarity of thought and a good head to really understand the problems of the generation in which you live…The Chassidim hardly spoke, because they held that the one who speaks has to be on fire! But minimal speaking kept the issues alive and fresh."

He went on to say that the fruit born from minimal speech is very valuable, and he used the Satmar Rebbe, R' Yoel Teitelbaum, as an example. Despite his *geonus,* the Satmar Rebbe addressed the needs and issues of his *kehillah,* primarily survivors, on a rudimentary, simplistic level. Yet even the "simple" speech of a man of such stature and greatness contained much depth. We see the fruits of the Satmar Rebbe's labor, concluded R' Freifeld, by what the Satmar community has developed into, how *chashuv* it is.

R' Chanina was a talented speaker. When he stood in front of a room full of people and opened his mouth, the entirety of his presence took over the room. And he had a presence: He was a large man, with a full beard, and significant stature. Furthermore, there was something unique about his delivery. He spoke with fire, confidence, and conviction.

Even so, he kept it simple.

Whether he was speaking at a

bar mitzvah, or in his shul, or at another venue, R' Chanina frequently began with "*Rabbosai,* I want to learn with you a *shtickel pasuk* in Chumash with a Rashi," or "*Rabbosai,* let's learn a Midrash together," or "*Rabbosai,* I want to share a beautiful piece in the *Sfas Emes*." The *pasuk* would come alive, the Midrash would become part of the heart and soul of the listener, or the *Sfas Emes* would become a battle cry for growth in *avodas Hashem*. The beauty was in its simplicity, the brilliance in its delivery, the *gadlus* in how he always knew what the people needed to hear.

R' Chanina was an accomplished *talmid chacham,* capable of giving complicated *derashos* packed with *mareh mekomos* and thoughts that could wow the listeners with his command of Tanach, Chazal, and various *mefarshim.* Nevertheless, he did not reveal his true knowledge. Instead, he cherished every opportunity to communicate a message that matched his listeners.

To R' Chanina, every opportunity to speak to a crowd meant an opportunity to inspire them to grow, to become bigger, to further their connection with the *Eibishter*. In his words, "One has to put his ego aside and speak to the people."

R' Chanina's *sefarim* shelves were filled with the classic *sefarim* of the previous generations. At the same time, he possessed numerous *sefarim* from contemporary *mechabrim*. Any *sefer* that he thought would help him express himself and connect to those to whom he would be speaking— he had to have.

"When speaking in public, one should imagine he is speaking to *tinokos shel beis rabban,*" he would say. "Everything must be prepared and laid out for them, without any complexity of thought. The speaker's job is to take complicated ideas and simplify them so they are enjoyable. Don't speak too long; the *derashah* should be brief and the message timely. Speak well and leave your listeners wanting more. Then the message will stick with them, injected into their hearts and minds."

R' Chanina's sister, Sharon Maslow, was once asked to speak in a public forum. She called R' Chanina for advice, and he shared four points:

- Speak about what you know.
- Speak about what you love.
- Speak from the heart.
- Keep it short.

THERE WAS YET ANOTHER FACTOR IN PLAY HERE. ONE OF R' SHLOMO'S oft-repeated quotes originated from Shakespeare. "This above all, to thine own self be true." R' Shlomo emphasized to his *talmidim* that all their actions should reflect who they really are, that the greatest mistake in *avodas Hashem* is when one mimics another individual's *avodah*.

To Thine Own Self Be True

In an address to alumni of Yeshiva Toras Chaim, R' Chanina pointed out that the phrase *"lech lecha"* (*Bereishis* 12:1) means: go for yourself. This is the key to growth. Each individual must take a long, hard look to see where he himself is holding.

Hashem asked Adam (ibid. 3:9), *"Ayekah*? Where are you?" Do we think that Hashem didn't know the whereabouts of Adam? Rather, He was asking: *Where are you holding?*

Every Yid must periodically ask himself: *"Ayekah*? Where are you? Do you know what you want to do? Do you know what your desires and aspirations are?"

That is the only way to remain true to oneself.

R' Chanina made it a lifelong *avodah* to ensure that he stayed true to himself. Around a decade before R' Chanina's *petirah,* Eli Herzberg and his family traveled to Florida during winter break, and invited their parents to come along. R' Chanina and his wife were pleased to accept, eager to spend time with and revel in the joy and *nachas* of their children and grandchildren in a relaxed setting, where R' Chanina would have time for additional learning.

One afternoon, Eli noticed that a Minchah *minyan* was being organized in the park they were visiting, and he asked his father if he would be joining. R' Chanina quietly demurred, stating that he would daven later near the car. Unsure why his father was refusing, Eli prevailed upon him to be a part of the *minyan,* until he eventually agreed.

Later that evening, as everyone was unwinding in the villa where they were staying, R' Chanina beckoned his son over and told him, "Eli, I want you to know that today was the first time in 40 years that I davened (Minchah or Maariv) without wearing a hat." This revelation was unusual in and of itself, as R' Chanina rarely spoke about himself and his *avodas Hashem,* but generally taught through action. Eli apologized for causing his father to forfeit his commitment, yet R' Chanina waved away the apology with a pearl of wisdom. "Yiddishkeit is not about contests; it's not about streaks."

R' Chanina was self-aware. He taught himself how to live with himself, without a need to be around others; he learned how to do without outside recognition or validation. As a menahel and a rav, R' Chanina was a larger-than-life figure in the community. However, he was constantly performing "self-checks," to assure he did not become "lost in the limelight." Whenever possible, he dodged any form of honor.

At *simchos,* he usually chose to sit with his friends rather than at the rabbanim's table, and at large community gatherings he tried his best to avoid being seated on the dais. By the same token, R' Chanina's family knew that at every *chuppah,* they could find their father sitting toward the back.

In any *derashah* R' Chanina gave to *talmidim* at a yeshiva event or at a bar mitzvah, he concluded with a *berachah* that they grow up to be *ehrliche Yidden,* loosely translated as faithful, upright Jews. To R' Chanina, it did not mean merely that a person should be truthful and honest to Hashem and to his fellow friend; it meant that a person must be truthful to oneself, as well.[12]

R' Chanina retold a story about the Satmar Rebbe, R' Yoel Teitelbaum. A *badchan* was performing at a *mitzvah tantz,* and after asking permission from the Rebbe, he impersonated him. The *badchan* was extremely disturbed when he noticed R' Yoel crying during his performance. He ran over to the Rebbe, apologizing profusely. "Rebbe, I'm so sorry! Please forgive me!" The Satmar Rebbe brushed off the apology. "There is no reason to feel bad! I saw how you did such a spot-on imitation of me, and it made me realize that perhaps there are times when I am merely mimicking myself!"

We must all be true to ourselves, and to our capabilities. To that end, R' Chanina would also relay the famous story of R' Zusha of Hanipol on his deathbed. He lay there and wept, as his Chassidim asked him, "Rebbe, why are you so sad? You accomplished so much in terms of Torah and mitzvos! You will surely receive a great reward in Heaven!"

R' Zusha answered, "When I arrive in Heaven, I know Hashem is not

12. This idea is expressed (*Sefer Pirkei Avos: Generation to Generation,* R' Nosson Muller, ArtScroll, p. 83) in the name of the Novominsker Rebbe, R' Yaakov Perlow: "The term 'an *ehrliche Yid,* a faithful Jew' is used quite liberally these days. But what exactly does that title mean and represent? One must appreciate and understand that its definition is not limited to just being honest and truthful between man and his Creator, and man with his fellow friend. Rather, it encompasses being truthful to oneself, too. Every person has an obligation to be honest to his own core, ensuring that the decisions he makes and the actions he performs are in perfect line with the ideals and views the Torah has set forth for him to live by. That is the true and ultimate definition of an *ehrliche Yid.*"

going to ask me, 'Zusha, why weren't you more like Moshe Rabbeinu?' or 'Zusha, why weren't you more like Dovid HaMelech?' Rather, Hashem will ask, 'Zusha, why weren't you more like Zusha?' And then what will I say?!"

R' Chanina saw a real-life example of this in his rebbi. One Erev Pesach, R' Chanina went to visit R' Shlomo. Several months earlier, R' Shlomo's first rebbetzin had been diagnosed with the illness that would take her life and the situation was grave. R' Chanina found R' Shlomo sitting in a chair, looking dejected. Seeing that R' Shlomo's *peyos* were wet, R' Chanina understood that his rebbi had already gone to the *mikveh,* so he didn't offer to take him. Instead, he asked R' Shlomo if he could make him a coffee, and he accepted. As R' Shlomo drank the coffee, he seemed lost in thought. Afterward, R' Chanina offered his services and R' Shlomo asked his *talmid* to take him to the *mikveh.*

Though the request seemed strange — R' Chanina was sure R' Shlomo had already gone — he did his bidding and drove him to the *mikveh.* On the way, R' Shlomo remained melancholy and pensive, far from his regular jovial self. After they returned to R' Shlomo's home, he suddenly perked up and regained his vibrant, vivacious, energetic persona. He then asked for another cup of coffee and as R' Shlomo drank it, R' Chanina finally asked the question that had been bothering him. "I could see that Rebbi had already gone to the *mikveh,* so why did you ask me to take you again?"

"I'll tell you the truth," R' Shlomo replied. "When I came home from the *mikveh* earlier, the whole Erev Pesach atmosphere was lacking. The sights, the sounds, the scents. There was no last-minute hustle and bustle, no noise from children and grandchildren, no aromas from cooking and baking. My rebbetzin is not able to prepare for Pesach and we are eating with our children in their home. I was very down, and even more despondent about the fact that I was down.

"As I sat here, contemplating the whole situation, I chided myself, 'On Erev Pesach, a few hours before the Seder, Klal Yisrael's *geulah,* who gave you the right to feel so dejected?' Soon after, you came in, R' Chanina, and made me a coffee. I began to think some more and I asked myself, 'Who am I? Am I Shlomo of Breslov? Am I Shlomo of Izhbitz? Am I Shlomo of Lublin? No! I am Shlomo Freifeld from East New York, and I have to do the best that *I* can do! Hashem doesn't expect me to be R' Nachman of Breslov, or the Izhbitzer, or the Chozeh of Lublin. I'm just me, facing what I'm facing, and I must do the best I can do under the circumstances.' So, R' Chanina, I asked you to take me back to the *mikveh* so I can *toivel* with this *kavanah*."

R' Shlomo taught us that it is up to us to do the best *we* can do!

R' Shlomo averred that the first step in spiritual growth is not to know Hashem, it's to know yourself! When internalized, this concept affects every aspect of our lives.

The Herzberg children grew up during the technology revolution, but through it all, R' Chanina didn't cave in. He never owned a smartphone, didn't know how to text from his flip phone, and although he did allow a computer in the house, he didn't even know how to turn it on!

The PTA at Yeshiva Toras Chaim sponsored a computer for R' Chanina's office. R' Chanina was faced with a dilemma. On one hand, he was uncompromising in his stance not to use a computer. But on the other, if he didn't install it in his office, he would hurt the feelings of the PTA members. R' Chanina came up with the perfect solution. He kept the screen on his desk and got rid of the hard drive!

When the need arose to have his own yeshiva email address, R' Chanina had his email controlled by Mrs. Monika Weinberg, his long-time trusted secretary. Mrs. Weinberg would print out every email that

Purim in R' Shlomo's house (seated, l-r): Unknown, R' Shmuel Brazil, R' Shlomo, Mr. Allen Schiller, R' Chanina. Standing (l-r): Heshy Markovits, R' Moshe Lieber, R' Moshe Dov Stein, R' Yehoshua Kurland

R′ Chanina received, and R′ Chanina would dictate his responses to her.

One of his children asked him, "Abba, why are you so adamant about having nothing to do with technology? Your job would be so much easier if you were technologically savvy."

His answer made a lasting impression. "I know myself. If I learn how to use a computer, I'm going to waste my time, and time is too precious to waste."

The rav of a prominent shul in the neighborhood was retiring, and the board of directors approached R′ Chanina, asking him to accept the position as their new rav. R′ Chanina, however, refused. His reason: "The rav of your shul has to be a *posek,* as well. I'm no *posek.* My *tafkid* is to be an elementary school menahel." Instead, he suggested a *chaver* of his, an accomplished *posek,* for the position, and they appointed that *chaver* as their new rav.

At R′ Chanina's *hakamas matzeivah,* his son Mendy addressed the assembled. "My father was a big *chacham,* a very wise man. But perhaps his biggest *chochmah* was the fact that he knew when he didn't know and therefore needed to ask someone else. I remember when they came out with the first electronic organizer. Since he wasn't technologically savvy, he gave me a bunch of papers with names and numbers to enter into the organizer. As I was entering the names and numbers, I noticed that he had the name and number of almost every big rav and rosh yeshiva at the time, including R′ Dovid Cohen, R′ Feivel Cohen, R′ Hillel

R′ Chanina and his *mechutan* R′ Yehuda Kaplan with R′ Nota Greenblatt (center) at their children's *chasunah*

With his son Yudi greeting R' Dovid Feinstein

Escorting R' Yitzchok Scheiner into Yeshiva Toras Chaim

With his grandson Aaron Herzberg greeting R' Shmuel Kamenetsky

David, R' Zelik Epstein, R' Dovid Feinstein, R' Shmuel Kamenetsky, R' Avraham Pam, and R' Aaron Schechter. I asked my father, 'What do you need this for?' And he responded, 'At times, I need to call to confer with them on different issues.' This made a big impression on me. That was his *chochmah.* He knew a lot, and when he didn't know, he was true to himself and he knew he needed to ask."

Although R' Chanina was a gifted speaker, you hardly ever saw his name anywhere. Aside from speaking in Yeshiva Toras Chaim, or at a bar mitzvah or in his shul, he seldom spoke at other venues. His son asked him, "Abba, you are so talented. Why don't you speak? You can speak in many places, and people will listen."

His father's response taught him something important. "I have a *tafkid* as a menahel of a yeshiva, and that requires me to save my *kochos* for the yeshiva. If I give of my *kochos* to other places, it would take away from my ability to be *mechanech* there." He was true to himself, true to his goal, true to his mission. It was all about: "What is my obligation in this world?"

R' Chanina would constantly self-introspect, and if he found something within himself that he did not like, he would actively work on himself to fix the issue. Though he treated his rebbeim very well and expressed gratitude for the work they did, he always strove for perfection in his *avodas Hashem.*

One Yom Kippur after Kol Nidrei, R' Chanina arose to speak at the Ohr Shlomo Yamim Noraim *minyan*. He began to speak about character improvement, and how one must always look to grow in the realm of *bein adam la'chaveiro* and also *bein adam la'Makom.* He brought himself as an example of someone who needs improvement.

In his usual self-effacing manner, he recounted, "Recently, one of my close friends in yeshiva pointed out that when I ask the rebbeim to perform a task that is part of their job, I don't thank them enough. He told me that I take it for granted that the rebbeim will do what I say, because I'm their boss. I thought about it, and I realized he is correct. So I accept upon myself to show *hakaras hatov* in an improved manner."

In reality, R' Chanina, who was over 60 years old at the time, had never been remiss in this area. R' Yitzie Ross stated it clearly, "Anyone who knew R' Herzberg could tell you that his *hakaras hatov* was second to none. No matter what you did for him, he would always thank you."

R' Shlomo Drebin, special activities coordinator at Yeshiva Toras Chaim, elaborated. "When R' Herzberg would ask me to do something for him, he would introduce the request with: 'R' Drebin, I would like to ask you for a big favor, but I know you're very busy. If you think you might be able to give me a minute of your time, I would very much appreciate it. But only if you're not busy. I don't mean to bother you, but do you think you could just...' The request would usually be something extremely small and easy, and then he would thank me profusely!" R' Drebin added, "This type of thing happened all the time."

Nonetheless, his son Eli, who worked with his father for many years, noted, "I saw that after this conversation, my father made an extra effort to express appreciation to others!"

R' Chanina's close friend, R' Moshe Scharhon, communicated, "Though, as a rebbi where he was menahel, I worked for him, R' Chanina requested of me, 'If I'm doing something wrong, please tell me.' And if I happened to mention an area that I felt needed improvement, he was *mekabel*. He was willing to bend if he was wrong or could have done better."

R' Chanina would tell his children that *gaavah* holds one back from growth in *avodas Hashem*. It blocks a person from seeing his own faults and accepting criticism, which ultimately leads to stagnation in character development. The opposite is also true, and he would share a story to portray how "big people" are open to *mussar*.

R' Isser Zalman Meltzer once walked into a shul in Yerushalayim, where R' Aryeh Levin (who was about 15 years his junior) was giving a speech on according proper honor for one's wife. R' Isser Zalman sat down in the women's section to listen, as he didn't want to disturb the *shiur* by walking in in the middle.

Suddenly, the men heard crying coming from the other side of the *mechitzah*. R' Aryeh sent one person over to investigate if everything was okay. The messenger returned moments later. "Rebbi, R' Isser Zalman is sitting there crying!"

R' Aryeh immediately went to inquire. "R' Isser Zalman, did I say something wrong?"

"No," responded R' Isser Zalman, "I was listening to your *shiur* and I realized that I need to treat my wife better. When I wrote the *sefer, Even HaAzel,* my wife helped me by writing out the manuscript. At times, I noticed that she had not copied my notes accurately, and I would grow impatient. Now I see that I was wrong. Thank you, R' Aryeh, for helping improve my *shalom bayis.*"

R' Chanina turned to his children and said, "Believe me, R' Isser Zalman was a good husband! But he was able to realize that he needed to grow, and that is a *yesod* of Yiddishkeit!"

R' Chanina could have been speaking about himself.

Asking Mechilah

WHEN IT'S ALL ABOUT YOU, AND NOT ABOUT ME, ASKING FOR FORgiveness comes more readily. A young man once confronted R' Chanina and accused him of hurting his feelings. Many of the Herzberg family members in the room thought the individual was blowing the situation out of proportion. But to their disbelief, R' Chanina burst into tears. In a voice filled with sorrow, he asked for forgiveness. Afterward, family members asked R' Chanina why he even apologized when he was most likely in the right, and he replied, "It's not about me, it's about him." R' Chanina advised rebbeim, "Never be too proud to apologize to a *talmid.* Almost every time it will lead to more respect and a closer relationship between rebbi and *talmid.*"

R' Chanina's son accompanied him to a *chasunah,* where they met R' Chanina's mesivta rebbi from 45 years earlier. By mistake, R' Chanina addressed his rebbi with the informal Yiddish word for you, *"dihr,"* instead of the more formal *"ihr,"* which is often used when addressing someone in third person. As soon as R' Chanina realized his mistake, he went back to the rebbi to secure forgiveness for the slight in honor, and then he went back once more to be sure.

All those who knew R' Chanina will say that he was not a pushover. He was a very confident person. However, if he realized he made a mistake, there was simply no arrogance to hold him back from asking *mechilah.*

R' Chanina lamented to his children, "Do you know that families fall apart because people are too proud to ask *mechilah* or talk things out?" He knew human nature well, but he was still dismayed that people lose loved ones over *kavod* and pride. Whenever he heard that someone had done something silly because of jealousy, desire, or pride, R' Chanina would slowly recite the words of *Pirkei Avos* (4:28), in a singsong, *"Hakinah v'hataavah v'hakavod motzi'in es ha'adam min ha'olam* — Jealousy, desire, and pride remove a person from this world." In fact, with a smirk on his face, he once quipped to his children, "After 120 years, when I pass on from this world, if you children fight with each other, I will come back to haunt you!"

Back-Row Seats

IN 5762, YESHIVA SH'OR YOSHUV IN FAR ROCKAWAY MADE ITS MUCH-anticipated move to a magnificent new campus on Cedar Lawn Avenue, located on the border between Far Rockaway and the Five Towns. Preparations were underway for the overflow crowd that would be davening in the yeshiva for the Yamim Noraim, and the excitement was palpable. In those years, the *tefillos* were led by R' Moshe Dov Stein and R' Shmuel Brazil. The davening was inspiring and uplifting, injecting the *mispallelim* with renewed strength and fortitude to continue growing in their *avodas Hashem*. The "old building" on Central Avenue had been packed from wall to wall; the new building would allow for hundreds of additional seats. A crowd of over 1,000 people was expected, including many from the Lawrence community.

As a close *talmid* of R' Shlomo Freifeld, as well as a menahel in the community, R' Chanina had always been seated on the *mizrach vant,* in the front right of the *beis midrash,* with his five sons right behind him, both on Shabbos and Yom Tov, as well as the Yamim Noraim (before he had his own shul). Mrs. Herzberg, too, had always been right up front in the women's section, with her two daughters next to her.

On the first night of Rosh Hashanah, the first *tefillah* in the new building, there was anticipation in the air as R' Chanina and his boys made their way to the yeshiva. However, the Herzberg boys were in for a surprise. Instead of their regular seats at the front of the *beis midrash* right behind their father, they found themselves all the way in the back row, at the last table, near the door. An almost identical scene took place in the women's section, where Mrs. Herzberg was now in the second row and her two daughters, like their brothers, were seated in the back row next to the door.

R' Chanina's children didn't understand why they were placed all the way in the back row, instead of being seated in the front, right next to their parents, as had been done until then. They wondered, "Our father was a part of the founding group of *talmidim* of the yeshiva, a *talmid muvhak* of R' Shlomo. He is also a respected *mechanech.* Why are we now seated in the back?"

But R' Chanina and his wife didn't say a word. It was only after one of the boys approached their father and expressed his frustration that the truth came out. Years later, their father's response, and the message he delivered to his children that evening, still resonates.

"Let me explain what happened. You may not realize, but this beautiful new building is a huge strain on the yeshiva's budget, and they had to secure many new donors to help defray the costs. I called the seating committee and told them that if giving away my children's front seats and moving them to the back will open up front seats for potential donors and will be of help, they should not hesitate to do so. I said that my children will understand that this is what needs to be done for the good of the yeshiva. Even more, I let them know that if need be, Mommy doesn't mind moving back a bit in order to accommodate a donor."

But his son was not satisfied with the answer, persisting that the children felt slighted. At that point, R' Chanina, with a serious expression on his face, pointed toward an annex in the *beis midrash katan* in the back that was opened for the overflow crowd, and said in a stern voice, "You see that man over there, all the way in the back? He's very sick, and according to the doctors, he doesn't have much time left. Look at him! Do you think he cares where his seat is? He's just happy that he's able to sit! In the big picture, where you sit makes no difference. This is what we have to do to help the yeshiva!"

That Yamim Noraim R' Chanina imparted an everlasting *chinuch* lesson to his children. At the end of the day, *kavod* plays no role in the decisions we make. No matter what, we need to do what's right. We must always look to help others, and we must do everything and anything to help a yeshiva.

R' Chanina and his wife taught their children another lesson in *avodas Hashem* at the time. Neither of them cared how others would look at them if their children's seats were all the way in the back. And Mrs. Herzberg didn't care if her own seat was not in the front row. This is the *chinuch* the Herzberg children received from their parents: The only thing that matters is, "What does Hashem want from us now?"

After R' Chanina's *petirah,* R' Yechiel Perr, rosh yeshiva of Yeshiva Derech Ayson in Far Rockaway, asserted, "The community didn't just lose a great *mechanech*; we lost a *tzaddik*."

Chapter 15

The Final Years: "I Am His!"

"The Talmidim Need Me..."

IN JANUARY OF 2017 (5777), R' CHANINA WAS DIAGNOSED WITH CANcer. As the doctors outlined a protocol for chemotherapy, they expressed hope; the disease was treatable and R' Chanina's prognosis was encouraging.

Despite his illness and the debilitating treatments, R' Chanina went to yeshiva whenever humanly possible. There was no such thing as relaxation for R' Chanina. When his wife and children tried to dissuade him from going, urging him to rest and take it easy, their pleas fell on deaf ears. "The yeshiva is my life!" he insisted. "They need me there. The *talmidim* are waiting for me!" It was for this reason that he and his wife spent hours each day making sure his faux-beard, which replaced his full one that had fallen out as a result of treatment, was in order. It was all about the *talmidim,* and he wouldn't let them down.

Purim 2017

By August of 2018 (5778), following a battle that lasted a year and a half, R' Chanina was slowly getting back to himself, and the doctors declared his disease in remission. Even his hair and beard had grown back. He was looking forward to the new school year, to be back at his position as menahel in full force, to continue his lifelong mission of being *mechanech Yiddishe kinder.*

The yeshiva was his life

It was not meant to be.

In mid-August, R' Chanina again began feeling unwell and was admitted to the hospital. He was informed that the illness had returned in an even more aggressive form. Statistically, the chances of beating the disease a second time were very low. R' Chanina, for his part, cared only about the upcoming school year. Taking hold of the religious doctor's hand, he pleaded emotionally, "But Doctor, I need to be in yeshiva! It can't affect my *harbatzas Torah*. It can't affect my *harbatzas Torah*!"

The pain, the discomfort, the side effects, the fear of the unknown were non-issues to R' Chanina. It was all about his calling as a menahel and as an *oveid Hashem.* When confronted with his inability to perform mitzvos or daven properly, that's when R' Chanina broke down. A few months before his father's *petirah*, Eli was helping R' Chanina don his *tefillin.* As he recited the *berachah* and said *Shema,* R' Chanina began sobbing like a baby. After, he explained to Eli, "You think I'm scared to die? I am not scared to die. I had a rebbi, and my rebbi showed me how

August 2018

With R' Avrohom Yachnes, with whom R' Chanina spent many summers

The last picture taken with a *talmid*

to live, and my rebbi showed me how to die. I'm only bothered that I can't perform mitzvos properly." In any way possible, he still showed his love for the mitzvos. When he was in the hospital, he wasn't able to wear *tzitzis,* so he asked his children to spread them out over him.

Through it all, R' Chanina's lips were constantly murmuring *tefillos* and reciting *Tehillim.* Connecting to Hashem was so ingrained in R' Chanina, *tefillah* was such a part of his being, that even when the disease engulfed him — or, rather, specifically when the illness overtook his body — his *neshamah* attached itself even more to *tefillah.* As Dovid HaMelech stated (*Tehillim* 109:4), "*Va'ani sefillah* — But I was prayer." Especially at the end of his life, R' Chanina personified *tefillah.*

His son-in-law, Shua Nachman, remembered, "During the first round of his illness, Abba came home from the hospital after a particularly difficult chemo treatment on Pesach. He gathered himself and said with gusto, 'I thought of a *vort* in the hospital, and I have to share it with you.'" R' Chanina quoted two *pesukim* from *Hallel* (*Tehillim* 118:17-18), and translated them phrase by phrase.

"*Lo amus* — I will not die; *ki echyeh* — rather, I will live; *va'asaper maasei Kah* — and I will speak of the *maasim* of Hashem. *Yasor yisrani Kah* — Hashem has given me difficulties; *v'la'maves lo nissanani* — but He did not give me over to death."

R' Chanina expounded, "*Misah* in this *pasuk* is not speaking about actual physical death. It's talking about *ruchniyus* death, spiritual death. *Lo amus* — I will not die a spiritual death; *ki echyeh* — I will live spiritually; *va'asaper maasei Kah* — and I will speak of the *maasim* of Hashem. *Yasor yisrani Kah* — I can handle *yissurim; v'la'maves lo nissanani* — but *ruchniyus* death, I cannot handle."

"I have to be with my *talmidim*!"

"Certainly," Shua continued, "in the last couple of years, Abba had more than his share of *yissurim,* but when you live the spiritual life that my father-in-law lived, when every moment is dedicated to *avodas Hashem,* spiritual death is impossible. Throughout

Abba's battle with his illness, I heard him say, and we all heard him say many times, 'I have to go back. I have to go back to yeshiva. I have to be with the *talmidim*; they need me.' He would constantly check in. He would speak to the rebbeim, he would speak to the menahalim. They would give him updates, and he lived for that."

"Cheers!"

R' CHANINA'S *EMUNAH* WAS REAL, ALMOST PALPABLE, THOUGH NOT grandiose. In short, he possessed *emunah peshutah.* He took everything in stride, with the attitude of: *If this is what's happening, then this is what the Eibishter wants, and I'll make the best of it.* He never questioned or complained. He merely moved on, emphasizing repeatedly that though we may not understand, if this is what the *Eibishter* decided, then it is good. A common phrase of his was "It'll be good," and he meant it.

Yet he took it further. Dr. Jason Ostreicher, internist and cardiologist in Cedarhurst, is also a *talmid* of Yeshiva Toras Chaim. As R' Chanina's personal physician, he was given a close-up view of his former menahel's matchless *simchas hachaim* and inherent greatness.

"What struck me most when I treated R' Herzberg was his upbeat demeanor in all situations. Whether his illness was relapsing or he was in the midst of remission, he always kept this positive attitude about him. And I understood his sense of calm because he had unrivaled *emunah.* What I didn't understand was his expression of joy in such a difficult time.

"At his *levayah,* his children mentioned that he gave individualized bar mitzvah messages to each of the *talmidim.* So I went back to my parents' house, took out the old VCR, put in the video, and there was R' Herzberg more than 25 years earlier, with his long black beard, sharing the following message."

Dr. Ostreicher proceeded to repeat the speech R' Chanina had given at his bar mitzvah. It was three days after Avraham's *bris,* and he was in terrible pain, when Hashem appeared to him. But the Torah doesn't employ what would seem the respectable expression of "*Vayeira Hashem el Avraham.*" It simply says (*Bereishis* 18:1), "*Vayeira eilav Hashem* — Hashem appeared to him," with no mention of Avraham's name. We would think that if there was ever a time that Avraham deserved to be recognized by name, it was then. He had just sacrificed his body and his health for Hashem. Why would he receive the "second-class" treatment?

At Jason's bar mitzvah, R' Chanina went on to answer the question in the name of his rebbi, and in an address to Yeshiva Toras Chaim alumni, he delved even deeper. "The word תורה comes from the word הוראה, to show, to teach. When the *Ribbono shel Olam* appears to Avraham Avinu, he's not coming only to Avraham Avinu. Jews have *nisyonos* their whole lives. We all have tests: in learning, *parnassah, middos*. When the *Ribbono shel Olam* gives you a *nisayon* and you pass, then *'Vayeira eilav Hashem,'* Hashem appears to you. Hashem didn't appear only to Avraham Avinu, but He appears to each and every Yid who passes a *nisayon,* and puts sweat and tears into the mitzvah... We all have obstacles, but Hashem wouldn't give us a test we can't overcome. And when we do overcome, we grow from it, we become bigger from it."

After citing R' Chanina's words from his bar mitzvah all those years earlier, Dr. Ostreicher brought it all together. "That explains R' Herzberg's smile. He didn't look at his downturns in health as a tragedy. He looked at them as an opportunity to grow closer to *Hakadosh Baruch Hu.* It's one thing to say it in a bar mitzvah speech, but to actually live it is the mark of a true *tzaddik.*

"I always viewed R' Herzberg as a larger-than-life character. But it was remarkable to see that 'R' Herzberg the man' was even more special than 'R' Herzberg the mythical figure,' who stood in front of us, who gave us speeches... I think it was amazing to see his humanity. He was real — and that was even more impressive.

"This ability to accept whatever comes to you, to be able to sit with a smile in the good times and the bad, to know it's Hashem's plan and whatever Hashem plans for you is the best, is rare... We talk about it, we read about it in *gedolim* books, but to actually see it firsthand is truly amazing."

Years earlier, when he was hospitalized with coronary issues, R' Chanina demonstrated not only his joie de vivre, but also his ability to spread joy. R' Chanina had to take a medicine with a horrifically bitter taste. Since he was unable to drink it plain, the nurse mixed it with a cup of water and handed it to R' Chanina. R' Chanina took the cup and with a big smile on his face, raised it in a toast, as he called out, "Cheers!" before proceeding to drink the medication, bottoms up.

Sheer Willpower

LOUIS GREENSPAN, R' CHANINA'S PHYSICAL THERAPIST, WHO WORKED with him during both bouts of his illness, described R' Chanina's incredible *ratzon,* how he made extraordinary strides in physical therapy out of sheer willpower, harnessing all his inner *kochos.* All so he could be independent, so he could go back to yeshiva, so he could spend time with the congregants in his shul, so he could be less of a burden on his devoted *eishes chayil.*

"Every time R' Chanina reached a milestone," Mr. Greenspan recalled, "he would say, 'Let's move to the next step.' Even though it was questionable whether R' Chanina was ready to move to the next level, I would take the chance based on his *koach* and *ratzon.*" In physical therapy, Mr. Greenspan explained, there is a scale with which to test muscles and judge their capabilities. In order for a patient to climb steps, his muscles need to be at a three-plus. R' Chanina, however, was only at a two-plus. Even so, he climbed the steps. This made no sense on a purely physical scale. This is an unheard-of feat in the field of physical therapy. Mr. Greenspan stated that aside from when he worked with R' Chanina, he witnessed this type of true *ratzon* and inner *koach* only when working with *gedolei Yisrael.*

R' Chanina's son-in-law, Aharon Kaplan, shared a similar example. The last Succos of R' Chanina's life, Aharon asked him, "Are you sure you want to go to the succah? It's hard. You have to go down the steps, and steps are challenging for you."

Undeterred, R' Chanina responded, "No, you are going to help me, and we are going to go. I am going to eat in the succah."

And he ate every meal in the succah.

When the illness returned before the school year of 2018 (5778-5779), the doctors all but gave up hope, and it became a dreadful waiting game. Nevertheless, R' Chanina kept fighting, and those doctors who had abandoned hope were astounded at his perseverance, at his ability to hold onto life by a tiny thread.

Before long, the unimaginable took place.

Despite the odds, despite the statistics, in November of 2018 (5779), the doctors informed R' Chanina that the illness had disappeared.

His devoted family and friends breathed a sigh of relief, and became filled with optimism and hopefulness as R' Chanina was admitted to a rehab center to convalesce after the ravaging treatments.

Passing It On

SOON AFTER, HOWEVER, R' CHANINA CONTRACTED AN INFECTION and was transferred to the hospital; he was *niftar* a few days later, on December 16th, 2018 (8 Teves, 5779), shortly after Shabbos.

Not from the cancer, not from the infection, but from a heart attack.

The heart that pumped *chiyus* into his family, his thousands of *talmidim,* his *mispallelim,* and all those who had the *zechus* to come into contact with him; the heart that wept with the pain of every Yid and exulted in the joy of every Yid; the heart that flowed with *ahavas Yisrael, ahavas Hashem,* and *ahavas Torah;* the heart that felt the pain of the *Shechinah* in *galus* and truly longed for the *geulah*... the heart of R' Chanina Herzberg had stopped beating.

Yet all those individuals he affected can carry on his *avodah.*

In a *hesped,* R' Chanina's son Yitzchok quoted a *vort* from R' Aaron Schechter, which R' Aaron had communicated at the *sheloshim* of R' Shlomo Freifeld, R' Chanina's rebbi.

"Vayeitzei Yaakov mi'Be'er Sheva vayeilech Charanah — And Yaakov left Be'er Sheva and went to Charan" (*Bereishis* 28:10). Why must we mention Yaakov's departure from Be'er Sheva? Wouldn't it have been sufficient to write: *"Vayeilech Yaakov Charanah* — And Yaakov went to Charan"?

Rashi explains, *"Yetziyas tzaddik min hamakom oseh roshem."* We are accustomed to explaining these words to mean that when a righteous person departs from a place, he leaves a void, which, R' Aaron granted, is certainly true. But if that's what Rashi is telling us, then why does he say that when the *tzaddik* departs, *"oseh roshem,"* he makes an impression, and not *"oseh challal,"* he creates a vacuum?

R' Aaron elucidated. Although when a *tzaddik* departs, he leaves a void, it's not an empty, desolate void. Rather, it's a *challal* that has a *roshem.* It has the *tzaddik's* imprint on it; his *chosem,* his mark, is there. The *tzaddik* left something that needs to be filled, to learn from him and continue in his ways.

Yitzchok punctuated, "My father, R' Chanina Getzel ben R' Moshe, left his mark!"

During his stay in the rehabilitation center, R' Chanina had been treated by a nurse, Sheila,* who began working in the center that same week. Sheila informed the family that a while before, she had converted to Orthodox Judaism. However, after going through some difficult times, she had reverted to a non-Jewish lifestyle. An excellent nurse, she became acquainted with several of the Herzberg family members over the brief rehab stay.

A few months later, after R' Chanina's *petirah,* R' Chanina's son Yitzchok was set to spend Shabbos with his family at his in-laws. He was informed that there would be a guest for Shabbos, a woman named Sheila, who had been placed there by Shabbat.com. As Yitzchok entered his in-laws' home, he was dumbfounded to discover that it was the very same Sheila from the rehabilitation center! However, now she was living according to halachah; she had returned to a Torah lifestyle.

"I can't believe you're also here for Shabbos!" Sheila exclaimed in tearful joy, as she immediately recognized the Herzberg family. "Your father is the reason I recommitted to living an Orthodox lifestyle."

After everyone recovered from their surprise, Yitzchok asked Sheila, "Was there a specific behavior of my father that caused you to become religious again?"

"It was merely being in your father's presence that made me rethink the decisions I was making in life," Sheila responded. "I started thinking to myself, there has to be a reason this rabbi is here. And as I spent time with him, I noticed that he was always so friendly, with a kind good morning and good evening to others; always so quick to apologize if he was hampering my work in any way. I started feeling upbeat again about religion. He impressed me so much that the very same week I went out and purchased candlesticks for Shabbos, since I had thrown away my first pair. Slowly but surely, I made my way back. All thanks to R' Herzberg."

True, R' Chanina left a huge void in the hearts of his family, his yeshiva, his shul, his community, his fellow Jews. But he also left his *roshem* upon these same people, and as they follow in his ways of *menschlichkeit,* of being a "big Jew," of passionate *avodas Hashem,* of effervescent *ahavas Yisrael,* of *chinuch* with the child in mind, they will fill that vacuum to overflowing.

When R' Shlomo Freifeld was hospitalized shortly before his *petirah,* his childhood friend, R' Yaakov Perlow, the Novominsker Rebbe, came to visit. R' Shlomo gestured at the picture of the rebbi they shared, R' Hutner, which he kept on the table near him, and pronounced, "*Ich bin zeine,* I am his."

On 6 Teves, as R' Chanina fought for his life, his children showed him a video of his rebbi, R' Shlomo, speaking. Despite his weakened state, R' Chanina sat up in his hospital bed, a *talmid* before his rebbi, listening intently to the message of R' Shlomo, and his children snapped a picture. Less than 48 hours later, he returned his *neshamah* to his Creator.

The picture speaks volumes.

"*Ich bin zeine,* I am his. I am forever a *talmid.*"

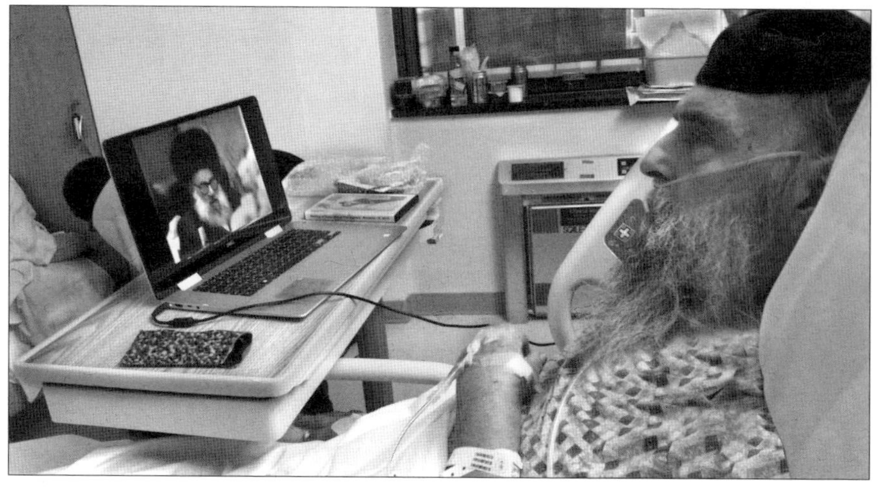

Forever a *talmid*

R' Chanina's *matzeivah* in Beth Israel Cemetery, Woodbridge, New Jersey

R' Pam stated that the true *kavod acharon* for a rebbi takes place at the last second of his *talmid*'s life, when it is clear that the *talmid* lived his entire life the way his rebbi dictated.

R' Chanina's life, up to his final moments, was a true *kavod acharon* for R' Shlomo.

R' Chanina passed on the *mesorah* he received from his rebbi, which continues through his children, his extended family, his *talmidim*, and the thousands of people he impacted over the course of his life. They recognize the *roshem* he made upon his *talmidim,* his *mispallelim,* his *mishpachah,* his community, and they commit to filling the vacuum he left as he departed.

And now they can point to the image of R' Chanina Getzel Herzberg and state proudly, "*Ich bin zeine,* I am his. I am forever a *talmid.*"

Glossary

Acharon shel Pesach — the last day of Passover
achdus — unity
achrayus — responsibility
adam — person
adam gadol — great person
adam hashalem — complete, whole person
afikoman — matzah eaten toward the end of the Passover Seder, which is hidden until then
Aggadeta— non-legalistic or narrative material of the Talmud
ahavah — love
ahavas — love of
ahyom v'nora — frightful and awesome
al cheit— portion of the Yom Kippur confession in which one bangs on his chest
Aleinu — prayer at the end of the service
aleph — top academic grade (A)
aleph-beis — Hebrew alphabet
aliyah — the act of being called to recite a blessing at the public reading of the Torah; personal growth
almanah, almanos — widow(s)
ameilus baTorah — toiling in Torah study
amel baTorah — one who toils in Torah study
amud — column where the one leading the prayer service stands
Anan — Cloud of Glory
Aron — Holy Ark
Asarah Harugei Malchus — Ten Martyrs (great sages killed by Hadrian of the Roman Empire)
asifah — gathering
askan — one involved in community affairs
aveilus — mourning
avel — mourner
Avihem she'ba'Shamayim — their Father in Heaven
Avodah — portion of the Yom Kippur service that speaks about the service in the Temple on Yom Kippur
avodah — service; prayer
avodas — service of
avodas hakodesh — holy service
avodas hatefillah — the service invested into prayer
avos — forefathers
ayin tovah — good eye
azkarah — memorial ceremony
b'achdus — in unity
b'al peh — by heart
b'darchei — in the ways of
b'derech hateva — based on the laws of nature
b'eimah u'v'yirah — with dread and fear
b'ezras Hashem — with the help of G-d
b'iyun — in depth
b'koach — potentially
b'lev va'nefesh — with heart and soul
b'simchah — in joy; happy
ba'avonoseinu harabbim — due to our numerous sins
baal chesed, baalei chesed — one(s) involved in acts of kindness
baal eitzah — adviser
baal habayis, baalei batim — householder(s); layman/ laymen

baal korei — one who reads the weekly Torah portion aloud on behalf of the congregation

baal simchah, baalei simchah — one celebrating a joyful occasion/ those celebrating a joyful occasion

baal tefillah — one who leads the prayer

baal tovah — one who does someone a favor

baalas chesed — woman involved in acts of kindness

baalas habayis — woman of the house

baalei kishron — intellectually gifted individuals

baalei mussar — those who toil in the study and teaching of ethical conduct

bachur, bachurim — unmarried young man/ men

badeken — (Yid.) ceremony at a wedding, where the groom veils the bride

bakashos — requests

baki b'Shas — expert in the six orders of the Talmud

baruch Hashem — blessed is the Name of G-d

bas Yisrael — daughter of Israel

bechinah — test

bedieved — ex post facto

bein adam la'chaveiro — between man and his friend

bein adam la'Makom — between man and the Omnipresent

bein hazmanim — between scheduled learning periods in yeshivah

beis din — Jewish court

beis haknesses — synagogue

Beis HaMikdash — Holy Temple

beis midrash — study hall

ben Olam Haba — one who is worthy of the World to Come

ben Torah — one who studies Torah and observe its teachings

bentch — (Yid.) bless; recite Grace After Meals

berachah, berachos — blessing(s) recited before performing a mitzvah and before eating; blessing(s) bestowed on a person

bigdei Shabbos — special attire in honor of the Sabbath

bimah — lectern used during the reading of the Torah

Bircas HaChamah — the blessing of the sun, recited once every 28 years

Bircas HaMazon — Grace After Meals

bitul Torah — waste of time that can be utilized for Torah study

blatt — (Yid.) folio of the Talmud

bnei Torah — those who study Torah and observe its teachings

Borchu — opening prayer of the evening service

bren — (Yid.) fire, fervor

bris, bris milah — circumcision

chaburah — group (usually a group that learns together)

chacham — wise man

chalav Yisrael — milk that has been supervised by a Jew from the time of milking

Chamishah Chumshei Torah — Five Books of the Torah

charoses — mixture of wine, nuts, fruits, and spices on the Seder plate

chas v'shalom — G-d forbid

chashivus — importance, significance, prominence

chashuv, chashuve — important, significant, prominent

chassan, chassanim — bridegroom(s)

Chassidish — (Yid.) Chassidic

chasunah, chasunos — wedding(s)

chatzos — exact moment of midnight (which varies by the day)

chaver, chaverim — friend(s)

chavrusa — learning partner

Chazal — our Sages; a saying of our Sages

chazarah — review, repetitive study

chazer — to review

cheder — lit. room, boys' elementary school

cheilek — part
cheishek — desire, longing
chesed — act of kindness
cheshbon, cheshbonos — accounting(s); calculation(s)
chesronos — deficiencies
chevrah — group of friends
chiddush, chiddushim — novel thought(s)
chinuch, chinuch habanim — Jewish education; the obligation of a parent to train a child to perform mitzvos
chitzoniyus — externals
chiyus — life, vitality
chizuk — encouragement
chochmah, chochmos — wisdom, pieces of wisdom
Chol HaMoed — intermediate days of Passover and Succos
Chumash — a volume of the Five Books of the Torah
chuppah — wedding canopy; marriage ceremony that takes place under a canopy
churban — destruction
chutzpah'dik — (Yid.) demonstrating audacity
dalet — low academic grade (D)
dalet amos shel halachah — four cubits of halachah, i.e., in a yeshiva
daven — (Yid.) pray
derashah, derashos — lecture(s); sermon(s)
derech — approach, method
derech eretz — respect
derhoiben — (Yid.) elevated
dinei nefashos — laws involving lives
divrei — words of
dvar Torah, divrei Torah — lesson(s) from the Torah; short speech(es) on Torah topics
dveikus — attachment, connectiveness
ehrlich, ehrliche — (Yid.) upright, honest, conscientious, faithful
Eibishter — (Yid.) the One Above
eishes chayil — woman of valor; righteous wife
eitzah, eitzos — idea(s); advice/ pieces of advice
emes — truth
emes'e — (Yid.) true
emunah peshutah — simple faith
epes — (Yid.) somehow
Erev — the eve of
eved — servant
farher — (Yid.) oral test
frum — (Yid.) religious, Torah observant
gaavah — arrogance
gabbai sheini — assistant/ backup to the sexton
gabbai, gabbaim — synagogue sexton(s); personal attendant(s)
gadlus— greatness
gadlus ha'adam — greatness of man
gadol hador, gedolei hador — great Torah sage(s) of the generation
gadol, gedolim — great Torah sage(s); giant(s)
galus — exile
Gan Eden — Paradise
gartel — (Yid.) belt worn by (Chassidic) men for davening and performing certain mitzvos
gashmiyus — materialism
gavra — person of stature
gedolah — big
gedolei Yisrael — sages of Israel
Gemara — Talmud
gemilus chasadim — acts of lovingkindness
geonim — Torah geniuses
geonus— Torah genius
geshmak — (Yid.) enjoyable, delightful, zesty; enjoyment, delight, zest
geulah — redemption
gimmel — mediocre academic grade (C)
giyores — (f.) proselyte
gurr chashuve zach — (Yid.) very significant thing
gut — (Yid.) good
hachna'ah — deference, submissiveness
hadrachah — guidance
Hakadosh Baruch Hu — The Holy One, Blessed is He (G-d)

hakamas matzeivah — erecting of a monument
hakaras hatov, hakaras tovah — appreciating the good; gratitude
hakodesh — the holy
halachah — Torah law
halevai — if only
hanachas tefillin — the first time a boy of bar mitzvah age dons his phylacteries
HaNasi — the prince
hanefesh — the soul
hanhagah — behavior
hanhalah — school administration
harbatzas Torah — Torah dissemination
has'chalas Chumash — celebration in school when young children receive their first Chumash
hashalem — the whole, the complete
hashkafah — outlook, ideology, perspective
hashkafas hachaim — outlook, ideology, perspective on life
hashpa'ah — influence, effect
hasmadah — diligence in learning
hatzlachah — success
hatzne'a leches — behaving modestly
havanah — comprehension
haYahadus — Judaism
heimish — (Yid.) homey, familiar; with an old-world flavor
hesped — eulogy
hiddur, hiddurim — beautification(s), enhancement(s)
hishtadlus — effort
ikar — main point
im yirtzeh Hashem — G-d willing
inyan, inyanim — topic(s); important point(s)
k'nip — (Yid.) pinch
kabbalah, kabbalos — commitment(s), resolution(s)
Kabbalas Shabbos — prayer welcoming Shabbos
kallah — bride
kapota — (Yid.) caftan
kasher — make kosher
katan — small
kavanah — intent, concentration, focus; proper thought during prayers or performance of mitzvos
kavod — honor, respect
kavod acharon — final honor, respect
kedushah — holiness
kedushas Shabbos — holiness of Shabbos
kehillah — congregation, community
keilim — vessels
kesher — bond, connection
kesser shem tov — crown of a good name
kevurah — burial
kibbud av va'eim — the mitzvah of honoring one's parents
kibbud, kibbudim — honor(s), specifically distributed at a joyous occasion
Kiddush — blessing that speaks of Shabbos or festivals; gathering at which Kiddush is recited
kiddush Hashem — sanctification of the Name of G-d
kinder — (Yid.) children
kinderlach — (Yid.) affectionate term for children
kiruv — outreach, the act of drawing near
kishke — (Yid.) filling added to cholent
kishkes — insides, depths
kishron — intellect, talent
kittel — (Yid.) long white garment worn by men on the High Holidays and at the Passover Seder, symbolizing purity and holiness
klal — the community
Klal Yisrael — the community of Israel
klap — (Yid.) bang
klei kodesh— lit. holy vessels, indicating those who dedicate their lives to serving the Jewish people, mostly as Torah teachers and rabbis
koach, kochos — strength(s), power(s), ability/ abilities
kodesh — holy
kollel — institute for advanced Torah studies, usually for married men

kriah — Hebrew reading
Krias Shema — recitation of Shema, in which we accept G-d's Kingship upon us and declare His Oneness
kuntres — pamphlet, small Jewish book
kvod — honor of
kvod habriyos — honoring other people
l'chaim — a toast to life
l'fi kevodo — as befits his dignity
l'havdil — lit. to separate, i.e., leaving aside the obvious differences
l'ilui nishmas(o) — for the elevation of (his) soul
l'olam va'ed — forever and ever
l'sheim Shamayim — for the sake of Heaven
l'yedideinu hanechbad — to our honored friend
l'zecher — in memory of
lamdanim — analytical Talmudic scholars
lashon hakodesh — the holy tongue, i.e., Biblical Hebrew
Leil Shabbos — the eve of the Sabbath; i.e., Friday night
lein — (Yid.) read the Torah portion; read; recite
levayah — funeral
lichvod Shabbos — in honor of the Sabbath
limud Torah — Torah study
limud, limudim — lesson(s); study/ studies
limudei kodesh — Jewish studies
lokshen — (Yid.) noodles
lomeid Torah — one who studies Torah
maalah, maalos — virtue(s); merit(s); advantage(s)
maamar — discourse
Maariv — evening prayer service
maaseh — story; action
maavir sidrah — review the weekly portion
madreigah, madreigos — level(s)
maftir — the final honor given during the reading of the Torah
maggid shiur — Torah lecturer
Mah Nishtanah — passage in the Haggadah, also known as the Four Questions, usually recited by the children at the Seder
makkas choshech — plague of darkness
makpid — particular, strict
malach Elokim — angel of G-d
malach, malachim — angel(s)
malchus — kingdom, empire
mamash — really
manhig — leader
mara d'asra — rabbi
marbitz Torah, marbitzei Torah — disseminator (s) of Torah
mareh mekomos — sources
maror — bitter herbs, placed on the Seder plate
masechta, masechtos — tractate(s)
mashgiach— staff member in a yeshiva who supervises the students' behavior and gives ethical discourses
Mashiach — Messiah
mashpia — person of influence; to influence others
matanos la'evyonim — gifts given to the poor on Purim
matzliach — be successful
mazel — fortune
mechaber, mechabrim — author(s)
mechadesh — come up with a novel thought; innovate
mechanech, mechanchim — educator(s); to educate
mechaneches, mechanchos — (f.) educator(s)
mechazek — strengthen
mechilah — forgiveness
mechitzah — partition separating men and women
mechutan — father-in-law of one's child
meforash, mefarshim — commentary/ commentaries
Megillas Eichah — Scroll of Lamentations that is read on the Ninth of Av
mehalchim — human beings, who walk

mehalech hachaim — way of life; approach to life
meis — the deceased
mekabel — accept; receive
mekarev — draw close; draw close to Judaism
mekubal — one who learns and delves into Kabbalah
melamed — teacher
melaveh malkah — meal to escort the Sabbath queen after the Sabbath
menachem avel — comfort a mourner
menahel, menahalim — principal(s)
menschlichkeit — (Yid.) the quality of being a mensch, exemplifying integrity, respect, and kindness
menuval — despicable person
mesader kiddushin — rabbi who officiates at a wedding ceremony
mesame'ach — make others happy
mesayem — finish; make a *siyum,* a celebration upon completion of Torah study, usually of the Talmud
mesibah — party
mesiras nefesh — self-sacrifice
mesivta — high school
mesorah — tradition
metziyus — existence; essence
mevatel — nullify, invalidate, negate
mezonos — food upon which the blessing of mezonos is recited, e.g., cake and cookies
mezuzah, mezuzos — parchment(s) affixed to one's doorpost
midbar — desert
middah tovah, middos tovos — positive attribute(s), character trait(s)
middah, middos — attribute(s), character trait(s)
Mikdash — Holy Temple
mikveh, mikvaos — ritual bath(s)
min haShamayim — from Heaven
Minchah — afternoon prayer service
minhag, minhagim — custom(s)
minyan, minyanim — quorum(s) of 10 men for prayer
misah — death
mishloach manos — gifts of food sent to friends on Purim
Mishnah, Mishnayos — teachings of the Sages known as Tannaim
mishpachah, mishpachos — family/ families
mispallel, mispallelim — congregant(s); to pray
mitzvah tantz — (Yid.) special dance at the end of a wedding, generally practiced by Chassidim
mitzvah, mitzvos — commandment(s)
mizrach vant —(Yid.) eastern wall (where the rabbis and prestigious members of the congregation sit)
moed — festival
mofsim — wonders
morah, moros — (f.) teacher(s)
mosdos haTorah — Torah institutions
moser nefesh — sacrificing oneself; totally and wholeheartedly devoting oneself
Motza'ei Shabbos — Saturday night
motzi — enable another person to fulfill his obligation
muhn — (Yid.) to challenge
Mussaf — additional prayer recited after the morning prayer, on Sabbath, the new moon, and holidays
mussar — (Yid.) lecture on ethical conduct; speech on proper behavior; ethics
n'eemus— sweetness, pleasantness
nachas — pleasure, joy, gratification, usually from one's children or students; gentleness
narishkeit — (Yid.) foolishness
nashim tzidkaniyos — righteous women
ne'eman — trustworthy, faithful one; trustworthy, faithful
nebach — (Yid) poor; unfortunate
neshamah, neshamos — soul(s)
netilas yadayim — hand-washing ritual
niftar — passed away; one who passed away
niggun, niggunim — Jewish tune(s)

nisayon, nisyonos — test(s), challenge(s)
nusach hatefillah — style of prayer
olam — world; social group
Olam Haba — World to Come
Olam Haba'dik — (Yid.) belonging to the World to Come
oveid Hashem, ovdei Hashem — one who serves Hashem/ those who serve Hashem
pachad — fear
parashah — Torah portion of the week
parnassah — livelihood
pashtus — simplicity
pashute — (Yid.) simple
pasken — (Yid.) to render a halachic ruling
pasuk, pesukim — verse(s)
pasul — invalid
penimiyus — internals
Pesukei DeZimrah — verses of praise recited toward the beginning of the morning prayers
petirah — passing, death
peyos — sidelocks
pikchus — clarity of thought; cleverness; insight
piyutim — poems
posek — halachic decisor(s)
rabbosai — gentleman
Ramban — Nachmanides, medieval commentator
Rashi —Rabbi Shlomo Yitzchaki, main medieval commentator
ratzon — will, willpower
rav, rabbanim — rabbi(s)
Rebbe — Chassidic leader
rebbetzin — (Yid.) rabbi's wife
rebbi muvhak primary teacher
rebbi, rebbeim — Torah teacher(s)
regesh — emotion, feeling
reshus — permission
retzon Hashem — the will of G-d
Ribbono shel Olam — Master of the World
Rosh Chodesh — new moon
rosh yeshiva, roshei yeshiva — dean(s) of a yeshiva
roshem — impression, imprint
ruach — spirit, atmosphere
ruchniyus — spirituality
ruchniyus'dike — (Yid.) spiritual
sandak — one given the honor of holding the baby during a circumcision
seder hayom — day's schedule
seder, sedarim — order(s) of the Mishnah; study period(s)
Sefer Torah, Sifrei Torah — Torah scroll(s)
sefer, sefarim — book(s), especially on a Torah topic
segulah — spiritual remedy
seichel — common sense, insight
semichah — rabbinic ordination
seudah hamafsekes — final meal before the fast of the Ninth of Av and Yom Kippur
seudah, seudos — festive meal(s)
seudas hoda'ah — meal to express gratitude
seva ratzon — satisfaction
s'gan menahel — assistant principal
Shabbos Nachamu — the Sabbath following the Ninth of Av
Shabbos Shuvah — the Sabbath between Rosh Hashanah and Yom Kippur
Shacharis — morning prayer service
shailah, shailos — halachic query/ queries
shalom — peace
shalom aleichem — greeting, meaning: Peace be upon you
shalom bayis — marital harmony
shalosh seudos — third meal of Sabbath, eaten on Sabbath afternoon
Shamayim — Heaven
Shas — (six order of) the Talmud
shayach — relevant, related, on the level
she'ifah — spiritual aspiration
she'tichyeh — may she live
Shechinah — Divine Presence
Shehecheyanu— blessing said on a holiday or something new, e.g., a new garment or new fruit

sheigetz — (Yid.) non-Jew
sheliach tzibbur — representative of the congregation, i.e., the cantor
sheloshim — 30 days of mourning observed for a close relative; gathering after the 30 days of mourning
shemiras halashon — guarding one's speech
Shemoneh Esrei — prayer that forms the central core of the prayer service
shevach v'hoda'ah — praise and thanks
shidduch — match, i.e., for marriage
shimush talmidei chachamim — serving Torah scholars
shitah — opinion, outlook, creed
shiur, shiurim — Torah lecture(s); class(es)
shivah — seven days of mourning observed for a close relative
shlita — may he live long and well
shmooze — (Yid.) chat
shmuess, shmuessen — (Yid.) lecture(s)
shomer Shabbos — Sabbath observant
shomrei Torah u'mitzvos — those who observe Torah and its commandments
shoresh — root
shtar mechirah — document of sale
shteig — (Yid.) advance in learning and personal growth
shtell tzu — (Yid.) cite, refer to
shtender — (Yid.) lectern
shtetl, shtetlach — (Yid.) town(s), village(s)
shtick, shtickel — (Yid.) piece, bit
shtreimel, shtreimlach — (Yid.) fur hat worn by Chassidic males on the Sabbath and festivals
shul — synagogue
Shulchan Aruch — Code of Jewish Law
Shulchan Orech (Haggadah) — portion of the Passover Seder in which the festive meal is eaten
shurah — row
shvitz — (Yid.) sweat
siddur, siddurim — prayer book(s)
sidrei hayeshiva — study periods of the yeshiva
simchah, simchos — joy; time(s) of joy
simchas beis hasho'eivah — celebration on the festival of Succos, commemorating the drawing of the water in the Temple
simchas hachaim — joy of life
sippur Yetziyas Mitzrayim — the story of the Exodus
siyata d'Shmaya — Heavenly assistance
siyum — celebration marking the completion of a portion of the Torah
siyum haShas, siyumei haShas — celebration(s) marking the completion of a portion of the Talmud
sofer — scribe
succah — temporary home for the festival of Succos
sugya — topic; conceptual unit in Torah study
taanah, taanos — complaint(s); objection(s)
tafkid — purpose, role
taharah — purity
takeh — (Yid.) indeed
tallis — prayer shawl
talmid chacham, talmidei chachamim — Torah scholar(s)
talmid muvhak, talmidim muvhakim — primary student(s), primary disciple(s)
talmid, talmidim — student(s), disciple(s)
Tanach — acronym for Torah, Neviim, Kesuvim — Torah, Prophets, and Writings
techunos hanefesh — personal characteristics
tefillah, tefillos — prayer(s)
tefillin — phylacteries
Tehillim — Psalms
teitch — (Yid.) translation; translate
teshuvah — responsum; repentance
tikkun hamiddos — correcting one's character traits
tinokos shel beis rabban — small children who learn Torah

Tishah B'Av — Ninth of Av, anniversary of the destruction of both Holy Temples
tochachah — rebuke, reproof
toivel — immerse
Torah'dike — (Yid.) in connection with the Torah, connected to Torah
Tosafos — medieval commentators on the Talmud
tovah — favor
trop — (Yid.) cantillation
tzaar — pain, sorrow
tzaddik, tzaddikim — righteous man/ men
tzarah, tzaros — problem(s); painful, difficult situation(s)
tzibbur — congregation
tzitzis — fringed four-cornered garment; the fringes on a four-cornered garment
tzubrochene — (Yid.) broken
U'Nesaneh Tokef — prayer recited on High Holidays, in which we speak about G-d's strength and power
upsheren (Yid.) — 3-year-old boy's first haircut
vaad — group of men or boys who get together to work on improving themselves
vatran — one who yields or gives in to others
vort — (Yid.) word; small Torah thought; engagement party
yachas — relationship
yachid — individual
yahrtzeit — (Yid.) anniversary of someone's death
Yamim Noraim — High Holidays
yedid nefesh — close friend
yedidim — close friends
yediyos klaliyos — general knowledge
yegiah — effort, toil
yerei Shamayim — one who fears Heaven
yeridah, yeridos — descent(s), decline(s)
yesod, yesodos — foundation(s), fundamental(s), basic principle(s)
yesodos hachaim — foundation(s), fundamental(s), basic principle(s) of life
yetzer hara — evil inclination
Yetziyas Mitzrayim — Exodus from Egypt
Yid, Yidden — (Yid.) Jew(s)
Yiddishe — (Yid.) Jewish
Yiddishkeit — (Yid.) Judaism
yimach shemam — may their name be blotted out (in reference to our archenemies)
yirah — fear
yiras — fear of
Yisrael — Israel; a Jew
yissurim — suffering
yungerman, yungerleit — (Yid.) young married man/ men, usually referring to those learning in a yeshiva or kollel
zechus — a merit
zman — time; semester in yeshiva
zocheh — to merit

This volume is part of
THE ARTSCROLL® SERIES
an ongoing project of
translations, commentaries and expositions on
Scripture, Mishnah, Talmud, Midrash, Halachah,
liturgy, history, the classic Rabbinic writings,
biographies and thought.

For a brochure of current publications
visit your local Hebrew bookseller
or contact the publisher:

Mesorah Publications, ltd
313 Regina Avenue
Rahway, New Jersey 07065
(718) 921-9000
www.artscroll.com